ALSO BY THOMAS J. MOORE

Lifespan
Heart Failure

DEADLY MEDICINE

Why Tens of Thousands
of Heart Patients Died
in America's Worst Drug Disaster

THOMAS J. MOORE

SIMON & SCHUSTER

New York London Toronto Sydney Tokyo Singapore

SIMON & SCHUSTER
Rockefeller Center
1230 Avenue of the Americas
New York, NY 10020

Designed by Irving Perkins Associates

Manufactured in the United States of America

10   9   8   7   6   5   4   3   2   1

Library of Congress Cataloging-in-Publication Data

Moore, Thomas J., date.
    Deadly medicine : why tens of thousands of heart patients died in America's
worst drug disaster / Thomas J. Moore.
        p.   cm.
    Includes bibliographical references and index.
    1. Myocardial depressants—Side effects.   2. Flecainide—Side
effects.   3. Pharmaceutical policy—United States.   I. Title.
RM347.M66   1995
615'.716—dc20   94-43501   CIP
ISBN 0-684-80417-4

For Winston Cook Moore

CONTENTS

Part Three **MEDICAL USE**

Caution

THIS BOOK DESCRIBES various drugs that can cause cardiac arrest and other adverse effects. However, stopping or changing the dose of the antiarrhythmic drugs described in this book should be undertaken only in consultation with a physician.

A Note to Readers

PRESCRIPTION DRUGS HAVE two names, a generic (or chemical) name and a brand name. For example, one drug described in this book has a brand name of Tambocor and a chemical name of flecainide acetate. To avoid confusion I have used only one name for each drug, usually the brand name. Even within quotations I have taken the liberty of substituting brand names for chemical names.

To preserve the narrative flow of story, attribution and source citations have been kept to a minimum in the body of the book. A notes section and bibliography provide documentation and a guide to other sources. An appendix contains all the names of the drugs, both generic and brand.

PROLOGUE

THIS BOOK TELLS the story of America's worst medical drug disaster. Over just a few years, an estimated 50,000 people died from taking drugs intended to prevent cardiac arrest. After hundreds of thousands of patients routinely took these drugs, a definitive medical experiment proved they did not prevent cardiac arrest as doctors had believed. Instead the drugs caused cardiac arrest. Often the effect was so sudden and unexpected that people literally dropped dead while going about their normal lives. The result of this single medical misjudgment about the properties of these drugs produced a death toll larger than the United States' combat losses in wars such as Korea and Vietnam. If one were to total the deaths from every commercial airplane crash in the history of U.S. aviation, the sum would not approach the number of deaths from this episode. Today our modern medical system stands capable of producing catastrophes of a magnitude unequaled by any other human endeavor except war and genocide.

These stark statements understandably trigger an avalanche of questions. Is there convincing evidence such a disaster occurred? Why wasn't there a widespread public outcry? How could the Food and Drug Administration have overlooked the dangers of these drugs? What have the health authorities been doing since 1989, when the lethal properties of these drugs were first documented, or since 1992, when many remaining questions were resolved?

The answers to these and to larger questions can be found in this story of a family of drugs for irregular heartbeats. The story unfolds over more than two decades, and involves how researchers test drugs, what companies do to sell them, and what doctors know—and don't know—about the drugs they prescribe and we all consume.

Part One

TESTING

Chapter 1

A GENIE GETS LOOSE

A GREAT TRAGEDY in modern medicine began on a note of optimism. On November 7, 1985, the 3M Company had rented a small room at the National Press Club in Washington, D.C., for a press conference. With only twenty chairs and a lectern, it was clear only a modest turnout was expected. 3M was already famous for Scotch tape and Post-its, sandpaper and adhesives. In surveys it ranked as one of the nation's most admired corporations; at number 47 on the Fortune 500 list, 3M also was one of the world's largest. Its annual corporate revenue exceeded the entire economic output of Kenya. However, 3M had been only a minor player in the most profitable of all U.S. businesses, prescription drugs. Fifteen years earlier it had bought a small pharmaceutical company called Riker Laboratories. Now, after more than a decade of research and development, 3M had its first major new drug.

The drug was called Tambocor, and it was for people with irregular heartbeats. This medical problem was no rival of cholesterol as a popular topic of discussion. Nor could it compete with cancer as a source of outright fear. Nevertheless, the condition created a market of surprising size. Irregular heartbeats accounted for 3 percent of all doctors' office visits. In the previous year, more than 10 million prescriptions were written for drugs to combat this problem. For 3M, Tambocor had another key feature. Some of the most important drugs in the medical arsenal are so effective they are taken for only a short time. Antibiotics are the textbook example. The largest profits, however, come from medication that does not cure a disorder, but merely holds it at bay. Such drugs have to be taken indefinitely. Prime examples are drugs to lower blood pressure, to treat ulcers and to prevent the rejection of organ transplants. Tambocor worked the same way. It suppressed several kinds of irregular heartbeats—including some very dangerous ones—but if the patient stopped taking it, the problem returned. Tambocor was a new member of a growing family of agents called Class I antiarrhythmic drugs.* In profit terms, it had the look of a major money-maker.

It had taken thirteen years from the creation of a new molecule to the public announcement at the National Press Club. Tambocor had been studied in mice, rats, rabbits, pigs, dogs, cats and baboons. It had been given to 1,330 patients in 38 different studies; it was already sold in seven other countries. The Food and Drug Administration had spent 34 months evaluating 3M's New Drug Application, a document so extensive and detailed that it filled an entire bookcase.

The featured speaker at the press conference didn't work for 3M. For this pivotal task the company had recruited a 40-year-old heart specialist named Joel Morganroth. He was a compact, wiry man with so much suppressed energy that he seemed perpetually impatient with how slowly the rest of the world moved. Morganroth was a cardiologist and professor at Hahnemann University in Philadelphia. As a specialist in irregular heart rhythms, he was a major figure on a very small piece of medical turf. Morganroth was a paid consultant for 3M. Over the coming months, the company would pay him more than $100,000 for lectures, presentations, and publicity work.

"Tambocor is a major advance in antiarrhythmic drugs in terms of efficacy, safety and patient compliance," Morganroth said. "Tambocor is also the first antiarrhythmic drug to provide twice-a-day dosing with an extremely high degree of efficacy." This was an important part of Tambocor's sales potential. The dominant drug in the market, quinidine, had to be taken three or four times a day and often produced unpleasant symptoms in the digestive tract.

Morganroth also explained why he believed Tambocor was potentially such an important new drug. Every year, he said, more than 400,000 persons died from an event called sudden cardiac death. Many deaths ascribed to a "heart attack" also involve disruption of the rhythmic electrical pulses that trigger each contraction. In a normal heart, these pulses appear as the spikes on an electrocardiogram. If these electrical pulses are disrupted, the heart stops pumping blood. This is called cardiac arrest or, as Morganroth put it, sudden cardiac death. It is a breakdown of the electrical system of the heart, and is invariably fatal unless the normal rhythm is soon restored through a brief electric shock.

*The classes and names of the various drugs are described in an appendix.

Morganroth was among the cardiologists who believed that even mild irregular heartbeats could trigger a lethal cardiac arrest, especially in already damaged hearts. Therefore, Tambocor's ability to suppress even mild disturbances of heart rhythm might save thousands of lives, and earn 3M hundreds of millions of dollars. However, Morganroth was careful to note that this was a medical theory, not a proven scientific fact.

"Tests that prove that Tambocor, or any other antiarrhythmic drug, will prevent sudden death have not been conducted," he said. What he didn't say, however, was that thousands of doctors, including himself, were certainly not waiting until this theory was proved conclusively; they were going to prescribe Tambocor in hopes it would prevent cardiac arrest. It would be taken by patients whose irregular beats were so mild they could not be detected without medical testing.

On this day in November 1985, in an office just five miles from the National Press Club, another medical doctor was thinking about this same theory. His name was Lawrence Friedman and he worked for the National Institutes of Health, the world's premier biomedical research organization. A soft-spoken, intense man, Friedman was managing a $40 million medical experiment. He hoped to learn whether Tambocor and two similar drugs would, in fact, prevent cardiac arrest in patients with electrically unstable hearts. At its core, Friedman's study was simple. Half the patients recruited would take one of the active drugs, while the other half would get a harmless placebo. If the drug worked as expected, fewer cardiac arrests would be counted among patients on the active drug, compared with those taking the placebo. It only sounded easy. His project would take five years, feature a cast of more than 300 researchers, and involve screening tens of thousands of heart patients. At $40 million, it would cost about as much as 3M had spent to develop Tambocor.

Why was Friedman testing a medical treatment already widely accepted among heart rhythm experts? So eager are America's doctors and patients for the latest advances in medical research that new treatments are routinely provided to hundreds of thousands of patients before their benefits are clearly established. It was Friedman's life work to test such theories, to measure the precise extent of the benefits of promising new medical treatments. Also, the project was assumed to be too big and too expensive for a single drug company, even an industrial giant like 3M. The experts who already accepted the theory were nevertheless enthusiastic about obtaining definitive scientific proof to buttress their more circumstantial case.

3M believed it was indeed fortunate to have its drug included in an impartial clinical trial intended to document its life-saving benefits.

Back at the press conference it fell to Gary Gentzkow, 3M Pharmaceutical's youthful medical director, to describe the unhappy dimension of Tambocor, its adverse effects. The slender, sandy-haired doctor had embarked on a career in the drug industry after abruptly quitting his advanced medical training. He had become the chief medical officer of 3M's drug subsidiary by age 35. He had husbanded Tambocor through its most difficult moments.

"As with any drug," he told the assembled reporters, "side effects do occur." Dizziness and blurred vision were seen frequently. In about 7 percent of the patients who took Tambocor, the irregular heartbeats got worse instead of better. In this respect, he said, Tambocor was no worse than other drugs. At the press conference, Gentzkow confined himself to a dry recitation of the clinical data. Soon, however, 3M would emphasize the drug's safety.

Another medical doctor had worried a great deal about the safety of Tambocor. His name was Robert Temple, and he worked at the Food and Drug Administration headquarters in nearby Rockville, Maryland. He held one of the most important and demanding jobs in all of American medicine. As director of the FDA's Office of Drug Evaluation, Temple made the final decision to approve Tambocor. In three years in this pivotal job, he had never been overruled in a decision to approve or reject a new prescription drug. In fact, it had never occurred to him to consult anyone at a higher level. There were at least two secrets to Temple's great power. He had abilities that ranged from skill at bureaucratic infighting to the capacity to cite from memory the smallest details of a company's clinical testing results. Also, hardly anyone else wanted this thankless and demanding job. If a drug provided wondrous new benefits, the drug company and the doctors who helped develop it would line up to reap the praise and the profits. If anyone paused to consider the contribution of the FDA, it would be to criticize the agency for not approving the drug more quickly. If, however, a drug turned out to have unexpected adverse effects, rarely would the doctors who helped develop this drug be held responsible. The blame would fall on the FDA in general, and Bob Temple in particular. It takes an unusual person to relish such a job. And even the comparatively few people who didn't like Bob Temple would instantly agree that he was an unusual person.

Temple had stayed up late at night worrying about Tambocor, with the thick medical review and other documents spread out on his dining room table. He had written his own lengthy safety analysis and sent it back down to the FDA doctor in charge of evaluating cardiovascular drugs. But ultimately he had allowed Tambocor on the market. It was one of twenty new drugs approved in 1985.

The Washington press conference officially marked the launch of Tambocor. Back at 3M headquarters in St. Paul, Minnesota, the employees who had worked for twelve years to make this drug a reality were getting ready for a party in the cafeteria of Building 265. A celebration was also planned for the Northridge, California, factory where Tambocor was being manufactured.

The announcement was duly recorded in a short article buried on page 20 in the business section of *The New York Times*. At this point, however, media coverage was not important to the future of Tambocor. The battle for acceptance was going to be fought in the minds of America's doctors. The real rollout of Tambocor would begin a few weeks later. It would include multipage color advertisements in medical journals, and special symposia in Dallas, Miami, New York, Chicago and Boston. There would be exhibits at medical meetings, and videos for those who couldn't make the symposia or meetings. Company sales representatives—known as drug detailers—would call on doctors around the country offering free samples, brochures and other giveaways.

The pharmaceutical industry spends more to persuade doctors to prescribe its drugs than it does on research. To influence a doctor's decision about what is best for a patient, the companies wage expensive and highly sophisticated sales campaigns, spending more than $14,000 a year for each doctor in clinical practice. Gifts and other inducements range from elaborate office computer systems to trinkets, theater tickets and ski caps. 3M knew the rules of the selling game and was ready. It could not afford to lose its advantage in having the first of a new generation of drugs for irregular heartbeats. Bristol-Myers Squibb was coming along soon with a similar drug called Enkaid. The German pharmaceutical giant, Boehringer Ingelheim, was going to market Mexitil, which it had sold for a decade in Europe. DuPont owned an interesting drug obtained from the Soviet Union called Ethmozine. And three other companies had antiarrhythmic drugs far along in development. 3M had not been alone in discovering the rapidly expanding market for antiarrhythmic drugs. Now the race for profits and market share had begun in earnest.

It would be fortunate if life were so simple that the wise use of prescription drugs depended solely on selecting effective agents or avoiding dangerous ones. For example, poisons with a wide variety of devastating effects have important medical uses. Hundreds of thousands of patients take a small dose of rat poison every day to prevent blood clots. A synthetic version of curare, the paralytic ingredient in poison arrows of South American Indians, is routinely used in surgery. At the other extreme, widely used and beneficial compounds such as aspirin and penicillin have highly toxic effects in some people. Aspirin was given for decades before doctors realized that it could sometimes cause serious internal bleeding. Even penicillin triggers potentially fatal allergic reactions in some people. The safety and effectiveness of drugs, therefore, depends on the larger system by which drugs are discovered, tested, sold to doctors, and prescribed for particular medical purposes.

All the major players in that larger system were in evidence at the debut of Tambocor. At center stage was 3M, a corporate giant with millions invested in an important new product. In our society, most new drugs are developed by large private businesses, for profit. However, even for a press conference announcement, 3M relied on Morganroth, an expert from a medical school research center. The nation's medical education and research centers, and their specialists, also play an essential role in helping to develop and test drugs, and in persuading other doctors to use them. Little happens in the world of pharmaceuticals without these medical opinion leaders. From the first human test patient, the federal government was intimately involved. The FDA evaluates, approves or disapproves the drugs; perhaps even more important it sets the standards for how much clinical testing must be done. The other major player was the federal government's National Institutes of Health. Its job is to assemble the building blocks of medical knowledge from which sound decisions about drugs and medical treatments can be made. The main focus of this entire system was the doctors in daily medical practice. It was they who would decide to prescribe Tambocor, an alternative, or perhaps no drug at all. With great care, and at enormous expense, the drug companies would woo the doctors. The medical experts would advise them. The FDA declared which medical uses of a drug were proven and which were not. From this mass of information—ranging from careful scientific studies to misleading product propaganda—each doctor had to judge what was best for the patient.

. . .

Deciding whether a drug is helping a patient is another critical task that proves much more difficult than it sounds. In many ailments, most patients recover whether they get a drug or not. Many drugs are given in hopes of preventing heart attacks or other events that will probably not occur anyway. (They are said to "lower the risk" of the event.) Countless studies show that when given a completely inactive placebo, about one third of patients improve anyway. Those who want to trust their physician's judgment about how well drugs work often do not realize how often a doctor—no matter how observant and experienced—simply can't tell.

From the beginning, one property of Tambocor put medical judgment to a severe test. Even during the early clinical testing of Tambocor, many patients experienced sudden cardiac death or cardiac arrest. They dropped dead while dancing, at a picnic and playing tennis. They died while asleep in bed, just after eating breakfast, and while sitting quietly in a living room chair. In the most carefully studied cases, their hearts had stopped beating while in the hospital, and wired to cardiac monitors that sounded an urgent alarm. Equipment to shock the heart back to a normal rhythm was used immediately. With such a rapid medical response it is normally possible to reverse a cardiac arrest. But many of these patients could not be resuscitated, or only with great difficulty. In every case these patients already had at least a minor heart problem, often a very serious one; otherwise they wouldn't have been taking Tambocor or a similar drug. But was the drug to blame?

The case of a 16-year-old boy taking Tambocor because of a congenital heart defect illustrates the problem. The youth was running laps around a baseball field during physical education class. Feeling weak, he stopped and asked the teacher if he could rest. The teacher said no. As punishment for stopping, he was ordered to do twelve push-ups. When he couldn't complete the push-ups he was ordered to do twelve sit-ups. After a few sit-ups he turned pale, his heart stopped beating, and he collapsed. The boy got emergency medical care fast. Paramedics were on the scene within 10 minutes. He was rushed to a hospital equipped to deal with a major cardiac emergency. It proved unusually hard to restore a normal heartbeat. But the medical team refused to give up on this boy even after the initial shocks failed. After 65 minutes, his heart started beating again. In that period, he suffered severe brain damage from which it is unlikely he will ever recover.

Did the boy suffer cardiac arrest because he had a congenital heart defect? Should the blame fall on the physical education teacher who was woefully ignorant of the boy's medical history? Or was the culprit a drug that causes a cardiac arrest that is especially difficult to reverse? When a drug causes completely unrelated side effects, they are easier to identify. If a baby girl takes a drug for an ear infection and suddenly suffers massive liver damage, the drug is the immediate and obvious suspect. Only a few such reports are required to build a case against the drug. But if a patient being treated for a heart problem then dies of a heart problem, the natural tendency is to blame the patient's illness, not the drug. In such circumstances it takes systematic scientific study of groups of patients to implicate the drug.

This was the situation with Tambocor, and it was by no means unique. Critics blame some psychoactive drugs for causing suicide and psychotic behavior, while proponents say such episodes are only to be expected in a patient population with mental illness. Many drugs used in cancer chemotherapy are known to cause cancer themselves. In 1993, a clinical trial of a drug to combat liver infection had to be hastily canceled when it was discovered the drug was highly toxic to the liver. In 1975 a nation-wide test of an already marketed cholesterol lowering drug was halted amidst evidence it caused heart attacks rather than prevented them. On the day Tambocor's approval was announced, 3M's medical director, Gary Gentzkow, was careful to point out that the drug made about 7 percent of the patients worse instead of better. He did not, however, mention that it could make some patients so much worse that they died of cardiac arrest.

Tambocor was a bright new star in the growing constellation of drugs for almost every conceivable biological purpose. Every day people take drugs that affect their blood, bladder, liver, heart, brain, bones, lungs, muscles, sex organs, skin, stomach, kidneys, and a variety of glands—thyroid, pituitary and adrenal. In fact, very few human biological processes have been clearly defined without a drug soon appearing to manipulate them. Also, some drugs alter body processes not readily understood. For example, no convincing explanation exists for why general anesthesia works. However, no one would seriously propose to do without it.

While the beneficial effects of new drugs have been widely celebrated, few have paused to consider the growing dangers that flow from this power over the most fundamental biological mechanisms. Thirty years ago some wise words on this subject came from Louis Lasagna, a medical doctor and Tufts University professor who studies the evaluation and regulation of drugs.

"The mind of man has removed the stopper of the bottle from the medicine jar," he told a conference in San Francisco. "The chemical genie formerly imprisoned within now stands before us. He is a spirit known to work miracles, but also to wreak havoc—to improve life or destroy it.

"It is not clear that we are yet sufficiently wise to control the genie adequately. It is quite clear that we can never wish him back into the jar." The story of Tambocor and other antiarrhythmic drugs is an account of what happened when the genie got completely out of control.

Chapter 2

DISCOVERY

LATE ONE NIGHT in 1972, the phone rang, interrupting the sleep of a young physician named Roger Winkle. Like the other interns at Barnes Hospital in St. Louis, he was so tired he could barely see straight. Winkle pulled on his white coat and grabbed his stethoscope, an indispensable tool and badge of office that distinguishes a doctor from other hospital workers.

The call to Winkle was from a night nurse in the seventeen-story Queeny Tower, a section of the sprawling Barnes Hospital complex. Barnes, with ties to the medical school at Washington University, ranks among the most famous teaching hospitals in the United States, in the same league with Johns Hopkins in Baltimore and the Harvard-affiliated Massachusetts General.

Soon Winkle's stethoscope was pressed against the chest of a man in his late 40s. The sounds that Winkle heard indicated a very rapid heartbeat. Instead of contracting about 70 times a minute, the heart was beating more than twice that fast. The man had been admitted to the hospital earlier with heart problems. As Winkle examined his patient and checked over the chart, he was optimistic. Except for a rapid heartbeat he looked good, he was conscious and alert, and the rest of his vital signs were stable.

The next morning Roger Winkle's patient became the focus of an essential ritual of medical training. In the hallway, or near the nurses' station, the interns and residents gather around a senior attending physician and present the patients that they have admitted or treated. One of the skills that young doctors master is the ability to recite the mass of medical information about a patient in a rapid-fire, tightly organized manner. The show-offs do this entirely from memory. From his crisp presentations and clear grasp of the essential facts, it was already clear that Winkle was going to be a very good doctor. After each intern presents a patient, the attending physician grills the young doctor, and then often gives a short talk enlarging on some aspect of this patient's condition and care. In the case of Winkle's patient, the topic was the prognosis or future prospects.

Winkle was quite surprised to learn that his patient was in great danger of dying. Several obvious things can go wrong with the human heart. It has four essential valves that must open and close about 100,000 times a day. This patient's valves worked fine. While the muscle cells are sometimes killed or weakened, enough heart muscle must survive to squeeze the left ventricle—the main pumping chamber—with enough force to maintain adequate blood pressure and output. A heart attack had killed some of Winkle's patient's muscle cells, and they could never be replaced. But enough probably remained. A third critical component is the electrical system. It ensures that the millions of individual cells contract in a precise sequence and timing. An electrical problem was endangering the life of Winkle's patient. He had, in effect, a short circuit.

Normally, the contraction of the left ventricle is triggered by an electrical impulse rippling across it. Then the heart rests for the better part of a second while the pumping chamber fills again with blood. Then the next signal to contract arrives. It originates in the heart's built-in clock, a small node of tissue called the pacemaker of the heart. Unfortunately, Winkle's patient's heart wasn't waiting for the next signal from the pacemaker. Instead the electrical pulse took on a life of its own, traveling perpetually around the heart, causing the very rapid beat. The patient's heart was beating so rapidly that the left ventricle didn't have time to fill properly before each contraction. Therefore it wasn't pumping enough blood. Soon this would damage the lungs, the kidneys and the brain. Also, the rapid beat can degenerate into a complete electrical breakdown, leading to cardiac arrest and death.

Winkle's patient was transferred to Barnes's special coronary care unit, established a few years earlier as one of the first in the country. However, without effective interventions, a special unit and space-age electronic monitoring can only provide a more detailed view of the inevitable conclusion. And Winkle learned that when it came to effective treatments to slow down the racing heartbeat, the cupboard was nearly bare. There was a drug called quinidine, so old that it had been first described by the great Louis Pasteur more than a century earlier. It was a chemical relative of quinine, the malaria drug. Another was procainamide, a variant of the first local anesthetic, procaine or Novocain, which was discovered in 1904. It was a classic case in which a drug used successfully for one purpose proves useful for a totally different medical problem. But both drugs had severe limitations. In some patients these drugs didn't work at all. In others there were serious adverse effects. Sadly, neither could save Winkle's otherwise healthy and vigorous patient. Seven days later he was dead.

The death had a profound effect on Winkle, who in turn would ultimately play a dramatic role in the development and testing of antiarrhythmic drugs. This patient sparked Roger Winkle's interest in the electrical system of the heart. Before going to medical school, Winkle had been an honor student in electrical engineering at Cornell University. So he was already knowledgeable about electrical systems. Also, Winkle wanted something more from medical training than to memorize the nuts and bolts of the daily grind. He hoped to get into research. He wanted to learn how to save the next patient who woke him up in the middle of the night with a dangerously rapid heartbeat.

Winkle's experience was just a blip in the medical life of the United States of America, circa 1972. But it illustrates a beginning point for many new drugs: a perceived medical need. A series of new monitoring devices was revealing a wealth of information about the electrical system of the human heart. Bright young physicians such as Winkle were going to study it intensively. And the more they learned, the more they were going to demand new drugs and other tools to manipulate and control the electrical pulses so central to life itself.

In St. Paul, Minnesota, during that very same year, a research scientist named Eldon Banitt was looking for a new drug. Banitt was a medicinal chemist who specialized in creating molecules that might become new medicines. He worked for the 3M Company and labored daily in a laboratory tucked away in one of the buildings scattered across 3M's sprawling headquarters complex. 3M was one of America's largest and most successful business corporations. From a shaky beginning in sandpaper products it had become a global manufacturing and sales organization so effective it was a model for textbooks on modern business organization and management. In an era of technological progress, 3M made it an important goal to get 25 percent of revenues from new products. As business leaders increasingly realized they were part of a world economy and a global marketplace, 3M could boast that almost half its sales came from outside the United States. When critics charged that America's biggest corporations had become slow, clumsy behemoths, 3M tried to create a flexible confederation of entrepreneurs managing their own businesses. This was a company that promoted from within, tried to nurture new ideas, and said it regarded failure as an inevitable price of trying something new. And while 3M had a dazzling array of products, ranging from mundane masking tape to exotic fibers for spacecraft, in the early 1970s it was trying to expand a small foothold in pharmaceuticals, one of the largest and most profitable businesses in the world.

By deliberate public policy, the search for new medicines is undertaken by businesses seeking profits. The reason is not immediately obvious, since medical research is such a public enterprise. Most of the money to pay for biomedical research comes from public sources, with the lion's share coming from the National Institutes of Health. The research work is mostly conducted at nonprofit medical schools and research centers, although the bill is variously paid by government, drug companies and charitable foundations. The discoveries from this research establishment, even from private drug company laboratories, are published in the open scientific literature where anyone can read about them.

The patent is the instrument through which public scientific knowledge is converted to private gain. Some drugs are so essential that people will pay almost anything to get them. A patent guarantees that no other company can supply them and opens the door to charging the maximum price that the market will bear. This legal monopoly has been the major influence in spawning a multibillion-dollar global pharmaceutical industry. Patent rights are remarkably broad. Current law encourages scientists who develop drugs with government funds to patent them and reap the benefits personally. Genentech, the California pioneer in genetic engineering, patented a chemical so universal that every human body on earth manufactures it to dissolve blood clots. Harvard has patented a mouse. A controversy raged about the millions of dollars earned by Burroughs Wellcome for its patented AIDS drug AZT. It was sitting on a shelf in a North Carolina research laboratory until the government's National Cancer Institute discovered its important effects. Since Burroughs Wellcome owned the patent, it reaped the financial benefits. The National Cancer Institute is spending $60 million to test Merck's prostate drug Proscar but will not share in the profits if, as the sponsors hope, it prevents prostate cancer.

A single patented drug can sustain an entire multinational corporation. For example, cyclosporin, which prevents the rejection of transplanted organs, supplies almost 30 percent of the revenues of Sandoz Pharmaceuticals. SmithKline Beecham's breakthrough ulcer drug Tagamet once provided one quarter of the company's total revenues. For several years Genentech stayed afloat on its blood-clot-dissolving drug, Activase.

These patents make possible the most profitable industry in the world. Measured as the return on its stockholders' investment, pharmaceutical companies are more than twice as profitable as the typical American manufacturing corporation. Compared by return on sales, the profits of the drug industry were higher than all 26 other industries tracked by the Pharmaceutical Manufacturers Association.

For decades such results have delighted investors and fueled a torrent of angry criticism of the industry, which has remained a favorite populist target. In defense, the industry says these billions in profit finance the search to find new drugs. Pharmaceutical companies spend more than seven billion dollars a year to develop new drugs, and pay a global army of 10,000 scientists and researchers. This huge enterprise produces about twenty-five new drugs annually. Most are quite similar to ones that already exist.

Although the question of whether incentives to the industry are appropriate or excessive will be long debated, one fact remains clear. Discovering, developing, testing and supplying a new drug is a mammoth enterprise requiring many years, vast expertise, and millions of dollars. The U.S. Congress Office of Technology Assessment estimated that it took direct cash outlays of about $65 million to bring a new drug to market in the 1980s. New drugs today aren't likely to be discovered by idealistic young doctors working in the basement on weekends.

The events that led to the discovery of Tambocor began in Eldon Banitt's laboratory at 3M in St. Paul. Banitt's tools were simple glass beakers, tubing, filters and smelly solvents. But in Banitt's lab, organic chemistry was revealed truly as the work of gods. Banitt was taking incredibly tiny molecules and twisting them into new shapes. He could attach long chains of atoms or rip off whole blocks of matter like a mechanic stripping down an engine to rebuild it. Banitt hoped to create a molecule with unique and powerful properties, a new drug. Traditionally, the drug companies scoured the globe looking for compounds with unique biological properties. In the remote Amazon, biologists collected rare tropical flowers. Near the Arctic Circle, they packed dirt into plastic bags in hopes the soil might harbor tiny life forms capable of making beneficial compounds. One famous drug was developed from an ancient deadly poison, arsenic, after thousands of chemicals were tested. Another breakthrough drug was an orange dye for fabrics that happened to kill the bacteria that often cause pneumonia. Today, however, a major fraction of the search for new drugs is concentrated in organic chemistry laboratories where medicinal chemists like Banitt try to shape new molecules they hope will make the sick healthy again. Even given interesting compounds from the plant and animal world, they synthesize more potent or less toxic variants. Literally thousands of organic chemists do this every day.

It is a task with an overwhelming chance of failure. An industry rule of thumb holds that researchers must test 10,000 compounds to find one new drug. In 1970, somebody actually counted and reported that the industry screened 703,900 distinct compounds. That same year the FDA approved just 11 drugs that were unique new molecules. (Since the compounds screened in 1970 would not have been tested and approved for a decade or more, the comparison is not an exact one.)

Banitt worked with carbon molecules, the central ingredient in all compounds found in anything alive. Its six protons and six electrons are so configured that carbon combines in an infinite variety of form and function. Hooked together in long chains of 10 or 20 atoms, carbon forms compounds we call fats. Join a carbon and nitrogen atom, and this is the beginning point for the 20 amino acids from which all proteins are constructed. Proteins in turn are the raw materials from which skin and muscles, blood and brains are built.

In searching for a new drug, Banitt was using six carbon molecules formed in a hexagonal ring. The simplest form results in the chemical solvent benzene. It is a remarkably flexible and powerful beginning structure. It looks something like a hexagon made with Tinker Toys. At each point on the hexagon are two locations where additional pieces may be attached. Banitt could attach long complex side chains or tack on single hydrogen atoms.

That flexibility was the central problem for Banitt, and it is one reason why drug research is so expensive and so much a lottery. With great facility he could attach an extra oxygen and carbon group and have a weak acid. And he could add side chains of simple or intricate design. But what effect would this molecule have circulating in the bloodstream of a human being? How did Eldon Banitt know what kind of molecule to make, or imagine how his new creation might work?

A powerful but simple way to think about this problem was devised nearly a century ago by one of the great pioneers of pharmacology, the German scientist Paul Ehrlich. Long before anyone had a clear idea of the inner workings of cells, Ehrlich theorized that cells must have receptors. And what all drugs did was react with a unique cellular receptor. The easy way to visualize this is to imagine that the cell receptor is a lock and the drug is the key. Some drugs worked like a kind of skeleton key, turning locks all over the body. Others would work in only one lock, affecting one, very narrow function such as the absorption of sugar from the bloodstream. Decades of scientific progress produced abundant specific examples to validate Ehrlich's theory. The outer membrane of every cell is packed with special receptors that recognize molecules of a particular size and shape. Receptors also float in the fluid inside the cell. And still others lurk in the cell nucleus, ready to restrain or unleash some process described in the genetic code of DNA.

In modern pharmaceutical research and development, it is increasingly possible to create idealized pictures of the cell receptors, and then to fashion a molecule with a matching shape. But in the late 1960s and early 1970s when Eldon Banitt was working in his 3M lab, the process was less deliberate. He made a whole bunch of keys with new shapes and then tried them in a lot of different locks. This was why about 10,000 novel compounds had to be tested to come up with one drug. Many medicinal chemists work a lifetime creating new molecules without ever making a winner.

One day Banitt's starting point was a white powder called salicylic acid. Ten dollars will buy pounds of it at any chemical supply house. This cheap chemical boasts a rich history: It is the active ingredient in the willow bark prescribed by physicians back as far as Hippocrates himself. A simple alteration of this molecule yields a vastly more pleasant-tasting compound called aspirin, one of the most beneficial medicines ever discovered. However, Banitt was not interested in a new kind of aspirin. Salicylic acid was merely a convenient molecule built on a central structure containing the benzene ring of six carbon molecules. Banitt dissolved the salicylic acid in a common solvent called acetone.

Next Banitt concocted a second chemical brew. It was rich in an element with such unusual properties that it formed the central focus of a special research program at 3M. The element was fluorine. 3M already had created numerous products through skillful manipulation of fluorine atoms. One was its Scotchgard treatment to protect fabrics from grease stains. Fluorine would become the key ingredient in the linings of microwave popcorn bags, it protected hoses in auto engines, and it was an important constituent in the blankets of foam sprayed to quench aircraft and oil fires. The company considered itself a master of fluorine chemistry and was now trying to apply this expertise to pharmaceuticals. This scientific cross-fertilization was the hallmark of the technical innovation that 3M systematically nurtured as its commercial lifeblood.

The key components in Banitt's second chemical mixture were three fluorine atoms clamped to a carbon atom. Fluorine is interesting because it is so similar to, but also subtly different from, the ubiquitous element hydrogen. With a single proton and an electron, hydrogen is ready to attach almost anywhere that a vacant electron orbit offers a safe harbor. But lightweight hydrogen is also readily detached and lured to some more powerful mate. Even with its nine protons and electrons, fluorine has almost the same propensity as hydrogen to combine readily with many other atoms. However, unlike the easily detached hydrogen, fluorine clings more tightly in place, yielding more stable compounds. Stability was an attractive property for a drug. For oral administration, a drug had to survive being bathed in stomach acid, resist the assault of digestive juices, and be protected against the liver enzymes that divide large molecules into smaller pieces. Fluorine had other valuable properties as well.

Banitt's carbon and three fluorine atoms were at the moment part of a much more elaborate sulfur compound, a nasty white powder with the chemical name of *2,2,2-trifluoroethyltrifluoromethanesulfonate*. This too can be bought readily from a chemical supply house. Now came a critical part of the medicinal chemist's art. Banitt had to engineer a chemical reaction in which the cluster of carbon and three fluorine atoms was removed from the sulfur compound and then reattached to the benzene ring exactly where he intended, at carbon number 5. To achieve this, the sulfur and fluorine compound was dissolved in acetone, along with a third agent, potassium carbonate.

Now came the first major step in making the new molecule. Very, very slowly, the salicylic acid mixture was stirred into the heated fluorine-rich brew. It took two full hours of slow, patient work just to combine the two mixtures. To complete the chemical reaction for the 40 ounces of liquid and dissolved chemicals required 24 continuous hours of boiling. To avoid the obvious problem that it soon would boil dry, Banitt used a condenser tube to capture the escaping vapors and cool them to a liquid which then drained back into the flask.

After 24 hours, the hot mixture was filtered, and the liquid removed by evaporation. The residue was a thick yellow syrup. Banitt still had to purify the mixture to remove all the remaining original agents and by-products. To do so, he used a paper filter to remove some impurities; others were dissolved in chloroform and then evaporated. Step by step he removed all the other compounds until only his new chemical remained.

Banitt still was not done. To his first product he attached a nitrogen atom to the benzene ring. And the nitrogen, in turn, acquired a side chain, which was stripped away from another molecule. Eldon Banitt now had a finished new molecule of his own design. But once again he faced many laborious steps to extract the new molecules from his mixture, and then turn them into crystals. As a final step, he would send out the new crystals for tests to confirm the compound's molecular weight and basic structure.

What happened next, when a new molecule was finally in hand, reveals much about the development of new drugs. Banitt put the white crystals—a meager handful of white powder—into an amber medicine bottle. He labeled the bottle with a diagram of the new chemical structure that he had created. Then he started all over again. Next time the fluorine group would be moved to a different position on the hexagon of carbon molecules. Sometimes he attached two fluorine groups. And the side chain sprouting from the nitrogen would have different shapes and lengths. He changed reactants and experimented with different chemical techniques. These acts of creation were too prosaic to deserve a name. They just got a number, beginning in 1966 with R-1. It was not until years later, and R-799, that Eldon Banitt really hit pay dirt.

Before Banitt reached R-799, a fortuitous event affected the entire course of the research project. One original goal was to find a new, better local anesthetic. Banitt had started with a prototype molecule with properties of an anesthetic, and then developed interesting variants. One prototype molecule was procainamide, a relative of the first local anesthetic, Novocain. What happened next was exactly what is envisioned in business school textbooks about managing innovation.

One day a 3M pharmacologist named Jack Schmid had a bright idea. As a pharmacologist, he specialized in understanding how molecules functioned as medicine, how they were absorbed into the body, what dose should be used, what their therapeutic effects and side effects might be. Schmid suggested that some of the would-be anesthetics that Banitt had created might work as antiarrhythmic drugs for people with irregular heartbeats. Two leading antiarrhythmic drugs—procainamide and lidocaine—were both local anesthetics. Equally important was the mechanism by which they achieved their pain-deadening effect. Nerve cells transmit signals of pain through electrical impulses that ripple in waves along the cell membranes, leaping from fiber to fiber. The two local anesthetics altered the electrical properties of the nerve cells, slowing the conduction of these electrical pulses so much that the pain signal was not propagated from cell to cell. In the human heart, similar waves of electrical pulses trigger the contraction. Perhaps a drug that slows conduction might help, for instance, that patient of Roger Winkle's who had an electrical short circuit that created a heartbeat so rapid that it soon killed him. Thanks to Schmid's idea, Eldon Banitt had an entirely new potential use for this series of new fluorine compounds. Now the problem was finding whether any of them worked.

In this critical screening phase, much depends on the disease process and what medical science knows about it. In well-characterized disorders, screening is a straightforward routine. If the goal is a drug to kill bacteria, each compound can be put on a petri dish where the bacteria grow. Then the rare compounds that show activity can be given to mice to make sure they don't kill them too. At the other extreme, some biological processes are so poorly understood that it is difficult to devise any feasible screening test. For example, hidden among the hundreds of thousands of novel compounds already created by the pharmaceutical industry might be several that greatly enhance conceptual thinking. But except in large-scale human tests, how would the experimenter know? For many medical problems, an animal model is developed. There are inbred mice strains with no immune systems, which grow human tumors that are surgically implanted. Another mouse is prone to heart failure and provides a model for testing drugs to increase cardiac output. None of these animal models accurately reflects the disease process in humans. However, as a screen, the models produce a manageable number of possibilities. Thus, one reason 3M decided to look for an antiarrhythmic drug was the existence of an animal model well documented in the open scientific literature. This is how it worked.

For each compound, the 3M team used ten female Swiss-Webster mice, an inbred laboratory strain. Each mouse was given a large (for its size) oral dose of the test compound, dissolved in water and gum arabic. Then the mice were placed in glass beakers. The first test was elementary. If the drug was highly toxic, it killed the mice or caused other easily observable harm. Next a wad of cotton saturated with chloroform was added to the beaker. As might be expected, the first effect was to put the mice to sleep. The anesthetic was so concentrated that the mice soon stopped breathing.

What happened next provided the basis for the animal model. Soon after the mice stopped breathing, the physiological stress quickly led to a complete collapse of the electrical system of the mouse's heart. Under some circumstances a mammal heart will continue beating even when removed from the body. But the stresses of this particular protocol in these mice caused an electrical breakdown, and the rhythmic, coordinated waves gave way to electrical chaos. Individual cells contracted randomly and spasmodically in the pattern called ventricular fibrillation.

The anesthetized mouse was removed from the beaker. Its chest was cut open, and a researcher could then observe if the heart was quivering chaotically in ventricular fibrillation. That meant the compound had had no effect on heart rhythms. Sometimes the researcher would observe a heart that was still pulsing with normal, but perhaps slowed contractions. This was the first sign of a possible winner.

Any compound that showed antiarrhythmic activity was then tested again at half the dose in ten more mice. This continued until the researcher established the lowest dose at which the chaotic pattern of ventricular fibrillation was prevented in half of the mice tested. The lower the dose, the more potent the drug. Testing began with two well-known existing drugs, procainamide and quinidine. This benchmark allowed the 3M team to match their own data with the results published in the scientific literature. The comparison had another central purpose. A drug that didn't work better than the two already on the market was of little interest.

Banitt and his colleague, the pharmacologist Jack Schmid, identified more than 20 fluorine compounds that didn't kill the mice and appeared at least as effective as quinidine. The results also allowed Banitt to graduate from a blind search for activity into a targeted process of design. Now he could begin to see which specific molecular structures worked.

Banitt learned that attaching two separate clusters of carbon and fluorine atoms worked better than using just one. The best results came when these two clusters were attached to the hexagon at carbon atom number 2 and carbon number 5. It resulted in a drug four times as potent as quinidine. But Banitt was still the blind locksmith. He was creating the key to turn an unknown switch off or on. Specifically which cell receptor was involved, and how it affected the function of cardiac muscle cells, remained a mystery. The key that worked best in this mysterious lock was R-799.

Banitt experimented extensively with the side chain. The side chain on R-799 was exactly like procainamide. It was quite long, and branched at a second nitrogen atom like the fork of a tree branch. The team worried that the two branches of the side chain might have a serious disadvantage in a drug. A salable antiarrhythmic drug needed to have a long life in the body. The two branches of the side chain looked vulnerable to the liver enzymes, which might sever them. It was just possible the researchers might have a better drug by taking the ends of the two branches and joining them to form a ring. Several compounds were created with a side chain that terminated in this ring structure. One, numbered R-818, was effective in mice, almost as good as the original leading candidate, R-799. Two or three others worked nearly as well, and many were as good as quinidine.

The 3M team now owned a collection of keys that without doubt fit some important locks—at least as defined by the animal model. The perfect drug fits only the cell receptor of interest to the pharmacologist and none other. Unfortunately there are no perfect drugs. So often they fit locks in unexpected locations. This can be a bonanza to the researcher. A drug developed to combat motion sickness became important in the treatment of severe mental disorders. Iproniazid, a drug used against tuberculosis, was discovered to be an antidepressant when patients reported to their doctors that not only were their lungs better, they felt just terrific. But most often when a drug fits too many different receptors this causes unacceptable side effects, a terminal problem for uncounted numbers of otherwise promising drugs.

With R-799 in the lead, the 3M development team began more extensive tests in animals. Dogs were given an intravenous infusion of ouabain, a paralytic agent once used in Zulu poison arrows and a fast-acting form of the heart drug digitalis. In the toxic doses used, ouabain caused a whole spectrum of heart rhythm disturbances, ranging from occasional premature ventricular contractions to ventricular fibrillation, the total disorganization of the electrical system. Then the researchers measured how effectively the test drug prevented these rhythm disorders. In these and other animal models of increasing sophistication, R-799 still looked more potent than any drug then on the market.

Then one day R-799 died. This is how most pharmaceutical research and development ends. While it was remarkably effective in all the animal models used, it failed a critical test. When administered to mice for a longer time it proved too toxic to the central nervous system. That is just the kind of problem one would expect from a potent drug originally modeled on a local anesthetic, a deadener of nerves.

Just a small handful of compounds remained. One of them was R-818, practically identical with R-799, except for the curious ring shape at the end of its side chain. It was not quite as effective in the animal models as R-799. But it was seven to twelve times more potent than any drug then on the market. For the 3M team, that would ultimately prove to be good enough. In time, R-818 would become a drug called Tambocor. The year was 1972, and development was just now beginning in earnest. 3M had been researching novel fluorine compounds for six years.

Chapter 3

A RACE BEGINS

A MODERN METROPOLIS of medicine stands on the east bank of the Mississippi River, tucked into an enclave between Minneapolis and St. Paul. Almost six thousand medical care professionals labor daily among the fourteen buildings that make up the University of Minnesota Hospital and Clinic. From the main hospital complex, one can go by tunnel underneath Church Street to the student health center. In the basement is a lab where cardiologists perform a diagnostic procedure called an exercise stress test. The patient walks on a treadmill while the physician takes an electrocardiogram. The test measures the electrical response of the heart to the stress of increasing levels of exercise. One day in 1975, a University of Minnesota cardiologist named Arthur Leon wanted the lab for a special study.

Leon was about to give a human volunteer the very first dose of Tambocor. 3M's fledgling drug had crossed an important boundary. Tambocor was no longer just an interesting molecule with an unusually potent effect on the hearts of dogs, cats, pigs, mice and rats. The company was now ready to test it in living humans. With an advertisement aimed at the University of Minnesota campus population, Leon had recruited a 24-year-old student willing to participate for $100. All the volunteer had to do was lie on a couch in Arthur Leon's lab for eight hours. First he was hooked up to the EKG machine. Then he extended his arm so an IV needle could be inserted into a large vein that leads a short distance back to the heart. A clear plastic tube was attached to the needle; at the other end was a container filled with water, sugar and the first dose of Tambocor. As soon as the stopcock was turned, the mixture flowed down the tube. Within seconds it would reach his heart.

Before testing in humans, drug companies must get a permit from the Food and Drug Administration. It is called an IND (*i*nvestigational exemption for a *new d*rug) and technically what it allows is the shipment of an unapproved drug in interstate commerce. In filing for an IND, the company describes the animal tests that have been completed and outlines a plan for testing in humans. Explicit approval is not required. If the FDA does not object within 30 days, the company may proceed. In the case of Tambocor, there were no objections. Leon also had to get approval from his own medical center's Institutional Review Board, a committee that regulates experiments in human subjects. Each volunteer is informed in writing of the nature of the experiment, and provides written consent.

Although a serious responsibility, this was not a novel situation for Leon. Before joining the University of Minnesota, he had directed a special drug testing unit at the College of Medicine and Dentistry of New Jersey. The unit was funded by Hoffmann-LaRoche to test the company's new drugs. Leon had given the very first dose of L-dopa, a drug used to treat Parkinson's disease. Leon got the job of testing Tambocor through Donald Hunninghake, a University of Minnesota medical colleague. Hunninghake had trained 3M's head of clinical pharmacology, Donald Kvam. When Kvam needed someone to test Tambocor, he went to his former professor. Hunninghake, a professor of pharmacology and medicine, had designed the protocol but left the actual study to Leon. All these connections illustrate the close relationship between the pharmaceutical industry and the doctors who do research at medical schools.

After Tambocor was administered over five minutes, Leon closely observed his patient, focusing particularly on the EKG tracings. He observed nothing unusual. If the experiment went as planned, he hoped to observe nothing whatsoever. He was conducting the first of what are called Phase I trials. It was too early in drug development to think about a therapeutic effect. Leon had loosed a molecule of a brand new design into the human body, itself a chemical factory of great complexity and power that assembles and breaks down molecules with a facility that medicinal chemists only dream of. The purpose of Phase I testing was to find exactly what happened to that molecule from the moment that it entered the body. Without this critical information, pharmacologists lacked the factual foundation on which to build an answer to the question of whether Tambocor was safe.

Before giving Tambocor to the first human volunteer, 3M had completed some, but by no means all, of the animal testing required for a new drug. One important animal study that was completed before Leon administered the first dose of Tambocor was the acute toxicity study. The goal of this study is to find the smallest dose that is immediately lethal to one half the animal subjects. Pharmacologists call it the LD_{50}, or dose lethal to 50 percent. These experiments showed that while Tambocor seemed more potent than competing drugs, it was also more toxic. For the first human, Hunninghake and Leon had set the initial dose of Tambocor at one-fortieth of the LD_{50} in beagle dogs.*

In the first patient absolutely nothing happened, not even a slight change in the EKG. However, the most important results from the experiment were not immediately available. Leon had taken nine blood samples, including four in the first hour. These would be sent over to 3M's lab near St. Paul to be analyzed on its gas chromatograph, which measured the concentration of the drug in the blood. The researchers couldn't find a therapeutic dose for Tambocor until they could plot its distribution through the body over time. If the body broke down the drug quickly, large and repeated doses would be required to maintain adequate levels of the drug. However, if the body had great difficulty breaking down the drug, then repeated doses could accumulate into toxic concentrations. Large differences existed among drugs for irregular heartbeats. Quinidine was broken down so quickly it had to be taken three or four times a day. A drug called Cordarone could be detected in the blood more than 200 days after the last dose. Thus, learning Tambocor's pharmacological profile was the essential first phase of human testing. All this looked routine to Arthur Leon as he infused the drug to the first eight volunteers. After two patients had tolerated one dose level, he would slowly increase it. Again, the blood samples were bundled up and sent over to 3M.

Leon's experiments produced an important discovery about 3M's new drug. He learned that humans break down Tambocor eleven times more slowly than the beagle dogs used in the toxicity tests. Dogs broke down one half the Tambocor circulating in just one hour. In Leon's healthy human volunteers, it took eleven hours.

While a longer-acting drug improved Tambocor's commercial prospects, it created a dangerous moment during testing. The ninth and last patient in Leon's test series received about one half the LD_{50} for dogs. But because humans break down Tambocor so much more slowly, the drug reached concentrations in the blood much higher than what had frequently killed the beagles. Apparently nothing happened. Asked about it years later, Leon would remember only that "the experiment went very smoothly."

*All such dose calculations are also adjusted for differences in body weight.

. . .

For two years the Phase I testing of Tambocor continued at a modest pace. 3M researchers learned that the drug was eliminated in urine and does not accumulate in the body. When a large molecule like Tambocor is broken down by enzymes in the body, the large pieces are called metabolites. In drug development these metabolites are a source of both pleasant and ugly surprises. The very first sulfa drug turned out not to be the patented compound called Prontosil that was actually administered. The body quickly broke down Prontosil into the more common compound called sulfanilamide. In some drugs, the metabolites could also prove toxic and might accumulate in various tissues. Tambocor was mostly excreted unchanged. Researchers tested the oral form of Tambocor to make sure that the digestive juices and liver didn't destroy it, as they do many drugs. Unless it was truly unique and beneficial, a potential best-seller needed to be available in oral form.

It was not until 1978, almost six years after the discovery of Tambocor, that 3M crossed another important boundary. Now reasonably convinced they understood Tambocor thoroughly enough to judge its safety, 3M researchers were free to address the seminal question: Did it have a benefit? The studies to establish the effectiveness of a drug are called Phase II trials. Once again it fell to Donald Kvam of 3M to pick a medical center to conduct the first Phase II trial, to find out whether Tambocor worked effectively in humans.

Kvam selected Pitambar (Pete) Somani, a physician and pharmacologist who had been born and trained in India. Somani had helped develop new cardiovascular drugs for Abbott Laboratories in North Chicago before returning to the academic world at the University of Miami. In the small community of cardiovascular drug development, Kvam and Somani were already acquainted and had been talking about working together on Tambocor since human studies began in 1975.

Somani was delighted when Don Kvam asked him to conduct the first effectiveness study. Highly motivated research doctors seem no less driven to be "first" than Olympic athletes. Most were tough competitors from an early age; in medical school they were ranked at the top of their class; after medical school they were the residents who stood out from the crowd during advanced medical training. Then these medical success stories would compete with greater intensity at academic medical centers because only some would win tenure. Medical research is one of the most intensely competitive meritocracies in the world. The pressures to achieve have led a few competitors to fabricate research. On occasion the successful competitors develop egos of monumental proportions. Somani, in fact, is a soft-spoken man. But he would patent four new drugs, become a senior medical school professor, and eventually the director of health for the state of Ohio. He achieved all this in addition to mastering the culture of an adopted country.

But in 1978 Somani was pleased enough just to be the first to test the effectiveness of Tambocor. He was then professor of clinical pharmacology and medicine at the University of Miami and had a special lab at Jackson Memorial Hospital. The need to find patients with precisely defined illnesses is another of the forces that drive the pharmaceutical industry into such a tight partnership with academic medical centers. As a cardiovascular specialist in drugs, Somani would have referred to him patients with difficult heart rhythm problems that couldn't be solved using the few drugs available in 1978. So Somani could supply the patients.

The first ailing patient to get Tambocor was a 37-year-old man with a long-term problem with PVCs or premature ventricular complexes. Also called premature beats, they occur when the main pumping chamber contracts before it has had time to fill completely. Occasional premature beats are quite common and usually can't be detected without an EKG. Somani's patient, however, had an exceptionally large number of PVCs, an average of 12 every minute. The reasons why this particular patient had an electrically unstable heart were not known; his heart was otherwise undamaged. Before getting the drug, he had been hospitalized for a day on Somani's Pharmacology Research Unit.

"We were quite excited being the first clinical trial," Somani remembers, "the whole team, my research nurse, the physician assistant. We were all anxious to know whether it would work." 3M was also excited. A company monitor was present to observe the experiment, and Donald Kvam wanted to know the outcome immediately.

As the drug was administered, Somani could watch exactly what was happening on the electrocardiogram. The patient's problem was remarkably easy to see. In a normal heart, Somani would see spikes march with regularity across the lengthening strip of graph paper, one for each contraction. Typically the spikes occur at intervals of about one second. In this patient Somani could see each premature beat as an extra spike on the EKG. They came quite regularly, about one-half second after a normal beat. The stopcock was turned and the drug rushed toward the patient's heart.

For ten minutes nothing happened. Then, very slowly, the interval between the regular beat and the premature beat began to widen, from a half second to about three quarters of a second. Suddenly the premature beats disappeared entirely. All that remained were the spikes of a normal heartbeat marching across the EKG strip. "I never saw anything this dramatic before," he recalled. Somani had been counting the premature beats and plotting them quickly on a piece of graph paper. He phoned Donald Kvam at 3M. "I let them know quite excitedly that the drug had abolished the PVCs."

Somani would repeat the experiment in nine more patients. In the tenth patient, Tambocor didn't work. Since this family of drugs was known for its hit or miss effects, this was expected. Suppressing PVCs in two out of three patients might well be acceptable; 90 percent efficacy was a new record. Somani noted only one adverse effect. Five minutes after the Tambocor was infused, the first patient reported chest discomfort. Since Somani observed no confirming signs in the electrocardiogram, he attributed the symptoms to the patient's anxiety over participating in this experiment.

Thus, the most notable therapeutic benefit of Tambocor was evident in the very first patient. It would quickly become known as amazingly effective in suppressing premature beats, better than anything researchers had ever seen before. An unequivocal superiority was the mark of a new drug that might go the distance. But even to Somani back in 1978, it was already clear that 3M was in a close race with other competitors. Somani's research unit was about to test its first samples of Bristol-Myers' new investigational drug, Enkaid. It too would show impressive power over PVCs. "There was a race going on," Somani recalled. "It was a question which drug would make the clinic first."

Chapter 4

THE MAKING OF A MARKET

WHILE TAMBOCOR PROVED remarkably effective in suppressing premature beats, it was not immediately obvious why this was useful. Overall, it would be hard to define a more benign disorder of the human heart. Only in a tiny minority of cases did an individual with PVCs have symptoms disturbing enough to spur a trip to the doctor. Those with frequent PVCs might occasionally detect a momentary pause, as if the heart were considering whether it wanted to pump again or not. A few would awake at night with palpitations. However, most people with PVCs felt nothing. In fact, a majority of the adult population had at least a few premature beats each day, and the frequency increased with age. The growing medical interest in premature beats in the 1970s was not inspired by swelling legions of patients begging their doctors to stop their premature beats. This was a problem identified by doctors doing medical tests, and they were the ones who worried. Even the grounds for physician concern were not self-evident, since by themselves, premature beats are not inherently harmful. Why, then, was the pharmaceutical industry developing new drugs to treat a condition that did no harm, and could not be detected by most patients?

Part of the answer lies in the broader spectrum of electrical disorders of the heart, of which premature beats are the most benign and common (see Figure 1). At the most serious extreme is the complete electrical breakdown of the heart, ventricular fibrillation, in which the rhythmic pulses degenerate into electrical chaos. Death occurs inevitably in the absence of an electric shock, which usually can reestablish a normal rhythm. Next to a complete breakdown, the most dangerous condition is a sustained rapid heartbeat, the electrical short circuit that killed Roger Winkle's patient at Barnes Hospital,

FIGURE 1. The Pulse of Life: Basic Heart Rhythms

Normal heart
The sharp spikes mark the contraction of the main pumping chambers.

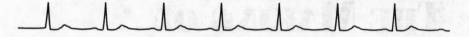

Premature beat (PVC)
The contraction has occurred early. In this case a pause occurs.

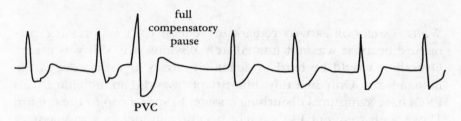

full
compensatory
pause

PVC

Sustained rapid beat
Contraction occurs too quickly to pump adequate amounts of blood.

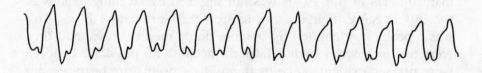

Ventricular Fibrillation
Electrical chaos. The heart no longer pumps any blood. Only an electrical shock can restore a normal beat.

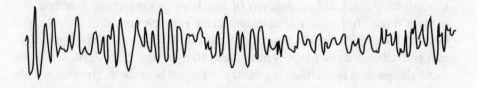

and inspired his interest in cardiology. This usually proves fatal within a matter of days unless the rapid beat can be halted. In between the benign premature beat and a life-threatening short circuit are a graded sequence of intermediate patterns. Sometimes PVCs occur in pairs or triplets. Other patients experience several seconds of a rapid heartbeat, but the rhythm disorder halts of its own accord. However, symptoms are rare except in the continuous rapid beat.

The decision to treat PVCs sprang from the fear that these premature beats might somehow trigger a lethal episode of fibrillation and cardiac arrest, a sequence called sudden death. From a drug company perspective, this was a vitally important theory because cases of sustained rapid heartbeat were comparatively rare—and drugs often did not work. However, hundreds of thousands—perhaps even millions—of people had premature beats and 3M had a remarkably effective drug that suppressed them.

But did suppressing these mild premature beats in fact prevent the lethal event, sudden cardiac death? The medical thinking behind that theory was articulated in a landmark speech to the annual convention of the American College of Cardiology in 1978—the same year Pete Somani discovered Tambocor's dramatic effects on premature beats. The speaker was an important cardiologist named Bernard Lown.

In a long and colorful career, Lown had been both a social visionary and a pioneer in researching the electrical system of the human heart. After World War II, he had been expelled from medical school at Johns Hopkins for refusing to segregate the blood of blacks and whites. (He was readmitted after a student protest.) He had become famous for publicizing the terrible medical consequences of a nuclear war, and at the height of the cold war promoted medical cooperation between the United States and the Soviet Union. He was also one of the early experimenters with using electric shocks to reverse the otherwise fatal electrical breakdown of the heart, ventricular fibrillation. The device, called a defibrillator, can today be found in coronary care units, ambulances and operating rooms. The defibrillator was a symbol of the nation's rising faith in the great power of medical innovation, a tool capable of restoring life in the face of otherwise certain death.

In 1978 Lown had another soaring idea for the 15,000 physicians who had assembled in Anaheim, California, for the annual gathering of the nation's heart specialists. He was going to outline an electrical theory to explain the most important malfunctions of the human heart. He would pull together not only his own discoveries, but the thinking and innovations of dozens of others in the field.

In Lown's vision, great danger came from an electrical breakdown of the human heart. His lecture was titled, "Sudden Cardiac Death: The Major Challenge Confronting Contemporary Cardiology." As always, his thoughts were ready to rise to high altitudes.

"In the industrially developed countries, sudden cardiac death is the leading cause of death," he proclaimed. "It was recognized at the dawn of recorded history and even depicted in Egyptian relief sculpture from the tomb of a noble of the Sixth Dynasty approximately 4,500 years ago." By Lown's count, sudden cardiac death was killing more than 400,000 people every year and accounted for 32 percent of all deaths among adult men under age 65.

These were mostly the same deaths that the American Heart Association was counting when it talked about heart attack victims, and warned about high cholesterol. Lown's electrical theory and the American Heart Association's cholesterol-based approach were like blind men touching different parts of an elephant and describing quite different animals.

The urgent challenge to cardiology, in Lown's view, was to prevent sudden cardiac death. It claimed, he said, 1,200 human lives a day, almost one every minute. The electric shock from defibrillators was already saving lives by reversing cardiac arrest. But whether used in coronary care units or by paramedics in ambulances, the equipment had to be used within a very few minutes or the patient would suffer irreversible brain damage or die. These emergency stopgaps could never solve the problem of sudden cardiac death. Those who experienced one cardiac arrest were prone to have another, and next time help might not be immediately at hand. Also, too many cardiac arrests occurred without warning symptoms that might trigger a call for emergency help or a trip to the hospital.

The only solution, Lown believed, was to prevent the electrical accident that caused cardiac arrest rather than trying to rescue those whose hearts had already stopped beating. The first step was to identify those at greatest risk. At that instant those seemingly benign premature beats, or PVCs, moved directly to center stage. Premature beats indicated an electrically unstable heart; surely the electrical accident of cardiac arrest was more likely to occur in people who experienced PVCs. Several studies seemed to support this proposition. The National Heart, Lung, and Blood Institute had studied more than 8,000 survivors of heart attacks. Those with PVCs were twice as likely to die in the next three years as those who had none. A

New York state insurance company study of heart attack survivors found that among those with large numbers of PVCs, 15 percent died over three years' time. Thus, Lown concluded that PVCs identified the population at risk—especially if they had already had a heart attack. Antiarrhythmic drugs were the solution to the problem.

"Any prophylactic program against sudden death must involve the use of antiarrhythmic drugs to subdue ventricular premature complexes [PVCs]," he declared. This was the essence of the arrhythmia suppression hypothesis. The central idea was that eliminating the milder rhythm disturbances would prevent the life-threatening breakdowns. It would never become as familiar as the theory that lowering cholesterol levels might prevent heart attacks. But Lown's theory would lead to hundreds of thousands of patients taking drugs for irregular heartbeats for the rest of their lives.

Lown readily conceded that the PVC suppression theory had never been tested in a clinical trial. However, he saw no need to delay until the proof was in hand. As he explained it, "In medicine, great rewards have flowed from partial answers and usually have preceded complete solutions. This is the case with sudden cardiac death."

By 1978 the suppression hypothesis was already widely accepted in cardiology. Lown had laid out key elements as early as 1971; others had contributed important studies. In this speech, he was trying to move the theory to center stage for the cardiology community. Cardiology had to reduce the terrible toll of sudden cardiac death. Suppressing PVCs with antiarrhythmic drugs was the treatment to use.

Already, this approach had such serious weaknesses that it is amazing that so few physicians demanded it be tested first to establish that the expected benefits, in fact, existed. Irreversible damage that occurs in a heart attack might also create electrical disorders. The greater the damage, the more PVCs. Since the heart could not be repaired, it might be pointless or even harmful to suppress the premature beats. Every doctor had been taught that an association between two events does not prove a causal link. In this case it was equally plausible that premature beats were nothing more than a telltale indicator of underlying, permanent damage.

The most serious blow to the suppression theory had come from another pioneer in cardiology, Leonard Cobb of the University of Washington in Seattle. Cobb had organized the nation's first teams of paramedics to rush to the scene with defibrillators to reverse sudden cardiac deaths occurring outside the hospital. Cobb had studied sixty-four patients who had experienced cardiac arrest. He found three quarters of them were already taking antiarrhythmic drugs! Just how much protection could such drugs afford if a large majority of the cardiac arrest victims were already taking them?

Lown and other supporters of the theory had a response that was to determine the fate of Tambocor and bring American medicine a new generation of drugs for irregular heartbeats. The problem, he concluded, was that the drugs had not effectively suppressed the premature beats. In fact, that was his main message to the American College of Cardiology. Physicians needed to be more systematic in making sure that the drugs actually eliminated the PVCs. He urged much wider use of the newly developed heart monitors that made a 24-hour recording of the heart rhythm. It was a major advance over the traditional doctor's office EKG, which captured just a few minutes of electrical activity. Rather than simply prescribing the drugs and hoping for the best (in medical terminology, empiric therapy), Lown wanted doctors to use the new monitors to guarantee that the drugs were performing as expected. Lown's suggestion of additional testing to ensure that the drugs were working was certainly reasonable. But did it explain why Cobb had found so many cardiac arrest victims already taking antiarrhythmic drugs? Lown's explanation was plausible, but still an unproven answer to a major question about an untested hypothesis. But as the increasing sales of drugs for irregular heartbeats showed, Lown's theory was rapidly gaining acceptance in the medical community.

A few words of caution also appeared. One such warning came from Roger A. Winkle, who had come a long way since seeing his first patient with a rapid heartbeat as an intern at Barnes Hospital in St. Louis. Winkle completed his internal medicine residency at Barnes and went on to train in cardiology at Stanford. It was a logical choice for a young physician interested in the electrical system of the human heart. The head of cardiology at Stanford, Donald C. Harrison, was one of the senior figures in antiarrhythmic drugs. At the completion of his cardiology fellowship, Winkle was invited to remain at Stanford, beginning on the lowest rung of the faculty ladder, acting instructor. By 1979 Winkle had become an assistant professor and was studying the new generation of antiarrhythmic drugs. He had done some early studies with Tonocard, another antiarrhythmic drug being developed for the growing market. In 1979, the year after Lown delivered his stirring call to arms against sudden cardiac death, the much more junior Roger Winkle also published an appraisal of the problem. Writing in the *Annals of Internal Medicine* he noted that it was pointless to give antiarrhythmic drugs without follow-up testing to determine their effect.

Winkle disagreed with Lown about the wisdom of treating patients on the basis of the unproven suppression hypothesis. While Lown urged physicians to act on "partial knowledge," and treat high-risk patients with PVCs, Winkle took a skeptical view. "Its clinical value remains unproven," he declared. He noted that "in no situation" had suppressing premature beats been shown to prevent death or other cardiac events. Despite Winkle's article, the first of many warnings, the use of antiarrhythmic drugs to prevent cardiac arrest continued to grow. It was not merely a question of Winkle's junior rank, compared with Lown's world renown. In American medicine, words of caution rarely slow the rush to treatment.

At 3M headquarters in St. Paul, the year 1979 was also decision time for Tambocor. Don Kvam had been shepherding the drug through preliminary human trials for nearly four years. While no commitment had been made to complete development of the drug, the growing size of the market was encouraging. The number of prescriptions written for antiarrhythmic drugs had expanded by 50 percent since 1970, reaching an annual total of nearly 12 million by 1979. But even more eye-catching to the 3M team was the dramatic success of the only new drug for irregular heartbeats introduced during the whole decade. Searle had introduced Norpace in 1977, and in just two years it commanded a market of one million prescriptions a year. Such rapid growth proved how eager physicians were for a safer, more effective drug. The old-timer quinidine still dominated the market. But it had such frequent side effects that one third of the patients couldn't tolerate it.

To help make a decision that involved investing tens of millions of dollars, 3M asked three outside consultants to evaluate Tambocor. One expert they turned to was an up-and-coming young doctor and pharmacologist at Vanderbilt University in Nashville. His name was Raymond Leon Woosley, Jr., and by age 38 he was already consulted frequently by companies with new antiarrhythmic drugs.

As Woosley put it, he had always liked small ponds. He had spent his early childhood deep in rural Kentucky at a crossroads store where his family lived and worked. Woosley's soft-spoken southern manners concealed an intelligence and drive that would take him straight to the top. However, after being first in his high-school class, he still wanted a small pond, turning down an appointment to the

Air Force Academy to attend a small Kentucky college in Bowling Green. With no aspirations to be a medical doctor, he studied pharmacology at the University of Louisville. Armed with a doctorate, Woosley found another small pond. He turned down a job offer from Upjohn, where he would have been the 500th pharmacologist hired. Instead he accepted an offer from a Fort Lauderdale drug company so tiny that he was its only pharmacologist. It was not long before Woosley noticed that the most important drug development work was done by medical doctors—who could test drugs in patients. In just two years time, Woosley had his own M.D.

His first assignment in advanced medical training at Vanderbilt University set his professional course for life. His mentor was a doctor and pharmacologist named John Oates. Right at the dawn of the interest in antiarrhythmic drugs, Oates had had a bright idea. One of the drugs doctors knew best was lidocaine, which was used extensively in the newly developed coronary intensive care units. But lidocaine could only be given intravenously, so its use was limited to patients in a hospital setting. The emerging need in treating arrhythmia was for a drug that could be taken indefinitely. Oates told Astra Pharmaceuticals that it would be quite simple to make a molecule with the properties of lidocaine, but in oral form. It involved a fairly simple reshaping of the molecule. Astra was interested and the clinical testing of the new drug was assigned to Woosley. The drug was Tonocard, the same agent that Winkle also studied at Stanford.

Woosley's next drug, Enkaid, came from Bristol-Myers. The company was about ready to drop out of the race to the clinic. Early testing at Stanford had shown that the body broke down half of the circulating Enkaid in two or three hours time. This seemed a fatal limitation because the company believed a marketable drug needed a convenient, twice-a-day dose schedule. Bristol-Myers wanted Woosley's opinion. He quickly saw that the body did metabolize—or break into pieces—Enkaid in a few hours. However, as he studied the individual pieces, the metabolites, he discovered that two of the most important ones were effective antiarrhythmic drugs in their own right. Therefore, the effects persisted for eleven hours.

Woosley uncovered another unusual property of Enkaid. In roughly 10 percent of the patients, the drug behaved quite differently. These individuals apparently lacked the enzyme that split apart the Enkaid molecule so easily. Such biological differences among individuals are still another factor that makes drug development, and drug safety, so complex. The Enkaid itself worked well in those patients who couldn't rapidly break down the drug. Woosley told Bristol-Myers they had a good drug. It was this kind of pharmacological detective work that made Woosley a star in this area, and brought 3M to his door. If Lown was the godfather of the suppression theory that created the market for these drugs, Woosley was the godfather of their pharmacology.

As Woosley examined Tambocor, he liked what he saw. He realized its molecular structure somewhat resembled another old-time drug, procainamide, but without the particular configuration he suspected caused frequent side effects. It was just as effective as Enkaid in suppressing premature beats, but not metabolized so quickly. He told 3M that in oral form it ought to be even better than Enkaid, the best antiarrhythmic drug he had ever tested.

Back at 3M headquarters in St. Paul, Don Kvam and medical research director Terrance Coyne drew up a plan for clinical development of Tambocor. In Phase I testing they had learned much about what happened to the drug inside the human body. Somani's Phase II study had been repeated at the University of Minnesota with equally dramatic results in suppressing PVCs. But beyond Woosley's exploratory assessment, they had done little with Tambocor in the oral form. Consequently, Kvam and Coyne had to draw up a complete development plan for the oral product. They would have to find the correct dose for Tambocor in tablet form. They would pay for elaborate clinical trials to compare Tambocor with the most important competitors already on the market: quinidine and Norpace. They planned to complete the clinical research program over the next five years and have a New Drug Application ready for the FDA in 1984. Starting almost from scratch with the oral product had an interesting advantage. They could test their potent new drug in many different academic medical centers around the country, spreading money and excitement throughout the cardiology community. It was a quantum leap for Tambocor, a jump from the backwater of a few limited studies to a major clinical development program that would involve dozens of hospitals and hundreds of patients.

Chapter 5

THE RISE OF MORGANROTH

IN EARLY OCTOBER 1980, 3M medical research director Terrance Coyne headed toward Philadelphia for a meeting. It was important enough to draw not only the company's senior research doctor, but also three other members of the Tambocor development team. 3M was among 23 drug companies sending high-ranking representatives. The industry contingent, in turn, was greatly outnumbered by research physicians from academic medical centers in the United States, Britain, Germany and Japan. The federal government was also represented. The Food and Drug Administration had sent J. Richard Crout, its senior doctor responsible for drug evaluation. The 145 participants were going to spend two days talking about a single subject: new drugs for irregular heartbeats. As one British doctor put it, the world's medical elite in this specialized area had gathered. Tambocor was just one among a new generation of drugs now being tested in medical centers around the world. The rapidly expanding market had spurred great interest among the drug companies; the large turnout demonstrated the intensity of that interest. But what clinical testing should be done to ensure these potent new drugs were safe, and to judge their effectiveness? What questions should be answered before they were prescribed for hundreds of thousands of people around the world? That was the issue before this assembled medical elite.

It was an amazing feat to have gathered all the players in one room. It marked a particular triumph for Joel Morganroth, the 35-year-old Philadelphia doctor who had arranged the conference. He had a shrewd eye for technical issues. Also, as he was now demonstrating, he had a flair for making himself useful to the major players. As

Tambocor and other drugs like it moved ever closer to the market, his ambition would lead him into a role of major importance.

Joel Morganroth's drive to succeed had been evident from an early age. He grew up in the Detroit suburb of Oak Park, surrounded by all the essential elements that defined the American dream in the 1950s. He was the second of four boys, raised in a neighborhood that included both factory workers and professionals. His father owned a furniture store and his mother raised the family. It was an era of drive-in root beer stands, American-made cars with soaring tail fins, and steadily growing prosperity. In the suburban heartland at least, there were unlimited opportunities for young people inclined to grasp them.

Even by his high-school days, Joel Morganroth was a youth so inclined. His report card was so filled with As that he ranked at the top of his class. However, he was really not a nerd, one of those sickly, brainy kids with thick glasses, bent over a rack of test tubes or table full of electronics equipment. He was an athlete, good enough to be state champion in wrestling in the 133-pound weight class. Wrestling attracts boys with a special combination of skills. Unlike football or basketball, it does not require great size, coordination, grace or teamwork. The wrestler can be a skinny kid weighing in at barely one hundred pounds or he can be a burly giant. But wrestling requires the guts and the drive to stand up in front of a crowd in a direct physical confrontation that yields just one winner and one loser. In one of his high-school years, Morganroth didn't lose at all. When he did lose, he didn't gnash his teeth or smash fragile objects. He just planned how to win the next match.

He was not the passionate or impulsive type. As Morganroth put it, "I get things done ahead of time. I prepare. I never do things at the last minute." To make top grades, he did the work. The Morganroth home was not the kind of place where a parent checked every homework assignment, or relentlessly pressured the boys to compete and perform. From as early as he could remember, the desire to excel had come from within.

Joel Morganroth decided he wanted to be a doctor during his second year of college at the University of Michigan. Some doctors are truly called to their profession, as are many ministers. For Morganroth, it was just one of those career choices that college students make, and he was not a person who had difficulty making up his mind. Medicine involved working with people, and it involved science. He liked both. Morganroth was soon enrolled in a special program that allowed him to take medical school courses during his undergraduate years. It shortened the trip to an M.D. by one year. It was just the thing for a young man in a hurry to make good.

During medical school at the University of Michigan, Morganroth rose to meet the greater demands and tougher competition. He was ranked first in his medical school class, and named the valedictorian. In his senior year he wrote a prize-winning paper that he read at a national convention sponsored by the American Medical Association. It was also printed in the AMA's prestigious medical journal.

"Let us be perfectly clear that medical technology today, right at this moment, has the capacity to visit both benefit and incomparable mischief upon mankind," he wrote.

"Have we the audacity to assume that the proper utilization of these techniques will be guaranteed by such professional platitudes as 'We seek to alleviate human suffering'?"

It would have been a most appropriate message for his meeting about new drugs for irregular heartbeats. Morganroth had assembled in Philadelphia in 1980 a group of people with the "capacity to visit both benefit and incomparable mischief upon mankind."

A medical school graduate with Joel Morganroth's impeccable record gets his pick of hospitals for an internship. He chose the Harvard-affiliated Beth Israel Hospital in Boston. It was at Harvard and Columbia and Hopkins that the very brightest and most competitive medical students would become doctors. It is perhaps at the Harvard-affiliated hospitals that American medicine's high opinion of itself reaches fullest flower. Most of the senior professors consider themselves the world's preeminent authority in their subject. Some of them really are. The Detroit kid named Morganroth did not love Harvard. As he put it, "The atmosphere was a little thin."

Thin atmosphere or not, he won a spot as one of five clinical associates named each year to train at the National Institutes of Health. An ambitious young doctor could combine the final year of a residency in internal medicine with a first year of postdoctoral research at the federal establishment that was the biggest spender for biomedical research in the world. A research fellowship at NIH was another important stop to get the ticket punched in the journey to the highest ranks of the medical establishment.

At NIH, Morganroth worked at the National Heart, Lung, and Blood Institute in the branch that was researching the role of cholesterol compounds in heart disease. And with hundreds of millions of dollars to award in research grants, the cholesterol branch could be confident that researchers would remain interested in this approach. Although he would work with two physicians who would later head the overall heart institute, Morganroth did not particularly prosper at NIH.

Soon he was undertaking more conventional advanced training in cardiology at the University of Pennsylvania in Philadelphia. There, nearly eight years after he had graduated from college, the central elements of his medical future finally began to take shape. Internal medicine is a specialty of medical practice. Cardiology is a subspecialty of internal medicine, focusing on the heart. Now, in seeking a niche in the world of academic medicine, Morganroth would end up in a subspeciality of a subspecialty. At Penn he was put in charge of the Heart Station, where he was responsible for a set of diagnostic tests in cardiology that are called "noninvasive" because they are performed from outside the body. Many of these tests focused on the electrical activity of the heart: the EKG, the exercise stress test, and the portable Holter monitor which records heart rhythms for an entire day. The Holter monitors were particularly useful in detecting premature beats, and establishing whether drugs eliminated them. Morganroth completed his cardiology training and was asked to stay on at Penn as a junior faculty member, still in charge of the Heart Station. He now had a position on the lowest rung of the ladder of academic medicine. He would not be there long.

Morganroth's career in antiarrhythmic drugs began the day that Sara Armstrong Mahler of DuPont Phamaceuticals came to Penn to talk about an unusual new drug. It was the direct result of still another of Bernard Lown's global visions. He wanted to "solve" the problem of sudden cardiac death. He wanted to reduce the dangers of nuclear war. He managed to combine both interests in a program of medical cooperation between American and Soviet doctors. One result of this program was that DuPont got a license to develop and sell a Russian drug for irregular heartbeats called Ethmozine. It was an international medical breakthrough in cooperation that made headlines. Although one of Lown's Harvard colleagues had spent months in Moscow studying Ethmozine, Mahler went to Penn for the initial clinical testing. The assignment went to the young faculty member who handled the Holter monitors. Morganroth's first job seemed elementary: find an effective dose.

Morganroth started giving Ethmozine to patients at the dose prescribed in Russia. Then he measured the results on a Holter monitor. Nothing happened. No adverse effects were found, but no observable results either. So he doubled the dose. Still nothing happened. Ultimately, DuPont would learn that a dose that effectively suppressed

PVCs was ten times higher than had been used in Russia. It was an illustration of Lown's argument; it wasn't enough to give an antiarrhythmic drug to patients known to have irregular heartbeats. Doctors had to ensure that the premature beats were in fact suppressed. Ethmozine had been given to tens of thousands of patients in Russia at a dose much too low to have a useful effect.

It was at exactly this point that Morganroth asked a key question that helped to make him a star in antiarrhythmic drug development. Suppose Ethmozine did an excellent job of suppressing PVCs, he said. "How would you know?" The answer sounds easy. The premature beats would disappear. But Morganroth knew from managing the Heart Station at Penn that PVCs had little regularity. Few patients were like Pete Somani's first Tambocor subject, who produced a consistent string of premature beats. Most varied day by day, hour by hour. A 50 percent reduction in PVCs occurred routinely as spontaneous variation. After making some tests, Morganroth concluded that it would take an 83 percent reduction in PVCs to be assured the drug was actually achieving an effect. He had a reasonable answer to a recurring problem in medicine. The severity of symptoms and disease vary widely from day to day, even month to month, even in disorders that inevitably worsen over time. Both patients and their doctors desperately want to interpret any short-term change for the better as evidence that the treatment works. Only the most objective and systematic methods of measuring the outcome of treatment prevent doctors and patients from fooling themselves.

At it happened, Morganroth's study of Ethmozine terminated abruptly. Because the drug had been so widely used in Russia, DuPont had persuaded the FDA to let it skip the animal testing phase. The FDA agreed but asked for a single long-term toxicity study in monkeys. When six of the twelve monkeys in the study died unexpectedly, DuPont hastily brought human testing to a halt.*

Although Morganroth lost his drug, he still made a name through his method for measuring whether it worked. He published his conclusions in the journal *Circulation*. It made him an instant celebrity in the narrow subspeciality of antiarrhythmic drugs. Given a modest success, Morganroth began to display his talent for maneuver in the world of biomedical politics.

As he discussed how to test drugs, Morganroth discovered that

---

*Development resumed several years later when DuPont persuaded the FDA that deaths resulted from errors in how the drug was administered to the monkeys; however, the animal studies were not repeated.

pharmaceutical companies were often reluctant to question decisions of the FDA, even when they didn't make sense. Yet when he called up senior officials at the agency and asked them an intelligent question, he got a reasonable answer.

This was how Morganroth befriended two important doctors at the FDA, Robert Temple and Raymond Lipicky. These two colleagues would, in fact, make the final judgments about the safety and effectiveness of a new generation of drugs for irregular heartbeats. Morganroth became a skillful middleman. He had a base at an academic medical center. He was attracting attention from the drug companies. He wasn't bashful about talking to the FDA. And he wasn't afraid to ask everyone scientific questions. Morganroth had a sure instinct.

Thus, Morganroth was able to recruit Temple and Lipicky to help plan the Philadelphia conference on how to evaluate this new generation of drugs. Because Morganroth had turned out the most important FDA officials who were going to judge these drugs, the conference became something of a command performance for the pharmaceutical companies. They needed to know *how* to test their drugs.

To open the conference, Morganroth echoed the words of Bernard Lown. "The solution to the problem of sudden cardiac death is the leading challenge to cardiology today," Morganroth said. His talk left no doubt that the new generation of antiarrhythmic drugs was now aimed at the large population with mild irregular heartbeats. The larger purpose of the assembled group, he declared, was "providing to the American public effective and safe antiarrhythmic agents which can eventually be used to prevent or decrease the epidemic of sudden cardiac death."

It was therefore not surprising when early in the conference one of the participants rose to question the still-unproven theory that suppressing premature beats would prevent sudden death. It came from one of Morganroth's Philadelphia colleagues, Irving M. Herling.

"We've seen that you can suppress [premature beats] and still have the individual sustain sudden death," Herling said.

Herling was, however, quickly cut off by Morganroth. "We cannot address the question in this symposium," he said. "We have to have effective antiarrhythmic agents that are well tolerated." Like Lown, he diverted the discussion of whether the whole concept had any basis in fact to the more technical issue of suppressing the irregular beats effectively.

In many ways the whole meeting was an elaborate presentation aimed at influencing a tiny audience: the four FDA officials in attendance. It fell to the most senior member of the FDA contingent to explain to the assembled elite the true source of the FDA's great power. The official's name was Dick Crout and he headed what was then called the Bureau of Drugs.

One great difference distinguishes the drug laws of the United States from the practices of other countries, he said. Many countries require that drugs be effective before being granted approval. For this audience, he didn't need to explain that in most European countries, that meant the most senior experts can assemble—as they had in this room—and simply agree among themselves whether a drug was effective. Many European countries were quite comfortable with the idea of being ruled by an elite, including a medical and scientific elite. The United States was different, and so were its drug laws, Crout said. To win approval for a drug requires "adequate and well-controlled clinical trials."

Crout was challenging those assembled. "If experts don't have an evidentiary base for their opinion," he said, "their opinion isn't worth it." He had touched the heart and soul of American drug law. It does not matter whether all the experts agree. They must prove their case with objective clinical trials, even if such studies are expensive and time-consuming. Crout seemed to be saying that if the assembled experts believed these new antiarrhythmic drugs would prevent cardiac arrests, they would be required to conduct the lengthy clinical trial needed to prove it. The arrhythmia suppression hypothesis remained a theory, plausible but unproven.

But no sooner had Crout described so eloquently the strength of the United States law than he opened a loophole large enough for everyone in the room to squeeze comfortably through. The law said that drugs had to be proven effective. However, the FDA exercised great flexibility in defining what "effective" really meant. For a painkiller, the sponsor had to prove it relieved pain. But if one had a drug to prevent cardiac arrests—and that was clearly the main purpose of these new drugs—it was *not* going to be necessary to prove it prevented cardiac arrests.

Crout could not have been more explicit. He was "not requiring they should do something to protect the patients or to improve mortality." As he put it, "We vary the ground rules depending on what experts in the particular field think." So if a drug "effectively" suppressed premature beats, that was enough for the FDA.

While the FDA would not allow experts to declare a drug effective based merely on their opinion, it would allow them to define the standards by which drug effectiveness would be measured. By allowing the companies to prove only that the drugs suppressed premature beats, rather than showing this made patients feel better or live longer, Crout had made it relatively easy to win FDA approval.

The rising interest in antiarrhythmic drugs evident at the 1980 Philadelphia symposium was not lost on the 3M development team. The company cut the development cycle for Tambocor in half. Instead of submitting its New Drug Application in 1984, the deadline was advanced to 1982. The faster schedule meant a shift in tactics. No longer would the testing of Tambocor proceed slowly in a few hand-picked medical centers. 3M would launch an all-out campaign to introduce all the major centers in cardiology to their impressive new drug.

Less than a year later, in August of 1981, Tambocor was introduced to America's doctors in the country's most prestigious medical forum, the *New England Journal of Medicine.* The journal is widely read and respected by doctors the world over, and publishes only a few hundred articles a year among thousands of manuscripts submitted. A seat on the editorial board, or even being asked to peer-review articles, is an important honor in medicine.

It was thus a great public relations coup for 3M when Tambocor became the subject of a scientific report so glowing that it read like an advertisement. Tambocor "appears to be a highly effective and well-tolerated antiarrhythmic agent," the article said. The discussion section described Tambocor as "an important addition to the current antiarrhythmic armamentarium." And it suggested its characteristics approached those of "an ideal antiarrhythmic drug." Furthermore, if Tambocor had serious adverse effects, these researchers did not detect them. In fact, they concluded their data suggest "a low potential for toxicity and adverse symptoms." Knowledgeable doctors were already aware that a new generation of drugs was in the pipeline. Once again the authors obliged 3M by proclaiming, "The results equal or exceed those reported for the most effective antiarrhythmic agents that are available or being tested."

Although this appraisal was based on just eleven patients, the report named nine coauthors. It is one sign how eagerly researchers sought to include on their resume a publication in the *New England Journal of Medicine.* Scientific articles routinely list so many coauthors that an unwritten code usually determines the order in which the names appear. The doctor who did the most work and probably wrote the article appears as the first-named author. In this case, it was Jeffery L. Anderson, a young cardiologist who had trained at the University of Michigan, and was then setting up his own research operation in Utah at the LDS Hospital in Salt Lake City. With such a glowing endorsement of Tambocor, he could count on winning research business from 3M in his new position. The unwritten code also provides that the last-named author is the "senior author." This is usually the head of the section or department, and it is another badge of rank in the medical hierarchy. In this case the senior author was Bertram Pitt, chief of cardiology at the University of Michigan. Getting an endorsement from one of the major figures in arrhythmia research was an additional bonus for 3M. Not only had Pitt attended the 1980 conference that Morganroth had sponsored to speed the approval of the new drugs, he would also be sitting on the FDA's advisory committee when 3M's application was presented.

A few months later, another medical journal would report the news that Tambocor was "highly effective in patients with high frequency arrhythmias." This time the publication was the *American Journal of Cardiology.* The study reported here was remarkably similar. In every important detail, it was exactly the same research protocol. The only difference was the academic medical center—this was one at Vanderbilt University. And it had another very important senior author, Raymond L. Woosley, the consultant who had earlier advised 3M to proceed with development. When the FDA advisory committee sat down to review 3M's new drug application, Woosley would also sit on this important panel.

The readers of *Circulation*, the flagship medical journal of the American Heart Association, would also learn about "the very effective antiarrhythmic agent" called Tambocor. This time the identical experiment was done at the University of Minnesota, where Morrison Hodges had picked up from Arthur Leon the testing duties for Tambocor.

What had occurred was surely a deliberate program to win publicity for Tambocor and to get endorsements from the most influential experts. 3M had designed and paid for a study of thirty-three patients conducted at three different medical centers. In 3M documents, the study even had the same number, R818-33. The "first" study establishing the dose of a new drug is considered an important paper, according to Dean T. Mason, the editor of the *American Heart Journal.* But once such a study is published, he said, no journal is likely to accept a duplicate. The authors of the Tambocor study apparently evaded this problem by submitting their manuscripts simultaneously to three different journals. Although 3M refuses to discuss the study, it is likely that the company orchestrated the campaign, designing the protocol and paying for the studies. It did the laboratory work to measure the levels of Tambocor in the bloodstream. And all three similar papers have a common author, Gordon Conard, who was 3M's supervisor of metabolic studies.

In all, 3M succeeded in publishing the same study six times. In addition to the three journal articles, both Jeffrey Anderson and Morrison Hodges presented their identical studies to the same scientific session of the American College of Cardiology, and their findings were published as abstracts in the college's journal. Woosley's were presented at the other major cardiology convention, the American Heart Association meeting. Although still a relatively new player in the pharmaceutical business, 3M had already demonstrated its skills in exploiting the system to its advantage.

In August of 1982 Tambocor passed another important milestone. Soon after the first oral dose studies were published in the United States, 3M won approval to sell Tambocor in Germany. Three other countries would soon follow suit. With rave reviews from important cardiologists in the United States, and approvals from foreign drug authorities, Tambocor was rolling rapidly toward approval on the accelerated schedule.

Chapter 6

TAMBOCOR IN TROUBLE

THE FIRST INDICATIONS of the dangers of Tambocor and similar drugs emerged in the same period that the medical journals were filled with enthusiastic reports. The most important finding came from Roger Winkle, the Stanford cardiologist who had questioned Bernard Lown's suppression hypothesis, and his grand scheme for preventing sudden death by eliminating the mild premature beats. Winkle was studying treatment of the immediately life-threatening rhythm disturbances—a sustained rapid beat that soon led to death unless it was halted. While Tambocor and its similar competitor, Enkaid, proved remarkably effective in suppressing the mild premature beats, they failed a distressing amount of the time in the severely ill patients.

During this period, one of Winkle's patients was a 67-year-old man with a weakened and enlarged heart. His failing heart was unable to contract with normal force, and its walls had ballooned out under the pressure of blood contained within. Such diseased hearts also can become electrically unstable. Winkle's patient was experiencing brief salvos of a rapid heartbeat, which then resolved into a normal rhythm. In hopes of controlling these rapid beats Winkle had prescribed Enkaid.

What happened next was a common medical mistake. The patient was on a low dose of Enkaid, one tablet every eight hours. By accident, he was given an extra tablet after just two hours. Within fifteen minutes, his cardiac monitor showed an alarming trend. For the first time, this patient was showing a rough, poorly organized and very rapid heartbeat, an irregular rhythm so serious that cardiac arrest might occur at any moment. Winkle was summoned.

Winkle had already seen cases where other drugs seemed to make a heart rhythm problem worse. But usually the drug-induced rhythm disorders were readily reversed. So when he reached the bedside of his 67-year-old patient, he expected to halt the rapid heartbeat immediately with a brief electrical shock. This time the shock had no effect. Another shock was given. Again it had no effect. After repeated shocks and cardiopulmonary resuscitation, Winkle finally managed to restore the patient's heart to a stable rhythm. Enkaid was stopped and the problem did not recur.

Winkle wondered whether Enkaid was responsible. The patient had a seriously damaged heart that was still deteriorating. He had not done well on another antiarrhythmic drug. Even with the extra tablet, the total dose of Enkaid was lower than for the typical patient. It was, however, enough to make a reasonable person suspicious enough to search for confirming evidence. Winkle went through the voluminous medical records of the 140 patients treated with Enkaid during testing at Stanford. He found ten serious incidents where Enkaid caused the rhythm to become worse.

One patient was a 60-year-old woman whose unstable heart was prone to lapse into long runs of rapid heartbeats. On seven previous occasions a normal rhythm was restored with a single electrical shock. Nineteen hours after taking the first dose of Enkaid, the woman again lapsed into a dangerously rapid beat. This time the Stanford doctors could not stop it. Repeated shocks didn't work. Other antiarrhythmic drugs had no effect. The women suffered cardiac arrest and died. Winkle found a similar pattern in a 72-year-old man; nineteen hours after taking Enkaid he experienced a rapid heartbeat that could not be halted. He also died. On this evidence, Winkle began to believe that Enkaid was a dangerous drug.

Winkle did next what all research physicians are trained to do when they believe they have found something important. He prepared a medical journal article describing the eleven cases. He submitted it for publication. As noted earlier, the medical journals are filled with repetitive—typically enthusiastic—reports about new drugs. Winkle was surprised to find his manuscript rejected. In fact, it was rejected for publication three times.

A less-concerned doctor might have given up. In one last try, he sent it to Dean Mason, a cardiologist who was based nearby in San Francisco and was editor of the *American Heart Journal*. Mason knew Winkle and respected his honesty. Mason was also active himself in the testing of this new generation of drugs and was quite enthusiastic about their prospects. Nevertheless, he decided it was an important finding and published it immediately. Winkle's report became widely known in the growing circle of cardiologists who were working with this new generation of drugs; it also caught the attention of the FDA doctors evaluating them. But his observations had come perilously close to being suppressed altogether. The text of one of his rejection letters was instructive.

"Because the literature does not at present contain an overall description of the antiarrhythmic efficacy of Enkaid, it seems somewhat inappropriate to include a separate article about this specific adverse side effect." This was the answer he got from the American Heart Association's journal, *Circulation*. However, Enkaid's efficacy had already been described in four lengthy reports, and all were cited in footnotes in Winkle's manuscript. Winkle's three rejections suggest that medical journals—all of them supported by drug company advertising—may not want to call attention to a new drug's adverse effects. Such conscious or unconscious biases help explain how, as noted earlier, doctors gave patients aspirin for fifty years without noticing that it could cause internal bleeding in some patients. Unless doctors were specifically looking for an adverse effect, they could easily overlook it. They would not be likely to look for an effect unless someone told them about it. And the main place that doctors learn such things is in medical journals.

Winkle's warning was indeed balanced by enthusiastic reports. Joel Morganroth described Enkaid in *Clinical Therapeutics* as a drug that "shows great promise as a potent antiarrhythmic agent." Raymond Woosley at Vanderbilt wrote in the *New England Journal of Medicine* that Enkaid was "a highly effective, well tolerated antiarrhythmic agent." In the world of biomedical politics, Woosley and Morganroth were making all the right moves to win the confidence of the drug industry. Winkle was making the wrong one. He heard nothing directly and did not suspect retaliation. But neither did any company approach him ever again to evaluate a new drug. Winkle was left believing the system rewarded people who put the best foot forward about a new drug. "They are free to go to the people who always say good things about every drug," he said.

While Tambocor was chemically quite similar to Enkaid, it might not necessarily have the same problems. Before the Enkaid incident, Winkle had in fact discussed testing Tambocor with 3M, but no agreement had been reached. The issue over which they differed—like many questions Winkle raised—proved later to be significant. Winkle wanted to test Tambocor in the sick patient population he was trying to help. However, 3M wanted to focus development on people who were fairly healthy except for their PVCs. He warned that it was a mistake to ignore the patients who needed the drug the most. 3M's clinical test program was already near completion when the company learned that the FDA was going to require studies focusing on the seriously ill population. That meant a serious push to meet the company's self-imposed deadline of submitting its New Drug Application to the FDA in late 1982. It also meant gathering additional data from the exact same patient population in which Roger Winkle had observed the malignant rhythm disturbances with Enkaid. The physician responsible for addressing these needs was the medical director of 3M Pharmaceuticals, Gary Gentzkow.

By November 1982, at the age of 35, Gary Gentzkow had restored the luster to a medical career that had once lain in ruins. Earlier that year he had been named medical director of 3M after his predecessor, Terrance C. Coyne, was promoted to head pharmaceutical research and development at 3M. For Gentzkow, it had been a rapid rise.

Gary Gentzkow had grown up in Salem, the sleepy state capital of Oregon. His parents were both clerks, his father in the post office and mother with the state tax commission. With two brothers and a sister, Gentzkow played along tidy, wooded streets of clapboard houses tucked into the scenic Willamette River valley. By his high-school days, Gary was handsome, bright, articulate and well groomed. Being of modest means and living in a small town, this was not a family that envisioned Harvard for the kids. But with the help of a scholarship, that was where Gary Gentzkow headed after public high school. He graduated from Harvard *cum laude*, and returned to Oregon for medical school at the University of Oregon Health Sciences Center in Portland. Once again he was an honor graduate. For his residency, Gentzkow chose the nearby St. Vincent's Hospital in Portland. But when he started to take care of his own patients, something went wrong. Occasionally it is the very brightest who have the imagination to see the endless possibilities for error that are missed by lesser minds more content to follow instructions. Some young doctors cannot keep the proper emotional distance from ailing patients and their families. It is rare among successful medical school graduates, but some just can't handle patient care. After his first year of residency, Gary Gentzkow quit the practice of medicine, never to return.

This decision left him without any clear direction in life. "I looked around for something to do with my medical training that didn't involve patient care," he recalled. "Nobody had any good ideas." Ultimately he settled on the pharmaceutical industry. He went to work for Abbott Laboratories in Chicago answering physician questions about drugs and helping handle the company's responsibilities for analyzing adverse reaction reports and forwarding them to the FDA. Soon he moved into drug research at American Critical Care, working on an antiarrhythmic drug called bretylium. It was used in emergency rooms to reverse cardiac arrests. He still recalls being delighted when in the Steven Spielberg movie *ET,* the movie doctors called for bretylium to resuscitate the alien visitor. On a more practical level, his work on bretylium led to a job at 3M. He became medical director just months after joining the company in St. Paul as associate director of clinical research.

It didn't take Gentzkow long to grasp how important Tambocor was to 3M's plans for a greater role in prescription drugs. "It was the corporate child. It was *numero uno*," he remembered. While 3M had literally thousands of other products, Tambocor was the star of the 18-year program to develop a major new prescription drug. It fell to young Gary Gentzkow, the newcomer at 3M, to face the serious possibility that this favored child, nurtured for a decade with millions of dollars of corporate cash, might die.

Physicians may obtain and prescribe new drugs for patients before they are approved or their safety demonstrated. The companies are not supposed to advertise or promote unapproved drugs, but they are available to physicians who contact the company and request them. Called a "compassionate use exemption," it is supposed to be reserved for life-threatening illnesses where approved drugs haven't worked. In return, the physician is supposed to report information about the patient and outcome of treatment. Thus the new drugs for irregular heartbeats had become widely available under a compassionate use protocol. Doctors were learning about Tambocor by word of mouth, at medical conventions where papers about the drug were presented, or by reading the enthusiastic reports that were appearing in medical journals. At some medical meetings, 3M had exhibits and handed out reprints of the published clinical studies.

By November of 1982 Tambocor was being used at 45 different sites, mostly large hospitals with medical school affiliations. Some of the patients were seriously ill; others had PVCs that produced symptoms described as "uncomfortable." More than 200 patients were being treated. Not only were these patients sicker and more vulnerable, it was a vast expansion of the total patient exposure to Tambocor. Only a few hundred people had taken the drug in controlled trials in the United States, many for brief periods. Pharmaceutical companies have mixed feelings about early compassionate use of drugs. The most moving testimonials for a new drug are those that come from doctors who found it saved a life when nothing else would work. These remarks build an early constituency of knowledgeable and enthusiastic doctors. On the other hand, it is in patients whose overall health is failing, and therefore tend to have a cascade of complex interrelated medical problems, that a powerful drug is going to produce previously undetected adverse effects. It is a regular source of nasty surprises for developers of new drugs, and that was exactly what Gentzkow received in November of 1982.

Nobody remembers who called 3M first. At one of the hospitals where Tambocor was being given under the compassionate use exemption, a patient had died. The physician thought that the drug might be responsible, because the patient was unusually hard to resuscitate from cardiac arrest, and this occurred soon after giving Tambocor. This surprised Gentzkow, despite being the person whom investigators should call if they observed some disturbing new adverse effect. Especially when compared with the widely used quinidine, he had found few adverse effects of Tambocor of any kind. Gentzkow asked for more information.

The next call came from Johns Hopkins University's medical school in Baltimore. A cardiologist named Lawrence Griffith was using Tambocor in a experimental treatment program targeted at the sickest of the sick. Griffith was using a technique in which irregular heart rhythms were deliberately induced with programmed electrical pulses. Then he would identify a drug that blocked the effects. It was trial and error. No drug worked consistently; in some patients, all the drugs failed. In still other patients, Griffith was unable to induce an irregular rhythm. Griffith's innovation was that he was focusing this protocol on patients who had already been resuscitated from a prior cardiac arrest. It was a long, arduous testing regime that could involve weeks in the hospital as Griffith tested drug after drug, trying to find one that would suppress the dangerous rhythms that he induced.

All this gave Lawrence Griffith an unusual perspective on cardiac arrest. On one hand, if one of his patients experienced a cardiac arrest, he would be among those least likely to blame a drug. Who would be more likely to die of cardiac arrest than someone who had already experienced one? On the other hand, it would be hard to find a physician in the United States so acutely aware of how easy it was to reverse an arrest, provided someone got there in time with an electric shock. Unless their previous cardiac arrests were reversed fairly readily, they could not have survived long enough to join Griffith's special protocol.

Therefore, one day in June 1982, Griffith was not initially surprised when a patient recently given Tambocor seemed to get worse, and then experienced a cardiac arrest. But this time, Griffith could not resuscitate the patient, a 75-year-old man who had suffered a previous heart attack. The immediate suspect was the patient's own severely damaged heart. It could pump out only about one third of the blood that flowed into the left ventricle. It was also so unstable electrically that the patient had long runs of a rapid heartbeat that at least twice had terminated in cardiac arrest. Still, Griffith had seldom seen an arrest impossible to reverse.

Griffith treated several more patients with Tambocor before he encountered another cardiac arrest where the patient could not be resuscitated. This one was a 61-year-old man with a lengthy catalogue of severe heart problems. The date was October 22, 1982. Just one week later, and in the very next patient getting Tambocor, it happened again, this time in a 55-year-old man whose heart was so severely damaged that its pumping capacity was about one fifth of normal. Two days after first taking Tambocor, the patient lapsed into an incessant rapid heartbeat that killed him. Repeated shocks and all other measures were of no avail. Griffith called Gary Gentzkow at 3M. He told Gentzkow this was something he had never seen before, despite his long clinical experience with the full array of antiarrhythmic drugs. If anyone knew, Griffith had to know that antiarrhythmic drugs sometimes made the patients worse instead of better. But the effects were typically reversible. In these three patients the usual resuscitative measures had no effect, and they died. He had no idea what the problem was, but he thought the doctors who were using the drugs had better sit down and see if they could find out what was happening.

This was the second call to Gentzkow in the same week about cardiac arrests where Tambocor was possibly responsible. He had now heard about four unusual patient deaths in a two-week period. It would be hard to imagine a worse time for such a problem to surface. Tambocor was already approved for sale in Germany. In just a few weeks' time, 3M planned to send the FDA the completed New Drug Application seeking United States approval.

As Gentzkow thought about it, he realized it was possible that nothing was wrong. The use of Tambocor had expanded rapidly in the patient population that were more seriously ill. Deaths had to be expected, and the number ought to rise as the use of the drug increased. "I could have rationalized it," Gentzkow recalled, "and said 'Gosh, this patient is at high risk of sudden death anyway.'" On the other hand, it was also possible that Tambocor was killing people. He knew about Winkle's paper, and heard the first rumbles that these drugs might have harmful as well as beneficial effects. He decided that on ethical grounds, he could not take that chance. He told his superiors at 3M that the new clinical use of Tambocor should halt until the deaths had been explained. Higher-level management at 3M accepted his proposal. Soon every hospital using Tambocor was notified to stop enrolling patients. 3M also notified the FDA. The central question now was whether Tambocor could survive.

Chapter 7

SUMMIT MEETING

AS THE BIG-NAME doctors came off the plane in the Twin Cities, they faced an arctic cold that had nudged zero degrees that December morning in 1982. From Philadelphia came Joel Morganroth, who was playing an increasingly important role in the development of Tambocor. He had written the most important study for marketing, showing that Tambocor was more effective at suppressing premature beats than the sales leader, quinidine. From Nashville came Raymond Woosley. Since publishing the dose-ranging studies of both Tambocor and Enkaid, his influence in the field had increased. J. Thomas Bigger, Jr., of Columbia University, flew in from New York City. Bigger's growing renown was earning him invitations to write the authoritative texts on antiarrhythmic drugs. He wrote the chapter in a major pharmacology textbook, Goodman and Gilman's *Pharmacological Basis of Therapeutics*. He wrote the chapter in the mammoth, 2,300-page *Cecil Textbook of Internal Medicine*, and had a chapter in the leading cardiology text. Lawrence Griffith, whose experiences helped trigger the meeting, represented Johns Hopkins.

3M had invited a large fraction of the doctors who had worked with Tambocor to help figure out what might have gone wrong. The date was December 12, barely a month after 3M had halted all new use of the drug. This was 3M medical director Gary Gentzkow's show, conducted in his open style of involving everybody. On this day, it was likely that Tambocor was going to either sink or swim, and along with it perhaps Gentzkow's future.

The Tambocor investigators gathered in a large conference room to review the situation, study by study.* The problem had first arisen in the compassionate use patients, a total of 228 individuals given

---

*The figures presented in this chapter are from a summary prepared later by 3M; the investigators may have heard slightly different figures.

the drug at 45 different hospitals. Most of these patients had structural heart damage in addition to an irregular rhythm. From another perspective, a rhythm disturbance was not an isolated malfunction. Electrical instability was simply one manifestation of an underlying structural problem. The results could not be regarded as clean data from a well-controlled study. Some investigators, such as Griffith, were using programmed electrical pulses to stimulate dangerous rhythm disturbances, then testing a drug. Some used 24-hour Holter monitors to measure effectiveness, others an exercise stress test. Some investigators checked the levels of drug in the blood, others did not. Whether the drug was effective or not was left to the judgment of the investigator, not to a uniform scientific standard.

By any measure, Tambocor did not look like a miracle cure. In 45 patients, the drug had little or no effect. For another 26 patients the side effects were so severe the drug was discontinued. These side effects included dizziness, nausea, headache, nervousness, visual disturbances, rash and fatigue. In 4 patients with heart failure, the drug made this low-output condition worse, and use was halted. In 7 other patients, the drug appeared to block conduction of the regular signal to contract that coordinates the overall heartbeat. Usually such conduction defects require an artificial pacemaker to maintain the rhythm, at least until the drug effects wear off. In 22 patients, Tambocor made the original heart rhythm problem worse.

The worst adverse effect, however, was what Lawrence Griffith had observed at Hopkins, and Roger Winkle had seen earlier with Enkaid. Sometimes it was extremely difficult or impossible to resuscitate a patient. Among the compassionate use group there were 10 such cases. Eight of these patients died. Among the 228 patients, a total of 27 were dead.

Because there was no uniform protocol, the compassionate use study was difficult to analyze. Overall, 38 percent of the patients in the compassionate use program were dead or suffered adverse effects. The obvious conclusion was that a large group of investigators with widely varying amounts of expertise and experience with Tambocor had observed a large number of deaths and adverse effects. However, 10 cases were set aside for further analysis. All of these patients were unusually difficult to resuscitate despite being hospitalized in sophisticated medical environments where all the necessary equipment was immediately at hand. All died soon after being given Tambocor.

A second, smaller study offered greater opportunities for discussion and analysis. In addition to the open-ended compassionate use patients, 3M sponsored its own controlled study in a similar patient population at 13 handpicked sites. Just 39 patients had been enrolled. As in the compassionate use group, the patients had other severe heart problems. The purpose of the study was to provide the FDA with data on how Tambocor worked in patients with more severe rhythm disturbances, that is, patients who had experienced a run of at least six premature beats in a row during a day's time. While Tambocor was dramatically effective against isolated PVCs, it had little effect on the more extended bursts of premature beats. In only 7 patients did Tambocor abolish the longer runs.

In terms of mortality, the death rate was even higher than among the compassionate use patients. Eighteen percent died, all but one from cardiac arrests from which the patient could not be resuscitated. From the two trials together, a total of 16 cases had been identified where the deaths were "associated" with Tambocor.

Those were the essential facts that confronted the Tambocor investigators in St. Paul on that chilly Friday in December. The first question was whether this truly constituted a problem. Were the deaths an expected occurrence in a sick patient population with failing hearts, and Tambocor had no important role? The 3M team had assembled evidence that spoke to this possibility. In compassionate use of the antiarrythmic drug Tonocard, 21 percent had died overall. A published study of Mexitil showed an 18 percent mortality rate. Perhaps these deaths had to be expected in a sick population? A darker possibility existed. Perhaps all drugs of this type were much more toxic than anyone yet realized. The truth was that with no untreated comparison group, different drugs and patient populations followed over varying lengths of time, no one could tell for sure. It all went back to the central point Dick Crout had raised at Morganroth's Philadelphia symposium. At the center of American drug law was the notion that expert opinion doesn't have much weight unless supported by objective scientific evidence gathered in well-controlled trials. At this meeting in St. Paul, the experts were proceeding without such evidence. On one hand, here was a gathering of important authorities in American academic medicine, each with extensive hands-on experience with the drugs in question. Their sincerity was not in doubt. They all meant well. On the other hand, collected in this room were the doctors who had been responsible for the increasing use of these drugs, whose research laboratories, careers and scientific standing depended on these drugs. They were physicians, sworn to preserve and revere life. Would they readily conclude they had been killing their patients? They were unusually bright. Would this gift give them superior insight in a dangerous situation? Or would exceptional intelligence simply provide unusual facility in creating a clever, plausible explanation, backed by the weight of their medical authority, but unsupported by scientific evidence? It was amidst these pressures, absent the essential scientific evidence from well-controlled clinical trials, that the process of medical guesswork then proceeded. It would determine the fate of Tambocor.

As the experts examined the data, they absolved Tambocor of most of the deaths. They ruled out any drug involvement in the heart attack deaths, even though a heart attack frequently causes electrical instability, and this instability might have been made worse by Tambocor. More than one half the deaths occurred out of hospital, some as soon as four days after the first dose of Tambocor. These out-of-hospital deaths were also discounted, although a few investigators thought that in some cases Tambocor could "possibly" be involved.

Nevertheless, 12 deaths remained. This is how a document prepared by 3M for the FDA described it. "Twelve represented cases that were early in the course of Tambocor treatment and no other explanation was apparent. The difficulty of resuscitation was unusual, suggesting a drug relationship," the report said. As the language suggests, the group considered only those cases where another candidate for the blame could not be found.

Having concluded that Tambocor was responsible in a few cases, the critical question for the group was preventing future deaths. The options were few. One possibility was to define a precise group of patients who should avoid taking the drug. As the investigators examined the deaths, the major characteristics that the victims shared were damaged hearts and more severe heart rhythm disturbances. To exclude these patients was a little like having an antibiotic that was useful unless the infection was serious. The second choice is to adjust the dose. Every doctor learns in pharmacology class that the difference between a drug and a poison is the dose. A consensus began to emerge among the investigators that they had made a mistake on the dose.

In the smaller, controlled trial, the protocol called for an initial dose of 400 mg per day. It could be increased to 600 mg if needed to suppress the irregular beats. It now occurred to the investigators that these doses—established in Raymond Woosley's dose-ranging study—might be excessive in patients with severely damaged hearts. In some patients the researchers also had measurements of the concentration of Tambocor in the blood plasma. These are measured in one billionths of a gram per milliliter, or ng/ml. Therapeutic doses were found to range from 300 ng to 1,000 ng. As they examined the records of the deaths linked to Tambocor they found patients with blood levels that were double the maximum therapeutic levels.

Gentzkow explained later, "This crystallized the perception that the doses of Tambocor that had been well tolerated in previous trials might not be appropriate in this population with more serious cardiac disease." As Woosley put it, combining both approaches: "I think there is a profile of the patient who is at increased risk. . . . That patient was one with a very bad ventricle who had been given rapidly increasing doses of the drug."

With a possible answer now in focus, 3M took other steps. The company terminated compassionate use of Tambocor. It was not going to let just any doctor who asked use this potentially lethal drug in sick patients even though exactly that would happen if Tambocor were approved by the FDA. Gentzkow did not need any more phone calls like the ones that led to the halt in new use of Tambocor. Second, the 3M team designed a revised study for the sicker patient population. It would be conducted only in selected medical centers with special expertise, and with a new and more cautious protocol. The starting dose was to be cut in half, and would be increased very slowly, with the blood levels carefully monitored.

While a new protocol made sense, the data available to the investigators suggest it was not a convincing answer why Tambocor patients were dropping dead and could not be resuscitated. Among the 12 cases that the investigators concluded were related to Tambocor, 4 cases were found with high blood levels. But others on the list had clearly not been given excessive doses. For example, a 66-year-old man had died after taking Tambocor for two months. His blood level was only 418 ng, which is at the low end of the therapeutic range of 300 to 1,000 ng/ml. Among the 12 Tambocor-related deaths were 3 patients with blood levels below 600 ng. Three more patients on the list had come from Griffith's program at Johns Hopkins. Blood levels weren't measured in that protocol, but Griffith said he didn't think the doses were too high. He thought the problem might have been an interaction with another drug. The dose and blood level problem explained 4 deaths among the 12. The investigators had absolved Tambocor in 23 additional deaths where the drug might have been involved. The exclusion of out-of-hospital deaths seemed particularly arbitrary. Why would Tambocor cause cardiac arrest in the hospital, but not outside it? Equally arbitrary was the idea that cardiac arrests had to come soon after first giving Tambocor. It contradicted what the investigators had learned about the electrical accident of cardiac arrest. Electrical instability of the heart varied spontaneously and was notoriously unpredictable. If a drug that profoundly altered conduction put the heart at greater risk of an electrical accident, by what logic should that accident occur immediately? If deaths blamed on Tambocor occurred two months after the first dose, why exclude deaths after five months or eight months?

While the consensus explanation was tidy and convenient, there were many signs of deeper doubts among the investigators. At this meeting an important concept burst into full flower. The participants started to realize that not only did this family of drugs have beneficial effects on heart rhythms, it also had harmful ones. The drugs were known as *anti*arrhythmic drugs. The harmful effects thereafter were described as *pro*arrhythmic effects.

The way the medical mind copes with the overwhelming uncertainties of life and death is to confine them within emotionally manageable categories with medical names. So the possibility that these well-meaning doctors had inadvertently killed a dozen of their patients was described as the task of establishing the extent of the *proarrhythmia* caused by Tambocor.

Having defined the new problem of proarrhythmia, the next step was an effort to measure its extent. 3M planned to send a questionnaire to all the investigators who had used Tambocor, asking if they had observed cases where the drug made the heart rhythm worse. The questionnaire later became the basis for claims about the extent of proarrhythmia. This approach made excellent sense from the standpoint of medical politics. It would flush out any potential critics with concerns about the safety of Tambocor. If some doctor was ready to do for Tambocor what Roger Winkle had done with his paper on Enkaid's malignant rhythm disturbances, 3M would find out. From a safety or scientific point of view the survey was of limited value. As a 3M document prepared for the FDA put it, "The approach will not capture one class of proarrhythmic events at all, those being sudden death. These could represent proarrhythmic events but there is no way to know this in the absence of a control group."

Twelve days after the investigators' meeting, 3M submitted its completed New Drug Application asking FDA for approval to market Tambocor. It would be four months before the company would have results from the investigators' questionnaire, and at least a year before a new study was complete. The results of this still-unfinished research might either improve Tambocor's safety profile or identify even more serious problems. In the race to the clinic, 3M was not waiting to find out.

Bristol-Myers had also been forced to halt enrollment in a clinical trial of Enkaid after unexplained patient deaths. Eight medical centers had been randomly assigning patients to receive either a placebo or one of three doses of Enkaid. In one of the centers, a 45-year-old woman developed an abnormal electrocardiogram after her second dose of Enkaid. It was the highest dose given in this trial, a 50-milligram tablet three times a day. However, it was well below the therapeutic maximum. Two days later the left ventricle of her heart began to flutter, rather than contract. This degenerated into fibrillation, and then to the complete electrical death of the heart, called asystole. She did not survive. A second patient in the high-dose group initially seemed to respond well to the drug. Seven days later he suffered cardiac arrest and died. This also happened to one patient on the very lowest dose, 25 mg. In response to the deaths, the company stopped enrollment in the high-dose group. Bristol-Myers later asked chief of cardiology at Stanford, Donald C. Harrison, to review all patient deaths. Harrison concluded that one of the three was "probably related" to the drug.

Bristol-Myers also made Enkaid available for compassionate use, and the results were as disturbing as with Tambocor. Of the 496 patients on Enkaid, 18 percent died, a total of 91 patients. Like the Tambocor investigators, Harrison discounted deaths that did not occur soon after the first dose of the drug. A Bristol-Myers summary of drug testing, prepared under FDA direction, said:

"Deaths that occurred late in treatment were generally not attributed to Enkaid; in 16 cases, however, death occurred within 10 days in circumstances where a relationship to Enkaid could not necessarily be ruled out. Evaluation by Harrison considered eight of those possibly or probably related to Enkaid treatment."

The more Bristol-Myers analyzed the data, the fewer the deaths that were attributed to the drug. A report prepared for the FDA said that Harrison found a "direct, clear link of proarrhythmia to death" in only three cases. One case was in Roger Winkle's paper. One case was the woman in the dose ranging study. A third case occurred in a study in Belgium.

When Bristol-Myers later presented the safety data to a group of doctors invited to Scottsdale, Arizona, to hear about Enkaid, the number of deaths shrank still further.

"The only case directly linking proarrhythmia to death occurred in Belgium...," said Lester F. Soyka of Bristol-Myers' medical staff. If the definition was expanded to include "possibly or definitely" related to Enkaid, then "worst case analysis" total reached twelve deaths, he added. The limitations of this arbitrary scheme were apparent to Bristol-Myers, in the FDA-supervised report.

"Obviously this estimate could be low or high as the determination as to whether an early sudden death in a patient with a history of arrest is or is not drug related is very much a matter of judgement," the company's summary said. The overall 18 percent mortality rate among compassionate use patients must have seemed high on purely intuitive grounds. The company justified the death toll by telling the FDA it was comparable with the experience with its competitor, Tambocor.

The Philadelphia cardiologist Joel Morganroth would later remember this period vividly. "Clearly, we were finally catching on that these drugs kill people," he said.

Chapter 8

A QUESTION OF BENEFIT

By EARLY 1983 Joel Morganroth was a pivotal player in antiarrhythmic drugs. 3M had entrusted him with the sensitive assignment of characterizing the proarrhythmic effects of Tambocor. He would analyze the questionnaires 3M had sent, asking the investigators to report incidents where the drug made the heart rhythm problem worse. He would present the results to a special symposium planned to showcase the drug to a select group of influential physicians. It was the kind of assignment Morganroth loved. He liked consulting assignments for the drug industry where the information could later be reshaped for scientific papers. And here was proarrhythmia, an emerging medical issue that required careful definitions, criteria, a rational approach. As the first serious concerns about the safety of these drugs rippled through the cardiology community, he was positioned on the leading edge of the wave. He had now worked on four different antiarrhythmic drugs. His increasingly close ties to 3M had not prevented him from also developing a relationship with the company's chief competitor in the race to the clinic, Bristol-Myers. He was beginning to work not only with Enkaid but with another Bristol-Myers antiarrhythmic drug, sotalol.

His activities also expanded in other directions. In the previous year he had published seventeen scientific papers, and delivered eleven more at medical meetings. He published two books and gave twenty-five invited lectures. While mostly he lectured at hospitals and symposiums for the Pennsylvania medical community, he also spoke at Harvard and at a symposium in Italy. He was also involved in civic affairs. The American Heart Association is a medical special interest group controlled by cardiologists and other medical specialists interested in heart disease. Morganroth paid his civic dues, serving as a member of the association's local program committee and chairman of its education committee. Morganroth was also developing business interests. He was a consultant for a local Holter monitor company, Cardio Data Systems, and got to know the management of its parent corporation, United Medical. His interest in Holter monitors had spawned an interest in computers, which were used to analyze the results of 24 hours of continuous EKG monitoring. He befriended a Philadelphia heart surgeon, Harold W. Kay, who shared his fascination with computers. Together they formed a company to use computers to assemble and analyze data from medical research.

One notable hitch had endangered Morganroth's upward rise. It occurred at Lankenau Hospital, which he had joined after leaving Penn. Lankenau was affiliated with Thomas Jefferson Medical School, where Morganroth held an appointment as associate professor of medicine. This medical complex also had a clinical research unit for testing new drugs, and it was one center of activities for Morganroth. The unit was supervised by Eric Michelson, a young doctor who was also taking advanced cardiology training at Lankenau, partly under Morganroth's supervision. The two were coauthors on several scientific papers. Morganroth had a patient on the research unit, a woman who was being given a drug to measure its effects on blood pressure. Michelson, the day-to-day supervisor, concluded that the woman's blood pressure had dropped dangerously low and demanded that the experiment be halted immediately. Morganroth refused, saying the drop in blood pressure was an expected effect of the drug. Michelson insisted. Morganroth demanded that Michelson be removed as supervisor of the research unit. Michelson made a formal complaint to the hospital's Institutional Review Board, which supervises research involving human subjects.

This dispute involving a complex question of medical judgment was referred to an outside consultant for an evaluation, and considered by the hospital medical authorities. Lankenau ruled in favor of Michelson and his concerns about the patient's safety. A great deal of legal and other maneuvering then followed. In the medical tradition that values secrecy in the consideration of medical mistakes, all parties were sworn not to reveal the incident. The FDA was informed, but there was no change in Morganroth's status as doctor authorized to do clinical investigations with unapproved drugs.

Morganroth did no further clinical research at Lankenau Hospital. However, he quickly developed two other alternatives for his drug studies. In a southern New Jersey suburb of Philadelphia he established his own drug-testing facility, the National Cardiovascular Research Center in Haddonfield. He ultimately left Lankenau in 1982 and joined Hahnemann University medical school, and its affiliated hospital. He was promoted to full professor of medicine and pharmacology at Hahnemann.

In addition to reaching senior faculty rank in 1982, Morganroth enjoyed a great success in his third Philadelphia symposium for the world's medical elite in antiarrhythmic drug research. This time the cast was even more glittering with stars than the original meeting in 1980. The Food and Drug Administration contingent was led by none other than the commissioner himself, Arthur H. Hayes, Jr. Again the pharmaceutical industry turned out in force, including Merck and Searle, CIBA-Geigy and Sandoz, Abbott and Eli Lilly, Hoffmann-LaRoche and SmithKline Beecham, Upjohn and Burroughs Wellcome. The contingent from the medical schools included virtually all the major figures in electrophysiology, including those beginning to wrestle with emerging evidence that sometimes this family of drugs made heart rhythms worse. So the meeting included the doubter from Stanford, Roger Winkle. From Columbia came Thomas Bigger, Lawrence Griffith came from Hopkins. Gary Gentzkow represented 3M.

Although there was no discussion about the risks of antiarrhythmic drugs at the third symposium, major questions were raised about their presumed benefits. Roger Winkle of Stanford talked about his research among patients with the most serious disorders. He told the group that, quite frankly, disappointing results were achieved in over 300 patients. In Winkle's approach antiarrhythmic drugs were not used unless they successfully suppressed dangerous rhythm disturbances induced by programmed electrical stimulation. In two thirds of the cases, he said, no drug could be found that worked. In those patients where the drug seemed to work, many had serious side effects. Among those patients who could tolerate the drug, some still died of cardiac arrest. It was time, he said, to consider a different approach to the problem.

Doubts also surfaced about whether these drugs really did prevent sudden death when used to suppress the mild premature beats. Ronald W. F. Campbell from Britain observed that several clinical studies had been conducted without demonstrating any benefits in preventing death. He noted, however, that the size and design of the studies might be at fault. Others were even more direct.

"I would like to raise the fundamental question of whether or not sudden death can be prevented by antiarrhythmic drugs," said Frank

Marcus, a cardiologist from the University of Arizona Medical Center. He said that he had just reviewed the records of 100 heart attack survivors who had died later. While many were classified as "sudden deaths," in most cases the death resulted from other underlying causes the drugs couldn't possibly have affected.

Another participant, Jay Cohn of the University of Minnesota, was even more direct. "We sit here making these glib assumptions which are probably not warranted." In some patients, he said, "We can actually view antiarrhythmic therapy as potentially increasing the risk of muscle damage and perhaps death. . . ."

The participants also heard a warning from the doctor with the real power over these still unapproved drugs, Robert Temple of the FDA. He was Morganroth's friend and, as head of the Division of Cardiovascular-Renal Drug Division, was going to make the decision whether to approve Tambocor, Enkaid, and other drugs in development. "The largest portion of drug therapy," he noted, was to prevent sudden death rather than to deal with the already serious cases.

It was time, Temple said, for a controlled study to demonstrate the benefits of antiarrhythmic drugs. A consortium of hospitals in an area the size of Philadelphia or New York City, he noted, could recruit enough patients for the experiment. "The answers that would emerge," he said, "would be well worth it both to the public, and perhaps to a group of commercial sponsors willing to provide support."

He also held out the carrot, noting that with blood pressure drugs, successful clinical trials had led to an explosion in their use. "Depending on their results, documentation of a real benefit from antiarrhythmic therapy in asymptomatic people would be expected to provoke a similar response," he said.

Temple also had a warning for the assembled doctors and drug company officials. "Enthusiastic treatment of patients *before* such demonstrated life-prolonging benefit is shown has a substantial potential for doing no good or causing harm," he said. It was, on one hand, a serious warning. But like Dick Crout two years earlier, he hastened to assure the audience that the FDA would not require such studies before approving the drugs. Suppression of mild and generally benign premature beats would be sufficient. And as Temple knew, doctors in steadily increasing numbers were already treating patients without symptoms.

·   ·   ·

These remarks were not lost on Joel Morganroth. As Bob Temple had suggested, Morganroth realized it might be possible to mount a controlled clinical trial right in the Philadelphia area. It would be a scientific coup of the first order to emerge with the long-sought proof of the arrhythmia suppression hypothesis. It would create a large new market for the drugs. It would please the FDA. If Robert Temple's remarks were an indication, the agency was beginning to worry about certifying as "effective" drugs that had no proven therapeutic benefits to most patients. It was just the kind of idea that appealed to Morganroth's sophisticated sense of medical politics. He decided to launch a clinical trial.

Academic cardiologists like Morganroth were, of course, doing studies all the time. Typically they would involve ten or fifteen cases picked from the stream of ailing patients referred to their medical center. If a whole group of doctors kept careful records over several years, the patient total might reach two or three hundred—as Roger Winkle and his colleagues at Stanford had. What Morganroth envisioned now would involve a half-dozen hospitals and nearly a thousand patients. He saw an opportunity to join the project to his emerging interests in the computer business. All the patient and safety data would be entered into computers using software he would develop. It was an opportunity to develop further his ties to the FDA. The researchers would put terminals with the data right in the FDA offices in Rockville, Maryland, outside Washington, D.C. To do all this Morganroth needed money, a lot of it, perhaps a million and a half dollars. He went to Bristol-Myers and he got it.

Morganroth's idea was an objective test of three quite different drug approaches to preventing sudden death. He would recruit heart attack survivors. These patients were already in the hospital and attended by cardiologists, so they were accessible for a study. This group also had roughly a 10 percent chance of dying in the next year, with cardiac arrest the main danger. In this group, many deaths would occur without effective treatment; drugs that worked would save lives.

One third of the patients would take Enkaid. One third would receive a beta-blocker, another kind of heart drug often prescribed to lower blood pressure. Morganroth selected timolol, a beta-blocker which Merck agreed to supply free of charge. The final third of the patients would take sotalol, another antiarrhythmic drug Bristol-Myers was developing. Sotalol also worked directly on the electrical system of the heart, but its principal effect was different from that

of Tambocor and Enkaid. Sotalol lengthened the brief period when
the muscle cell does not respond to an electrical signal to contract.
Intellectually, it was a tidy study, comparing three different families
of drugs, each with a different effect. Bristol-Myers, which had two
drugs in the trial, agreed to pay the bills. Morganroth worked with
two colleagues at Hahnemann, Leonard Horowitz and Scott Spielman,
and with Harold Kay, his heart surgeon partner in computers.

In roughly nine months' time, the team had entered 55 patients
into the study. The results for timolol, the beta-blocker, were instructive. Of the 20 patients randomly allocated to receive this drug, only
8 were taking it. The others experienced side effects serious enough
to discontinue it. In Morganroth's mind this illustrated the chief
drawback of most of the heart drugs on the market—too many patients couldn't tolerate them. The dropout statistics were better with
Enkaid. Only 6 of 18 couldn't tolerate the drug. But with the third
drug, sotalol, disaster struck. Within two weeks of starting the drug,
almost half of the 17 sotalol patients either died or developed serious
rhythm disturbances.

"We made an error in selecting too high a dose [of sotalol] in very
sick patients," Morganroth said. "That was the end of the trial." While
the trial failed, he believed it vindicated his interest in monitoring
clinical research with computers, because the immediately accessible
data allowed them to identify the unexpected adverse effects. However, proof of the arrhythmia suppression hypothesis did not emerge.

Morganroth was not the only cardiologist interested in proving that
suppressing premature beats would prevent sudden cardiac death,
nor was Bristol-Myers the only drug company to appreciate the commercial value of such evidence. A group of cardiologists from five
nations got an unrestricted grant from a German company, Boehringer Ingelheim, to test its drug Mexitil. It was the major European
rival of Tambocor and Enkaid in the race to the clinic. Like Morganroth's study, the trial was focused on survivors of recent heart attacks.
The experiment had to answer a more basic question before testing
Mexitil's ability to prevent cardiac arrest and death. Could enough
patients tolerate the drug, and did the drug work effectively enough
to suppress most premature beats? It was not possible to prove the
arrhythmia suppression hypothesis without first proving the arrhythmias were in fact suppressed. After measuring suppression, the study
might be extended to determine whether the drug worked to save

lives. The preliminary study continued for one year and included 630 patients, half getting a long-acting form of Mexitil, and half getting a placebo.

This study also failed. "In spite of a marked reduction in cardiac arrhythmia," the study chairman reported, "there were more deaths" among those taking Mexitil than those on the placebo. However, the difference in deaths (7.6 percent versus 4.6 percent) was so small that it could have occurred by chance. The study neither proved nor disproved the arrhythmia suppression hypothesis. One reason lay in the design of the clinical trial. The drug had been prescribed to all enrolled heart attack survivors on the presumption that it would be beneficial. However, only about one third of the heart attack victims had large numbers of PVCs, and Mexitil was not always effective. Critics argued that benefits would be observed only in the small fraction of cases where Mexitil effectively suppressed frequent PVCs. On the other hand, beta-blockers had demonstrated benefits under these circumstances. And if the effect of drugs like Mexitil were large, benefits might be observed despite the limitations of the study. The drug didn't have to help every patient. It simply had to help sub-stantially more patients than it hurt. The Mexitil trial provided no evidence of such benefit, and a dark hint that it just might be harmful.

As the drug companies began to complete their clinical testing of the new generation of antiarrhythmic drugs, serious questions re-mained about both the safety and efficacy. Not only had testing been marred by unexplained patient deaths, the efforts to demonstrate real benefits to the patients had failed. It would prove instructive to see how the system responded to these clear warning signals.

Chapter 9

SHOWTIME

IF JOEL MORGANROTH was acquiring the right tickets for entrance into the highest circles of American medicine, his colleague J. Thomas Bigger, Jr., had unmistakably arrived at that destination by the summer of 1983. It was an impressive achievement for a soft-spoken southerner whose career could be summarized so simply: Soon after medical school, Bigger had gone to Columbia University and stayed there.

Bigger was about ten years older than the other doctors who were shaping the future of antiarrhythmic drugs. He was the established figure in the field, surrounded by a constellation of rising young stars such as Morganroth, Roger Winkle at Stanford, and Gary Gentzkow at 3M. If Bigger lacked the global vision and social passion of a Bernard Lown, he made up for it in his practical mastery of the machinery that runs modern medicine.

A graduate of the Medical College of Georgia, he had arrived in New York City in 1960 to undertake an experience that has since become the dramatic material for countless books, articles and movies. He became an intern at Bellevue Hospital, New York City's medical last resort for countless numbers of poor, the critically injured, and the desperately ill. Responsibility for Bellevue is shared by New York University and the Columbia College of Physicians and Surgeons. It was a hellish training ground for young doctors, who had to treat an endless stream of patients under terrible conditions. With lack of sleep, lack of equipment and incessant demands, only the toughest prospered in this environment.

After two years at Bellevue, Bigger moved uptown to the vastly more patrician Presbyterian Hospital, which was also affiliated with Columbia. At Presbyterian, he completed his training in internal medicine and began to specialize in cardiology. He and two colleagues would strike back against the sleep and other deprivations of phy-

sician training. While some Bellevue graduates wrote gripping nar-
ratives of their ordeal, the research-oriented Bigger dealt with the
experience by beginning a study. Working with two colleagues, he
collected evidence showing that sleep-deprived interns made almost
twice as many mistakes reading an EKG as did those with a normal
night's sleep. He got the study published in the *New England Journal
of Medicine*, where it was received with the same restrained amuse-
ment that the elders of a college fraternity reserve for an earnest
undergraduate report about hazing abuses. (An accompanying editorial quoted Shakespeare and dubbed it "food for thought.")

As he neared the end of training in cardiology at Columbia, Bigger
had assembled the ingredients of a major medical career. He had an
affiliation with a prestigious medical school. He was in on the ground
floor of the rapidly evolving field of electrophysiology. And he had
a powerful and important mentor in Brian Hoffman, chairman of the
Columbia Department of Pharmacology, and one of the founding
fathers of research into the electrical activity of the human heart.
Most of Hoffman's research was at the cellular level. With elaborate
and specialized monitoring equipment, Hoffman sought to understand the precise electrical responses of isolated animal cardiac cells.
Some of Hoffman's young proteges worked with live animal models.
Bigger decided to move another step up the biological ladder and
try some of the experiments in patients who were already in the
catheterization laboratory for the diagnosis of other heart malfunctions. He became one of the early experimenters with programmed
pulses of electricity to the human heart—work Roger Winkle and
Lawrence Griffith would try to turn into practical treatments. By
1983 he was a textbook example of the exercise of power in the
decentralized world of medical care in the United States.

Individual patients share with their doctor extraordinary powers
over their own bodies. At their doctor's urging they will undergo
the most drastic imaginable surgery or take a powerful drug for the
rest of their lives, with possibly profound effects on the quality of
their life. Consider beta-blockers, one of the most widely prescribed
heart drugs. In one study, 45 percent of the patients taking the beta-
blocker propranolol reported the drug decreased their overall sense
of well-being. One quarter said it caused sexual dysfunction. A mental
test documented a significant decline in the cognitive abilities of
those taking the drug. Beta-blockers, generally speaking, are among
the safest and most benign cardiovascular drugs. But a doctor's brief
notation on a prescription pad confers tremendous power over the
fabric of a patient's life.

Who, in turn, guides the decisions of doctors? They all went to medical school and studied for demanding board and medical specialty exams. As noted earlier, Thomas Bigger wrote major textbook chapters they would study. As doctors continue in practice, medical journals form an important source of new information. By 1983, Bigger was on the editorial board of four medical journals. The truth of day-to-day medical practice is that for many medical judgments, only a fraction of the needed information is known. Who decides what medical questions have priority for medical research? Once again, Bigger had won seats on the powerful committees that evaluate new research proposals from doctors seeking funding from the National Institutes of Health. By the middle of 1983 the National Heart, Lung, and Blood Institute was exploring the feasibility of a major clinical trial to test the arrhythmia suppression hypothesis. Chairman of the new steering committee was J. Thomas Bigger, Jr. In day-to-day medical practice, two thirds of all patient visits involve prescribing a drug. To influence those decisions, the pharmaceutical companies employ an awesome variety of techniques. One of the most effective is to recruit the major authorities in the field. Thus it was a great coup for 3M when it recruited Bigger to chair a major symposium on Tambocor. For such work drug companies typically pay doctors honoraria that range from a few hundred to thousands of dollars.

The Bermuda Beach Hotel rises like a castle above the brilliant green of a surrounding golf course. In the distance the ocean is a perfect rich blue. Bermuda is not nearly as tropical as the travel brochures imply, but in June the weather is often lovely. It was an idyllic setting for a symposium on Tambocor. The island had more lavish hotels than the Bermuda Beach, but it was suitably luxurious for the discriminating tastes of the research elite of medicine. They were accustomed to regular visits to premier resorts around the world. Along with first-class travel and fine food, it was one of the ways that the pharmaceutical companies courted the most influential medical school faculty. (Morganroth, for example, had already appeared that year at Snowmass Mountain, Colorado; Scottsdale, Arizona; Lima, Peru; Cologne, Germany; and San Francisco.)

Medical symposia are an important tool the pharmaceutical industry uses to influence medicine. A 1988 Congressional study reported that eighteen large drug companies sponsored 34,688 symposia, or 95 such events every single day. Another survey estimated 175,000 to 180,000 physicians attend such events—or about two out of five doctors. Medical symposia run the spectrum from the most blatant direct sales promotions to legitimate scientific exchanges. What they share in common is that virtually all are funded by the drug industry, and company involvement ranges from subtle influence over the agenda to complete control over the entire affair. Although Bigger would chair the event, the Bermuda symposium was very much a 3M showcase for its new drug Tambocor. It was a cross between a coming-out party and a celebration for a job well done. 3M had invited thirty cardiologists to Bermuda, all expenses paid. Many had helped develop the drug, but other influential figures had also been invited. For example, editors of two major journals, William C. Roberts, editor of the *American Journal of Cardiology*, and Dean Mason, of the *American Heart Journal*, had joined the group. 3M had also invited Roger Winkle from Stanford, better known for his questions about these drugs than his enthusiasm for them. Ten more cardiologists, including Bigger, were the paid faculty, and faculty members were expected to write a paper and deliver a fifteen-minute summary at the conference. Faculty such as these typically receive $1,000 to 3,000 each, and the chairman more. Later, the assembled papers would be published in a medical journal as a "supplement." In this case they would appear in Roberts's journal with the same typeface and layout as the regular editorial content. Critics called this drug company advertising masquerading as scientific research.

Three of the five days of the symposium were business days. The program began at 8:30 A.M. and adjourned by 1 P.M., leaving plenty of time for golf, sailing, scuba diving, fishing or other entertainment. In the evenings, the company sponsored a handsome dinner. Bigger chaired the conference and guided the twice daily discussion periods.

Bigger opened the conference with an overview of treatment of heart rhythm disturbances. It was information everybody present already knew, but his paper would be valuable to distribute to less-expert doctors when the drug was marketed. Three company men from the 3M team described the history, early development and animal testing of Tambocor.

Raymond Woosley of Vanderbilt summarized the three dose-ranging and effectiveness studies that had been initially published separately, and included long-term follow-up results. Despite the December investigators' meeting, he remained enthusiastic about Tambocor. "Tambocor has many advantages over currently available antiarrhythmic drugs," he said.

Woosley also had a piece of news for the conference. He was also a senior investigator for a project sponsored by the National Heart, Lung, and Blood Institute. It was a study of a study, to determine if it were feasible to mount a clinical trial to test the arrhythmia suppression hypothesis. The steering committee, of which Woosley was a member and Bigger was chairman, had decided that Tambocor would be among four drugs evaluated. The record doesn't indicate whether Woosley mentioned another piece of news. He would soon be taking a seat on the FDA's advisory committee that would consider the Tambocor New Drug Application.

For the most sensitive subject—the safety of Tambocor—3M devoted one half of one morning—from 8:30 to 9:45 A.M. Joel Morganroth led the program.

Tambocor had taught researchers, Morganroth said, that toxicity of this family of drugs was not limited to unrelated side effects affecting other organs of the body or those producing clear symptoms. It could also make an already abnormal electrocardiogram worse. "Almost every agent tested has the potential for proarrhythmia," he said. In his view, Tambocor and Enkaid might be safer than not only the old-line drugs but also newer potential competitors such as Mexitil.

He described the December investigators' meeting to an audience that included many who had attended. But Morganroth sounded uncomfortable with the idea that the patient deaths could be blamed on excessively high doses or elevated blood plasma levels. "Plasma levels varied greatly among patients, and even for the same dose level, and therefore no absolute relation could be obtained," he said. Still he recommended a cautious approach to using Tambocor in patients with damaged ventricles, starting with a low dose and increasing it slowly.

Morganroth also reported on the 3M survey of investigators. Among 588 patients, the investigators could recall 44 cases where the heart rhythm disturbances became worse. (Such a survey, however, could not capture the adverse event that had most worried the group—the sudden deaths—because investigators could not separate events caused by the drug from those caused by the underlying illness.) He ended on a note of optimism, saying, "We hope that these effects will not limit the potential usefulness of these drugs."

Philip R. Reid reviewed the Tambocor cases from the Johns Hopkins protocol that he and Lawrence Griffith used for patients with a

previous cardiac arrest. It was Griffith's cases that had helped trigger
the December meeting. They had been forced to discontinue Tambocor in 81 percent of the 36 patients in which it had been tried,
he said. This total included five deaths that occurred within four days
of the first dose of Tambocor, and a cardiac arrest that could not be
reversed despite prompt attention. After advising caution in this patient population, Reid also endorsed Tambocor as "a highly effective
antiarrhythmic agent."

As the conference proceeded, it was possible to see the excessive
dose theory win acceptance.

3M medical director Gary Gentzkow said it was his working hypothesis that a lower starting dose and slow increases in dosage were
"a much safer approach."

Joel Morganroth was not so sure. "We have no ability today to
predict a proarrhythmic effect by dose or blood level," he said.

Nevertheless, safety concerns did not dim the enthusiasm of Jeffrey
Anderson, another of the rising stars of arrhythmia research. While
working with Bertram Pitt at the University of Michigan, Anderson
had performed one of the three original dose and effectiveness studies, and written the most glowing endorsement. Anderson had now
moved to the University of Utah in Salt Lake. In a talk describing the
proposed clinical use of the drug, he said that Tambocor "will frequently be the drug of choice when medical treatment is indicated."

It was just as Roger Winkle had said. The drug companies were
free to go to researchers who said good things about drugs. And at
the Bermuda symposium, the paid faculty had all said good things
about Tambocor. While Roger Winkle had not been asked to make
a presentation, the open-minded 3M had invited him to attend. As
the symposium rolled toward a close, he did have a comment. Once
again, it was not what a drug company would like to hear. And once
again it would prove prophetic.

"After listening to all these presentations, I'm still left with a tremendous concern about the safety of Tambocor," Winkle said. "I
don't want to tar Tambocor with the Enkaid brush, but there are just
too many similarities between Tambocor and Enkaid."

Winkle continued, "What concerns me is how these drugs will
actually be used when they are approved in this country. It's a very
seductive drug because it does give dramatic improvement in ventricular arrhythmias. I have a lingering concern that we've just heard
about the tip of the iceberg here, e.g., people who get arrhythmias
on the treadmill and can't be resuscitated. I'm not even sure that

putting the people in the hospital will protect against some of these adverse reactions."

Gary Gentzkow, 3M's medical director, rose to defend his drug. "I would like to reassure everyone that [3M] is not taking lightly the potential negative effects of Tambocor. The data presented indicated this drug has been studied intensively already and will continue to be." He was becoming convinced that cardiac arrest was not a serious problem. After 10 months of marketing in Germany, he said, they had "some episodes of cardiac failure, a few, and by 'few,' I mean less than five cases of sudden death that were reported out of a patient experience in excess of 10,000 patient exposures so far."

Two European doctors rose to suggest that maybe everyone was worrying too much. John Kjekshus of Norway said, "We are making deductions about adverse findings seen in uncontrolled studies. High-risk patients are more likely to die, but we need controlled studies before blaming Tambocor." Kjekshus was correct, but the lack of data from controlled studies was a sword that cut both ways. It also meant that the German experience that Gary Gentzkow cited provided no reliable indication of the drug's safety. It meant German doctors didn't blame the drug for cardiac arrests; it did not indicate whether the drug might cause cardiac arrest.

Stanley Taylor of Leeds, England, was even more sanguine about the safety of Tambocor. "Certainly if you take a dying patient, there are very few drugs that can confer immortality upon him."

It was left to the conference chairman, Thomas Bigger, to sum up the proceedings.

"I made a long list of studies that we need to do in the future," he said. "However, we do not need to hold up marketing of the drug until we have all of this information."

Bigger, the senior doctor present, gave his own assessment. "I have a very positive feeling about the efficacy and safety of Tambocor in most patient groups."

He closed the conference with a little joke, playing on Taylor's earlier comment that Tambocor couldn't confer immortality on a dying patient

"It was Galen who made the following statement: 'All those that drink of this remedy will recover in a short time. Those who do not recover will die; therefore the remedy is of no value in the incurable patient.' "

The assembled doctors then adjourned to golf and the other recreational lures of Bermuda. Except for the still uncompleted study in seriously ill patients, the clinical testing and development of Tambocor was now complete. A group of experts from important medical centers around the world was solidly behind it. Despite unpleasant surprises Tambocor had been a great success in the competitive, action-oriented world of academic medicine. The critical issue now was what kinds of questions would be asked by the Food and Drug Administration. The FDA was all that stood between 3M and the large and lucrative United States market.

Part Two

APPROVAL

Chapter 10

QUESTIONS FOR TEMPLE

For DERVA DAVIS, it was literally a rude awakening. As an epidemiologist at Johns Hopkins University, she was unusually knowledgeable about medicine and drugs. Therefore, she knew something was seriously wrong when her heart suddenly began to race ahead while she lay quietly in bed one night in 1983. She woke up her husband and asked him to get her the *Physicians' Desk Reference*. It is a compendium of information about prescription drugs, and Davis had an immediate suspect. Twenty-three minutes earlier she had taken a Zomax tablet to relieve the pain of a broken foot. After finding the book had no hint that Zomax might cause such a reaction, she called the hospital emergency room. She was advised to come in immediately. She was experiencing a potentially fatal allergic reaction called anaphylaxis. Just as Davis was trying to ease a shoe onto her broken foot, she blacked out and began to tumble down a flight of stairs. Fortunately her husband caught her. After awakening, she would not forget the worried faces of her two small children, aged 3 and 6. At the emergency room doctors brought her allergic reaction under control. The nurse told her they had seen twelve cases just like it in the past month.

For the Food and Drug Administration, Davis's story was not going to be easy to deal with. A few months later she was repeating the episode at a public hearing of a subcommittee of the United States House of Representatives. It was chaired by Representative Ted Weiss, a New York City liberal with a keen interest in the FDA. A former prosecutor, Weiss knew how to ask hard questions, and his subcommittee staff had already investigated the drug. On this day in 1983 he wanted to know why the Food and Drug Administration had approved Zomax without learning of these allergic reactions.

After 923 such cases were reported, the manufacturer, the McNeil Pharmaceutical Company, had voluntarily withdrawn the drug. Weiss also wanted to know why the FDA had approved Zomax despite evidence that it caused cancer of the adrenal glands in rats. After the case against Zomax had been laid out in dramatic detail, it was the FDA's turn to respond.

In the center seat at the witness table sat the FDA commissioner, Arthur H. Hayes, Jr. The head of the FDA is appointed by the President and rarely serves as long as his chief executive. Zomax had been approved before Hayes became commissioner in 1981, and he would leave the agency before the end of 1983. By tradition—if not by necessity—the commissioner is the public face of this diverse regulatory agency. With 7,300 employees and a $362 million budget in 1983, the FDA was responsible for the safety and labeling of most foods, additives, cosmetics, soft drinks, bottled water, and spices. It also regulates equipment that emits radiation, ranging from lasers and x-ray machines to microwave ovens. Its jurisdiction includes products for animals as well as humans. However, the FDA's embrace is tightest in the medical arena, where it regulates drugs, vaccines, and medical devices. So it was Hayes's job to field questions about the Zomax controversy, even though he had had no role in the original decision, and would not have been consulted during the approval process even had he been commissioner.

As he sat at the witness table in the House hearing room, Hayes was flanked by seven subordinates. First among them was Robert Temple. As head of the Office of Drug Evaluation he had the authority to approve or reject new prescription drugs. Temple was of medium height. His round, almost cherubic face was framed by steel-rimmed glasses. Although Temple was only the acting director of drug evaluation, there was nothing tentative in his manner as the Zomax hearing proceeded.

Hayes summarized his prepared testimony for the committee, outlining the agency's actions in approving the drug. He explained why the allergic reactions had not been discovered during clinical testing. Hayes's testimony unmistakably hinted that the FDA might allow Zomax back on the market. This drew immediate fire from an amazed Ted Weiss.

"Let me start out by asking you what your judgment is as to restoring Zomax to the market," Weiss asked.

Hayes replied, "I have made no judgment on that point. Perhaps Dr. Temple can tell you where we are in our review and the various concerns and considerations, both scientific and clinical." The speed with which Hayes referred the question illustrated the true responsibilities. While Hayes was in charge of the FDA, Bob Temple was in charge of Zomax. Weiss quickly shifted his questions to Temple.

"I think the conclusion jumps out at you that this is not a product that should be restored to the market," said Weiss. Here was a drug that might cause cancer and certainly caused serious allergic reactions.

Temple would not be pinned down. "In deciding the question of whether the drug should be made available for long-term use—as opposed to the short-term uses now stressed in the labeling, for example—you would have to reach a number of conclusions before that would appear to be an intelligent thing to do." He noted that even a painkilling drug suspected of causing cancer might be valuable in terminally ill patients, or those who already had cancer. A drug that triggers an allergic reaction might be safely used in a hospital setting where countermeasures could be immediately taken.

Weiss pressed again. "You have to bear in mind your basic charge as an agency, which is to protect the lives and safety of the American people and not to allow the public to use drugs which, in fact, may jeopardize their lives. The product you are talking about is not a lifesaving product. . . . It is a painkiller." He still wanted Temple to admit that Zomax should not be returned to the market.

"I'm sorry, I don't agree with that," Temple said. "It is possible, I suppose, to say that pain is no big deal. I don't do a lot of practicing myself, but what people who deal with pain tell you is that you do need a variety of drugs to treat it."

Zomax would never return to the market. In that House of Representatives hearing room, in the full glare of television camera lights, the 42-year-old acting director of the Office of Drug Evaluation was putting on a little demonstration. When it came to balancing the risks and benefits of a specific drug, he was in charge. It was not the senior man next to him, Arthur H. Hayes, commissioner of the FDA. It was not a powerful and well-informed member of Congress. It was Robert Temple, M.D. He held one of the most important and demanding jobs in American medicine. Unlike some of the nation's premier research doctors, he was neither routinely featured on the evening news nor a regular subject of adoring magazine profiles. However, it would be hard to name another doctor whose medical judgment affected the safety and well-being of so many millions of patients.

The hearing continued only a few minutes more before another reason for Temple's dominant position became apparent. Representative Weiss wanted some details about the adverse reaction reports on Zomax, and the FDA official in charge of adverse drug reaction reporting could not answer the question. After waiting a tactful interval, Temple recited a complete breakdown from memory. It was another little demonstration. Not only was Bob Temple in charge, he was a very smart man. In ten years he had risen from a junior medical officer to one of the most powerful positions in American medicine, with the authority to tell the nation's 525,000 doctors which drugs they could and could not use. The job demanded someone willing to make hard decisions under pressures that seldom abated. On one side were the giant pharmaceutical companies, with years of effort and hundreds of millions of dollars invested in a promising new drug. They wanted their drugs approved, and were masters of all the modern tools of political pressure and media manipulation. On the other hand, if Bob Temple routinely caved in to the industry, and something went wrong, he would quickly find himself at the witness table explaining his mistakes to a critical and aggressive committee of Congress. For decades, a long and distinguished line of crusading senators and representatives had investigated the FDA and the drug industry. In this environment, the Food and Drug Administration, and Robert Temple in particular, had to make some of the most difficult and complex scientific decisions that governments must make.

The Food and Drug Administration's 18-story headquarters towers over the commercial suburban sprawl of Rockville, Maryland, near Washington, D.C. From the outside it looks like an oversized but nondescript office tower sheathed in black and silver aluminum. Inside, it resembles a nightmare vision of a faceless government bureaucracy. Narrow corridors with featureless beige walls and linoleum floors stretch for a city block. At regular intervals the monotony is broken by metal doors. Open any of these doors and the sight is similar—a rabbit warren of plain steel desks crammed into tiny inner offices, packed with cheap metal bookcases and filing cabinets. However much FDA employees might like their job—and many are deeply committed to protecting the health and safety of the public—almost all detest this graceless, cramped and isolated building. In these tiny offices and unadorned conference rooms, the fate of Tambocor will be decided. The final decision whether to approve it would be made by Robert Temple, director of the Office of Drug Evaluation.

Although he held one of the most important jobs in American medicine, and was a senior grade civil servant, Robert Temple rated only the slightest improvements on the overall austerity of the FDA building. He had a fourteenth-floor corner office overlooking a massive expanse of asphalt parking lot. It was large enough to accommodate not only a desk, but a small round conference table, which was typically heaped high with documents. The stark decor was leavened by ivy and rubber plants flourishing in the extra light of a corner office. But they were a pale reflection of the large collection of orchids that Temple nurtured in the greenhouse attached to his living room at home in northwest Washington.

Temple favored blue blazers and gray slacks, a typical uniform for doctors, who avoid business suits to distinguish themselves from lawyers and bankers. He arrived at the office each day at 8:30 A.M., usually burdened by an armload of documents in cardboard binders, far too much paper to fit into even a large briefcase. Like all the doctors who worked in drug evaluation, he punched in like a clerk or factory worker.

Robert Temple grew up in the New York City suburb of Merrick, Long Island. His father was a manufacturer's representative for a lamp company, and his mother taught English in the local schools. In the way that even the most normal lives are studded with odd coincidences, this small area of Nassau County, New York, would produce not only Bob Temple but two FDA commissioners—Hayes and David Kessler. By the time Temple graduated from the community's public high school, he was already known as one of the smartest kids around. He went to Harvard University, which collects smart kids from high schools all over the country and then pits them against each other. Even in that environment, Temple was still smart enough to publish as an undergraduate a scientific paper about the metabolism of *E. coli* bacteria. A professor urged him to go into microbiology. But he still wasn't sure what he wanted to do. One summer while at Harvard, he went home with a classmate and met a woman who looked strangely familiar. Her name was Bonnie Streifer, and she went to Radcliffe. She looked familiar because they had been in a Harvard class together for the past year. In three years they would get married.

Temple still didn't know what he wanted to do. He was not convinced he wanted pure science. He took the law boards. He applied to medical school. "I could never tell people to their satisfaction that I burned with desire to heal people. You could see they wanted to hear that," he recalled. These doubts notwithstanding, the smart kid

from Harvard had a good enough record to be admitted to medical
school at New York University on a full scholarship, plus a $3,000
stipend.

Many successful doctors will reveal that they hated their formal
classes in medical school. The volume of material that must be quickly
mastered is often daunting, even to excellent students. It is mostly
rote memorization. A major examination—a standardized national
test—guarantees that medical school harbors no gentlemen scholars.
Temple loved the classes. If you needed lecture notes, Bob Temple
was the man to see. If you needed answers, Bob Temple was the
man to ask. He had good enough answers to rank first in his medical
school class.

He remained in New York City for his internship and residency.
Like Thomas Bigger, the arrhythmia specialist who chaired the 1983
Tambocor symposium in Bermuda, Temple trained in the Columbia
University program at Presbyterian Hospital. It was total immersion
in the world of direct patient care, and Temple found it not entirely
to his liking. "I don't think I was bad at it, but I found it very stressful,"
he recalled. "I was very afraid of making a mistake because I hadn't
learned something, because I didn't know enough."

While training at Columbia, Temple learned his first lesson in the
complicated business of regulating prescription drugs. The country
was then experiencing a rising tide of sentiment for Laetrile, an
unproven cancer drug extracted from apricot pits and almonds. Organized medicine had denounced it as a quack treatment, and the
FDA had never approved it. But clinics were springing up all over
the United States, often headed by doctors who said they saw mi-
raculous cures. Temple was part of a team of medical activists who
traveled to states that were considering legalizing the drug. To make
a case against legalizing the unproven drug, the team had a dramatic
presentation. It included a case study of a young woman with op-
erable cancer of the cervix, who was going to leave five small children
without a mother because she had taken Laetrile instead of undergo-
ing surgery. "It was so appalling, I couldn't get through it without
choking," he said. "Then I would finish. They would heave a huge
sigh of relief, and they would go and make Laetrile available like they
already planned to." It was an object lesson, because a drug without
proven benefit could nevertheless produce patients who attributed
their survival to it. Experienced doctors who witnessed this often
endorsed the treatment.

For three years after his residency, Temple did research in endo-
crinology at the National Institutes of Health. It was an ideal form of

alternative military service for Temple, and a useful start on what he presumed would be a career in academic medicine. "Most of the smarter people in the class thought that's what they were going to do," he remembered. "It was the distinguished thing for doctors to do." He was a member of a moderately radical group of young doctors who were supporting Senator Edward M. Kennedy's efforts to create a national health system modeled on England's. He often got into arguments with another young NIH doctor in the same group named Sidney M. Wolfe. Wolfe would join Ralph Nader to form the Public Citizen Health Research Group and would become an effective public critic of the FDA and the drug industry.

Temple did well at NIH and stayed on past the end of his two-year alternative service fellowship. However, medical research, as he put it, "didn't light my fire. I didn't think I was going to get a Nobel prize." Now he dreamed about a challenge exciting enough to wake him up at night. It seemed to him that scientific research meant focusing obsessively on an extremely small piece of the puzzle. Temple craved the chance to work on big pieces.

One day in 1972 Temple met Dick Crout, the director of what was then called the Bureau of Drugs at the FDA. Crout, perceiving a smart but restless young doctor, tried to interest him in evaluating drugs for the FDA. Intrigued, Temple agreed to give it a try, and was soon reviewing drugs that affected metabolism and the endocrine system. He wondered just how much a youthful newcomer would be allowed to do. Soon he learned that the workload was so heavy that his colleagues were simply delighted to have another person to help.

One of his first drugs was calcitonin, a hormone that helps regulate calcium levels in the blood. The calcitonin he was evaluating was extracted from salmon, and its main use was in a rare bone disorder called Paget's disease. He judged it reasonably effective. The evidence was more problematic for a second proposed use—to lower elevated calcium levels in the blood. As he read through the massive file, Temple noted the results were inconsistent. Some study centers got a good response to the drug, and blood calcium levels fell. At others, little or no effect was found. Intrigued, Temple got out the case records and began looking at the test results, center by center, patient by patient. As he began to analyze the details, a little light went on. He saw something that the experts who designed the study had overlooked. All the centers tended to give the drug at the same time, at 7 A.M. each morning. But the blood samples to measure the calcium levels, and therefore the effect of the drug, were taken at different times. The only cases in which the drug worked were when the blood sample was taken almost immediately after the drug was given. The effect of salmon calcitonin was too transient to be medically useful for this purpose. Temple was thrilled. Numerous others had reviewed the same set of data, but no one else had seen the pattern. In the reams of scientific data that are routinely unloaded on the Food and Drug Administration, Robert Temple would find plenty to challenge his talents.

The legal boundaries of Robert Temple's job as a medical officer were set in a 1962 law that is surprisingly straightforward. It requires a pharmaceutical company to provide scientific evidence that a drug is safe. As noted earlier, the law also demands "substantial evidence" that a drug is "reasonably effective," and this proof must come from well-controlled clinical trials. Neither the endorsement of enthusiastic experts, nor anecdotal accounts of dramatic results in individual patients is acceptable. Both the safety and the effectiveness of the drug must be well-enough documented to be described in a detailed disclosure statement called the drug's label or package insert.

The drug label for a common rat poison called warfarin illustrates the importance of the disclosure statement. Doctors prescribe warfarin for tens of thousands of human patients every year. DuPont sells the drug under the trade name of Coumadin. Warfarin kills rats by blocking the capacity to form blood clots. As a result, the animals hemorrhage and die. Coumadin provides a textbook example that the difference between a poison and a drug is the dose. At the right dose, Coumadin can prevent unwanted blood clots from forming in the blood. After a heart attack, and certain other cardiac events, some individuals are at great risk that the blood may coagulate and form a small clot. If this clot lodges in the brain, the result is a stroke. Clots can also form in the lungs, in veins of the legs and other extremities. The drug label for Coumadin describes its ability to prevent clots, its dose, and warns of dangers.

A drug that inhibits the formation of blood clots could be enormously beneficial—but under what circumstances? When is the risk of a blood clot high enough to warrant taking a small dose of rat poison? This question of effectiveness is established in a controlled trial. A group of similar patients at risk of being damaged by blood clots is randomly assigned to get either Coumadin or a placebo. If the drug is effective, the treatment group should suffer fewer strokes

and other events caused by unwanted blood clots. The trial participants are systematically monitored for other adverse effects of the
drug, such as excessive bruising, hemorrhage, paralysis, shock, and
gangrene. These studies form the scientific basis to define those conditions in which the benefits are proven to outweigh the risks. This
is the central concept in approving any drug. In the drug label, this
is the indication. It identifies the specific medical uses in which the
benefits are proved to outweigh the risks. Often specific circumstances are identified in which the drug is harmful. These are
contraindications. Coumadin's capacity to inhibit blood clotting, for
example, would be dangerous in candidates for surgery.

This scientific disclosure statement about the safety and benefits
of the drug also gives the FDA flexibility. The drug label can be loaded
with warnings and disclaimers—as was Coumadin's. In the case of
Zomax, the FDA approved the drug despite finding that it caused
cancer in rats. The label described the study, and recommended
restricting the drug to short-term uses. However, physicians have no
obligation to prescribe a drug in accordance with the FDA label
indications and warnings. Within the standards of community practice, they are free to exercise what is customarily described as their
"independent medical judgment." Doctors need not inform patients
that they are going to be taking a drug for a medical purpose the
FDA specifically warns against. To help protect physicians against
troublesome questions from patients, the label or package insert is
removed before the drug is provided to the patient. (However, patients can ask for the package insert at the pharmacy.) Most of these
disclosure statements are published in the *Physicians' Desk Reference*—which is the book Derva Davis checked when she suspected
she was having a reaction to Zomax late one night.

Bob Temple had barely gotten his feet on the ground at the FDA
when he found himself at a party with the FDA official who recruited
him, Dick Crout, director of the Bureau of Drugs. Crout asked him
how he liked the work. Temple said the work was terrific, but he
had a problem. He didn't have enough work to do. In an organization
that was groaning under an excessive workload, that was all the boss
needed to hear. Crout said he would find plenty for Temple to do.
In short order, Temple was working part-time as Crout's personal
assistant on a government task force that had been formed to promote
the use of blood-pressure-lowering drugs. Bob Temple was soon

demonstrating that not only did he know how to analyze the minutiae of drug-testing studies, he also had the sure instinct for organizational politics that often leads straight to the top.

A good sense of politics, however, provides little help with some of the difficult medical judgments a medical officer must make. Temple could absorb the lessons from past successes and failures. One of the most famous episodes concerned a broad-spectrum antibiotic called chloramphenicol, first introduced in the 1950s. It was unusually potent, and also worked against some of the toughest tropical diseases. It was approved by the FDA and embraced by physicians with enthusiasm. Only after it had been taken by hundreds of thousands of patients was it learned that chloramphenicol could produce a life-threatening adverse effect. In perhaps 1 in 25,000 patients, the drug attacked the bone marrow, causing a frequently fatal condition called aplastic anemia. This adverse effect opens a whole new perspective on the balance between risk and benefits. Chloramphenicol was undoubtedly effective against several dangerous infections. But was that worth a 1 in 25,000 risk of a crippling or fatal disorder? The FDA left the drug on the market, but it was labeled with dire warnings not to use it except when other antibiotics had failed. Temple boiled the case down into a rule of thumb. He was fond of saying that a drug that caused aplastic anemia in 1 percent of the cases was not approvable. In practical terms, that meant the margin between benefit and risk must be large. The case of chloramphenicol highlights another of the great balancing acts in drug approval. How large should safety studies be? To find an adverse effect as rare as found in chloramphenicol would require a controlled study with more than 100,000 patients. As a practical matter, the FDA did not expect to identify side effects this rare before approval. In most drugs, testing was limited to a few hundred patients.

Robert Temple soon had to grapple with another problem that faces every new medical officer at the FDA. One job is to review the adverse reaction reports that are submitted for already-approved drugs. From these reports may emerge the first clues about side effects too rare to have been identified in clinical testing. Sometimes it means that a mistake was made in approving the drug. To make matters more difficult, adverse reaction reports are an uncertain and unreliable indicator of the extent and nature of the adverse reactions to a drug. In the controlled trials required for approval, adverse reactions are monitored systematically and uniformly. After approval, some ad-

verse effects go undetected for decades. Others might be overre-
ported because of a burst of publicity from a medical journal report
or news story. In this uneven and sporadic flow of adverse reaction
reporting, Robert Temple observed a troubling trend.

For two decades, a drug called phenformin had been prescribed
for milder cases of diabetes, called Type II. It was usually given to
individuals who still produced insulin, but nevertheless had moderately elevated levels of blood sugar. Temple found repeated reports
of lactic acidosis among patients taking phenformin. Lactic acidosis
is a disruption of the delicate balance between acid and base in body
fluids. Mild cases produce fatigue and compromise the function of
muscles. Serious cases can be fatal.

Temple decided to move against phenformin, hoping to get it off
the market. He got an outside consultant to present the evidence to
the division's advisory committee of experts drawn from the medical
schools. However, without a systematic study it was hard to make a
compelling argument. Mild cases of lactic acidosis were difficult to
detect without lab tests. Severe cases might be wrongly blamed on
sudden heart attack. Temple got nowhere with the advisory committee. "The committee barely believed the relationship was real,"
Temple recalled, "and they certainly didn't want to get rid of the
drug." While the committee served a purely advisory function to the
FDA, it was an excellent bellwether for the sentiment among specialists in diabetes. Rebuffed, Temple did not pursue his safety
concerns.

More than eight years elapsed before the FDA ordered the drug
off the market as an imminent hazard to health. It acted on a petition
from Sidney M. Wolfe's Health Research Group. Wolfe argued that
phenformin was causing from 1,000 to 4,000 deaths a year through
lactic acidosis. Wolfe and Temple, the two young doctors who had
been fellows together at the National Institutes of Health, would
devote much of their careers to the role of drugs in the medical
system. Wolfe remained the outside critic and reformer. Temple was
an organization man, working patiently within the system, apparently
comfortable with its limitations.

The FDA world in which Robert Temple worked was, as insiders put
it politely, "very much a mixed bag." Some who worked in drug
evaluation were stereotypical, time-serving bureaucrats. Others were
foreign medical graduates. Foreigners are readily admitted to the
United States to work the long shifts on the housestaff of hospitals.

But no matter how talented, many foreign-born doctors find it difficult to build an office practice. As a consequence, some were lured by the regular hours and regular pay of the FDA. Other medical officers were idealists who wanted to police the industry more aggressively, and regarded it as their democratic responsibility to make public FDA shortcomings they observed and could not remedy. Their freedom to speak their mind was protected by civil service regulations.

Robert Temple had been at the FDA just two years when director of the Bureau of Drugs, Dick Crout, asked him to become a special assistant. No sooner had the director's protege become his full-time aide than Crout gave him a task that was a deserving test for the brash young doctor who complained he didn't have enough work to do. He was assigned to handle an administrative and legal monstrosity that in FDA jargon was known as the Drug Efficiency Study Implementation (DESI) list. In 1962 Congress had greatly strengthened the legal requirements for approving drugs, insisting that a drug be proven both not only safe but also effective. For three previous decades it had only been necessary to show that a drug did no harm. Therefore none of the hundreds of drugs on the market had been evaluated for effectiveness. Congress gave the drug industry two years to demonstrate the effectiveness of existing drugs; otherwise the FDA was empowered to order them withdrawn. Fourteen years later, when the problem landed on Robert Temple's desk, little progress had been made. National Academy of Sciences expert panels had reviewed scores of drugs and issued reports. The FDA had been sued for failing to remove ineffective drugs from the market and was under court order to act.

Temple loved his assignment. For a lover of raw data, the DESI list was a feast, an education in every kind of study that could be conducted, and a lesson in every conceivable error. To get an ineffective drug off the market without an elaborate hearing required fancy legal footwork, summarizing the drug testing data accurately but with just the right legal language. Temple learned he was not only smart with data, he was quick with words and could use both to achieve the ends he desired. "I thought we did a good job on the DESI list," he said later. In reality, Temple was one of the few people who thought so. Unproven drugs—supposed to be off the market by 1964—are still being sold thirty years later, despite lawsuits, court orders, critical government studies, and congressional complaints.

Temple also helped Crout handle a rebellion from medical officers and other specialists who evaluated drugs. A group of eleven FDA employees or consultants had testified in a 1973 hearing that they had been transferred and suffered other consequences for being too tough on the drug industry. They were dubbed "the conscientious objectors" and their complaints got widespread media attention. The new FDA commissioner, Alexander M. Schmidt, was appalled, and testified that the charges were false. He insisted the FDA had not caved in to the drug industry and promised to produce a report to document his statements. This began one of the saddest and most divisive chapters in FDA history. Temple, still Dick Crout's aide, contributed to the lengthy report that Schmidt ultimately delivered to buttress his position. However, Schmidt's report was received skeptically in Congress and triggered a lengthy rebuttal from the eleven outraged conscientious objectors. Years of effort and millions of dollars were spent resolving the issues. The end result was that the conscientious objectors' charges were found substantially accurate, although they may have overstated the intent of the FDA management to cooperate with the drug industry.

When Robert Temple took over the Cardio-Renal Drug Division in 1976, he had arrived at a key position in American medicine. Of the more than $30 billion spent each year for prescription drugs, one quarter went for cardiovascular drugs. Cardiologists in particular used drugs intensively. A typical heart attack survivor left the hospital with a prescription for three to five different drugs. The Cardio-Renal Drug Division controlled what new drugs would be available for millions of patients. Temple was 35 years old, and in his fourth year at the Food and Drug Administration.

Some might see Temple's new job as an extraordinary responsibility for a bright young man. To others, including Temple himself, he was now in charge of a fractious and troubled office. The division had been a center of the conscientious objectors' rebellion, and was deeply divided. It had had no full-time director for several years. The responsibility for being acting director rotated among a chemist, a toxicologist and a medical officer. No new drugs had been approved for almost five years.

Temple finally had enough work to do. And at the end of the day he would take home armloads of documents and sit up until 1 A.M. reading them on the dining room table. In some divisions, a group leader coordinates the work of several medical reviewers. Temple never had a group leader and never wanted one. He went a step further. He asked the medical officers to submit rough drafts of their reviews, and he would return them with comments, corrections and analysis. A draft of a medical review could run to hundreds of pages. Because of the FDA's perennial shortage of secretaries, these documents were often handwritten. (So limited was the secretarial support that the FDA is one of the few government agencies where until recently even senior officials sent lengthy documents in handwriting.)

For eighteen long months, the Cardio-Renal Division still approved no new drug. When approvals finally began to flow, disaster struck. The drug was Norpace, the first newly approved antiarrhythmic drug in twenty years, the drug whose rapid growth in sales had helped persuade 3M to bring Tambocor to market. Temple realized that Searle's Norpace had not been well studied in patients whose failing hearts could barely pump enough blood to sustain body function. But the application had been pending for a total of fifty-four months. So Temple compromised. He recommended approving the drug. But the label carried a warning that it had not been studied in patients with this condition, called heart failure. He also extracted a commitment from the company to conduct the missing study after the drug was marketed. The follow-up study was never finished. A flood of adverse reaction reports made it clear Norpace frequently contributed to the death of patients with low cardiac output. It was Temple's first major crisis. Whether it was luck, or Temple's growing political skills, the Norpace mistake was managed quietly in the cardiology community. A warning in boldface type was added to the label. But Temple did not find himself at a witness table explaining his actions to a committee of Congress.

It must have been a lesson. First the division had acted too slowly; it was unable to act on Norpace for a period of four and a half years. However, neither was there safety in acting quickly. In hindsight Temple knew he should have required an additional study, even if it meant another year's delay. There was only one way to evaluate drugs, and that was to do it right. In 1980, Temple was at a cardiology meeting and under attack from August Watanabe, a doctor who was chairman of the committee on cardiovascular drugs for both the American Heart Association and the American College of Cardiology. Watanabe complained that Norpace had been available in Britain five years before it was approved in the United States. He named several other cardiovascular drugs that were also available more quickly in Europe. Watanabe was sounding a familiar drug industry theme— describing the so-called drug lag.

With the Norpace mistake fresh in his mind, Temple joked about the fifty-four months it had taken for the FDA to act. "It is obvious that at least half the audience thinks that we acted too quickly on Norpace, not too slowly." For a group of cardiologists who already knew they had helped speed the death of some of their heart failure patients by giving them Norpace, it was a painful joke.

Robert Temple learned that neither hurry nor delay offered a safe refuge. Relations with the drug industry could be polite and comfortable, or they could be hostile and adversarial. All that really mattered was getting the right answer, and the only way to get the right answer was to conduct the right kind of study. It would become almost a religion for a man who loved data. When the New Drug Application for Tambocor ultimately reached his desk, few people in the entire country were as capable of analyzing it as Robert Temple, M.D. But before the Tambocor application could reach Temple for action, it had several more hurdles to overcome.

Chapter 11

THE TAMBOCOR REVIEW

WHEN SUGHOK CHUN was a little girl in Korea before World War II, she got rheumatic fever. The disease left her with an irregular heartbeat. Sometimes these rhythm disturbances were so severe she had to squat down to try to catch her breath, wondering whether this was the moment she was going to die. When the New Drug Application for Tambocor reached Sughok Chun's desk fifty years later, it went to an FDA medical officer with both personal and professional experience with heart rhythm disorders. By late 1983 the application was complete enough for her to begin her evaluation of the drug.

Chun had been the original medical reviewer for Norpace, the first new antiarrhythmic drug approved in nearly two decades. Since Norpace was introduced in 1977, antiarrhythmic drug sales had nearly doubled, from six million prescriptions a year to nearly twelve million. However, this rapidly growing figure represented only a fraction of the potential market. One major limit on growth was that many patients simply couldn't tolerate the two leading drugs.

Quinidine was the market leader, in use since Sughok Chun was a schoolgirl. Quinidine is discontinued in one third of the patients because of adverse effects on the GI tract, specifically diarrhea, nausea and vomiting. Furthermore, the difference between a therapeutic and a toxic dose is small. "Constant vigilance is required in every patient taking the drug," cautions a major pharmacology text, *Goodman and Gillman.* In most preparations, it had to be taken four times a day, which was inconvenient for lifetime therapy.

The second-place best-seller, procainamide, seemed an even more dangerous drug. "The incidence of adverse effects is high when procainamide is used clinically," declares *Goodman and Gillman.* The drug sometimes suppresses one family of white blood cells, called granulocytes, compromising the immune system and opening the door to fatal infections. The careful physician might detect this problem with periodic blood tests and by paying great attention to any complaints of a sore throat or fever. This problem occurred in 1 in 200 patients, killing one quarter of those so affected.* A second adverse effect also involves the immune system and is much more frequent. It produces effects similar to the disease lupus. Symptoms of this disorder include pain in the joints, inflammation of the sac that encloses the heart, enlarged liver and fever. Unlike drugs that destroy bone marrow, these adverse effects of procainamide are reversible when the drug is discontinued. However, the most serious immune reactions involving the heart can be fatal. About 15 percent of patients developed symptoms of this immune disorder, and 60 to 70 percent show evidence of an immune response in lab tests.

One has to wonder how two drugs with so many serious adverse effects could have been approved in the first place. The antiarrhythmic properties of quinidine were discovered in 1912, and it spread into clinical use even before its safety had to be proven. Procainamide was approved under the more primitive 1938 law, and its adverse effects were not clearly understood until the early 1960s. Only for new drugs approved since 1962 has the law required that risks and benefits be compared with scientific evidence from well-controlled trials. Cardiologists familiar with drug development doubt that quinidine and procainamide could be approved under current law. However, the FDA was not going to take away two drugs used by tens of thousands of doctors for decades. Some doctors believed that the safety of old-line drugs had been proven through years of clinical practice. In fact, the safety of many old-line drugs has never been adequately studied, and some, like quinidine, are among the many dangerous drugs routinely given to patients. Whether it is a promising new drug or a long-established old drug, the dangers emerge only when they are thoroughly tested.

It was against this backdrop that Sughok Chun began to evaluate the safety and effectiveness of Tambocor. 3M would argue to Chun that Tambocor was a better and safer drug than quinidine and procainamide. Although a plausible argument, given the record and history of these two drugs, it was a questionable standard of reference. It was Sughok Chun's responsibility to judge these claims.

---

*This serious disorder is an apparent adverse effect of at least 77 different prescription drugs.

· · ·

Chun's father always wanted to be a doctor. But his family didn't have the money for medical school and he became a high-school math teacher in Seoul, Korea. He worked hard to make available to his daughter Sughok the opportunity to become a doctor that he himself had been denied. She finished medical school in Seoul in the chaos and destruction of the Korean War. Her residency at the Seoul National University Hospital was conducted under primitive conditions, and training in a medical specialty was not available. This brought her to the United States. She completed a three-year residency rotating among three Washington, D.C., hospitals, and then began advanced training in cardiology. Her fellowship was in the hospital affiliated with Howard University, which had one of the nation's first predominantly black medical schools. She did not finish training until 1964, 12 years after getting her M.D. degree.

After training she found work in the hospital coronary intensive care units that were being established in hospitals across the country. She worked first in Howard University's unit, and then became director at Holy Cross Hospital, in the Washington suburb of Silver Spring. She also was an assistant professor of cardiology at Howard, and was raising two children.

One day she met FDA medical officer E. D. Belton, a doctor who taught at Howard one day a week. Allowing outside medical activities one day a week is one incentive the FDA uses to attract doctors to government employment, despite pay that is much lower than a lucrative clinical practice. Belton worked on cardiovascular drugs, and told her the division needed a cardiologist.

Chun was tired. She had a family and a medical career. A slender woman, she had to wear a heavy lead-lined apron for many diagnostic studies, working hours on end on her feet. This made drug evaluation at the FDA appealing. "It was a desk job. I thought I might like it," she recalled. Her second assignment was Norpace, and it began an association with antiarrhythmic drugs that would last for two decades. She had monitored Tambocor from the time the human testing began in 1975.

When Sughok Chun needed information from 3M, she contacted a company division called "regulatory affairs." As in most drug companies, its job was to deal with the FDA. Other members of the 3M development team weren't supposed to talk to the FDA without going

through regulatory affairs; similarly when FDA officials wanted anything from the company, they were encouraged to contact regulatory
affairs. This arrangement gives the company centralized control over
what the FDA hears and when. 3M had a $50 million investment in
Tambocor at stake, and this provided a great incentive to win every
ounce of good will and cooperation possible from Sughok Chun.

For the Tambocor New Drug Application, 3M had designated one
person to be liaison to Chun for Tambocor. She was a pharmacologist
named Florence Wong, a dark-haired woman of Taiwanese extraction.
Chun found her a pleasure to deal with. Not only was Wong likable—
which was typical—she also had a strong medical background, which
made her quick to understand what Chun wanted. And 3M's responses were equally rapid, often within the hour. Chun and Wong
would talk on the phone almost every day. Much as an intelligence
service case officer does each time he contacts one of his agents,
Wong prepared reports of the conversations she had with Chun and
other FDA officials.

It was through Wong that Chun had first learned of the Tambocor
crisis in 1982. Wong telephoned to report the unexplained sudden
deaths, and medical director Gary Gentzkow's decision to stop enrolling new patients. She gave Chun a detailed briefing. "I smelled
something," Chun recalled. "Everything [adverse] happened within
two or three days [of starting the drug], so maybe you are giving too
much drug, so maybe too much dose." As she thought about it, Chun's
concerns moderated. "Bad things do happen to people. Some people
dropped dead on other drugs too." She recommended that 3M try
cutting the initial dose in half.

Thereafter 3M had a good reason to assume that the FDA would
accept the explanation that excessive doses explained the patient
deaths. Chun had been among those who originally proposed the
idea. The 1982 crisis was almost a year past when Chun began a
formal review of the Tambocor New Drug Application. It was a job
that would take six months.

One of the first documents available to Chun was an analysis of
the now completed animal studies. It came from Charles A. Resnick,
an FDA pharmacologist and toxicologist in the Cardio-Renal Drug
Division. When testing began in human volunteers back in 1975 only
the short-term animal studies were complete. The FDA allows companies to complete the longer studies at the same time human testing
proceeds.

The Tambocor animal studies provided grounds for serious concern. To study the effects over the long term, Tambocor was admin-

istered to hundreds of Charles River laboratory mice for eighteen months. In mice, no significant adverse effects were observed.

Over a two-year period, Tambocor was also given to 400 rats, at various doses. The rats, however, did not tolerate the higher doses as well as the mice. Some rats experienced urinary incontinence; others failed to gain weight normally as they matured. The highest no-effect dose in rats was the same as the maximum dose proposed for humans.

The findings were no more reassuring among animals biologically closer to man. When given to beagle dogs, electrocardiograms documented irregular heart rhythms at the higher doses. Once again the highest no-effect dose was about the same as for humans. At higher doses, the dogs lost weight, and when sacrificed for animal autopsy, abnormalities were found in lung tissue.

Tambocor dissolved in orange juice was also given to Senegalese baboons at the 3M testing facility in France. Once again the highest no-effect dose was similar to that for humans, and adverse effects occurred over the six-month term of the study. A particularly troubling finding occurred among four baboons getting the highest dose. After just seven days of taking Tambocor, one of the four baboons died suddenly. An animal autopsy disclosed no abnormality or signs of disease. This is exactly the finding expected in a drug that caused cardiac arrest. Of the eight beagles taking the highest dose of Tambocor, one died suddenly at thirteen months. No evidence of disease or other abnormality was found.

3M was also required to study the effects of Tambocor on the reproductive systems of mice, rats and rabbits. High doses of Tambocor produced birth defects in the form of clubbed paws, abnormal hearts and deformed skeletons in newborn New Zealand rabbits, but not in Dutch belted rabbits. The drug was also tested for its capacity to produce cell mutations in studies that ranged from *Salmonella* bacteria to the bone marrow of rats. Here no adverse results were found.

Resnick was concerned about the results. In his review, he concluded, "There is no margin of safety when extrapolating the baboon and canine toxicity study data to man." Resnick also examined the early studies in which irregular heartbeats were artificially created in dogs. When he compared the effective dose with the lethal dose in dogs, he noted "a further indication of a small margin between effective and toxic doses of Tambocor." Resnick said later that had he seen these data before human studies had started, "I would be disturbed about it."

The issue of animal studies has been debated for decades. Some critics—for example, Sidney Wolfe's Health Research Group—argued that all animal studies should be completed before any human testing began. The FDA, however, requires that only short-term toxicity studies be completed before short-term studies in humans begin. Therefore, in the case of Tambocor, the troubling long-term oral toxicity studies were not finished until human testing was nearing completion. If the FDA warning about the small margin of safety had come before human testing began, it might have prevented the twelve patients deaths that were attributed to excessive doses. Not only did the animal studies fail to prevent the deaths, 3M did not communicate the safety concerns later expressed by the FDA. This is what Gordon Conard of 3M told the doctors who attended the 1983 symposium in Bermuda:

"Long-term oral administration of Tambocor . . . does not produce any consequential toxic effects or any evidence of carcinogenicity." Conard's seeming clean bill of health for the animal studies was directly contradicted by the concerns that were later voiced by Resnick at the FDA.

The FDA policy over animal studies was adopted to shorten the development cycle of new drugs. In the worst case, requiring that long-term animal studies be finished before human studies begin might add two years to the existing cycle of eight to ten years for drug approval. Even with careful scheduling it might still add a full year to the cycle. However, it ought to make the overall process ultimately more efficient by focusing human drug testing on safer and more effective drugs.

Another major cost of not doing the animal studies first is more subtle. Once extensive human testing begins, the animal results tend not to be taken seriously. After millions of dollars have been invested, and a drug is nearing approval, it is extremely hard to kill it on the basis of animal tests alone. As noted earlier, Zomax animal studies returned typical positive results for cancer in the long-term animal study. With millions at stake, the company had a huge incentive to get into a technical argument over minute details of the animal study, rather than accepting the finding.

An even more serious case involved an animal study for Eli Lilly's antiarrhythmic drug, aprindine, another promising member of the same chemical family as Tambocor and Enkaid. After human testing was under way, Lilly discovered a dangerous effect in dogs. To mimic the effects of a heart attack, one of the small coronary arteries was tied off with surgical thread, abruptly halting the blood supply to an area of heart muscle tissue. However, ten of thirteen dogs getting aprindine experienced fibrillation, compared with just two on placebo. And in a pattern strikingly similar to Tambocor and Enkaid, the fibrillation was unusually difficult to reverse with an electric shock. Nevertheless, clinical development of aprindine continued for several years and numerous patient deaths were experienced.* Several years later, Eli Lilly abandoned aprindine. All this illustrates an underlying principle. If the animal studies are completed prior to human testing, a bad result means just another of the hundreds of compounds that are discarded. Once a drug is tested in hundreds of humans, and millions of dollars invested, it is difficult to prove that a drug is dangerous on the basis of animal studies alone.

Thus when Sughok Chun began to review the Tambocor New Drug Application she focused primarily on the dozens of volumes of human data. The main standard of comparison was the two long-established drugs, quinidine and procainamide. Her first key responsibility was to review the safety of Tambocor.

When a new molecule of human design is loosed in the complicated chemical machinery of the human body, a lot can go wrong. Halothane, an anesthetic, can destroy the liver. Declomycin, an antibiotic, can make the skin so sensitive to the sun that a severe burn results from a brief exposure. MER/29 creates cataracts in the eyes and makes hair fall out. Zomax triggered potentially fatal allergic reactions. Chloramphenicol attacked the bone marrow. Lopid, a cholesterol-lowering drug, can cause gallstones. The blood pressure drug bendrofluazide is linked to gout. The painkiller Oraflex made fingernails separate from the finger. The blood pressure drug Capoten has been associated with impotence, and priapism has been reported among Coumadin patients.

Numerous drugs on the market cause cancer in animals; only a few—such as the synthetic hormone DES (diethylstilbestrol)—have been studied extensively enough to establish cases in humans.

Sometimes the side effects of a drug are logical and a medical reviewer finds evidence for concern by looking in the right place. Taking the cholesterol-lowering drug Questran is the functional equivalent of swallowing sand, so constipation and other GI tract

*This also illustrates how unwise the Tambocor investigators were to absolve the drug of involvement in heart attack deaths. In this case an animal model of a heart attack showed disastrous effects with a similar drug. It was observed in others in the family as well.

distress is a reasonable and expected effect, and is observed in two thirds of patients. Other adverse effects are just weird. Why would a painkiller cause the fingernails to separate from the finger? Given all these possibilities, how did Chun cope with the formidable task of evaluating the safety record of Tambocor?

The key is systematic observation of the patients required during clinical testing. The hunt for adverse effects is anchored in the bed-rock of clinical medicine—a complete physical examination and patient history. After taking the drug, each patient is examined and interviewed for evidence of an adverse effect. A patient reports a rash. Does the patient have a history of skin problems, or is this the telltale sign of a possible allergic reaction or other drug effect? A significant fraction of the time, a patient detects the symptoms of the adverse effect. If asked, and if the doctor is listening carefully, the patient suggests the first clues to a possible adverse effect.

Laboratory tests provide evidence to confirm and enlarge on patient reports. Nausea just might indicate that a drug is damaging the liver. A blood test can detect unusually high levels of unique proteins released into the blood when liver cells die. Counts of the various red and white blood cells will reveal cases where the drug damages the bone marrow, or one of the kinds of blood cells. Chest x-rays might highlight fibrosis of the lungs—a potential problem noted in animal studies of Tambocor. All this raw data make a New Drug Application such a massive document. If the information is clear and well organized, the medical officer's job is much easier. But reviewing it still takes months of work. In the case of Tambocor, Chun recalled, "It was the best NDA I ever had."

The principal adverse effects reported were logical in a drug that altered how both muscle and nerve cells transmitted electrical pulses. Tambocor appeared to stimulate the central nervous system—a tendency observed in the earliest animal screening tests. (This was the problem that had eliminated the somewhat more effective R-799.) Approximately one third of the patients who took Tambocor reported dizziness. A slightly smaller number reported episodes of blurred or distorted vision. Most of these effects were temporary, and overall patient acceptance was good. While one third of patients couldn't tolerate quinidine, only about 8 percent discontinued Tambocor. These findings were limited to the population who were reasonably healthy except for premature beats. Overall, Chun was greatly impressed, especially in a class of drugs where serious side effects were routine. "None of the drugs were good until Tambocor came up," she recalled.

The greatest safety questions surrounded the cardiac arrests and large numbers of deaths in the seriously ill population. The application contained the full details of these events, and Chun was fully aware of them. However, she was less certain how to interpret the events.

"You could not tell anything because this was the patient population that had [cardiac arrest] before," Chun said. "Most had coronary heart disease. I read each case study to see if it was the drug or one of those things that was going to happen in those kinds of patients. You don't have a control group [for comparison], so you just didn't know." The question of a controlled trial in the most seriously ill patients had come up at Joel Morganroth's symposia for the research elite of antiarrhythmic drugs. From those discussions it was clear the cardiology community had never been willing to conduct a placebo-controlled trial in this population where so many deaths had occurred. The researchers were so certain of the value of these antiarrhythmic drugs they were unwilling to deny the benefits of these drugs to a placebo group. Therefore Chun could not tell whether a 12 percent death rate for these patients was excessive or only to be expected. There was no comparable group of untreated patients. As Chun said, you just didn't know. On grounds of safety, Chun judged Tambocor acceptable. She still had to consider the question of effectiveness.

Back in 1962, reformers wanted the law to require evidence of *therapeutic* effectiveness. Under such a standard, a drug must produce demonstrable health benefits to the patient. It had to relieve the symptoms, pain or suffering, to cure a disease, or prevent damaging events such as heart attacks or strokes. But the word "therapeutic" never made it into law, and this one omission had profound consequences for the kinds of drugs that would become available and how they were tested. It opened the door to entire families of drugs that provided theoretical benefits to the patient rather than proven good. These unproven benefits were called surrogate endpoints. They are effects believed to be surrogates or substitutes for actual therapeutic benefits.

A classic example of a surrogate endpoint can be found in drugs for diabetes. The main evidence of this disorder is elevated blood sugar. In juvenile-onset or Type I diabetes the cause is inability to make insulin, and replacing the missing insulin provides lifesaving benefits. However, in adult-onset or Type II disease, insulin is present and the reasons why blood sugar levels rise are not known. Nor is it clear that elevated blood sugar itself causes the complications of diabetes; it could be a marker for a deeper underlying disorder. Is a drug that lowers blood sugar beneficial? It proved to be reasonably inexpensive to develop drugs that lowered blood sugar. However, it would be expensive and require years to prove that the drug that lowered blood sugar produced measurable health benefits—prolonging life or reducing the complications of the disease. Nevertheless, many doctors embraced these agents. At least one—phenformin, proved to lower blood sugar, but as noted earlier, also produced fatal lactic acidosis. The FDA accepts the surrogate endpoint, or theoretical benefit of blood sugar lowering, even though health benefits have never been demonstrated for any such drug. Cholesterol-lowering is another surrogate endpoint, in this case for the therapeutic benefit of preventing a heart attack. Nevertheless a clinical trial of one approved cholesterol-lowering drug—a thyroid hormone—was halted amid fears it caused heart attacks. Another, Atromid-S, was shown to increase the chances of death by 29 percent.

The surrogate endpoint for anticancer drugs is reduction in tumor size. Treating a cancer could logically have two objectives—to increase survival or to improve the quality of remaining life. Cancer drugs are approved without demonstrating either benefit. Reduction in tumor size is sufficient. Patients do not necessarily feel better or live longer because some malignant tumors are slightly reduced in size. As a group, chemotherapeutic agents are among the most toxic in the entire arsenal of drugs. Because survival and quality of life studies are not routinely required, there is no way of knowing which agents do more harm than good.

Defenders of surrogate endpoints argue that requiring proof of direct benefit to the patient would increase the already enormous expense of developing new drugs, and inevitably reduce the number of new drugs available. Even when a surrogate endpoint does bring a flood of new drugs, it creates a new problem. Blood-pressure-lowering drugs are a case in point. Epidemiological studies show modest elevations of blood pressure increase the risk of heart attack and stroke. The FDA therefore approves drugs that lower blood pressure, another surrogate endpoint. When actual benefits to the patient were later tested in large, government-sponsored clinical trials, the drugs had little or no effect in preventing heart attacks. If high blood pressure signals an increased risk of heart attack, why doesn't reducing it provide a benefit? Nobody knows. The drugs do cut the risk of stroke, but the benefits are small, requiring treatment of 850 people for a year to prevent just one stroke. However, these disappointing direct benefits don't curtail their widespread use, and the huge market stimulated a flood of more than 60 drugs. Some drugs employed new mechanisms for lowering blood pressure—but because of the surrogate endpoint there was no way to tell whether they might be more or less effective in preventing strokes. Were there some mechanisms by which lowering blood pressure might cause heart attacks, just as one mechanism for lowering cholesterol had caused heart attacks? No one knows the answer to these questions. The inexpensive surrogate endpoint did encourage the development of dozens of new drugs. But what is the value of stimulating the development of so many drugs without finding out whether one is better or worse than another? Once drug regulation departs from the fundamental principle that a drug must be proved to benefit the patient—therapeutic effectiveness—there is no end to the potential difficulties created.

In the case of Tambocor, however, the presence of a surrogate endpoint made Sughok Chun's life easier. The main yardstick for gauging the effectiveness of an antiarrhythmic drug is the ability to suppress PVCs. On one level it makes sense. The most common and benign of all heart rhythm disorders provides an accessible and inexpensive vehicle for documenting the antiarrhythmic activity of Tambocor. Years earlier, it took Pete Somani just one patient and ten minutes to observe its dramatic effects on premature beats. The problem, of course, was that most patients don't even know they have premature beats, and don't feel any different once they have been treated. While the surrogate endpoint for judging Tambocor was probably the pivotal policy decision that the FDA made about antiarrhythmic drugs, it was not the result of any orderly deliberative process. When Sughok Chun got the Norpace New Drug Application, it was the first antiarrhythmic drug to be evaluated under the 1962 requirement for effectiveness. She and Robert Temple, then the division director, were venturing into uncharted waters, and many of the decisions were arbitrary. Temple and Chun knew what was needed. A surrogate endpoint should be defined in a clear set of written guidelines approved by the division's advisory committee. But in the pressures to get drugs out the door, the job never got done. In the absence of guidelines, Temple had set a precedent with Norpace:

"It remains true that the reduction in [premature beats] has not been shown to correspond to increased survival," Temple wrote. "This, however, is true for all anti-arrhythmic agents, none of which has been shown to increase survival. While I believe the labeling should reflect this fact, demonstration of this kind of 'ultimate' effectiveness should not, in my view, be a prerequisite to approval of a new anti-arrhythmic agent."

This was the policy that Chun worked under, and by this standard she concluded that Tambocor was a very effective drug. "It was the cleanest drug by way of having less side effects and cleaning up the EKG," she recalled. "It was an amazing drug."

Tambocor was not so successful in meeting an additional requirement, added almost as an afterthought. 3M also had to show that Tambocor suppressed rapid heartbeats deliberately triggered through programmed electrical stimulation. This was the technique that Roger Winkle at Stanford had found initially promising, and then discouraging. Chun was not impressed with the Tambocor results. "The people who responded are no more than 20 or 30 percent," she said. "At the end of the study not that many patients were left. They are either dead or taken off the medication because of side effects." Tambocor, however, was not significantly worse than other similar drugs. This was also the argument that 3M used to explain the many cardiac arrests recorded among Tambocor patients.

Nevertheless, Chun was enthusiastic about Tambocor. She thought its main properties were well documented in a clear and crisp analysis. She believed it was both more effective and better tolerated than the last drug she had handled, Norpace. She recommended that Tambocor be approved for use for a wide range of heart rhythm disorders, from simple PVCs to life-threatening disturbances. Tambocor had passed its first major hurdle to FDA approval. However, as the application was considered at higher levels, the questions were going to get harder, not easier.

Chapter 12

THE EXPERTS SPEAK

IN EARLY MAY, tourists are not yet clogging the double ribbon of highway that leads down the narrow peninsula to Woods Hole, Massachusetts. Soon they will jam the narrow streets of Woods Hole before boarding ferries for the summer playgrounds of Nantucket and Martha's Vineyard. While it is still early for tourists, May marks the beginning of the squid season at the Woods Hole Oceanographic Institution. This event triggers a more manageable annual migration of scientists who study the electrical activity of nerve cells. Each year they arrive at Woods Hole, accompanied by truckloads of computers and other specialized equipment. Included in this migration is Raymond Lipicky, M.D. When Lipicky is not studying voltage changes in squid nerve cells, he is director of the Division of Cardio-Renal Drug Products for the FDA. It was his desk on which Sughok Chun's review of Tambocor would land.

At Woods Hole, Lipicky in fact does study antiarrhythmic drugs. From the freshly caught squid, he removes two nerve cells, or axons, each almost three inches long. They are the largest nerve cells found in nature—and control the siphon through which the squid pumps seawater to achieve movement. The huge squid axons are just big enough for the experiments Lipicky wants to conduct. He spreads one out in a circular chamber, and attaches electrical probes. With a special minicomputer so fast it can capture events measured in millionths of a second, Lipicky plots the electrical responses of the squid nerve axons before and after the drug is administered. In a perfect world for Raymond Lipicky, he would spend full time conducting pure scientific experiments at the laboratory bench, pursuing knowledge for its own sake. But the world has forced Lipicky to compromise. He cut a deal with Robert Temple while Temple still headed the cardio-renal drug division. Lipicky was a full professor of medicine and pharmacology at the University of Cincinnati, and disillusioned by the constant pressures to hunt for research grants to support his laboratory. Lipicky agreed to spend half his time evaluating cardiovascular drugs for the FDA if he could spend the other half in a laboratory the FDA provided. Lipicky and Temple became close colleagues, and when Temple ascended to head the Office of Drug Evaluation, Lipicky took over Temple's old job.

Lipicky's special interests were a staple of the pharmaceutical industry gossip circuit, where it was said that if you wanted to get a New Drug Application approved, it was important to build a schedule around squid season. Office directors such as Lipicky were so powerful that the companies invested time and effort in learning their foibles, personal preferences and schedules. He was a tall, gangling man who towered over six-footers. He peered down at the rest of the world through half glasses in a manner that suggested that from his altitude, he was responding to mysterious forces others couldn't quite perceive.

When it came to reviewing drugs, Lipicky didn't have Robert Temple's passion for data. Lipicky worked more by triangulation, listening to ideas from various sources, questioning here, and probing there, watching the conflicting ideas collide like billiard balls. That was how he handled the Tambocor approval. He had Sughok Chun's medical review. He could talk to the company. The special sounding board that Lipicky particularly valued was the division's advisory committee. Depending partly on the preferences of the division director, such committees can play a critical role in drug approval. A series of objections from the advisory committee could halt Tambocor's steady progress toward approval.

In the early 1990s the FDA had forty-one advisory committees. They provide scientific and technical advice across the spectrum of medical activities that the FDA regulates—medical devices, vaccines and other biological products and prescription drugs. Members are mostly drawn from the world of academic medical research. They meet twice a year for one to three days, and get paid $150 a day during committee sessions. For the doctors of the academic medical establishment—often earning several hundred thousand dollars a year—it is obviously not the pay that makes seats on the advisory committee a sought-after honor. Advisory committees are important crossroads of medical research, and the major players like to be where the action takes place.

The FDA's advisory committees sometimes meet to consider a specific controversy—such as the widely publicized concerns about the safety of silicone-gel breast implants. They also can help make policy—such as drug approval guidelines. The committees' most important function, however, is their role in the ritual of drug approval. Even though the drug companies often seek publicity for their new drugs in development, and publish many studies, they have persuaded the Congress and the FDA that New Drug Applications ought to be closely held trade secrets. Therefore, company submissions and the agency's internal deliberations are closed to public view. Only when an advisory committee meets in public to consider a New Drug Application does the outside world get the first peek under the official curtain of secrecy. The company gets two hours to present its case for the safety and efficacy of the new drug; it comes with a battery of experts and trays of color slides portraying every aspect of the data. The advisory committee members are provided with fat briefing books stuffed with data. The powers of an advisory committee are quite narrowly proscribed. The committee addresses specific questions posed to it—normally in writing. Its conclusions and recommendations are not binding on the FDA. However, a recommendation for approval places pressure on the FDA to act; committee opposition usually torpedoes a drug's chances for speedy approval.

The Cardiovascular and Renal Drugs Advisory Committee was under the reasonably firm control of Raymond Lipicky. While senior physicians and medical researchers with tenure at medical schools don't follow orders from anyone, the committee was nevertheless one tool Lipicky could use to help manage the flow of new cardiovascular drugs into medical practice. Although members were technically appointed by the secretary of Health and Human Services (more recently the FDA commissioner), Lipicky proposed the members' names. A different director than Raymond Lipicky might have wanted senior, cautious doctors with no ties to the drug industry. Lipicky, with a background in research, wanted activists, as he put it, "at the cutting edge." It didn't bother him that such individuals would almost inevitably have close ties to drug companies and be testing their drugs. As a result, when the Tambocor New Drug Application came up, committee membership would include two men with an important role in developing the new generation of antiarrhythmic drugs: Raymond Woosley from Vanderbilt and Bertram Pitt from the University of Michigan. Both names appeared on the first dose-ranging studies of Tambocor; both attended Morganroth's Philadelphia gatherings of the research elite of antiarrhythmic drugs. The committee membership also typically included a pharmacologist and a biostatistician. Lipicky not only controlled the membership of the advisory committee, he also set the agenda. The committee usually considered questions that Lipicky specifically posed to them. They considered a New Drug Application when he was ready to advance the drug another step on the march toward approval. Over the years, various panels and commissions have proposed that advisory committees ought to have much more power and independence—and even their own staff. But to date, they have remained under the control of division directors. So it happened that six weeks after the beginning of 1984 squid season, the Cardiovascular and Renal Drugs Advisory Committee convened in Washington to consider the New Drug Application of 3M's Tambocor.

When public interest in an advisory committee meeting is high, the crowd can easily outstrip the limited facilities at FDA headquarters. With a front runner in a new generation of drugs under consideration, it was necessary to move the June 1984, meeting to the Lister Hill Auditorium at the National Institutes of Health. The move from the FDA's bleak tower in Rockville to the NIH's beautiful wooded campus in Bethesda, Maryland, freshly reminded the FDA employees that they performed one of the most difficult jobs in medicine under the worst conditions. The Lister Hill Auditorium was part of the strikingly modern National Library of Medicine building. It was built like an old-time surgical amphitheater: the seats sloped sharply downward toward the stage where the advisory committee members sat.

Before considering Tambocor, the advisory committee first addressed a piece of unfinished business from its previous session. It would set the tone for the entire proceedings. The preceding November the committee had reviewed the New Drug Application of Tambocor's leading European competitor, Mexitil, from Boehringer Ingelheim. But Lipicky had thrown a monkey wrench into the company's well-prepared and polished performance. Lipicky had just learned about the IMPACT study that had used Mexitil to see if suppressing premature beats would prevent cardiac arrest and death. As noted earlier, the largest test of the arrhythmia suppression hypothesis had produced the opposite of the expected result. More deaths occurred in patients taking Mexitil than in a similar group taking an inactive placebo. The excess deaths caused the investigators to stop the experiment before a conclusive finding was achieved. One of the IMPACT researchers had given the committee a briefing.

Since the results were inconclusive, Lipicky had also invited a clinical trials expert from NIH's National Heart, Lung, and Blood

Institute. His name was Curt D. Furberg, and his job was a pivotal one. The committee was poised to consider approving a new generation of antiarrhythmic drugs. It was expected that most prescriptions would be written on the theory that suppressing premature beats and other mild rhythm disorders would prevent a lethal cardiac arrest. It was Furberg's job to summarize the clinical trial evidence testing this theory.

Furberg told the committee he had identified six long-term clinical trials, including IMPACT, that tested whether antiarrhythmic drugs did indeed prevent sudden death. All were conducted in recent heart attack survivors. Whether analyzed separately or taken together, there was no evidence the patients benefited. In addition, twenty-two much shorter experiments—some as short as one hour—were equally inconclusive.

Furberg put the situation bluntly. "There is no evidence that any of the drugs tested in the populations studied have any effect on mortality." Here were twenty-eight separate experiments involving more than 6,000 patients, and no evidence of the claimed benefit of antiarrhythmic drugs could be found. Animal experiments and other kinds of studies suggested that treatment "should be beneficial," he noted. This theory had spurred "a massive use of antiarrhythmics."

This might have been the turning point in the story of antiarrhythmic drugs. Hanging in the balance was the fate of a whole generation of new drugs—developed over more than a decade's time at costs measured in hundreds of millions of dollars. In a public hearing, the FDA's chosen experts were considering the central question: Was there evidence from well-controlled trials that the patients benefited? Furberg's answer was simple and direct. There was no such evidence.

There were three possible explanations why no benefits had been observed, Furberg told the committee. One answer was obvious: antiarrhythmic drugs don't prevent sudden death. A second possibility was that the drugs killed some patients and saved others, achieving zero net effect. However, it was in addressing a third possibility that Furberg, the clinical trials expert, really warmed to his subject. Perhaps they just hadn't yet done the right study. Most were too short. Almost all were too small. Sometimes patients who didn't have premature beats were treated. In other studies, the investigators didn't make sure the drugs actually suppressed the premature beats. One message was that future clinical trials needed to be larger, longer and better planned. And as he spoke, that kind of planning was under way in Furberg's division of the National Heart, Lung, and Blood Institute.

Even given the scanty, imperfect and conflicting evidence, Furberg still sounded worried. "If there is a benefit, you would have expected more trials to go in the favorable direction and have more trends in favor of treatment. That was not the case."

Furberg then volunteered a warning about Mexitil, the drug the committee then had under consideration. The drug had been included in three separate clinical trials where patient deaths had been reported. In each instance, more patients had died on the active drug than on the placebo. In no case, however, was the evidence conclusive in statistical terms. With some analytical techniques, he added, the excess patient deaths on Mexitil "could very well be close" to statistically conclusive evidence.

With Furberg's warning, the story of antiarrhythmic drugs crossed another key boundary. The FDA committee of experts was no longer considering a family of drugs whose theoretical benefits were as yet unproven. An expert had just told them that twenty-eight previous attempts to document that benefit had failed. Worse yet, the available evidence on Mexitil suggested it might kill some patients.

Raymond Woosley of Vanderbilt immediately attacked. "I have a great deal of difficulty taking nonsignificant changes in nonsignificant studies and trying to make significant conclusions," he said.

Furberg, a senior NIH official with a multimillion-dollar research budget, was angry at being so quickly dismissed

"Is that a comment?" he said.

The committee chairman, Jeffrey Borer of Cornell University medical school, tried to divert the discussion and prevent a conflict. But neither Woosley nor Furberg was deterred. Woosley was a medical godfather of this new generation of drugs. He had conducted the early major efficacy studies of both Enkaid and Tambocor, and had ties to both companies. He had studied Mexitil. Furberg was assailing the proposition to which years of Woosley's research had been devoted. It was Woosley, however, who pressed the issue of safety.

Woosley said, "We know that they will kill some people. We only hope they are going to be used in a situation where they would save more than they kill."

The issue was where to place the benefit of the doubt. In the absence of a conclusive finding proving the drugs were harmful, Woosley continued to believe in the benefits of the drugs he had helped develop. But Furberg believed the troubling findings suggested caution.

"In the absence of good data, what do you do?" Furberg asked. "You take the evidence that is there. And you have three negative trends [results] by chance alone. How often do you see that?"

The "negative" trend, as Furberg so politely described it, was excess deaths among patients taking Mexitil, compared with those taking an inactive placebo. This was not a question of benefit but the serious possibility of harm.

But Woosley would not hear of it. "I think that you stop doing poor studies like these." Woosley said that if you test penicillin in people without infections, the only effect observed will be harmful allergic reactions.

Furberg was angry to have his concerns dismissed in a joke. "The analogy is totally inappropriate," he said. "It has nothing to do with what I presented here."

At this moment Bertram Pitt of the University of Michigan stepped in, hoping to stop the argument. He agreed with both sides. "We would like to see that these drugs save more than they kill. And I don't think we can say that one way or another. Certainly there is an alarming trend and I certainly would agree that these are poorly designed studies." But Pitt refused to single out Mexitil. It "is probably no different than any other antiarrhythmic agent around," he said. "Until the proper studies are done, we are stuck with this data. And this data says be a little nervous."

Woosley was not convinced. He still blamed the studies. He said, "We all realize that these drugs are potentially lethal. I wouldn't be a bit surprised if you continue to give it to people who don't need it, you are going to show [excess deaths]."

Like so many committee meetings, the November session on Mexitil had sputtered to an inconclusive close. Lipicky did not try to resolve the issue. Instead he cut off the debate with a torrent of unrelated technical questions about the Mexitil dosing regimen. The committee put off the question of approving the drug until Boehringer Ingelheim could present additional information.

Thus the central issues concerning antiarrhythmic drugs were put forth with crystal clarity in a public session. More than two dozen attempts to document the main benefits of antiarrhythmic drugs had failed. These and other studies showed that these drugs were more dangerous than the experts has previously supposed. Whether it was the unexplained patient deaths on Tambocor and Enkaid, or the three disturbing clinical trials of Mexitil, researchers now openly acknowledged these drugs could kill. The law was explicit and clear. The sponsors must prove with well-controlled trials that a new drug's benefits are greater than its risks. With each additional piece of evidence the lethal risks of these drugs seemed clearer, and the benefits ever more uncertain. This seminal discussion at the previous meeting framed the issues that the committee would now address in the June 1984 session.

The committee had to finish with Mexitil before it could focus on Tambocor. This time Boehringer Ingelheim was taking care to have the test data available in every possible form. One of the presenters had prepared 50 backup slides, arraying the dose-response results in various configurations. To deal with the problem of the unexpectedly large number of deaths in the clinical trials, the company had hired Thomas Bigger of Columbia. Bigger had attended the Tambocor investigators' meeting in St. Paul, and chaired the Bermuda symposium on Tambocor the previous summer. Bigger was now working for Boehringer Ingelheim to reassure the committee about Mexitil's safety.

Before Bigger could speak, however, Bertram Pitt introduced the subject of the patient deaths. "I am still concerned about some of the data we saw the last time," he said. "There was no reduction in mortality. In fact there were a few more [deaths]—not significantly more—in the people who received Mexitil."

In six months time, however, Woosley had completely dismissed the study. "It is alarming as Bert said, but there are so many flaws in the study I don't think it means anything."

A few minutes later, Bigger was ready with a more elaborate case. "There are no studies designed with the power to detect any mortality effect," he said, summing up. "There are no studies that address the concern that Dr. Pitt raised."

In six months time—and with no new data—Furberg's concern that some members of this family of drugs might kill people was reduced to a "valid concern" for which no data yet existed. However, Bigger failed to mention the most important reason that the IMPACT study was inconclusive. IMPACT was intended as a pilot study to test whether Mexitil was safe and stopped the premature beats. Only if that effort was successful would it be expanded to test the larger idea that antiarrhythmic drugs prevented sudden death. When the investigators observed excess deaths in the pilot study, they stopped the study. Most doctors believe it is unethical to give medication to patients only to document the extent of harm, and the existing evidence suggested continuing would be harmful. Bigger and Woosley had reversed the burden of proof; they seemed to want conclusive evidence that the drugs harmed people, rather than convincing proof they were safe and beneficial. Such evidence seldom exists because researchers usually cancel a study as soon as indications of harm are apparent—but before the results are conclusive.

The immediate question before the committee in June 1984 was the future of Mexitil. It was Woosley, the committee reviewer, who summed up the evidence on the drug.

"I would like to first compliment Boehringer Ingelheim for having done a masterful job of pulling together the data," he said. "They have done a good job in surveying the world's literature and obtaining the best expert advice from around the world."

While Woosley recommended approval of Mexitil, he wanted a new warning on the label. Because of the lack of evidence the antiarrhythmic drugs prevented cardiac arrest, he wanted to warn doctors not to use these drugs in the majority of patients who had no symptoms.

But Raymond Lipicky, the division director, objected. How could the FDA warn doctors not to use these drugs when the clinical trials were inconclusive? The warning was ultimately limited to a bland statement of fact: "Like other antiarrhythmics, Mexitil has not been shown to prevent sudden death . . . also, like other antiarrhythmics, it has potentially serious adverse effects including the ability to worsen arrhythmias." The committee voted unanimously to recommend that Mexitil be approved. Tambocor was the next item on the committee's agenda.

After the intense debate over Mexitil, the Tambocor presentation seemed quiet, professional and well ordered. It was more a meeting of a club of colleagues than a formal proceeding with separate judges, expert witnesses, and a petitioner. To present effectiveness data, 3M had brought Jeffrey Anderson, who had trained in cardiology under committee member Bertram Pitt. After helping test Tambocor, Anderson and Pitt had jointly written an enthusiastic endorsement of the drug in the *New England Journal of Medicine*. Committee member Raymond Woosley had been a 3M consultant; his recommendation had helped launch the expensive Tambocor development program. To cover the safety issue, 3M had hired Joel Morganroth, who had worked closely with Raymond Lipicky, director of Cardio-Renal Drugs, planning the symposiums in Philadelphia where the FDA, the companies and the research elite gathered each year.

The 3M presentation was crisp and professional. Donald Kvam and Gordon Conard outlined the animal studies and the metabolism of Tambocor. Jeffrey Anderson described how effective Tambocor was in suppressing premature beats. Morrison Hodges of the University of Minnesota reported the study showing that Tambocor outperformed quinidine, the sales leader in the market.

The presentation rolled forward without major controversy, moving toward the toughest question about Tambocor. Many of those present were aware 3M had halted clinical testing of Tambocor after experiencing patient deaths that proved drug-related. They knew that patients had dropped dead right in front of investigators who could not resuscitate them. Had 3M resolved the safety concerns that this episode had created? 3M's medical director, Gary Gentzkow, reserved for himself the responsibility for taking the advisory committee across these treacherous waters.

Gentzkow gave the committee a detailed account of the disturbing results that led him to stop enrollment in Tambocor trials. He described the investigators' meeting and the theory that emerged: the deaths resulted from excessive doses in patients with already damaged hearts. Gentzkow also had something new—the results of the new study with a more cautious protocol, limited to a few carefully selected medical centers. (In fact, two thirds of the patients had been enrolled by Joel Morganroth in Philadelphia.)

Gentzkow developed his case carefully and methodically with 25 slides devoted to this one study. Overall these results were quite similar to the earlier experience. Of the 96 patients who got Tambocor in this special protocol, two thirds had a bad outcome. Either they died or the drugs had to be discontinued. There was, one difference, and Gentzkow was careful to point it out:

"There were no in-hospital deaths occurring in the first few days of therapy as we had experienced in the compassionate use program. None of those events occurred here." The overall death rate was quite similar to the early study but no deaths had occurred immediately after the drug was started. The committee had only a few questions. Gentzkow had reached safe ground. In a public session he had laid out the problems they encountered, and sold the advisory committee on the solution.

For an overview of the overall question of safety, 3M then turned to Joel Morganroth. He presented the data for Tambocor. Investigators had observed a cardiac arrest that proved unusually difficult to reverse in nearly 6 percent of the Tambocor patients. In all but one of these cases, the patients already had life-threatening heart rhythm disturbances. Therefore, Morganroth reasoned, Tambocor was quite safe to use in the majority of patients whose heart still pumped normally. It could be used with safety in patients without symptoms in hopes of preventing cardiac arrests. But extreme care was needed using Tambocor in the most severe rhythm disturbances, he said.

Morganroth was very confident about the safety of Tambocor. "I can assure you from the data that Tambocor doesn't increase death."

He also suggested a solution to the other problem that confronted the advisory committee. Repeated clinical trials had failed to establish that antiarrhythmic drugs prevented sudden cardiac death. Should Tambocor be prescribed for this purpose? Until an answer was available from a definitive study, he said, this question should be left to the medical judgment of the individual doctor.

"Should we not, in the medical community, have such a tool to use our best practice judgment with?" he asked. It was an argument likely to resonate with the FDA's Lipicky, who strongly believed the agency shouldn't tell doctors how to practice medicine.

Bertram Pitt, who had been the most concerned about Mexitil, immediately saw the danger of passing the buck to the individual doctors. He said, "What happens if it turns out, when the studies are done, that far more of the people died who got this drug?"

Once again, the central question of antiarrhythmic drugs was laid bare. What if definitive studies showed the drugs were unmistakably harmful? What risks was the FDA taking with the nation's health by releasing these drugs before such studies were done? What would they do if the studies showed the drugs caused cardiac arrests rather than prevented them?

"That is a decision to be made at the time those studies are done," Morganroth said. He noted that blood pressure drugs had been widely used before their benefits were fully tested.

No sooner did the committee stare directly into the stark face of potential disaster than they turned away. Over the next few minutes of discussion, the committee's concerns about the potential dangers of these drugs became distilled into a single word. The word was *symptomatic*. Previous drugs had been approved for use in treating "ventricular arrhythmias." The committee now proposed as an indication for medical use "*symptomatic* ventricular arrhythmias."

It was a curious, imprecise word to choose, but it happened to fit the committee's widely varying needs. Bertram Pitt was worried about safety, and wanted use of these drugs restricted. Since most arrhythmia drug patients didn't have symptoms, this word amounted to a restriction on the drug. Raymond Lipicky wanted the drug label to reflect scientific evidence; he was willing to let doctors decide how to use the drug. He said, "Physicians need to decide whether to treat PVCs. Why should we?"

The committee also indicated that it was not trying to single out Tambocor as particularly dangerous; the word "symptomatic" should be added to the labels of the other drugs as well. Thus a single word satisfied those who wanted to restrict the drug and those who did not: Those worried that increasing numbers of doctors were treating PVCs, and those who didn't think that was the FDA's problem. The truth was that buried in the fine print of a drug label, surrounded by thousands of other words, the single word *symptomatic* would have little or no effect of any kind.

It is the chairman's job to bring the committee's business to a vote. "Is there anyone present who would not vote approval for the drug for the indications that have been noted?" Borer asked. "I think you can note that it is a unanimous vote for approval."

Bertram Pitt was still nervous. While he didn't oppose approving Tambocor, he wanted the case reopened for all antiarrhythmic drugs. "We would like to suggest that the FDA perhaps review all the existing drugs on the market," he said.

Lipicky was against it, but not because he believed the existing drugs were safe. He thought they might be even more dangerous than Tambocor. "If they were being looked at today they wouldn't have a ghost's chance of making it," he said.

In the face of Lipicky's opposition, Pitt withdrew his proposal, and suggested a workshop. It was not voted on, and it was not held.

Tambocor had now to clear only one more hurdle before approval. It had to get by Robert Temple, director of the Office of Drug Evaluation, the man who loved data, and the kind of complexities that now surrounded Tambocor.

Chapter 13

TEMPLE DECIDES

IN THE TROPICAL Washington summer of 1985, the future of Tambocor and an entire new generation of antiarrhythmic drugs lay in the hands of one man: Robert Temple. His power and influence over drug evaluation and approvals had continued to increase. His position as acting director of the Office of Drug Evaluation was made permanent. He had won or shared in seven FDA awards, including a special citation from the commissioner. Most of the twenty or thirty new drugs approved each year crossed his desk. The early 1980s were a period of constant reorganization at the FDA with major changes in 1981, 1983 and 1985. But with each reorganization, Robert Temple's authority emerged unscathed, and often increased.

Temple's management style had changed little with his increasing responsibility. He no longer read handwritten rough drafts from medical officers, but he still lavished hours on each New Drug Application, writing his own detailed analysis and sending lengthy, fact-studded memos back to the division directors. The man who was first in his medical school class was not intimidated by the wide variety of drugs he now had to evaluate: agents to combat cancer, drugs that affected mood and behavior, or altered fundamental processes, such as cholesterol metabolism. He would appear at meetings and recite the detailed study results from memory.

Doing all this analysis for so many new drugs meant a brutal schedule. He seldom left the office before 7 P.M. When he did, he was carrying an armload of documents. Only when he was finally free of meetings and telephone calls did he sit down for serious study, working at his dining room table from 11 P.M. until 2 A.M. It was an enormous burden on a man who loved to carry the load. But clearly, if Temple was to review every drug in depth, something had to give. And the catch in this arrangement was that completed New Drug Applications, ready for approval, could sit on his desk for a long time.

As August of 1985 rolled around, 3M was extremely anxious about Tambocor. The advisory committee had recommended approval in June of 1984; it was not until the following May that the completed paperwork reached Temple. For three months the completed application sat on his desk. By August 1, 1985, five new antiarrhythmic drugs were near the end of the approval pipeline. Tambocor was first in line.

The day-to-day Temple watch was the job of Florence Wong of 3M regulatory affairs. In the years that Tambocor's application was pending, she had gotten to know the entire cast of characters in the upward chain of approval that led to Robert Temple's office. Her official liaison was Denver Presley, whose job title was consumer safety officer in the Cardio-Renal Drugs Division. Wong had frequent contact with Sughok Chun, the medical officer in charge of Tambocor. More rarely she could talk to Raymond Lipicky, the division director. And she had become familiar with the secretaries. Finally, on August 7, 1985, at 4:30 in the afternoon she got Robert Temple on the phone.

When Wong talked to the boss himself, she learned that Robert Temple was indeed focusing on Tambocor. In fact, he had spent the past several days analyzing the data, trying to zero in on the essential questions. As he went through the data, Robert Temple was worried. Specifically, he was concerned about the number of sudden deaths that had occurred among patients on Tambocor. Wong asked Temple if he would care to discuss his concerns with the 3M medical people. Temple didn't want to talk to 3M. First, he wanted to share his concerns with Lipicky and Chun in Cardio-Renal Drugs. What Temple said next must have sent a chill down Florence Wong's spine. He told her he was sure "major" changes in the Tambocor labeling would have to be made before he could approve the drug. This comment had to be an obvious sign of trouble ahead. The delays in approval were not the product of some pointless bureaucratic backlog. Robert Temple was reopening the case 3M had hoped that it had already won.

Temple had remained in touch with the controversies now developing around antiarrhythmic drugs. This meant he was also acutely aware of the pressures that were building. On one side, a new generation of drugs was waiting to flood into the marketplace. Most had been in development for more than a decade; hundreds of millions of dollars had been invested. On the other side of the balance was the rising tide of concern that the patients sometimes dropped dead soon after taking these drugs. The intensity of these pressures was already clear nine months earlier, when Temple, Lipicky and Chun had attended Joel Morganroth's annual gathering in Philadelphia of the elite of antiarrhythmic drug research.

Morganroth had made a pointed observation about the delays. "We believed this forum might help speed to market new antiarrhythmic agents to improve the drug armamentarium of physicians in the United States," he said. "Over the past five years no new antiarrhythmic agents have, in fact, been released."

As the session continued, however, it was increasingly clear many participants did not share Morganroth's impatience. Instead, increasing concern was evident about the safety of the drugs. Ronald Campbell, a British doctor had who tested Mexitil, argued the drugs should be the prime suspect when sudden death occurred. He stated bluntly, "arrhythmogenicity [should] be considered the cause of death until proven otherwise." His lecture title was equally direct: "Sudden Cardiac Death—Failure or Effect of Antiarrhythmic Drugs."

Sughok Chun, the FDA medical reviewer of Tambocor, said, "The problem really is the sudden death. That is the real problem we have." She said she had requested a count from the drug companies showing how many people had thus died.

However, Morganroth defended the drugs. "We don't know if the death is proarrhythmic [drug-related] or just part of the natural history. There is no way to tell which. I think that if the death occurs in about a week it might be proarrhythmic and if the death occurs after two or three months then it is probably not the drug."

Raymond Lipicky, the division director, objected to Morganroth's assumption that he knew which deaths were drug related and which were not. It was impossible to identify a drug-related death merely by when it occurred, he noted.

Another participant also challenged Morganroth's suggestion that drug-related deaths occurred only in the first week. "I would caution against using a break point and being so confident of it," said John Somberg of Albert Einstein College of Medicine. The group was moving toward assuming the drugs were responsible for all sudden deaths until the proper studies proved otherwise.

The final word in the discussion went to the man who would have to decide, Robert Temple. He defended the drug companies. "The consequence of merely counting every event as though it is really drug-induced is that companies that are willing to allow their drug to be used in relatively sick people will find that their drug is denounced," he said. But then Temple equivocated. "I'm not saying you should expose people to high lethal possibilities, but you do want to think about [whether] the event is really the drug or not."

Both Temple and Morganroth seemed to believe they could identify which deaths were drug related without a placebo-controlled trial. But to believe so was simply medical hubris.

By the first week of August 1985, Robert Temple was doing what he had proposed, thinking carefully about the Tambocor sudden deaths. Because of his conversation with Florence Wong, alarm bells were ringing at 3M. Temple's concerns had immediately come to the attention of Wong's boss, Roland Catherall, director of regulatory affairs. He in turn had consulted with Morganroth.

Catherall decided to bring in Jonah Shacknai, a Washington lawyer who specialized in pharmaceutical matters and was a friend of Robert Temple's. Catherall asked Shacknai to find out just how concerned Temple was over the safety of Tambocor, and learn how quickly Temple might act.

Shacknai soon had an answer for 3M. Temple was nearly done looking at Tambocor, and was about to go partway toward releasing it. He was going to send 3M an "approvable letter." If Temple were completely satisfied, he could simply send a letter approving the drug. An "approvable" letter indicated that he could approve the drug provided that certain concerns were met. Shacknai had more bad news for 3M. Temple thought that 3M "would have problems with what he is proposing."

The same day, August 14, 1985, Florence Wong tried a more direct approach to learning about Temple's intentions. She telephoned his secretary, Mary Duvall, and asked if she had seen a letter from Temple to 3M. Duvall told her that she had not gotten anything to type yet.

On the following Monday, Wong heard the message she had been waiting for. Mary Duvall, Temple's secretary, revealed that she had a 25-page memo to type. But it was not addressed to 3M. It was addressed to the Cardio-Renal Division. Still, this meant Robert Temple had made a decision about Tambocor. Wong immediately telephoned Denver Presley, the FDA consumer safety officer. Presley had good news for Wong. This week Lipicky was back from his squid axon studies at Woods Hole.

Wong reported to her 3M colleagues: "Lipicky is in this week, which is good because he should agree with everything Temple says. In case there is an unforeseen delay, Denver agreed to ask Lipicky to go to Temple's office to at least look at the draft on Friday before he goes off to Woods Hole again, so Denver could send the letter to us next week."

By the next Monday, August 26, Florence Wong had another news bulletin from Denver Presley. Lipicky had received Temple's memo and had written a reply before going back to Woods Hole. Wong relayed the new information to other members of the 3M team:

"Denver said the reply from Lipicky to Temple has been initialed by everyone.... It should go up today. I asked what Lipicky's position was. Denver said Lipicky maintained that it should be approved and that 'everyone here' thinks it should be approved. I asked if he would share with me what Temple's concerns were. He said he'd rather not, because everything is unofficial at this time."

Florence Wong and her 3M colleagues had to wait only three more days. On August 29, 1985, the letter from Temple was ready. The 3M team was optimistic that thirteen years after the first synthesis of Tambocor, success was nearly at hand.

Before deciding about Tambocor, Robert Temple had reviewed an immense pile of material. He had Sughok Chun's original medical review. He read the transcript of the advisory committee meeting and the thick volume of supporting material for committee members. He had a draft copy of another massive document, the Summary Basis of Approval, or SBA; it was for public release and described the testing and development of Tambocor in detail. (The finished version was 170 pages long.) It was drafted by the 3M team, but edited and revised by the FDA. Temple often rewrote the SBA himself.

The man who loved data then conducted his own analysis of the most critical question—the sudden deaths apparently caused by Tambocor. He went through this stack of material and extracted every cardiac death that had been reported during the clinical testing of Tambocor, and incorporated them into a memorandum. He listed patient number 028-59-101, who collapsed while playing tennis and died. He included 057-01-101, who died suddenly while gambling, and 057-06-007, who succumbed quietly at home. Patient 033-13-008 was at the ballpark when he died; another patient was at a picnic. Temple also looked at how long they had been taking the drug. The tennis player was on Tambocor for four days. The gambler, two and a half months. Another died in his sleep after fifteen and a half months of taking Tambocor. The tidy columns of patient numbers marched up and down the pages of his memorandum, each one marking a death.

Temple also wanted to know how sick the patients had been when they died. In one study, he found nine deaths where the patients had already experienced one cardiac arrest; in another study prior arrests were rare. He also listed the dose of each patient at death. Robert Temple was searching the data for clues to a pattern others might have overlooked. Mostly he accepted the investigators' crude judgments about which deaths were drug related and which were not; however, he also listed the other deaths.

Temple described the troubling questions about Tambocor that he couldn't answer with the studies and the other data at hand. He found well-controlled trials to demonstrate that Tambocor suppressed benign PVCs, but no studies to show that this was beneficial. He thought there was a better case for using Tambocor to halt severe rhythm disturbances, but had no controlled studies in this patient population. When it came to the seriously ill patients, Temple was worried. Tambocor "can both suppress life-threatening arrhythmias and cause them," he wrote. "The uncontrolled nature of these studies (probably unavoidable, and in any event standard practice) leaves uncertainty about the 'net benefit.'" In other words, Temple had no assurances from controlled studies that Tambocor did more good than harm.

To be unable to determine whether a drug does more good than harm ought to be grounds to reject it altogether. Temple, however, decided on a compromise. He believed the drug was of value in suppressing serious, life-threatening rhythm disturbances provided that it was started in the hospital with equipment to resuscitate the patient immediately at hand. He concluded that Tambocor might work in some patients when other drugs had failed. On the other hand, he wanted clear language on the label "to discourage the use" in patients for the unproven hope of preventing sudden death.

Temple also intended to extend the restrictions to other drugs in the same family. He wrote to Lipicky, "The suggested labeling is a major potential step towards revising labeling for this entire class of drugs. I need your candid comments on the entire analysis and labeling scheme." Temple was almost sure what he wanted to do. Before acting, he wanted the advice of his colleague and friend, Raymond Lipicky.

Lipicky was in Washington for only a week between research sessions at Woods Hole. He sent Temple a four-page, handwritten essay. It began with an apology.

"I am embarrassed by your having had to pull all of that death information and proarrhythmia information together into some digestible form," he wrote.

Lipicky could not decide whether he was in favor of Temple's restrictions or not. He said, "I am comfortable with the labeling indication as written. I am not sure any idea I have is any better than the one you have composed." Next he launched into a litany of reservations. "I am not sure it is not an overreaction to an uncontrolled set of observations." He proposed returning to the advisory committee's earlier recommendation. "One could say 'for symptomatic ventricular arrhythmias that deserve therapy,' " he wrote. Finally, he summed up his position in ambiguous language. "I guess, all in all, I view the labeling as constructed as alarmist. However, I must agree I am confused and alarmed. I have no reasonable alternative to suggest."

Now the moment of decision had arrived, Lipicky's concluding paragraph dramatized the monumental uncertainty of the director of the Cardio-Renal Drug Division.

"I probably have not helped much," he wrote to Temple. "I do believe Tambocor is approvable. You, I and the entire medical community are struggling with unknowns. No one knows why to use an antiarrhythmic, how to use them, or exactly how to develop them. However, no one (especially me) thinks they should not be available. 'Alarmist' labeling is an appropriate middle road given the circumstances. I am not convinced that it is correct."

Lipicky's memorandum had no effect on Temple's plans to restrict severely the medical use of Tambocor. He signed the letter to 3M without further changes. It was not an approval, but an "approvable" letter.

"Before the application can be approved," Temple wrote, "it will be necessary to revise labeling substantially in accord with the enclosed revised draft." He added, "The drug may not be legally marketed until you have been notified in writing that the application is approved."

The labeling changes Temple proposed were far-reaching. "We believe Tambocor should be indicated only for patients with life-threatening arrhythmias. Because of its proarrhythmic and other adverse potential it should not be recommended for use in less severe arrhythmias." Also the drugs would have to be started during hospitalization—vastly increasing the cost to each new patient.

Before 3M could pursue the large and lucrative market for suppressing PVCs, it would have to conduct studies to prove actual benefits to patients. "Additional study of Tambocor in patients with these arrhythmias, including further and longer-term comparison with alternative agents, will be needed before use in such patients can be recommended."

Temple signed the letter on August 29, 1985. The 3M team was soon flashing word throughout the company. They had a decision on Tambocor at last.

Chapter 14

PANIC AT 3M

BEFORE ROBERT TEMPLE's letter arrived at 3M, the company was already poised to begin the Tambocor product launch. A new drug does not leap by magic into the medical marketplace. It is a major project, involving manufacturing, packaging, distribution, advertising, sales and marketing. With more than 60,000 different products being sold in 50 countries, this was a job at which 3M managers believed they excelled. In these complex but concrete tasks, modern industrial corporations are enormously skillful. During the weeks while Temple pondered the safety of Tambocor, the product team was making elaborate preparations. At the Northridge, California, plant, the Kilian high-speed press was making trial runs with Tambocor. In test runs, the press could punch out 400,000 tablets an hour. One morning's run of a single Kilian press could supply 20,000 people with Tambocor for a month. Some batches of off-white Tambocor tablets had mysterious black specks. The sales and marketing people thought consumers wouldn't worry about it, but the safety office said it would require several months to figure out what the specks might be. The pills appeared to meet FDA specifications. Meanwhile layouts of the advertisements introducing Tambocor to doctors across the country and plans for symposiums were drawn up. The marketing people also wanted a smooth flow of "scientific" studies about Tambocor going into the medical journals.

Robert Temple's letter came as a devastating blow to this well-oiled industrial organization. Despite Florence Wong's intensive efforts to monitor the fortunes of Tambocor at the FDA, the 3M team had misjudged Robert Temple. They thought his concerns over sudden death would not jeopardize the drug. As the product team members absorbed the restrictions Temple had proposed for Tambocor, they were shocked and dismayed.

Roland Catherall, the director of regulatory affairs, was noncommittal in what he told others at 3M. "This event is a major milestone in the development of Tambocor and the organization should be congratulated on this accomplishment." He was guarded about the contents. "For business reasons a decision was made not to circulate copies of the letter to a broad audience. Presently, management is assessing the significance of the letter."

The key question management then addressed was how Temple's restrictions would affect the drug's profit potential. 3M ran the numbers to find the impact on the expected sales of Tambocor. The results were disastrous. "This labeling is most detrimental to the drug's marketing success and is indeed the worst case scenario," said a memorandum for 3M management. In fact, Temple's restrictions, or even a slight modification, produced a scenario with "little or no economic merit to 3M." The 3M team knew—as did many cardiologists—that the main market was patients with minimal symptoms or none at all. A scenario in which Tambocor could be sold for use in this larger market "could prove somewhat beneficial," according to the memo. Projected sales in the first year would be six times higher than in the "approvable" scenario. As the 3M team considered the impact on expected profits, their conclusion was simple. "In order to meet financial projections for the drug, it is imperative to have our original labeling approved," the memo said.

An elementary but central issue now surrounded Tambocor and the other drugs poised to enter the market. More than a decade earlier, cardiologists had developed the theory that treating minor indications of electrical instability might prevent the total electrical breakdown that resulted in sudden death. Troubling questions had emerged in the infancy of this theory. When Leonard Cobb's pioneering ambulance program in Seattle began to rescue the first victims of cardiac arrest, he found most were already taking antiarrhythmic drugs. Since then, medical researchers had mounted at least 28 recorded attempts to prove a measurable benefit to the patient taking these drugs. Every single attempt had failed. The published record of 28 failures did not even count attempts so unsuccessful they were halted prematurely without ever being reported. This was the fate of Joel Morganroth's trial with Enkaid and two other drugs. 3M also canceled its own Tambocor trial in heart attack survivors after enrolling just 10 patients. Rather than evidence of benefits, the growing body of clinical research produced increasingly troubling signs that these drugs were harmful, not beneficial. The first warnings had come from a handful of doubters, such as Roger Winkle at Stanford. Now concerns about safety dominated the meetings of the FDA advisory committee and Joel Morganroth's symposiums. In response to continuing failure to demonstrate benefit, and amidst increasing doubts about safety, Temple had proposed new restrictions, limiting these drugs to patients who already had life-threatening rhythm disorders.

Temple's proposed restrictions would eliminate the market where more than 80 percent of future sales were anticipated. If the company shared the safety concerns being increasingly voiced elsewhere in the medical community, now was the time to quit. Some companies, in fact, did. Eli Lilly dumped aprindine. If the company believed these concerns were unfounded, it could make the additional investment in placebo-controlled trials to satisfy the doubters. That was the moral if not the literal obligation of the drug approval law—to use all scientific means applicable to prove the safety of a drug. With a drug implicated in causing cardiac arrest, this was an important social responsibility. If the problem behind the failure of 28 previous attempts was a bad study design, the company could now conduct the proper controlled trial. This would be expensive, of course. But to abandon the project meant writing off the millions of dollars already invested. A major new clinical study meant spending several million dollars more, and might take years to complete. The only low-cost solution was to persuade the FDA to relax the restrictions on Tambocor. As the 3M team pondered its options during the first week of September, it already had indications such a strategy might work. It was probably 3M's only route to its profit target.

One day after receiving Temple's approvable letter, Florence Wong got a telephone call from Denver Presley, the consumer safety officer for Tambocor in Cardio-Renal Drugs at the FDA. "Denver called to tell me that the doors are open for meetings to discuss the approvable letter," Wong reported. "He suggested that I contact Lipicky at Woods Hole first, and gave me his phone number there."

Wong also wanted to know what their chances of success were. "I asked historically how often firms succeeded in convincing Temple in making major modifications in such an indication. He said it is always a give and take situation. Come prepared with your arguments and Temple will listen."

In Denver Presley 3M now had a friend inside the FDA, and that friend apparently did not want anyone else to know. Wong reported to her 3M colleagues, "Denver said he's willing to help as much as possible. However, I should not divulge the fact that he called and suggested negotiation." She had confided in Presley, "The letter was quite devastating."

With the entire fate of Tambocor at stake, Presley's suggestion was enough to trigger a systematic 3M assault on the FDA. The first stop was a telephone conference with the medical officer, Sughok Chun. Wong called along with the 3M doctor who usually dealt with Chun, David P. Ward. As usual, Wong circulated a report on the conversation:

"Dr. Chun said the approvable letter was as shocking to her as it is to us. She and Lipicky objected to the 'indication' and other wording. Temple insisted."

Chun, however, provided another piece of critical intelligence, suggesting it might be hard to change Temple's mind. "Temple said rewrite the labeling later."

This possibility worried David Ward. As Wong reported the conversation: "Dave pointed out that if we market with the current PI [package insert] we'll have a whole different population from other drugs and a lot of deaths probably."

Ward also asked whether Temple thought Tambocor was more dangerous than other marketed antiarrhythmic drugs. Chun thought that indeed was Temple's belief. Nevertheless, Chun encouraged them to press their case. "Temple was expecting to meet with us at least once or twice," Wong reported.

The next stop was Raymond Lipicky, division director. As they moved up the ladder, more senior 3M officials joined the campaign. For the conference call to Lipicky, Florence Wong's boss, Roland Catherall, joined in; and Ward's boss, Gary Gentzkow, took his place. They reached Lipicky in Woods Hole. Wong reported on the conversation:

"We told Dr. Lipicky we were surprised and disappointed by the approvable letter," her account began, "and would like some insight on the thinking behind it.

"Dr. Lipicky responded that, 'This drug kills people.' Don't quite know why, how ... therefore only people at risk are worth it. This is a reflection of general trepidation with respect to any antiarrhythmic therapy.

"When asked if similar labeling will be applied to quinidine etc., he said they'd like to, but the chance probably is 2 in 10 that it will happen. It certainly reflects the labeling of any antiarrhythmic in the future."

Lipicky seemed to take a firm position that the whole class of drugs was dangerous and should be restricted. But by the end of the conversation with 3M, he was backing off. While wanting Tambocor limited to life-threatening arrhythmias, he conceded, "We don't know how to define life-threatening, and Temple said we've got to put something there."

As the conversation drew to a close, Lipicky appeared to wash his hands of the whole matter. "I can be candid," he said. "When Temple first proposed this wording, I said he's an alarmist." Lipicky gave 3M his blessing to pursue the issue with Temple. "I think Tambocor should be approved. Any wording to get it approved is fine with me."

Gary Gentzkow, meanwhile, was also talking to Joel Morganroth, to see if he would help turn around the situation at the FDA. He began by asking, "How do you feel about the safety of Tambocor?" Morganroth told him what he said at the advisory committee meeting. He thought Tambocor was difficult to use in the most seriously ill patients, but very safe in the patients with premature beats. In his view, this was the logical patient population to take the drug. Since this group was also more than 80 percent of the potential market, this view must have been welcome news to 3M. Morganroth agreed to help Gentzkow persuade Temple that Tambocor was a safe and effective drug in this patient population.

After a week of frenzied effort by the 3M team, surprise and dismay had given way to cautious, if not outright, optimism. Roland Catherall sent forward a report with a revised outlook: "Based on discussions during the past week with the FDA and leading cardiologists, we are now convinced that differences in the letter between our expectations and the FDA's labeling recommendations are not as 'major and significant' as originally anticipated." Catherall told 3M management that the final labeling might be more restrictive but would prove "satisfactory."

A "satisfactory" outcome for 3M was one that would allow it to reach the larger market. Temple's proposed labeling, or package insert, constituted a kind of one-two punch. It not only limited Tambocor to "life-threatening arrhythmia" but also explicitly discouraged use in less severe cases. The most telling restriction was the requirement to hospitalize patients while starting the drug. To establish the correct minimum dose to suppress PVCs meant a week-long hospitalization for patients otherwise healthy enough to play tennis, attend a picnic or go dancing.

Medical opinion varied widely about the importance of these lengthy and technical disclosure statements on the package insert. One of Bernard Lown's proteges, Thomas Graboys of Harvard, would say later, "The bottom line is, who reads the package insert? I mean, only the most compulsive physician is reading the package insert." At the other extreme was Temple, who labored late into the night crafting each phrase, measuring the nuance of each word. In most cases, the truth fell somewhere in between. The label influenced how a drug was advertised and marketed, although it was in no way binding on physician practice. However, as then written, the Tambocor labeling restrictions were so severe they put a stranglehold on the drug's future. 3M could not succeed with a drug so implicitly dangerous that treatment could not be initiated without first hospitalizing the patient.

Temple had one more reason to lavish so much care on the wording of drug labels. If something did go wrong later, he was also writing his own defense. If physicians chose to disregard the warnings he wrote on the label, it would be hard to blame Temple.

In a conference call with Temple, the 3M team got more tantalizing hints it might prevail. Temple was starting to sound uncertain. "It's hard to know where to come down in a changing field," Temple told 3M. "I'm not arrogant enough to tell physicians how to practice." On the other hand, Temple was still plainly worried about Tambocor's safety. "Compared to other drugs I have seen," he told 3M, "the capacity for Tambocor to worsen arrhythmia—to be toxic—is more impressive." Temple closed out the conversation on a note of optimism. "It's worth looking at additional data," he said. "I think it will be a very productive meeting."

Unknown to 3M, though, Temple did not intend to open the larger market for Tambocor. He laid out his thinking in a memo to his own file. "I indicated that there seemed *some* room for modification in the labeling" (emphasis in original). But Temple still wanted Tambocor out of the very market that was essential to meeting 3M's profit target. "We all appeared to agree this was not a drug for people with frequent [PVCs] alone; that it is not a drug to 'treat the Holter.'"

What Temple meant about treating the Holter highlighted an ironic feature of antiarrhythmic drugs. The rhythm disturbance was usually detected by monitoring the heartbeat for 24 hours with a Holter monitor. The main effect of the drug—suppressing PVCs—was measured on the same equipment. The patient was typically unaware of the PVCs and could not detect the change. Critics said these drugs made the doctor feel better, not the patient. For 3M to make a profit on Tambocor would require "treating a lot of Holter monitors," with undetermined effects on the patient's health and lifespan.

The company had less than three weeks to prepare for the scheduled meeting with Temple, now set for October 8. To change Temple's mind, 3M medical director Gary Gentzkow would have to work with materials immediately at hand. It was not long before Gentzkow found something. 3M had hired two of Tambocor's most enthusiastic proponents—Joel Morganroth and University of Utah professor Jeffrey Anderson—to analyze the entire Tambocor patient data base for a medical journal article about safety. A draft manuscript was on Gentzkow's desk. Overall, it was similar to the material already forwarded to the FDA in the New Drug Application. However, 3M now had data on 550 additional patients treated since the Tambocor application was submitted three years earlier. The 3M team took Morganroth and Anderson's manuscript and adapted it to their now urgent needs. Just a week after talking to Temple, 3M sent forward a 55-page analysis and an 85-page appendix. Tambocor's commercial future now depended on this document, and Temple's reaction.

According to the new submission, the safety record of Tambocor had improved dramatically since the investigators met in St. Paul back in December 1982. Among the 1,330 patients who had taken Tambocor in 3M studies, "thirteen patients died of proarrhythmic events. All had structural heart disease. No patient treated for PVCs died of a proarrhythmic event."

According to this new analysis, Tambocor was implicated in the death of a single patient without a severe preexisting rhythm disturbance. The report pointedly described this patient in detail. "This 80-year-old man had severe coronary artery disease, a previous [heart attack] and severe congestive heart failure. . . . The patient had been admitted to the Hennepin County Medical Center 22 times." Nine days after taking Tambocor the man was admitted to the emergency room complaining of shortness of breath and fatigue. His electrocardiogram showed an irregular and rapid beat. Repeated shocks had no effect. He soon died. Although the man had had a previous heart attack, unsatisfactory cardiac output and severe heart disease, he had never had an irregular, sustained rapid heartbeat prior to the episode that resulted in his death. The number of drug-related deaths in this population had become a question of who was doing the counting. By the standard that Ronald Campbell had proposed at the last Philadelphia symposium, Tambocor should be blamed for all 41 cardiac arrests that had occurred in patients with mild rhythm disturbances. By Morganroth's count, the drug was absolved in all except the 80-year-old man, and the graphic presentation of his other ailments implied even this case was questionable.

3M also claimed impressive results in its study among patients who already had serious rhythm problems. This was the new protocol in which lower starting doses were tested to see if this reduced drug-related deaths. The study—which had had only 96 patients when 3M went before the advisory committee—was now four times larger. Out of 429 patients, just one patient death was blamed on Tambocor. Before starting doses were reduced, the submission said, drug-related deaths were "20 fold greater." Once again the results depended on who did the counting of drug-related deaths. While the drug was no longer being blamed in the new protocol, the overall death rate was similar to the original study. In the three years since the 1982 St. Paul investigators' meeting, only one additional sudden death had been attributed to Tambocor despite its being given to thousands of patients in the United States, England, Norway, Germany and Argentina.

This new analysis also spawned a medical truism that later played an important role in assessing the dangers of antiarrhythmic drugs. In trying to identify drug-related deaths, different investigators selected different, but equally arbitrary breakpoints. When Donald Harrison of Stanford first reviewed the Enkaid deaths, he thought a death within two days of starting the drug might count against it. At the Philadelphia symposium, Joel Morganroth was willing to implicate the drug for up to seven days. In this analysis, a new breakpoint of fourteen days emerged. It was equally arbitrary, since drug-related deaths could not be identified without an untreated control group for comparison. The fourteen-day standard became widely accepted in cardiology, but it would become a false source of assurance. Any drug-related problems, doctors would be told, would occur during the first fourteen days. After monitoring a patient carefully for two weeks, presumably they didn't have to worry.

Overall, the new safety analysis was a ringing endorsement of the safety of Tambocor, based on the work of Joel Morganroth and Jeffrey Anderson. The question now was whether it would persuade Robert Temple to relax the restrictions on Tambocor.

Chapter 15

PERSUASION

ROBERT TEMPLE DIDN'T think he was an easy mark in the influence game. "They have no way of influencing me," he said later. "Our sole job is to try to get it right. Lobbying doesn't work. They'll bring in the heaviest hitter they can find. They'll bring in the arrhythmia people. They'll bring in Joel [Morganroth] because they probably think we like Joel and trust him." On October 8, 1985, 3M intended to try its best to influence Temple. The company would also have to make its case to Lipicky and Chun.

On this day in October, Florence Wong might reap the benefits of the years she had spent building relationships with everyone from the lowliest FDA secretary to the director of drug evaluation. For this crucial meeting Wong would accompany her boss, Roland Catherall, and two senior 3M doctors, Gary Gentzkow and David Ward.

For Joel Morganroth this was also a pivotal occasion. His judgment had become so respected at the FDA that Lipicky had recently asked him to draft new guidelines for approving antiarrhythmic drugs. However, he had developed, promoted and tested antiarrhythmic drugs for seven years without seeing one approved. This meeting could change that situation at last.

Consumer safety officer Denver Presley had quietly suggested the strategy of negotiation to 3M. Now he had a seat at the table where the outcome of his behind-the-scenes assistance was going to be decided.

For two solid hours they all crowded around the conference table at FDA headquarters and argued about the data. The only record of the meeting is the minutes taken by Florence Wong of 3M.

Temple had not dropped his concerns about the safety of Tambocor. "Temple kept focusing on the proarrhythmic effects that trouble him," Wong reported. Safety was Joel Morganroth's department, and

he sought to reassure Temple. "Joel believes the potential for Tambocor causing trouble in very sick patients is greater; conversely,
Tambocor is safer than other agents in arrhythmia of lesser severity."
The medical director, Gary Gentzkow, also "kept emphasizing the
minimal risk."

Temple was not convinced. "He would not acknowledge the zero
or minimal risk we showed in PVC and nonsustained VT [three premature beats in a row] patients as acceptable," Wong reported. "He
commented that we saw what the data showed, and he saw what the
data failed to exclude." What the data showed was that by Morganroth
and Anderson's count, Tambocor caused only one death in nearly
1,000 patients with PVCs and other mild disorders. What the data
"failed to exclude" was the possibility that many more cardiac arrests
among Tambocor patients might have been caused by the drug.

At one point in the meeting, Lipicky and Temple began to argue
with each other over a critical finding about the most seriously ill
patients. Temple was persuaded the new study proved that lower
starting doses solved the problem of the proarrhythmic deaths. Lipicky argued the average doses had hardly changed in the new study.
(In retrospect, Temple said, "He's right. It wasn't that much.")

There came a moment when it must have appeared that 3M had
lost its case. Temple kept hammering away at the absence of controlled studies to demonstrate any benefit of treating PVCs to prevent
sudden death and to exclude the possibility the drug caused them.
To solve this problem, Temple proposed 3M launch a major post-
marketing clinical trial to find out whether Tambocor prevented
sudden death. "Don't tell me NIH can do it. I know you can do it
much cheaper and faster." If Temple insisted on an expensive post-
approval trial before opening the door to a larger market, Tambocor
might be effectively dead.

Unexpectedly, Temple dropped the subject. "He wanted to discuss
this later but the subject did not come up again that afternoon,"
Wong reported.

As the meeting rolled toward a close, the group began to focus
on the labeling. "Dr. Temple was somewhat sensitive to the commercial aspects of labeling," Wong reported. He did not write into
the label his concern Tambocor might be more toxic than other
antiarrhythmic drugs, persuaded apparently that there were no studies to support making such a distinction. The 3M team raised its
major concern, the restriction to life-threatening arrhythmias. At first
Temple seemed inflexible. "Dr. Temple said he would like to scare

them [physicians] a fair amount, and is perfectly ready to revise labeling likewise for marketed antiarrhythmics," Wong reported.

3M medical director Gary Gentzkow argued that trying to scare physicians might backfire. Physicians were already using antiarrhythmic drugs on a large scale, according to their own medical judgment. "We as a company cannot educate physicians on the proper use in arrhythmias not indicated for." Gentzkow noted, "They would use it anyway," he said. Rather bluntly, Gentzkow pointed out that experts like Morganroth and Anderson were going to be telling physicians something quite different from what Temple proposed on the label. "The credibility of labeling is reduced," Gentzkow said, "when physicians learn otherwise either through experience or through hearing from such people as Morganroth and Anderson."

In the end, Temple gave in. He agreed to new language that was very close to what 3M had sought. Tambocor was approved for "symptomatic" patients with PVCs. Temple's concerns were compressed into this additional sentence:

"Because of the proarrhythmic effects of Tambocor, its use in these less severe arrhythmias should be reserved for patients in whom, in the opinion of the physician, the benefits of treatment outweigh the risks." Temple also dropped the requirement to hospitalize patients with PVCs and other mild rhythm disturbances before starting Tambocor.

3M had won the day entirely. The door was open to the large market of patients with PVCs. The only limitation was encompassed in the single word "symptomatic." As Catherall reported back to 3M's management, "Despite a lengthy and arduous meeting, we successfully negotiated a mutually acceptable position. Needless to say, we are very happy to inform you about this achievement."

Since at the meeting only Temple pressed for the restrictions, it is worth examining a third possibility not considered. Should the Tambocor New Drug Application have been rejected altogether? The law, as noted earlier, requires that the safety of a drug be established by all applicable scientific means, and that it be shown to be effective in well-controlled clinical trials. This is often interpreted as requiring evidence that the benefits of a drug outweigh its risks. Practical good sense says the margin between benefits and risks ought to be large.

Tambocor was, first of all, approved for life-threatening arrhythmias, without the evidence of efficacy from well-controlled trials that the law seems to so clearly require. Lipicky later said that the case for this indication was self-evident. "You have someone lying in bed with sustained ventricular tachycardia," he said, "unable to maintain their blood pressure and certainly not able to get out of bed. You make that sustained VT go away. They can now get up out of bed and leave the hospital most of the time." However true, that is precisely the kind of anecdotal evidence that the law disallows, and for good reason. Convincing evidence also showed Tambocor could cause cardiac arrests, although opinions differed about the extent of the hazard. As Temple said in his own evaluation, Tambocor "can both suppress life-threatening arrhythmias and cause them." Or as Raymond Woosley said at the advisory committee meeting, "We know that they will kill some people. We only hope they are going to be used in a situation where they would save more than they kill." After trying to identify the cases where the drug might have been responsible for death, Sughok Chun said, "You just don't know." Three authorities publicly acknowledged they did not know whether the risks outweighed the benefits, nor could they define a patient population where Tambocor was manifestly beneficial. That should be the definition of an unapprovable drug.

Tambocor was also approved for less severe arrhythmias that were symptomatic. The advisory committee retreated to this concept amidst rising doubts whether Tambocor prolonged life, and Temple reluctantly embraced it. It was an effort to anchor approval on one of the three bedrock fundamentals of drug benefit: to prolong life, to relieve symptoms, or to reduce pain. This was the only potential claim that the Tambocor data might support. However, as Lipicky pointed out at the time, the Tambocor investigators had never collected any data on symptoms. As Temple acknowledged later, "We sort of assumed if the symptoms did go away, that would be of value." It is hard to believe such an assumption would meet the legal requirement to demonstrate effectiveness in well-controlled trials.

Finally, doctors were warned to limit the use of Tambocor in less severe arrhythmias to "patients in whom, in the opinion of the physician, the benefits of treatment outweigh the risks." To place such a warning in the Tambocor label was medically meaningless since neither the risks nor the benefits had yet been established. The accurate measurement of risks and benefit is the central function of the drug testing and approval process, and as Tambocor entered the marketplace it was already clear that process had failed.

As the future of antiarrhythmic drugs unfolded, Robert Temple would later regret his decision. "I guess I shouldn't have got talked out of my initial thought," he later said.

The approval of Tambocor was only one of a series of compromises that Robert Temple made in approving antiarrhythmic drugs. He also approved a drug called Cordarone without any of the normal clinical testing that the law seems to so explicitly require. Cordarone was an unusual drug with an unusual history. It was discovered in Belgium in the 1950s and was first tested by medical investigators who misunderstood its function and thought it might prevent constriction of blood vessels. Its antiarrhythmic properties were explored by the Indian-born American cardiologist Bramah Singh during his graduate work at Oxford. Cordarone proved unusually potent, and worked by an entirely different mechanism than Tambocor, Enkaid and other similar drugs, which slow conduction of electrical pulses. Cordarone lengthened the refractory period when a heart muscle cell cannot accept another signal to contract. It seemed to work in patients with a sustained, rapid heartbeat when all other agents had failed.

Cordarone, however, had no well-funded corporate sponsor willing to spend the millions of dollars required to complete the FDA-required clinical testing regimen. It was owned by the Paris-based Sanofi Research, which had no interest in marketing the drug in the United States. However, Sanofi gave the drug free of charge to American cardiologists, who used it extensively under investigational exemptions granted by the FDA. By the time Tambocor was approved, nearly 700 American physicians were prescribing the unapproved and untested Cordarone. Singh estimated that 10,000 to 20,000 patients were taking the drug. Almost all had severe, life-threatening heart rhythm disorders.

The FDA was unhappy about the widespread use of an unapproved drug; Sanofi was growing reluctant to give away such an enormous quantity of its drug and threatened to cut off the supply. Singh joined a delegation of cardiologists who went to Lipicky and negotiated a deal. American Home Products' major drug subsidiary, Wyeth-Ayerst, agreed to adopt Cordarone and submit a New Drug Application. In return, the FDA did not require the well-controlled trials outlined in the statute. Instead it accepted a review of the published medical literature, and the case records from 50 consecutive patients drawn from the files of five United States cardiologists. This is only a slight improvement over pure anecdotal evidence.

Cordarone was a poor choice for a gamble on safety. It was unusually toxic, even for an antiarrhythmic drug, and a pharmacologist's nightmare. Whatever its dangers, Tambocor had a clean, well-documented pharmacological profile. It was absorbed into the blood circulation in hours. The body eliminated half the dose in about 12 hours, excreting the drug in urine. Except for transient effects on the central nervous system, it seemed to have few effects on other organs of the body.

Cordarone, on the other hand, was different from Tambocor in almost every respect. The human body had such a difficult time breaking down the drug that in some patients, half the dose was still circulating 107 days later. The drug was eliminated in feces, but part of it appeared to accumulate in body fat and in the corneas of the eyes. Responses of individual patients varied widely, making it extremely difficult to establish a therapeutic dose. Some patients could eliminate half the drug in as little as 13 days. It could take anywhere from 4 to 10 days before any positive effects were observed.

A drug so persistent was especially dangerous when the drug had toxic side effects. Cordarone had plenty. It caused nausea and vomiting, malaise and fatigue, deposits on the cornea, tremors and other movement disorders, and damaged the thyroid, skin, liver and lungs. The greatest concern was its destructive effect on delicate lung tissue, where it caused fibrosis. At least 16 patients who took Cordarone had died and more than 100 showed evidence of lung damage.

Why would physicians even consider using—or the FDA contemplate approving—a drug with this safety profile? Cardiologists believed that Cordarone was effective in patients whose rhythm disorders might soon claim their lives. Cardiologists wanted Cordarone for a last ditch defense when other remedies had failed.

These many adverse effects hardly supported a claim that Cordarone was safe, and no well-controlled trials had been conducted to demonstrate that it was effective or to measure whether its benefits were greater than its risks. The FDA medical review said, "No prospective clinical trials were performed or data from such trials included in the NDA submission." Although it had a difficult pharmacological profile, the FDA medical review of this topic consisted of one sentence: "Prospective clinical pharmacology trials have not been performed by the sponsor."

With this background, it is instructive to observe how the FDA advisory committee for cardio-renal drugs handled this drug. Bertram Pitt of the University of Michigan, who had worried about Tambocor and Enkaid, was once again concerned.

"I just do not know whether the development of this drug has proceeded in the most responsible manner," Pitt said.

"It has not proceeded at all," Lipicky said.

Pitt said, "Here is a glaring example of where I think things have failed, and there is no reason for it."

Raymond Woosley, the enthusiastic supporter of Tambocor and Enkaid, entered the discussion.

"The health-care system of this country should have some mechanism to do studies that are needed."

Lipicky interrupted. "As I see it, the academic community here had an opportunity. It failed. Investigators who are leaders in the scientific area and in cardiology failed flat, and did not work this thing up worth a damn.

"Industry failed flat. Why did they fail? Because there was a profit motive and they did not see that there was any money at the end of the tube. So industry failed and academia failed."

Woosley had a partial defense of the experts. "We tried to do controlled trials with this drug, but it is a very difficult drug to study, and without funding it is almost impossible. . . . It is damned near impossible to do anything well with this drug."

Except perhaps for Morganroth, it would be hard to identify an expert from the medical schools who had done more for the new generation of antiarrhythmic drugs than Woosley. Yet oddly, it fell to Raymond Leon Woosley, Jr., M.D., Ph.D, to make a statement that distilled to its purest essence the entire story. His comments applied not only to Cordarone but to all the new antiarrhythmic drugs.

"There is a big compassionate plea that there are people out in this country that are going to die if this drug is not on the market, and, therefore, every one of us is about to vote for approval. I have a real concern that those same people are going to be told that here is a drug that will save your life. They will be put on the drug and it will work. But because we do not know how to dose it a lot of those people are going to die. Marketing this drug could cause more deaths than it saves. I am one of those people in academia who has not done my job. We have not done controlled trials. We can throw blame around for a long time, but the bottom line is we do not have the data."

As Raymond Woosley had foreseen, the committee voted unanimously in favor of Cordarone. Robert Temple approved it. The committee voted unanimously in favor of Enkaid, and Robert Temple approved it. And it backed Tambocor, Mexitil and two other similar drugs, Rythmol and Tonocard. Robert Temple approved them, every one. The new generation of antiarrhythmic drugs was now going to flood into the medical marketplace.

But because no one had done the proper controlled trials, people were going to die.

Part Three

MEDICAL USE

Chapter 16

SELLING TO DOCTORS

BY THE SPRING of 1988, the product managers for Tambocor had every reason to be satisfied with their sales and marketing performance. Two years after launch, pharmacists were filling 57,000 prescriptions for Tambocor every month. That was almost a 50 percent increase over the preceding year. 3M easily outdistanced its European rival, Boehringer Ingelheim; Tambocor's sales were nearly double Mexitil's. Even though Tambocor was 3M's first introduction of a major drug, the company remained comfortably ahead of the established pharmaceutical giant, Bristol-Myers, which had experienced delays getting to the market. However, with Bristol-Myers' huge presence and vast experience in the pharmaceutical marketplace, the Tambocor product team members should have been looking back nervously at the lumbering giant behind. The overall United States market for antiarrhythmic drugs had leveled off at roughly one million patients, but plenty of room for growth remained for the companies marketing the new generation of antiarrhythmic drugs. The older and more difficult-to-use generic drugs, quinidine and procainamide, still had 75 percent of the market. It was going to be a fight for market share, a commercial battle for the hearts and minds of doctors.

"Every time I take my heart medication I ask myself . . . how can something so small cost so much?"

Thus began an advertisement from the Pharmaceutical Manufacturers Association. It provided the expected answer—high prices result from the industry's heavy spending on research, about $6 billion in 1988. The advertisement failed to mention that industry spending on medical marketing and promotion easily outstripped research, totaling approximately $8 billion. The nature and intensity of the hard sell to doctors is as much a hallmark of the drug industry as its research might.

Pharmaceutical marketing is unique because the process is seldom visible to the ultimate consumer—the patients who take medicine. In a modern democracy most personal rights are retained by the individual, a notable exception being the right to choose a prescription drug. Only licensed medical doctors can decide whether a drug is appropriate and select among dozens of similar products with widely varying costs. Patients must depend on the doctor to make a wise choice on their behalf. This imposes a moral obligation upon doctors to consider only a patient's best interest while making a decision to prescribe a drug. But in 1988, drug companies spent nearly $14,000 for each active M.D. to influence and alter those decisions. The sternest critics of pharmaceutical marketing maintain that these efforts are, by definition, corrupt. They are intended to influence a decision in which each physician bears an undivided obligation to the patient. Defenders of pharmaceutical marketing argue that companies are merely providing information about their products, and say doctors are too honest to be influenced in this manner. The willingness of giant companies to expend one quarter of their total drug revenues on marketing demonstrates that the industry must believe that marketing works. A closer look at just how pharmaceutical marketing operates sheds light on the question of whether it is, by definition, corrupt.

The typical American visits the doctor several times each year. Three out of five doctors' office visits result in a prescription. On this most lucrative target, the pharmaceutical industry focuses its heaviest fire. An army of 20,000 sales representatives, or drug detailers, assaults the 395,000 doctors in office practice literally on a daily basis. A hard-working drug detailer hopes to see seven doctors each working day. Edward Roseman, who chronicles marketing strategy for *Medical Marketing & Media* estimated that detailers make 125,000 calls every day. This means doctors in office practice see several sales representatives a week, often one every day. (These are averages; some doctors refuse to see any detailers.) When drug detailers get those precious few minutes of a doctor's time, they do not simply pass the time away.

Almost every patient has seen the drug detailer's first-line sales tool—free drug samples. Few realize the scale on which samples are provided. In 1988, eighteen large drug companies gave away 2.4

billion samples: almost 10 free drug samples for every man, woman, and child in the United States. Just one company, Syntex, gave away enough samples to provide one to the entire United States population. Recent legislation that required doctors to sign personally for the samples may have reduced the volume. But it also likely increased the number of face-to-face contacts between detailer and physician.

The second tool is more insidious. Typically called a "reminder item," more plainly it is a gift. It includes almost any conceivable object that might influence a physician. For example, an informal survey turned up these gifts:

Hundred-dollar bills, lip gloss, beach bags, coffee mugs, stethoscopes, medical bags, notepads, clipboards, patient record forms, drug dose calculators, baseball caps, ballpoint pens, fruit baskets, pizza, audio cassettes, soap, Superbowl tickets, paperweights, personal computers, video cassette recorders, frequent-flyer miles, television sets, tennis match tickets, ice cream from baby formula, coasters, golf towels, cholesterol tests, tote bags, patient sign-in forms, murder mystery cruises, satellite dishes, skin cream, medical textbooks, gourmet dinners, magnifying glasses, Caribbean weekends, ski caps, ocean cruises, anatomical models, padlocks, custom videos, Mississippi riverboat trips, T-shirts, stuffed animal toys, umbrellas, gym bags, baseball game tickets, eyeglass holders, sunscreen, airline tickets, luggage tags, rulers, chocolates, wall posters, refrigerator magnets, medical journal subscriptions, prescription pads, calculators, videodisc players, wall calendars, diagnostic equipment, Post-its, coffee-makers, golf outings, monogrammed luggage, theater tickets, ski scarves, cameras, boxing tickets, golf balls, document cases, file cards, doorknob signs, shopping bags, leather attache cases, stickpins, symphony tickets, tennis balls, ski weekends, submarine sandwiches, infant formula, stuffed cats, magnetic paper clip holders, pencils, clocks, golf umbrellas, penlights, cellophane tape, laser light pointers, letter openers, three-ring binders, desk calendars, tickets for a reception with Dallas Cowboy cheerleaders, tennis towels, instructional slides, photo cubes, rock candy, free long-distance telephone calls, pocket pen holders, calipers, tape measures, basketball tickets, felt-tip pens, flowers, pillboxes, Swiss army pocket knives, and sweatshirts.

Many gifts are of modest value and go into office use. Several items—for example, frequent-flyer miles—triggered investigations about whether they constitute illegal kickbacks in cases where the government paid for the prescriptions. Some gifts were made at symposia, conferences and meetings.

The pharmaceutical industry will go to great expense to influence physician prescribing practices. For example, ten pharmaceutical companies launched an enterprise called the Physicians Computer Network. Participating doctors were given a $35,000 computer system to manage their office practices. In return, they agreed to watch thirty-two promotional messages per month on the computer, answering questions about what they saw. The network sponsors also expected to extract information from the doctors' computerized patient files for market research purposes. The patient record and physician response information provided the raw material for more effective efforts to sell drugs.

Another drug company consortium has bankrolled the Medical News Network, which puts a satellite ground station in doctors' offices free of charge. It feeds signals into an interactive television system in which doctors get customized news broadcasts about medical topics, interspersed with drug company advertising. Doctors can make program selections and enter requests for more information directly into the keyboard. A drug company sales representative will soon call for follow-up.

While some sales efforts proceed by sheer brute force, companies increasingly target specific doctors with data from elaborate, computerized national systems. When a patient fills a prescription, the pharmacist typically enters the information into a computer. Pharmacies, in turn, sell the computerized information to firms that tabulate and analyze the data. They calculate a company's sales and market share on a national, regional, and zip code basis. The most sophisticated systems provide data right down to the individual physician level. Thus, when a detailer sits down with a doctor, he might know how often that physician writes prescriptions for antiarrhythmic drugs, and which drugs he favors. The industry rule of thumb is that 25 percent of physicians write 75 percent of all prescriptions, and among detailers, a key part of the game is to hunt down the top prescription writers. (The biggest prescription writers see large numbers of patients who might need medication, and these doctors have a heavy hand with the prescription writing pen.)

Other schemes involve traditional sales gimmicks. For example, Wyeth Laboratories mailed knit ski caps to 19,000 general and family practice doctors, promising them a matching scarf if they saw the company drug detailer. According to *Medical Marketing & Media*, 44 percent of the doctors accepted the offer, and listened to a pitch for cough syrup.

Not only are the doctors' prescribing practices carefully monitored, the detailers' activities are also scrutinized. Some companies pay selected doctors (or their favorite charity) to secretly grade the sales presentations they listen to. Most companies closely monitor market share and total sales that each detailer achieves in a territory. Detailers also have to produce results to make bonuses, which in some companies account for a large share of total income. However, many in the industry believe that door-to-door drug detailing is in decline, along with the diminished importance of individual and group medical practices. Health Maintenance Organizations and other managed care systems often take over the selection of specific drugs within a class, and then negotiate discounts directly with the drug companies. While gift-giving practices have never been systematically surveyed, some industry observers believe that the size and value of gifts have been reduced, partly as a result of a 1990 voluntary code of conduct adopted by the American Medical Association and the Pharmaceutical Manufacturers Association. The other pressure to curb marketing excesses came from the public outcry generated after Sidney Wolfe of the Health Research Group disclosed a graphic series of what he called drug company "doctor bribery" programs at a 1990 Senate hearing. (The Physicians Computer Network was one of Wolfe's examples.)

The AMA code now declares "many gifts that are given to physicians by companies in the pharmaceutical, device and medical equipment industries serve an important, and socially beneficial function." It specifically authorizes physicians to accept meals, pens, notepads, and textbooks, but says they should be of "minimal value." (Medical texts, however, can cost several hundred dollars.) Doctors are not supposed to accept travel and lodging expenses for meetings (such as the Tambocor Bermuda symposium) or take honoraria unless they provide actual services. Pharmaceutical Manufacturers Association members also pledge to follow the AMA code.

The code is silent on another drug company marketing scheme— paying doctors to prescribe a drug as part of a pseudoscientific study. Wolfe uncovered an example where Roche Laboratories paid doctors $1,200 to prescribe a new and expensive antibiotic for 20 patients. One participating doctor estimated it took 4 minutes per patient to provide the company with a minimal description of the patient, diagnosis and outcome. Each doctor prescribing this new drug for 20 patients would bring an additional $11,400 in sales for the company. Wolfe denounced it as "bribing doctors to prescribe expensive antibiotics." The company said it is research that "helps demonstrate to physicians that the use of Rocephin is clinically effective and economical."

While 3M Pharmaceuticals fielded a smaller sales force than giants such as Merck and Bristol-Myers, the company proved skillful with another major marketing tool: the symposium. Drug detailers battle daily to snare just one or two minutes of a physician's time. The symposium offers the chance to influence doctors for an evening, a day, or longer. It is apparently so effective that, as noted in an earlier chapter, drug companies sponsor nearly 100 symposia every day.

A cute reminder gift and a glossy color brochure might capture the attention of a doctor for a minute or two, but for a lengthy symposium, heavier ammunition is required. No route of potential appeal is overlooked. One obvious inducement is to combine a presentation with golf, skiing or tennis or other recreation. A 1992 survey in *Medical Marketing & Media* ranked these as the top five symposia destinations during winter: Arizona, the Caribbean, Florida, Hawaii and various ski resorts. For the summer, European resorts, California and Canada are popular.

Although now frowned on by the AMA, some companies simply handed out $100 bills to symposium participants. Good food is essential. Despite the glitz and the crass appeals, the heart of a successful symposium is a subject of interest to doctors, presented effectively. For this crucial task, the drug companies turn to the superstars of drug promotion, the "marquee professors." These are the medical school doctors who are authorities in the field; their names are on journal articles and textbook chapters; they sit on important FDA or NIH committees. When 3M and Bristol-Myers needed marquee professors to promote their new antiarrhythmic drugs, they turned to doctors such as Morganroth, Woosley and Bigger.

Companies exercise little direct control over what these medical headliners choose to say at these occasions; marquee professors are free to express their medical judgment. However, the companies do recruit the audience, set the agenda, select the speakers, and often provide the illustrative color slides that are customary at such presentations.

Morganroth's activities during the three years that Tambocor and Enkaid were launched provide a vivid portrait of the life of a marquee professor. The doctor who had played such a major role to bring a new generation of antiarrhythmic drugs into the marketplace now found himself at the center of the medical stage. These activities made him rich, powerful and, in medical circles, famous. Morganroth's most prestigious job was professor of medicine and pharmacology at Hahnemann University. In addition, he received $150,000 salary from his medical practice centered at Graduate Hospital in Philadelphia, which is affiliated with the University of Pennsylvania. He received another $150,000 a year from the National Cardiovascular Research Center, an institution Morganroth founded to do drug testing for the industry. Because of a pivotal position in the field, the drug industry beat a path to his door. From 1986 to 1988 he did consulting work for Hoffman-LaRoche, Wyeth Laboratories, Merck, Burroughs Wellcome, Schering-Plough, Merrill-Dow, DuPont, Squibb, Upjohn, Sterling-Winthrop, ICI Pharmaceuticals, Bristol-Myers and 3M. Sometimes he was paid $1,500 for attending a single meeting. Other companies, such as Wyeth, guaranteed him $40,000 for a minimum of 20 days work.

Having developed such ties to so many drug companies also made Morganroth a potential dealmaker. A West German company, Cassella Pharmaceuticals, offered him $50,000 down, and $100,000 overall to find a United States licensee for one of its new drugs. Other deals were more honorary. 3M Pharmaceuticals paid him $5,000 a year to join a cardiac advisory board and Bristol-Myers $2,500 for a similar position.

This intensive work with the drug industry did little to curtail Morganroth's prodigious output of scientific publications. In the same three-year period he published 69 articles. Often he combined drug company and scientific work. In 1987 he published a comparison of Mexitil and quinidine in the *American Journal of Cardiology*. Boehringer Ingelheim paid him $4,000 to write the article. He published several comparisons of the new antiarrhythmic drugs that did not reveal his business relationships with the companies that marketed them. Even the medical journals that require authors to disclose their links to industry when the manuscript is submitted tell readers little or nothing about the authors' relationship in the published article.

At the same time all this activity was taking place, Morganroth went to work for the FDA as a part-time medical officer reviewing New Drug Applications. He was paid $32 an hour. The FDA work led to apparent conflicts of interests. For example, in 1987 Morganroth reviewed Merck's New Drug Application for a new indication for Prinivil, a drug used in high blood pressure and heart failure. In a 391-page report to the FDA, Morganroth recommended approval. From 1986 through 1988 Merck paid Morganroth $119,320 for drug studies and their expenses, for consulting, and to give a talk. The funds were received by Morganroth's professional corporation and the drug testing center he headed.

Morganroth, when asked about the conflicts, said, "The restriction that was placed on me by the FDA, which I bought, was that I could not review anything that I was working on as an investigator, or had a principal stake in." He said he "felt absolutely no bias" while reviewing the work of companies for which he also consulted. Asked if it was a good idea for an FDA medical officer to be consulting for the same company whose drugs he was reviewing, he replied, "In my particular case as an individual, I have no problem with that. I look on myself as being objective." He added, "I have no problem with the implication that I wear multiple hats as long as it is fairly stated that I didn't hide it." Morganroth did, in fact, disclose his multiple relationships to the FDA. Raymond Lipicky said his Cardio-Renal Drug Divison employed seven other part-time medical officers. Asked how many others had conflicts, he replied, "All of them."

The "hat" that was increasingly found on Joel Morganroth's head was that of paid drug lecturer for 3M and Bristol-Myers. When they needed a marquee professor for symposia, he was their man. Just weeks after Robert Temple approved Tambocor, Morganroth was ready to direct a Philadelphia symposium in January 1986. In June he starred in a nationwide symposia blitz, appearing in Dallas, Miami, New York, Chicago and Boston. The next year he spoke at several weekend symposia for Tambocor. Morganroth did package deals (getting $19,500 for the national symposium blitz) and he did piecework (getting $1,591 for a talk in nearby Monmouth, N.J., and $1,600 for one in East Orange, N.J.). For doctors who might have missed his lectures, he did an audiotape ($18,000) and other public relations work. In 1988, he also helped 3M in meetings with the FDA ($6,350) at the same time he worked part-time for the FDA evaluating other heart drugs ($6,254).

In Joel Morganroth 3M had more than a headliner for the symposium circuit. Under FDA regulations, 3M was not supposed to advertise Tambocor for the large population with premature beats, but no symptoms. Most patients with PVCs don't have symptoms. Furthermore, 3M drug detailers were required to stay within the FDA authorized indications in personal pitches to individual doctors. As a marquee professor, Morganroth was not limited by the restriction in the FDA labeling. He expressed independent medical judgment, which differed from the FDA's conclusions about Tambocor. In Morganroth's medical judgment, Tambocor was the near perfect drug for PVCs. "It doesn't hurt people; it's not so hard to use, it's tolerated well and it worked perfectly." In Morganroth's doctrine, patients with no other heart problems had "benign" PVCs, and didn't require treatment unless they had palpitations or other symptoms. However, in patients with heart disease, he regarded premature beats as "potentially lethal" even if the patient had no symptoms, and recommended using drugs. Like other cardiologists who advocated wider use of the drugs, Morganroth often pointed out the lack of definitive scientific evidence that this was beneficial. This was the broader message that Morganroth provided to doctors. Apparently, it was often persuasive; because as he put it, "That sustained the day."

The other great power of marquee professors was their ability to write assessments of the drugs they promoted for medical journals. Morganroth, for example, wrote a review of Tambocor for the *American Family Physician* suggesting how safe it was for patients with mild rhythm disturbances. "Proarrhythmic effects are uncommon in patients treated with Tambocor for benign or potentially lethal ventricular arrhythmias," he wrote. As is customary in many medical journals, in this article, Morganroth's financial relationship with 3M was nowhere disclosed.

Morganroth's promotion of Tambocor was consistent with his longstanding views. However, the promotion of Tambocor raised more difficult problems for prominent medical school experts who had already voiced doubts. A notable example was Raymond Woosley of Vanderbilt. When he wrote the original dose-ranging study of Tambocor he had been laudatory about the drug. That posture continued at 3M's Bermuda symposium. But while sitting on the FDA advisory committee he had voiced reservations. At one point, Woosley had proposed that the label warn expressly that "the treatment of asymptomatic PVCs is unjustified at this time." The committee didn't agree, but by early 1986, Woosley had more freedom to express his opinion, and perhaps even more influence over other doctors. He had won the assignment to write a review article about Tambocor for the *New England Journal of Medicine*, one of the most influential medical publications in the world. The Tambocor review article, appearing just months after marketing began, was an important first impression. It was an authoritative assessment of the first drug of the new generation. Would Woosley voice his doubts? Or his enthusiasm? He had a third choice. As an FDA advisory committee member, he could stick to the apparent spirit of label restrictions, which seemed to reserve Tambocor to the smaller market of more severely ill patients.

In the *New England Journal of Medicine* article, Woosley and coauthor Dan M. Roden endorsed Tambocor. In patients whose hearts still pumped normally, it "has been shown to be more potent and better tolerated than currently available drugs," the article said. This statement, in fact, became the highlight of an eight-page Tambocor advertising spread. In addition to supplying a quote suitable for 3M's marketing efforts, Woosley's article contained no language likely to slow 3M's push toward the larger market of patients with mild rhythm disorders. He warned only against using Tambocor in patients with "no symptoms" and "no known risk." Woosley remained silent on the pivotal question whether Tambocor should be limited only to immediately life threatening conditions, or extended to the vastly bigger patient population with heart disease and premature beats. Current theory held such patients were at higher risk for cardiac arrest. The *New England Journal* article also followed prevailing medical custom and did not refer to Woosley's relationship with 3M.

Other doctors joined Morganroth on the educational circuit. And as independent agents, not only were they free to differ with FDA label restrictions, they did not invariably confine their comments to their sponsors' products. For example, Thomas Graboys, who worked with Bernard Lown at Harvard, appeared at Saint Mary's Hospital in Long Beach, California, in May 1988. He was sponsored in part by A. H. Robbins, which sells a form of quinidine.

Graboys described his own practice of treating "potentially malignant" arrhythmias, as well as rhythm disturbances that were clearly dangerous. However, when Graboys identified a drug to suppress PVCs, he named Bristol-Myers' Enkaid. He said he also used Mexitil, procainamide and quinidine.*

A marquee professor must be prepared for challenges from the doctors in the audience. And at this occasion, one was forthcoming. Graboys was asked if he had evidence that suppressing PVCs would in fact prevent sudden death. He conceded this benefit had not been demonstrated. Based on the data available, he said, this was his own approach to treatment. On other occasions Graboys also warned against excessive use of antiarrhythmic drugs.

Roger Winkle, the Stanford professor who early warned of the dangers of Tambocor and Enkaid, also gave talks during this period. Without a powerful corporate sponsor, he made no national tours

---

*Graboys and other members of Bernard Lown's group at Harvard were unusual in donating the honoraria to research. Graboys estimated he donated $400,000 in drug company honoraria over twelve years.

as did Morganroth. But he was occasionally invited to speak by hospitals and other institutions that hosted educational programs. (The drug companies still paid the costs.) Winkle had quite a different message. His main theme was, "These are dangerous drugs." Winkle still remembers giving such a warning at a meeting in Reno, Nevada. As soon as he was finished, a drug company detailer rose to urge the doctors in the audience to pay no attention to Winkle's comments. Companies seldom, if ever, tried to silence dissenters such as Winkle, although there are cases where they have interfered with the publication of critical studies. But by sponsoring thousands of symposia each month, the industry could easily overwhelm the occasional dissenting voice.

Drug advertising, the third major tool of medical marketing, was a natural for a modest-sized operation such as 3M Pharmaceuticals. Advertising is an important element in drug marketing, typically accounting for one quarter of the marketing dollar. Pharmaceutical industry advertising supports more than 2,000 medical publications, but plays a paradoxical role in influencing physicians. When asked, physicians tend to deny that advertising influences their medical judgment. But the sheer volume of spending, as well as some provocative studies, suggests that drug advertising works.

The most intriguing findings come from a 1982 study written by Jerry Avorn of Harvard Medical School. The first question he asked a group of randomly selected doctors was how important advertising was in selecting drugs. Only 4 percent said it was "very important," compared with 62 percent who thought scientific papers were very important. Then he asked the same group of physicians about a specific case where the scientific literature and drug advertising were in conflict. He used the case of Eli Lilly's painkiller, Darvon, which numerous scientific reviews showed was little different from aspirin. However, the drug was advertised heavily as superior. Even though only 4 percent of the doctors thought drug advertising was a very important influence, 49 percent thought Darvon was a superior painkiller. Avorn also asked about two other drugs, with similar results.

Not only does drug advertising work, several studies suggest it is often misleading. The most widely publicized survey came from Michael S. Wilkes of the University of California at Los Angeles School of Medicine. Wilkes sent 109 full-page advertisements to a panel of experts in the subject matter and asked them to judge whether they complied with FDA guidelines. He found 92 percent of the advertisements failed to meet at least one standard, and 15 percent of the ads failed to comply with eight or more separate standards. The Wilkes study was widely reported in the news media and triggered howls of protest from the industry. (Typical complaint: the FDA cited officially only about 8 percent of ads for violations. The author's response: this might mean the FDA was significantly understaffed, or lacked subject matter expertise.) In a separate study, a group of Australian academics asked 10 pharmaceutical companies for references to support advertising claims. Writing in the British journal, the *Lancet*, they concluded, "None of the companies supplied clinical trial reports that are both scientifically valid and support the advertising claims."

The FDA has the authority to regulate drug advertising and requires that ads be accurate, "balanced" and reflect the approved labeling. Nevertheless, clearly misleading ads, even if cited by the FDA, can still bring a company major profits. Warner-Lambert propelled the cholesterol-lowering drug Lopid to a second-place market share in part on misleading advertising claims outside its approved indication. Although approved only for a rare lipid disorder, the FDA contended that the company advertised it for broader use. The company was required to acknowledge its error in a full-page corrective advertisement, but not before Lopid became the second best-selling cholesterol-lowering drug.

It was in this environment that 3M had been found in violation of FDA regulations even before Tambocor was approved. In 1983, Kenneth R. Feather, then chief of FDA drug advertising regulation, stopped by the 3M exhibit at the spring convention of the American College of Cardiology. He did not like what he saw, in particular a sign that said "Coming Soon" from 3M Pharmaceuticals "Tambocor (flecainide acetate) a unique achievement in cardiovascular medicine." The company was also handing out reprints of enthusiastic articles by Raymond Woosley and Jeffery Anderson. In a letter to 3M, Feather ordered them to stop promoting an unapproved drug. The company said Feather had "given them a better understanding of the intent of the guidelines" and promised to change any future exhibits.

In 1985, the FDA warned 3M again that it might be jumping the gun with two advertisements published before Tambocor was approved. One said, "Tambocor: An achievement without precedent." The other said, "A unique achievement in cardiovascular medicine." If 3M published the two ads together, the FDA said, it would be a violation. The company said it had no such plans.

The major controversy soon arose over which patient population ought to be taking Tambocor. On some level, the FDA hoped to restrict the drug to severe rhythm disorders; 3M was pursuing the larger market of patients with mild PVCs. Because of the negotiations with Temple reported earlier, the drug label language was ambiguous.

The FDA approved the product launch advertising with little comment. But within months, the FDA had dispatched an angry letter to 3M. It raised a series of objections about seeming violations of the labeling restrictions. As the FDA interpreted the labeling: "almost all sections place serious reservations over using Tambocor except in the most seriously-ill." The ads showed healthy-looking patients, and compared Tambocor with quinidine in its capacity to suppress PVCs. The letter continued, directing 3M "to discontinue any and all elements that even remotely resemble the 8/25/86 *Medical World News* ad."

3M, however, took the hard line. It pointed out that whenever it talked about PVCs, it inserted the word "symptomatic" as required in the labeling. (In fact, since the company didn't have data on symptoms, it simply inserted the word "symptomatic" before almost every reference to PVCs.) It argued that "it is not uncommon to advertise for one of multiple indications." After lengthy correspondence and a meeting, the result was an inconclusive agreement in which 3M conceded little but promised to pay more attention to warnings such as to use "only when benefits exceed the risks."

Within months, however, the FDA was complaining again about Tambocor ads. New ads not only emphasized the medical use in "symptomatic" PVCs; they omitted any mention of using Tambocor in seriously ill patients. Apparently acting on a complaint from Searle, the FDA also said the comparison with Norpace was unfair. 3M, once again, did not agree with the FDA charges. But it offered as a concession to put a reference to life-threatening arrhythmias in all future ads.

The fairness and overall impression made by advertisements is difficult to portray in words. It depends on subtle effects, on photographs, layout and type size. The author's impression of the advertisements is that 3M tried to reach the patient population with PVCs with every subtle device possible, while still complying with the letter of its ambiguous labeling. (This is in contrast to the many companies found to have made entirely unsubstantiated claims, or promoted its drugs for unapproved indications.) However, it would turn out that most Tambocor prescriptions were written for unapproved uses.

3M, meanwhile, had learned how to play the advertising game. It began to monitor closely the activities of its competitor, Bristol-Myers. When the product launch for Enkaid occurred—trailing Tambocor by more than a year—3M was ready with an advertising complaint. It rushed copies of Enkaid advertising and labeling to the FDA. In some copies of the label or package insert, the "warnings" section was in regular type instead of boldface. "More than a casual oversight," charged 3M.

Bristol-Myers later made the expected reply: a printer's mistake. But that was only the beginning of Bristol-Myers' rocky product launch, which had had problems since early 1987.

Chapter 17

ENKAID IN TROUBLE

SUGHOK K. CHUN was appalled. The Cardio-Renal Drug Division at the FDA had already clashed with 3M over the advertising for Tambocor. Now she had on her desk the first advertisements for Enkaid. As Bristol-Myers geared up for the product launch, it had submitted a seventeen-page brochure that the company's drug detailers would use in making calls on physicians. The material would also be used in a medical journal advertising campaign. It would make an important first impression on the physician community. The company was in a hurry when the proofs were finally complete in January 1987. It had to send the copy to the printer in twelve days.

"The material is totally unbalanced and unacceptable," Chun concluded. She took the brochure to Raymond Lipicky, the division director, and he agreed. It had taken Chun only five days to get to the ad, but the printer's deadline was just one week away. Chun then took her concerns to Bill Purvis in the Division of Drug Advertising and Labeling. It was already a few days after the copy deadline when Purvis arranged a conference call with Bristol-Myers officials.

"The drug is primarily intended for the seriously ill patient," Purvis told Bristol-Myers. The advertising failed to convey this, he noted. The advertisement, in fact, was plainly directed at the heart of the existing antiarrhythmic drug market—hundreds of thousands of patients with mild rhythm disturbances who were taking the best-selling quinidine in hopes of preventing a cardiac arrest. The theme of the Bristol-Myers sales pitch was "Classic therapy is now improved: The antiarrhythmic benefits of quinidine without significant GI distress." The advertising flyer devoted one page to proarrhythmic effects, but failed to mention the one adverse event that had most disturbed the company and the FDA: fatal cardiac arrests.

Purvis, however, was handicapped in his conversation with Bristol-Myers. Chun, who had gone over the flyer in greatest detail, was out sick, and her forty-seven specific objections were apparently not available to Bill Purvis. As had happened with some of the meetings about Tambocor ads, the telephone conference ended inconclusively. Bristol-Myers told Purvis the company would have its own internal meeting about the problem. Company officials would also be available to the FDA if needed.

The conflict over advertising and promotion seemed inevitable. As was noted earlier, 3M had concluded that it couldn't profit if Tambocor could be sold only for the population with serious rhythm disorders who comprised at best about one sixth of the potential market. Bristol-Myers' market research, presumably, had produced similar results. Further, Robert Temple's original restrictions on Tambocor showed he knew exactly what labeling language would confine these drugs to the smaller population. But Temple and Lipicky had compromised, allowing an indication that included "symptomatic" PVCs. Both companies were trying to squeeze through the loophole that the FDA had created. Without the loophole, the profit potential of the drugs would have been reduced by 80 percent, and the companies might never have marketed these drugs at all.

However, Temple and Lipicky were still worried about the safety of Enkaid, and they did not abandon their concern about Bristol-Myers' ads. But two more months passed before Lipicky, Purvis and other FDA officials sat down with senior executives of Bristol-Myers. Purvis's minutes of the meeting explained Lipicky's position:

"Dr. Lipicky was upset by the above-mentioned advertising flyer for Enkaid because he felt the overall thrust of the campaign was wrong. His reaction after reading the first nine pages of the flyer is that anyone now on quinidine should be switched to Enkaid. He felt that imparting this general thought to the medical community would be a tragedy. Enkaid is an agent for patients with severe arrhythmias. It is supposed to be initiated in the hospital."

Bristol-Myers representatives pointed out that 3M's Tambocor advertising was similar. Lipicky "agreed that they also targeted the same patients," the minutes said. As the meeting continued, the two sides fenced. Bristol-Myers said the advertising would be used only for cardiologists and internists. A different campaign would target general practitioners.

A practical problem emerged. While the FDA had initially responded quite rapidly, it was now two months later and the advertisements were already printed. Bristol-Myers' team said perhaps the company would use the advertisements, and then take whatever remedial action the FDA required. Kenneth Feather, the FDA chief of drug advertising, said Enkaid could be declared misbranded and seized. Lipicky, however, didn't back him up, and Feather conceded that seizing the drug was "probably unlikely." Two different compromise proposals emerged. The company wanted to add a cover letter. The FDA wanted changes in the opening page of the seventeen-page flyer. After consultation with Temple, the FDA position prevailed. But the advertising campaign ran with only modest changes to the first page, despite Chun's numerous objections to every page. The token changes in the Enkaid brochure left the door wide open to the larger and more profitable market. Meanwhile, Bristol-Myers had developed another promotional plan for Enkaid that was going to create problems that would dwarf this episode.

In early 1987, Bristol-Myers was far behind in the race to the clinic. FDA approval for Enkaid had come a full year after Tambocor. In the year that 3M was selling and promoting Tambocor directly to physicians, the best Bristol-Myers could do was sponsor an Enkaid symposium in Scottsdale, Arizona. It featured a glittering cast of marquee professors, including Morganroth, Bigger and Woosley. But that was still a poor substitute for drug detailers pushing Enkaid face-to-face to hundreds of doctors every week. Even when Robert Temple finally approved Enkaid in December of 1986, the company still wasn't ready with commercial quantities of the drug. With Tambocor winning over doctors, Bristol-Myers' solution was to launch a marketing program that was dressed in the trappings of a scientific clinical study.

It was called the "Enkaid Phase IV Post-Approval Study." Bristol-Myers was going to pay doctors across the country to switch their patients to Enkaid or to start new patients on the drug. The "objectives" of the study made the promotional purpose clear. It would "allow selected cardiologists to obtain premarketing experience." They would have the opportunity "to compare the effects of Enkaid to previous antiarrhythmic therapy." Each participating doctor was to enroll 10 patients and keep them on the drug for six weeks. The drug was provided free until supplies were commercially available. Doctors were required to attend a one-day symposium to learn about Enkaid and had to fill out seven patient information forms for each patient. The amount paid to each doctor to participate could not be determined, but doctors familar with drug research estimated payments to doctors in similar programs totaled several thousand dollars.

In scientific terms, the Bristol-Myers study could reveal little not already known from previous research. It had no control group. As might be expected in a marketing-oriented program, the definition of "success" was generous: relief of or improvement in symptoms, or a closer-to-normal EKG.

In marketing terms, the Enkaid study at first seemed successful. The company recruited 191 cardiologists to participate, and in just three months they enrolled 1,277 patients. Almost all the patients did have symptoms, as the FDA label required. However, most symptoms were minor, occasional palpitations (41 percent) and dizziness (19 percent). The rhythm disturbances tended to parallel the real market for Enkaid. Almost two thirds had PVCs. Just 8 percent had immediately serious heart rhythm disturbances—the population in which the FDA believed this drug was most appropriate.

However meager the scientific merits of the Phase IV Enkaid study, the reporting of adverse reactions was far superior to the usual system. Normally after approval, doctors who think they might have observed an adverse reaction are encouraged to report it either directly to the FDA or to the drug company. But without precise information about which patients are being treated, and all doctors watching for the same problems, this is a helter-skelter approach. In this case the Bristol-Myers marketing scheme happened to include systematic tracking of adverse reactions in a well-defined patient population with nearly 100 percent reporting. It was a model of the kind of procedure that should be routine for all new drugs. This happened because Bristol-Myers was not ready to market the drug and wanted to buy some early clinical exposure with its study.

As the results were tabulated, it was clear that a disturbing number of patient deaths had occurred. Even though these patients had taken Enkaid for only six weeks, 39 had died. Most were cardiac arrests. Overall about 3 percent of the Enkaid patients were dead. On a yearly basis, that would work out to a death rate of 26 percent, which is astronomical. For example, one highly vulnerable population that cardiologists routinely treat are heart attack survivors. In the first year after a heart attack the mortality rate is about 10 percent; after that the danger declines steadily. Twenty-six percent was an unusually high death rate even in patients with heart failure. Had the Phase IV trial been a useful scientific experiment, it would have been fairly simple to determine how many of the 39 deaths ought to be blamed on Enkaid. The treatment group could have been compared with a similar, but untreated control group. But there had been so few well-controlled Enkaid studies that not even comparable historical controls were available. As a consequence, Bristol-Myers turned to the medical school experts to evaluate which deaths might have been drug related. Once again, the companies were going to ask experts to answer a question that even the experts did not have the necessary data to answer. To review the Phase IV study deaths, Bristol-Myers hired Thomas Bigger of Columbia. He certainly had experience with the issue. In 1982 Bigger had joined the 3M investigators' meeting in St. Paul when testing of Tambocor had been halted over unexplained sudden deaths. In 1984, he had appeared for Boehringer Ingelheim to reassure the FDA advisory committee about the excess deaths observed with Mexitil. Bristol-Myers also recruited a close colleague of Joel Morganroth, a Philadelphia cardiologist named Leonard Horowitz. He was on the faculty at Hahnemann University with Morganroth and had written many papers with him. The third reviewer was William C. Roberts, then a coronary pathologist for the National Institutes of Health, and editor of the *American Journal of Cardiology.*

According to the three consultants' report, a total of 9 deaths were "probably related" to Enkaid. But a close reading reveals the three experts were unable to agree on a common set of guidelines for the review. Bigger and Horowitz wanted to use an arbitrary breakpoint and absolve the drug of any sudden death occurring more than 30 days after drug therapy began. Roberts did not agree. On the other hand, Bigger and Horowitz were willing to declare the drug "probably" responsible for certain sudden deaths occurring soon after patients started the drug. Roberts didn't agree. He was a pathologist who had conducted autopsy dissections of thousands of diseased hearts to identify the cause of death. When other potential causes of death were present—and that occurred in every single case—Roberts was willing to identify Enkaid only as a "possible" cause of death. The disagreement was understandable. When the results of the disease and the adverse effect of the drug are identical, the two cannot be separated without an untreated control group.

The consultants' count of Enkaid deaths depended not only on conflicting definitions but on the scorekeeping rules. Nine patient deaths were "probably related" if one counted cases where two consultants agreed. However, drug-related deaths increased to 22 if one included cases where at least one consultant believed the drug a possible cause. That still left 17 deaths where, according to the report, "the consultants unanimously agreed the death was not related to Enkaid therapy." Even this classification was questionable. For example, one patient died of unknown causes. The death was discounted because this patient was also being treated for leukemia. But without knowing the cause of death, the experts could not know whether the patient died of cancer or from a cardiac arrest. In another patient, the drug was absolved because "Insufficient data is presented to make a definitive statement about death and its relationship to Enkaid." Absolving the drug of blame in cases where no information was available to judge either way is a telling indication of the conscious or unconscious biases of these consultants.

The Enkaid study illustrates what happens during one of the most dangerous of all moments in medicine, when the door is opened to the possibility that hundreds of doctors are prescribing a drug that harmed their patients. The problem is that most doctors cannot bring themselves to believe they could have done such a thing. Sidney Wolfe, the Health Research Group physician who has spent more than two decades questioning the safety of hundreds of different drugs, eloquently describes what happens:

"Whether it is the doctor, the drug company, the FDA or the medical school doctor, everyone involved in medicine believes they have a net positive impact on the patient's health," Wolfe said. "As soon as you start putting forth examples in which they participated in something in which the risks did outweigh the benefits, they can't handle it. It completely contradicts their whole reason for being in medicine. The 'do no harm' principle is so inculcated in the minds of everyone involved they just don't believe they ever violated it."

The language of denial can be seen in the summary of the consultants' report: "It is possible that as many as nine patients died during the study of proarrhythmic effects of Enkaid. These patients appeared to have been in the highest risk group for proarrhythmic effects and may have been 'sicker' than the average patient in the study." This is almost invariably the second element in physician denial. The problem was not the treatment; the patient was too sick to be helped.

While Bristol-Myers had moved rapidly to get the Enkaid study started, the assessment of the deaths proceeded slowly and deliberately. By June of 1987 patient enrollment was complete. Another six months elapsed before the results were tabulated and the large number of deaths became painfully apparent. Bristol-Myers then launched its own review of the deaths, and that consumed additional weeks. The company took another month to present the data to its cardiovascular advisory board. (Morganroth was a member.) That led to a decision to ask Bigger, Horowitz and Roberts to review the deaths, but another month elapsed before Bristol-Myers got the data to the consultants. It was mid-May 1988 before an initial draft of the consultants' report was finished, and it took two more months to complete a final draft.

While Bristol-Myers considered the deaths caused by Enkaid on this measured schedule, the promotion and marketing were operating at full steam. When patient enrollment in the Phase IV study ended, just 2,700 Enkaid prescriptions were being filled each month. When the deaths were tabulated, sales had grown tenfold—27,000 prescriptions. By the time the consultants' report was finally complete, pharmacists were filling 50,000 prescriptions a month. The Bristol-Myers marketing machine was producing results.

More than one year after patient enrollment was completed, Bristol-Myers had not told the FDA about its Phase IV study results. At some point during the early spring or summer of 1988, Robert Temple heard about the the large number of deaths and was immediately concerned. By July, the FDA was pointedly demanding the results, and the wheels began to turn more quickly. Bristol-Myers sent the consultants' report to the FDA.

A company that was aggressively advertising "a low incidence of side effects within recommended dosage range" was understandably not eager to have the consultants' report on the 39 deaths known. It told the FDA, "The enclosed documents are considered to be CONFIDENTIAL by the Bristol-Myers Company, and should be afforded appropriate protection under the Federal Freedom of Information Act and applicable Federal Laws."

The consultants' report on the Enkaid deaths did not reassure Robert Temple. He demanded complete details and a briefing, and made no secret of his displeasure over the delays. It was the first week of August before a Bristol-Myers team came to Washington to brief Temple and Sughok Chun, the Enkaid medical officer.

Temple set the tone for the meeting. According to the minutes, he "summarized his initial concern that a drug being so vigorously promoted for non-life-threatening arrhythmia therapy should be implicated in what at first appeared to be a large number of deaths."

It fell to Leonard Horowitz, Morganroth's colleague, to explain the consultants' report, and the deaths. Horowitz pointed out that among the 9 "probably drug-related" deaths, 8 patients had heart failure—their hearts already too severely damaged to maintain normal body functions. Temple, who had lost none of his flair for numbers, was unimpressed. He noted that 4 percent of the 187 patients with heart failure had died within a month. "It is difficult to imagine that patients without Enkaid therapy could have done worse," Temple said. (If anything, he understated the situation. The one-month figures work out to a 36 percent annual mortality rate, more than double the typical death rate in this sick patient population.) "It would appear that the risk for patients with heart failure is very high," Temple said.

He ended the meeting on a note of displeasure, telling Bristol-Myers "whereas the firm had been within the regulations in not reporting the results of this study, the Agency likes to be kept informed." (Since this was a marketing exercise, the strict reporting rules for clinical testing did not apply.) However, Temple made no changes in the Enkaid labeling.

In an official summary of the study, Chun expressed no concern as medical officer for the drug, despite Temple's comments. "This Phase IV study result was similar to that of extensive premarketing experience with Enkaid. Under usual clinical conditions, this study confirms the efficacy and safety of Enkaid. . . ."

The discovery of the Enkaid deaths was an accidental by-product of the promotional scheme. For comparison, it is instructive to examine the results for Tambocor as seen through the FDA's regular adverse reaction reporting machinery. The first year on the market is a period requiring special vigilance from the medical officer. Consequently, Sughok Chun reviewed the adverse reaction reports and other new information on at least 10 occasions during Tambocor's first year on the market. Sometimes sudden deaths were reported. (One large group of 24 came in from an ongoing clinical study, where once again systematic reporting procedures were in effect.) Since they were expected, they were not of great interest to Chun. In June 1986 Chun had noted 3 sudden deaths without comment in a brief summary report. In the entire first year, one unusual case did capture her attention.

A 65-year-old man was being treated for chest pains and high blood pressure. While hospitalized, cardiac monitoring showed PVCs, and sometimes runs of three or more premature beats in a row. He was put on Tambocor. Five days after starting on the drug he was found unconscious on the floor beside his bed in the intensive care unit. His blood pressure and heartbeat were restored, but he remained "unresponsive." The case was unusual because the cardiac monitoring on this patient suggested he had not suffered the classic electrical breakdown, but some other form of cardiac collapse. It was unusual enough to capture Chun's attention and warrant a special summary. Chun was scanning the sporadic stream of adverse reaction reports for something unusual. (For example, she wrote up a case of incurable hiccups.) A sudden death was by now an expected event. The only significant finding in the first year of Tambocor marketing was a new caution about reducing the dose in patients with impaired liver function. Chun observed problems in such patients among the adverse reaction reports, and 3M submitted a study on the matter.

If Chun was looking for the unexpected, another FDA division conducted a more systematic count, screening all incoming adverse reaction reports. Because it was a newly approved drug, Tambocor also came to the attention of the FDA's Monitored Adverse Reaction or MAR system, which is part of another FDA division called Epidemiology and Surveillance. This early adverse reaction report spurred the division's interest:

"Shortly after breakfast, while visiting relatives, the patient collapsed without prior symptoms. Taken to the hospital, his family was told, 'He had a massive heart attack and could not be resuscitated.' No autopsy done." The report had all the earmarks of the cardiac arrests observed during Tambocor's clinical testing. "Massive heart attack" is a crude layman's translation, but could easily describe a cardiac arrest. However, when combined with two other reports, this led the division to track not cardiac arrests, but "heart attacks," or, in medical terms, acute myocardial infarctions. In the previous deliberations, the experts—perhaps too eagerly—had absolved Tambocor in any patient deaths where heart attacks or myocardial infarctions, were even suspected. Heart attacks were a plumbing problem, a blockage in the coronary arteries, not an electrical accident like a cardiac arrest. While Tambocor might make a heart attack worse, it was unlikely that it could cause a heart attack directly. Therefore, the computerized MAR system began systematically tracking the wrong adverse event, heart attacks rather than sudden deaths or cardiac arrests.

Since the system was looking for the wrong event, it was not surprising that no evidence of a problem was detected. After one year of monitoring, FDA analyst Joyce Creamer reviewed the results. The computerized MAR system picked out only nine additional adverse reaction reports mentioning a heart attack, or acute myocardial infarction. In the same period, doctors wrote 93,000 new prescriptions for Tambocor.

"I recommend that the MAR for myocardial infarction be placed on an END STATUS at this time," wrote Creamer. The reason: "lack of conclusive evidence to support either a claim of cause/effect or an association with myocardial infarction."

By mid-1988 both 3M's and Bristol-Myers' aggressive marketing was gaining the two companies a growing market share. More than 150,000 patients were taking Tambocor or Enkaid. The companies were getting the kind of patients necessary for their profit targets, mostly those with mild rhythm disturbances. Doctors were giving the drugs on the still unproven theory that they prevented cardiac arrests. If one occurred anyway, they would be unlikely to report it as an adverse reaction to the drug. Even if one did happen to get reported, it would provoke little interest from Sughok Chun. And the computerized MAR system was no longer following Tambocor.

On the other hand, if the death rate observed in the Enkaid marketing study were any indication of the potential hazard of these drugs, thousands of drug-related deaths might be occurring in a single year. Given the incomplete clinical testing before approval, and the meager system for tracking the results in clinical practice, there was no reason why thousands of excess deaths could not occur year after year without being detected.

Evidence was now abundant that at the FDA, Robert Temple, Raymond Lipicky and Sughok Chun knew that these drugs could cause cardiac arrest. This was equally apparent to 3M and Bristol-Myers, which had held worried sessions to examine troubling results. It was known to the senior medical school experts who had reviewed the deaths for the companies or pondered them at advisory committee meetings. These same experts were now promoting the drugs as marquee professors. What this group did not know was how many deaths the drugs might cause. They assumed any lives lost would be outnumbered by cases in which the drugs prevented cardiac arrests.

In the American medical system today, this is normally the end of the story. Serious questions arise about the safety of a widely used family of drugs. Whatever their inner doubts, FDA and medical school experts close ranks to reassure the public. This case has a different ending. An NIH division called the National Heart, Lung, and Blood Institute chose to spend a large sum of money to conduct a major medical experiment, a well-controlled clinical trial. The outcome was going to surprise everyone involved.

Chapter 18

THE FREAK OF CHANCE

ALBERT IGNATIUS MURPHY'S heart stopped beating on Memorial Day, 1988. His day had begun quietly enough with breakfast at home in the Washington, D.C., suburb of Beltsville. Although Murphy was a vigorous, passionate man whose life had been touched by great events, this particular day started in a mundane way. After breakfast, he drove to a nearby home improvement center to pick up a load of peat moss and some wooden logs. He intended to terrace the back yard of his tidy, red brick home. Despite the leisurely holiday morning, Albert Murphy was not entirely free of the pressures of his unusual occupation. For the preceding thirty-eight years Murphy had worked for the National Security Agency as a code-breaker.

Murphy had been involved in an epochal event of the cold war, the Cuban missile crisis of October 1962. As Soviet ships loaded with intercontinental ballistic missiles headed toward Cuba, Murphy was listening to their radio signals from a remote site in Scarborough, England. President Kennedy had vowed that the ships would not be allowed to pass a United States naval blockade of Cuba. Every hour the Soviet ships would radio back their position in code as they steamed toward Cuba with their lethal cargo. Murphy's station intercepted the signals and broke the code. As he read the latest position just radioed by the Soviet ship the *Kimovsk*, he immediately realized it hadn't changed in the past hour. "My God!" he exclaimed. "She's hove to." He dispatched to Washington the most urgent of all intelligence reports, a "flash" message. Within minutes, President Kennedy knew he had won a terrible and dangerous gamble. The Soviet ships would not challenge the blockade.

Murphy's problems at the National Security Agency also dated from that same remote intercept station. One of the other employees at the station had become angry at how Murphy had handled the work schedules. When he got back to the United States, he told NSA security officers that Murphy was emotionally unstable. It was many years before Murphy discovered the false charges, and persuaded the NSA to acknowledge they had no basis in fact. He had to sue the agency to force it to remove the allegations from his file. This legal victory had nevertheless led Murphy to fear for his future career prospects. On this day in May the pressures of work were a great burden.

He was 62 years old, in excellent health, but worried. As he hoisted a bag of peat moss into the trunk of his car, he felt something snap in his chest. It wasn't painful, but from some inner recess of his mind came the urgent message that he was in big trouble. He leaped into his car, and barreled home as fast as he could drive.

He called out to his wife. "Ann. Quick. Call 911. I'm having a heart attack." Murphy sensed he might be beginning a journey to a location more distant than the nearest hospital. Before he lost consciousness he took his rosary beads in his right hand, and put on his brown scapular, a religious token worn by the Catholic devout.

For the next minutes he was sometimes conscious and sometimes not. The medics arrived. A nitroglycerin pill was put under his tongue. The ambulance rolled and he heard the urgency in the medic's voice as he radioed the nearby Holy Cross Hospital. "Code Three. Code Three. Code Three."

The last thing Albert Murphy clearly remembered was the hospital chaplain, a man he knew. His thought was a trivial one. Murphy, a traditionalist, disapproved of the light blue shirt the chaplain wore with his clerical collar. He felt the chaplain's hand on his forehead; saw the crucifix held in front of his eyes. Then his heart stopped beating altogether in cardiac arrest.

From a vantage point above, Albert Murphy looked down and saw the doctor place the pads of a defibrillator on his chest. Then he looked upward, and he saw something unlike anything he had ever seen before:

"Call it an endless horizon of radiant green, so radiant that it looks like it is about to turn blinding white. It is a different and glorious state of being. I have no sense of time. Is this the edge of eternity? It must be. I hear music, soothing music. And then the beginnings of rapture. A warm, loving, nonthreatening presence is there, and it fills me with peace and joy. I feel there are people standing on both sides of me and behind me.

"Now I see what looks like a huge open book sitting on a lectern.

The pages are white. There are some symbols on the page, some at the top and an array spread across the bottom as though in the form of a footnote. I can't understand the symbols, but I'm not bothered. The beauty all around me is magnificent.

"I see a gray stone wall. Three horizontal lines, each about a foot thick, run along the wall. The top one is white, the middle line, dark green, and the bottom one, black. I wonder whether the lines represent the three options open to the soul at the moment of death, one of which the soul will choose of its own volition. I lean toward deciding to choose a line, but I'm wavering."

In the room below a nun took Murphy's wife, Ann, and his daughter, Ellie, into a separate room. The nun suggested that Ann should call the other children immediately. Albert was the father of eight daughters and one son, and had nineteen grandchildren.

Murphy, meanwhile, pondered whether he should make the final decision in life and choose one of the three lines running along the endless gray wall. "I know full well that by not choosing one of the lines I will give up the chance of greater unspeakable joy; and that by picking one of the lines along the gray wall I will leave behind my loved ones. How I love my family!"

Then a change occurred. "My sadness begins to fade and I am given to know with gentle clarity that I am going to be sent back." Next he heard an authoritative male voice command:

"Hit him again! Hit him again!"

With the shock of a defibrillator, Murphy opened his eyes, and found himself staring up directly into the eyes of a nurse with blonde hair.

"I just had the most extraordinary experience," he told her.

The nurse said, "You may have had some kind of experience, but you sure gave us a bad time."

Four days later Albert Murphy had been transferred to Washington Hospital Center. He was there to undergo cardiac catheterization for a diagnostic look at the condition of his coronary arteries, and other cardiac functions. It revealed permanent damage to the heart; impaired but adequate pumping capacity remained. While still at the Washington Hospital Center he was visited by a nurse named Diane Law. She wanted to talk to him about volunteering to participate in a medical experiment called a randomized clinical trial. It was part of a nationwide study involving 27 research centers and more than 100 hospitals. The National, Heart, Lung, and Blood Institute was sponsoring the clinical trial. The people who worked on it called it CAST, an acronym for Cardiac Arrhythmia Suppression Trial. A decade after Bernard Lown had formally described the arrhythmia suppression hypothesis, and after thousands of doctors had prescribed antiarrhythmic drugs in hopes of preventing cardiac arrest, the theory was finally being put to the definitive test. Diane Law wanted Albert Murphy to join CAST.

The randomized clinical trial is the product of the strange and uncomfortable marriage of mathematics and medicine. The doctor believes all life is precious. In a clinical trial, lives lost and saved are measured coldly, counted like beans out of a bottle. The doctor learns to trust his clinical judgment, a developed sixth sense that incorporates but sometimes transcends the available and always inadequate data. The clinical trial demands the doctor treat his patients blindfolded, unaware whether he is providing a lifesaving treatment or an inert placebo. The best doctors believe each patient is unique, deserving individualized treatment; the clinical trial demands strict adherence to standard rules and specific criteria. It is a wonder that doctors will participate in a cold and mechanical clinical trial; some indeed do refuse. However, the short history of clinical trials has repeatedly demonstrated how often doctors' clinical judgment and best intentions were simply wrong. As Sir George Pickering, a British doctor and medical research pioneer put it, doctors' clinical judgments are "victims of the freak of chance."

The tension between mathematics and medicine dates from the moment a French doctor first started to count systematically the results of treatment rather than to describe individual cases. Early in the nineteenth century, Pierre-Charles-Alexandre Louis came to doubt one of the major medical therapies of the day, bleeding or venesection.* Working before the discovery of germ theory, Louis found that bloodletting was more frequently employed in patients who died of typhoid fever than among those who survived it. His approach was opposed by other Parisian physicians, who argued against such "curious logical abstractions." They argued that simple averages from groups of patients should not be applied to complex individual cases. Since everyone was so different, a multitude of unique factors might well outweigh any gross conclusions derived from counting events in groups of patients. Louis's opponents argued

---

*A rich account of the history of the clinical trial appears in J. Rosser Matthews's new book, *Quantification and the Quest for Medical Certainty*, which was also a key source for this chapter.

that only the physician's clinical judgment is capable of weighing this multitude of seen and unseen factors in an individual case. It is an argument that resonates to this day. The doctors who helped develop Tambocor and Enkaid plainly became aware of their dangers. But they believed in their clinical judgment; they believed they could select patients who could benefit, and perhaps be saved. History teaches the error of that proposition.

If the knowledge and underlying assumptions of clinical judgment are incorrect, then the physician typically cannot see the results of error, no matter how bizarre the outcome of treatment. For one thousand years physicians allowed infected wounds to fester, untouched, because an authoritative Roman medical text had decreed erroneously that pus was beneficial to healing. Gross error, however, was hardly confined to medieval times. Paul Beeson, editor of the modern *Textbook of Medicine*, once reviewed the 1927 edition of the same volume. He noted in particular the prevalence of treatments that were manifestly harmful, such as arsenic, which was recommended for forty different diseases, or violent purgatives, which were prescribed for even the most fragile patients.

Not only can physicians remain blinded to direct harm; many patients get better when given treatments that are inert substances of manifestly no effect. In his classic exposition of the placebo effect, "The Lie That Heals," Howard Brody of Michigan State University noted that 30 to 40 percent of patients get better on a placebo. These effects are far-reaching and have been observed in hundreds of separate studies. Dramatic placebo effects are often seen in situations where the prime benefits are subjective—for example, patients given a placebo for panic disorder report fewer episodes. But measurable benefits have been noted among heart failure patients receiving a placebo instead of an active drug. In one 1990 study, 25 to 35 percent of those getting the placebo reported fewer symptoms, increased cardiac output, and the ability to tolerate increased levels of exercise. In another experiment, a placebo effectively suppressed PVCs in 35 percent of the patient population with at least 10 premature beats an hour. In many cases, the personal observation that lies at the heart of clinical judgment cannot separate a placebo effect from treatment benefits.

Selection bias is another confounder of clinical judgment, and can mislead even the most careful observer of patients. In *Minimizing Medical Mistakes*, Richard Riegelman warns the practicing physician about several specific dangers. The first problem is that the patients any individual physician sees are usually not a representative cross section of those who are ill with a particular disease. Often a doctor sees a very small number of patients with a specific disorder. In the emergency room of a public hospital, the doctor might encounter only the most severe cases; in a prosperous suburb, perhaps mostly the mildly ill. After diagnosis and treatment, the practicing physician often gets fragmentary and potentially misleading feedback about the outcome. Sometimes the doctor hears too much from treatment failures—because the successes do not return to complain. Sometimes the open gratitude of the few cured patients outweighs in the doctor's mind the perpetual silence of the many who died. The most thoroughly discredited treatments in the annals of medicine nevertheless produced anecdotal examples of seemingly dramatic results.

These manifest defects of clinical judgment long ago led those who wanted to make medicine more of a science into systematic counting of success and failure in treatment. No sooner had this process begun than the enormous difficulties of the approach became apparent. The fundamental problem is variability. Patients are not equally ill. Even those with a similar severity of illness do not respond uniformly to the same agent and dose. Each person's metabolism conducts thousands of interrelated chemical reactions, different in number and amount. Each immune system recognizes different definitions of self and distinguishes different microbial invaders. To study ailing humans systematically is to enter a world of nightmarish variability.

This central problem plagued the measurement of medical care until an American statistical genius came up with a surprisingly simple concept to harness the freak of chance. In the year 1935, R. A. Fisher had to confront a similar variability problem when comparing the yield of different varieties of grain. Would not small differences in soil, light and moisture have as much effect as one particular genetic strain of seed? By what technique could the two effects be reliably separated? He proposed the solution of randomly assigning the grains to small plots. The idea of randomization has an intellectual depth that reaches far beyond the elimination of conscious and unconscious bias. Randomization opens the door to a sequence of mathematical theories of probability that describe how much variability should be attributed to chance and how much to the intervention.

It was another eleven years before a British medical researcher applied Fisher's brilliant concept of randomization to an experiment with living humans. A. Bradford Hill was already a world authority in the infant specialty of medical statistics. In the year 1946, he devised an experiment with streptomycin, one of the first broad-spectrum antibiotics. One hundred and seven patients with tuberculosis were randomly assigned to receive either scarce supplies of streptomycin or the standard alternative treatment, bed rest. At the end of six months, 7 percent of the treated patients had died, compared with 27 percent of the untreated controls. Not only did the random assignment generally assure that the treated and untreated were comparable groups, the laws of statistics described the likelihood that the difference was a result of chance. Even though the clinical trial included barely more than 100 patients, Hill could say with confidence that the odds were less than 1 in 100 that the results occurred purely by chance.

In addition to randomization, the modern clinical trial contains other important elements. It must state a clear hypothesis in advance: Hill, for example, posited that the antibiotic treatment would reduce patient deaths (proved true), and would reduce fever (data inconclusive). A prospective trial inherently has greater power to convince than a historical study. The most convincing theory explaining yesterday's weather becomes compelling when it invariably predicts whether it will rain tomorrow. To prevent selection bias, each patient included in the study must meet stated entry criteria. All should be followed up systematically. Wherever possible the investigators should be unaware whether they were caring for a treated or placebo group patient—for example, when reading chest x-rays, deciding on a cause of death or making other judgments. Where practicable, randomized trials are entirely double blind—that is, until it is time to tabulate the results, neither the researcher nor the patient knows whether the patient is treated with the active agent or the placebo.

It was such a randomized clinical trial that led the research nurse Diane Law to Albert Murphy in his hospital bed at Washington Hospital Center. The heart attack and out-of-body experience already had had a profound effect on Murphy's overall outlook. "I will not fear death any more," he vowed. "I will look forward to it." He was also left with a renewed conviction to make the most of whatever time remained. When asked if he was willing to consider participating, he "was happy to be able to contribute."

Before he could do so, Murphy had to meet a long list of specific criteria intended to guarantee that everyone who participated was, in medical terms, similar. Murphy had met the first requirement for joining the CAST study: he had survived a heart attack. The stated purpose of the trial was to demonstrate that either Tambocor, Enkaid or Ethmozine (DuPont's Soviet drug) would prevent sudden death

by suppressing PVCs or premature beats. Such an experiment required subjects at substantial, but not astronomical, risk of experiencing this event. Heart attack survivors, with about a 10 percent
chance of dying in the first year, fell in the middle zone. The ghoulish
aspect was that having so many deaths expected over one year's time
limited the CAST trial to a manageable size—about 4,400 patients
overall to accumulate roughly 450 expected deaths or "endpoints."
The critical question Diane Law still had to answer was whether
Albert Murphy had enough PVCs for the drugs to suppress. She asked
Murphy to wear a portable Holter monitor that would record 24
hours' worth of heartbeats on a standard cassette tape. It was just
five days after Murphy's heart attack and brief voyage to the world
of brilliant green light.

In two days Diane Law had the results. The Holter had recorded
367 premature beats over a 24-hour period, or an average of about
15 an hour. Murphy had no runs of repeated premature beats, and
could not detect the relatively few isolated PVCs that he did experience. But that was a sufficient number of premature beats to meet
the CAST standard, 6 PVCs per hour. Diane Law was almost ready to
sign up Murphy.

No sooner were researchers around the world impressed by the
objective power of the randomized clinical trial than thoughtful physicians began to question its ethics. By an accident of fate, Bradford
Hill had faced no great ethical choices. Streptomycin was then in
such short supply that he used all that was available. In almost any
other circumstances, the structure of a randomized clinical trial
seemed to demand morally unacceptable actions: denying a valuable
treatment like streptomycin to one half the participants just to get
a comparison group. Looking on the other side of the coin raised a
related, equally troubling question. If the researcher suspected the
active agent might be harmful, how could one justify providing it to
those in the active treatment group, just to prove a point? Finally,
the randomized trial could not avoid the ethical complications that
had plagued discussions of the placebo effect for more than a century.
Part of the placebo effect must be attributed to the patient's trust in
a physician to cure him. Was it proper to breach that trust and fool
the patient about the medication? Can genuine health benefits flow
from knowing deception?

In the years that followed Hill's first randomized trial, the medical
community reached an ethical consensus; but like other aspects of

the marriage of mathematics and medicine, it was never an entirely comfortable union. The first solution was easiest. No patient should be asked to participate without being fully informed about the trial— including the placebo—and consenting in writing to participate. Second, the researchers must be genuinely uncertain whether a treatment is beneficial. It was regarded as unethical to conduct a randomized trial to prove harm. Also, if the physician is certain of the benefits, it is unethical to deny them to the control group, especially in cases of serious illness.

These ethical guidelines operate smoothly when new medical treatments are tested before spreading into widespread medical use. By definition the benefits of a medical innovation are uncertain. The randomized clinical trial is much more problematical when questions arise about medical treatments that have been widely accepted on the basis of clinical judgment, anecdotal evidence or medical tradition. Doctors believe in some treatments so deeply they cannot agree to deprive any patients of their benefits. But if one believes the treatment is harmful—as Louis did bloodletting—it is also unethical to conduct a clinical trial to prove the point.

Widespread physician belief in the benefits of treating PVCs came close to sinking the CAST study. Of those otherwise qualified to participate, nearly half had already been placed on antiarrhythmic drugs by their doctors. In another 20 percent of the cases, the physician refused to let the patient participate. No reliable figures are available, but CAST researchers reported that physicians refused primarily on grounds the placebo might deprive the patient of benefit. Among those otherwise qualified to participate in CAST, therefore, about two out of three were eliminated because physician certainty about the benefits of treatment made doctors unwilling to risk a placebo for their patients. The requirement for uncertainty about the benefits of treatment creates an ethical paradox that has never been resolved. The more firmly a physician's belief—whether correct or erroneous—is anchored in daily clinical practice, the less likely that the benefits can be established through a randomized clinical trial.

These were the factors that made the recruitment of Albert I. Murphy a significant achievement for Diane Law, Janna Harrison and Dulce Obias-Manno, the research nurses at Washington Hospital Center who worked on CAST. Every day they prowled the hallways, wards and intensive care units of eight Washington area hospitals, looking for eligible patients. Over three years they expected to recruit roughly 125 patients. Each day this same scene was repeated at 26 other sites, as far north as Calgary, Alberta, and as far south as Miami, as far east as Gothenberg, Sweden, and as far west as Seattle. To recruit 4,400 patients eligible and willing to participate was going to require screening roughly 166,000 heart attack survivors. (As another double-check against selection bias, the research nurses periodically reported every patient they screened, and the specific reason for excluding them.)

The 27 sites in the Cardiac Arrhythmia Suppression Trial were linked electronically by a telephone network of personal computers. The nerve center of the network was the CAST Coordinating Center, located in a nondescript office building on the northwest side of Seattle, near the University of Washington campus. The nurses at each hospital site could enter information about each patient into special forms that appeared on their computer screens. Once a week the central computer would poll all the computers in the network during the night and download the information. Electronic messages could be dispatched to the center at any time. The exception to this all-electronic data system was an event of special importance, the enrollment and randomization of a new participant.

Seven days after Albert Murphy's heart attack, Diane Law had completed the medical workup, obtained his informed consent, and was ready to enroll him in CAST. She telephoned the coordinating center to tell them the essential facts about Patient 0089-27-3 AMUR. In Seattle, Linda Stefan entered the information into the central CAST computer. At random, the computer selected the drug that would be given to Murphy. On this day in early June 1988, he happened to be selected to receive Enkaid. From a cardboard carton kept in a closet at the Washington Hospital Center, Law withdrew a bottle of labeled Enkaid tablets and sent Murphy home with them. Before the double-blind study could begin, the researchers had to address a preliminary issue.

The question was whether the drug would effectively suppress Murphy's PVCs. (Enkaid was successful in 69 percent of the patients, later results showed.) Earlier clinical trials to test the suppression hypothesis had been criticized on two grounds. In some studies the drugs were given to patients who didn't necessarily have PVCs, thereby exposing them to any possible adverse effect of the drug without any hope of benefit. In other studies, the drugs were given to patients with PVCs without follow-up testing to verify that the drugs had actually worked. In an attempt to provide definitive proof of the suppression hypothesis, the CAST trial design resolved both difficulties. Murphy did not become a candidate for the trial until after there was clear evidence he had numerous PVCs. However, he would not formally enter the trial until Holter monitoring showed that the drug had eliminated the premature beats. (Murphy, in fact, had been randomly assigned to a sequence of drugs. If Enkaid didn't work, the dose would be increased. If that failed, he would be given Ethmozine. If Ethmozine proved ineffective, he would get Tambocor.) This two-week trial period provided another benefit to those who believed in the suppression theory. The companies, the FDA and the research doctors who helped test these drugs had concluded that if the drugs were going to make the heart rhythms worse instead of better, these proarrhythmic effects would occur during the first two weeks. Deaths in the first two weeks when the effectiveness of the drug was being established were not counted in calculating the benefits of treatment.

For Albert Murphy, Enkaid proved effective at the lowest effective dose, a 25 mg tablet twice a day. The second Holter monitor tape showed that while taking Enkaid, he had experienced just five premature beats over a recording period of 22 hours, 59 minutes. Next occurred the key step in the clinical trial. Another call was made to the Seattle coordinating center. At the beginning of the trial, the CAST computer had performed the electronic equivalent of shuffling a deck of red and black cards. Now, as Albert Murphy's number came up, the computer selected the top card from the shuffled pack. It would determine whether he received Enkaid, or took pills that looked exactly like Enkaid tablets but contained inert ingredients. In Seattle, Linda Stefan read off her computer screen the serial number of a bottle of medication available at Washington Hospital Center. Stefan did not know whether it contained Enkaid or a placebo. The research nurses at Washington Hospital Center had no idea. Albert Murphy did not know. For emergencies, a key to the drug codes was listed in a blue binder, locked in a special cabinet in Seattle. But the drug codes were kept separate from the patient codes. At Washington Hospital Center the placebo or active drug status for each patient was sealed into a double envelope that also was immediately available for emergency use. (In a test drill, Diane Law produced a sealed assignment envelope in six minutes. Knowing whether a patient's drug was a placebo proved of critical importance during the pilot study for CAST when a child swallowed several capsules.)

What happened to Albert Murphy now was going to be important, rising beyond the customary value placed on a precious human life. At the end of the CAST trial, the results might depend on a difference as small as 20 individuals. With approximately one half of the nation's physicians already treating premature beats, any definitive result ought to have far-reaching effects on medical practice. If, as the investigators hoped, CAST demonstrated that antiarrhythmic drugs saved lives, then literally hundreds of thousands of new patients might potentially be treated. If the anticipated benefits failed to materialize, it would mean that hundreds of thousands of new patients were taking expensive and conceivably dangerous drugs for no useful purpose. The third alternative—that the drugs might prove harmful—was not part of CAST at the time Albert Murphy was enrolled. The statistical tests were designed only to identify the possibility of benefit or inform the investigators when the chances of success were too remote to continue.

CAST was going to be expensive: it would cost more than $40 million. It would involve 300 researchers, 27 sites, and take 5 years to complete. It would sometimes be tedious, requiring the research nurses to screen more than 30 patients for every one admitted to the study, and to fill out endless forms. However, it would be hard to define a medical research project more likely to produce important findings, no matter how the results turned out.

Chapter 19

A SIGNIFICANT DIFFERENCE

ONE OF THE most carefully guarded secrets of the Cardiac Arrhythmia Suppression Trial was the ongoing results. To protect the double-blind character of the trial, they were concealed from CAST Steering Committee Chairman Thomas Bigger, the Columbia University professor who had been a consultant for 3M, Boehringer Ingelheim and Bristol-Myers. The running totals were also not available to the vice chairman, Raymond L. Woosley, the Vanderbilt University professor and FDA advisory committee member who also had worked with most of the major drug companies. CAST had an independent Data Safety and Monitoring Board that met twice a year to assess the progress of the trial. But at its first meeting, the board decided to enter fully into the spirit of the double-blind trial—where neither the investigator nor the patient knows which is active medication and which a placebo. While the board had the duty of monitoring the ongoing results, it had voted to blind itself to the identity of the placebo and treatment groups. That decision was intended to render the board impartial. In making recommendations about the conduct of CAST, it would not know whether it was helping or hindering the proof of the arrhythmia suppression hypothesis. For example, the board learned the number of deaths in two blinded categories, simply labeled Group X and Group Y. Which group was getting the drug remained a secret.

Four months after Albert Murphy was enrolled in CAST, these closely held numbers were totaled in preparation for a meeting of the safety board. Without identifying which was active treatment and which was placebo, the results were:

Confidential CAST Results

	Group	
	X	Y
Sudden death*	3	19
Total patients	576	571

Status on Sept. 1, 1988

Until CAST reached its scheduled conclusion in 1992, the only reason for unblinding the data would be to consider calling an emergency halt to the trial. This could occur under two scenarios. The lifesaving properties of antiarrhythmic drugs might prove so impressive that it would be unethical to allow the placebo patients to continue without the medication. Several NIH clinical trials had been halted on this logic. Or the drugs might prove so dangerous that it was unsafe to continue the trial. This also had occurred in previous studies. Already the results were interesting. CAST had been designed under the hypothesis that antiarrhythmic drugs might reduce deaths by 30 percent. If "Group X" was getting the drugs, they appeared to be reducing mortality by a phenomenal 80 percent. The numbers so far included only 5 percent of the deaths expected to occur over the five-year course of the trial. If the trend continued, however, the disparity was large enough to raise the question of an emergency halt. While the Data Safety and Monitoring Board could express an opinion, it was a purely advisory body. Under the CAST protocol, a premature halt to the trial was a matter for the project officer. His name was Lawrence M. Friedman.

Friedman was the son of two New York City public school teachers. He had been among the flood of bright young doctors who met their military obligation during the Vietnam era with a research fellowship at the National Institutes of Health. After finishing his residency at Hartford Hospital in Connecticut in 1972 he was assigned to the National Heart, Lung, and Blood Institute. Friedman went immediately to work on the first randomized clinical trial that the heart institute had ever sponsored, the Coronary Drug Project.

With hundreds, or even thousands, of participants, a randomized clinical trial required a coordinated national effort often lasting a decade. It meant getting scores of fiercely independent doctors to

---

*This included cardiac arrests where the patients were resuscitated.

work together as a team. Dozens of hospitals were involved in each project. Each had its own paperwork, funding procedures and independent review boards. Thus the clinical trial was a new kind of research that produced a new kind of knowledge and required managers with an unusual combination of skills. It required patience and a team player, someone with medical knowledge, mathematical aptitude and managerial ability. Helping manage a large clinical trial was a brand new job in medicine, and it suited Lawrence Friedman so perfectly that he never did anything else.

He liked the complex questions that involved both advanced mathematics and medicine. He proved able to manage multimillion dollar research budgets. Most of all, the quiet and soft-spoken Friedman turned out to be a skillful consensus manager. At the National Heart, Lung, and Blood Institute, the buck rarely stops anywhere. It is referred to another committee.

Thus, it was under Friedman's patient husbandry, and through an endless sequence of committees, that CAST was first conceived, developed into a complete plan, and came to have an independent life of its own. When asked, Friedman did not remember who first suggested CAST, nor could he name any individual who had forcefully promoted it. It evolved from a workshop on sudden death held back in the late 1970s. It was endorsed by the advisory committee for the Division of Epidemiology and Clinical Applications, where Friedman worked. The proposal went up to the director's office, who referred it to his Advisory Council of prominent doctors. That led to a three-year pilot study, which was designed by another committee with several subcommittees.

Only one serious controversy rippled through this smooth flow of committee work, and that involved drug selection. Although Friedman was project officer, he did not choose which drugs would be tested. That was a question for the drug selection subcommittee, chaired by Raymond Woosley of Vanderbilt. One major faction wanted to include one of the drugs that most doctors used and trusted: quinidine or procainamide. This would make the results of the trial immediately applicable to existing clinical practice. Others advocated specific drugs. Bigger, who chaired the steering committee, wanted an antidepressant drug whose antiarrhythmic properties had been tested in his own lab, imipramine. Craig Pratt of Baylor University favored Ethmozine—the drug that Bernard Lown had brought back from the Soviet Union and Joel Morganroth had initially tested years before. Pratt was then working with DuPont on Ethmozine, on which development had resumed after a long hiatus.

Numerous committee members had experience with Tambocor and Enkaid. In the end the committee chose the new drugs that committee members had been recently testing rather than the established drugs that most doctors already knew. Bigger got imipramine. Pratt won approval for Ethmozine. Tambocor and Enkaid were easy consensus choices.

Before the main trial began, a pilot study was conducted to demonstrate that the four drugs selected could safely and effectively suppress premature beats under the demanding conditions of a randomized clinical trial. Like almost all clinical trials, the pilot study provided a few surprises. Bigger's drug, imipramine, proved something of a fiasco. It had the lowest rate of effectiveness (59 percent) and the highest rate of intolerable side effects (18 percent). Ethmozine was notably less effective than Enkaid and Tambocor but was well tolerated by most patients and remained a second-choice drug. In the pilot study, as in early clinical testing, Tambocor and Enkaid proved remarkably effective in suppressing PVCs and were well tolerated by patients. Joel Morganroth had joined the study as a principal investigator for the site in Philadelphia. So enthusiastic was Morganroth during this period that he wrote an editorial in the *Journal of the American College of Cardiology* titled, "Have We Reached Antiarrhythmic Nirvana?"

When the Data Safety and Monitoring Board gathered in Washington, D.C., in September of 1988, it learned of the difference in deaths occurring in Group X and Group Y. The board was chaired by a cardiologist named J. David Bristow from the Oregon Health Sciences University and included members from Harvard, Duke, Georgetown, the Universities of Wisconsin and Colorado. Thomas Bigger, as chairman of the overall trial, attended unless results were being discussed. Although it was only the second meeting of the board, the same group had monitored the pilot study and had worked together for years. As project officer, Friedman attended ex officio.

The most important task before the board that September was to set guidelines for halting the trial for safety reasons. Was 3 versus 19 sudden deaths an expected eddy in the river of data, or did it signal a flow of events already veering off on an entirely unexpected course?

That was in part a mathematical question, and to outline their choices the committee had available the CAST biostatistician, Alfred Hallstrom of the University of Washington in Seattle. He also managed the CAST Coordinating Center, and was responsible for the security, accuracy, and integrity of the data. Hallstrom was a numbers doctor, not a medical doctor, with a Ph.D. in mathematics from Brown University. He knew that before the safety board could define the conditions for halting the trial prematurely, it first had to agree on a definition of success.

While CAST investigators had already articulated a clear hypothesis—suppressing premature beats prevents sudden death—they were still lacking a specific definition of its proof. Such definitions are accepted as convincing only when they are specified far in advance of the results. They are normally calculated in terms of probability that the results achieved were just a nasty trick played by the freak of chance. The strictest customary standard allows only 1 chance in 100 that the results were a statistical fluke; the most lenient typically allows 5 chances, or a probability of .05. Like any standard, the more lenient the test, the easier it is to pass it.

CAST chairman Thomas Bigger, representing the 198 doctors who were CAST investigators, proposed the more lenient .05 standard. Then he recommended an additional specification to make it more lenient still. The investigators wanted to declare that the trial only sought to ascertain benefit. That meant Bigger believed the possibility of harm was so remote that it was not necessary to plan to detect it. In traffic engineering, this is the equivalent of purchasing half the normal number of traffic signs for a stretch of highway because you are convinced the cars will only move in one direction. This was Thomas Bigger's proposal.

That was the proposed definition of proof; the question of when to stop the trial early still remained open. The board had tentatively accepted a plan that also precluded the possibility of harm. The approach was called stochastic curtailment, and it was another game of chance. The trial would halt when the chances of proving benefit were too remote. Given the results at any particular point, Hallstrom could calculate the chances of proving the anticipated benefit. It was like a baseball game that allowed the home team to call off the game if it fell hopelessly behind.

While the CAST investigators were playing an honest game—and a difficult one—they did write the rules in their own favor. They were willing to settle for the smallest apparent benefit meeting commonly accepted scientific standards. And they wanted a structure that eliminated the possibility of ever proving that the drugs were harmful, even by accident. If the drugs were in fact harmful, convincing proof of this could not occur because the trial would be halted when the chances of proving benefit had become too remote. This was what Bigger and the CAST investigators wanted.

However, the safety board did not agree. What happened next was a kind of statistical sleight of hand. The board allowed the investigators to assume the trial was conducted only to prove benefit, but it insisted on a higher standard of proof. Instead of allowing 5 chances in 100 of a fluke result, it insisted on results definitive enough to allow only 2.5 chances. In the traffic analogy, the board would allow the investigators to order only enough traffic signs for one-way traffic, but they reduced the stretch of highway involved by 50 percent. If perchance the traffic did flow both ways, there would still be enough traffic signs for that stretch of highway. In the silken politics of medical consensus, the safety board had said "no" to the investigators so smoothly they could hardly tell. By an equally subtle maneuver, the safety board also established a specific advisory boundary for harm. Since the board had voted to remain ignorant of the identities of the treatment and placebo groups, both treatment and harm would, of necessity, be tested against the same boundary.

The safety board membership included David DeMets of the University of Wisconsin, a world-class statistician who had helped devise the formulas used to establish the advisory boundaries. Just as they adopted them at the September 1988 meeting DeMets noted that with 3 versus 19 sudden deaths, they must already be very close to the boundary. Those in Group Y were six times more likely to experience a cardiac arrest than those in Group X. The effect of these three antiarrhythmic drugs was already striking.

Lawrence Friedman, the project officer, asked, "Does it matter which way the trend is going?" He wanted to know if the safety board would stop the trial now if they knew treatment was beneficial. Or would knowing treatment might be harmful result in a different decision? The group decided unanimously that either way, they wanted to continue the trial. The differences were large but the absolute number of deaths was small.

Meanwhile, the death watch continued. On Thursday night of each week, the central computer at the Seattle Coordinating Center would automatically telephone the personal computers at each of the 27 sites and retrieve all the data collected and entered during the week. On Friday Hallstrom's programming staff would verify and test the data for accuracy and then update the center's master file of results. The following Monday a new value for deaths in Group X and Group

Y would be calculated. On Monday or Tuesday of each week Hallstrom would get the results. It was just a three-line report that showed deaths in Group X, in Group Y, and the likelihood the result had occurred by chance. Hallstrom said he never looked particularly for the report, and couldn't remember which day of the week it came. But with each passing week the number of deaths in Group X and Group Y slowly increased.

Among the CAST leadership, only Hallstrom knew which group was taking the active drug. He bore his secret knowledge comfortably; he was a plain-spoken mathematician and not prone to dramatic flourish. For a decade he had been the biostatistician for Medic-1, the pioneering emergency ambulance service in Seattle. Although he had helped collect and interpret the data about the dramatic resuscitation of cardiac arrest victims, he had never once gone out on an ambulance to observe what happened. ("It wouldn't have been productive," he said later.)

In late October 1988, Albert Murphy returned to Washington Hospital Center for his first follow-up visit. The visit had several purposes. He sat down for a interview with Diane Law, the nurse who had recruited him into the study. She went down a list of adverse effects. Did he ever feel dizzy? Nauseated? And so forth. Murphy had no adverse effects. Law also took his EKG, where she saw abnormal Q waves, the telltale electrical evidence of a prior heart attack. He also filled out a questionnaire about the overall quality of his life. The CAST investigators hoped that even if the medication did not prevent sudden death, they might still emerge with evidence that antiarrhythmic drugs improved patients' quality of life.

Murphy had also brought in his medication bottles, which had originally contained a four-month supply. Diane Law shook out the few pills remaining and made a count. He had taken 400 pills, during a period in which he should have taken 405 pills. This was 99 percent compliance, superior to the CAST average, which was about 80 percent. For a drug taken for a condition with few overt symptoms, even 80 percent is an excellent compliance rate. For the CAST investigators to demonstrate that the lives saved resulted from the medication, they needed proof that the patients, in fact, took the drugs. This was not always the case. In the heart institute's trial of the cholesterol-lowering drug Questran, it proved such an unpleasant drug that one third of the doses were never taken. As a result minimal cholesterol lowering and disappointing results were achieved.

Diane Law had another reason for checking Albert Murphy's medication. From the nearly empty bottle she took one of his pills. She wrapped it in cotton, sealed it in a plastic bag, and attached a sticker with Murphy's ID number, 0089-27-3-AMUR. During the month of October 1988, the same procedure was followed for every patient who came in for a follow-up visit. By month's end, Washington Hospital Center had 32 plastic bags with sample tablets. This was repeated at all 27 CAST sites. All the envelopes—almost 400 from the whole study—were sent to the Seattle Coordinating Center.

When all the envelopes were collected they were given to Surena Khatir, an Iranian-born data technician who worked at the center and was known for his meticulous work. He took all the pills into a room, along with a register of patient ID numbers. Then, one by one, he broke the pills in half. While identical from the outside, the placebos and the active drugs had different-color fillings. This was a closely guarded CAST secret; the staff was greatly concerned when a cooperating physician called to say he had taken it upon himself to reduce the dose for an elderly patient by one-half tablet. They worried that if he did this again he might happen to observe the different-color fillings, and the double-blind character of the trial would be broken. When Surena Khatir finished with the pills, his results were checked against the master register. There were no mistakes. In a trial that was already trending toward a definitive result, it was essential to be confident that those believed to be taking the active drug were actually doing so. With thousands of coded bottles scattered around the world, a medication foulup was possible.

As in any careful counting exercise, unforeseen events invariably arose. The center staff had to decide on the gender of a participant with a sex-change operation. (A male, they decided.) Another had a heart transplant. (He was censored, or removed from the study, on the date he had a new heart.) One patient suffered a cardiac arrest before taking a single dose of the study medication—although he had been previously taking the active drug to establish its effectiveness. The patient was resuscitated. Because technically he had entered the treatment group, the cardiac arrest was counted in the official results.

Just two weeks after the September meeting where the Data Safety and Monitoring Board set advisory boundaries for halting CAST, the Steering Committee gathered in Albuquerque. Everybody who worked on CAST was a member of the Steering Committee, and was invited to the twice-yearly meetings near one of the study sites. It was a fringe benefit, especially for the 84 research nurses who worked full-time on CAST. (Other meetings would be held at Banff, the scenic park in the Canadian Rockies near the Alberta site, and at Newport, Rhode Island.)

The participants heard a progress report. In the intervening weeks the number of participants and deaths had continued to increase. The Steering Committee, however, heard only the gross totals: 1,563 patients recruited, 91 had died, or 6 percent. There was not the slightest hint about the large difference between Group X and Group Y. Forty-one of these deaths had occurred during the two-week period while the effectiveness of the drug was being established, and therefore did not count toward proving or disproving the arrhythmia suppression hypothesis. The investigators also reported that doctors—responding to the drug marketing barrage—were increasingly insistent that their patients get antiarrhythmic drugs and refused to allow patients to participate in the trial. Morrison Hodges of the University of Minnesota told the committee that private physicians increasingly feared malpractice lawsuits if they didn't use antiarrhythmic drugs in their patients.

Meanwhile, week by week, Al Hallstrom got the printout with the totals for Group X and Group Y. In absolute size, the numbers got steadily larger as the total deaths mounted. However, the gap between the two groups did not diminish; there was no random change in direction. By January 1989, three months remained before the safety board's next scheduled official review of the data. Hallstrom decided he could not wait.

Chapter 20

NO LONGER BLIND

IN JANUARY 1989, CAST project officer Lawrence Friedman was attending a workshop on cost-benefit analysis in clinical trials. For a doctor who spent his career managing experiments that cost $10 million to $150 million each, the subject was a natural. These techniques might show that clinical trials could bring savings in medical care spending that far exceeded their substantial cost. The workshop was being held on the NIH campus in Bethesda, Maryland. During a break, Friedman ran into Al Hallstrom, who had come from the Seattle CAST Coordinating Center to attend the same meeting. Quietly, Hallstrom took Friedman aside.

"We've got some problems," Hallstrom said. Until then Friedman had been like the other board members, blinded to whether the emerging trend signaled accumulating benefit or increasing harm. Now Hallstrom revealed to Friedman that the results showed that the antiarrhythmic drugs were killing patients. He told Friedman the trend toward excess deaths among patients on the active drug had not reversed as he had expected. "We weren't seeing what you would expect," he said. "If the sicker people had died off in one group, they still should be available to die in the other group, and it ought to start to switch." This had not happened.

Hallstrom showed Friedman the totals, broken down by drug. "Should we be concerned?" he asked. Friedman wanted to take a closer look. As the two men sat down together, Friedman came up with thirty different ways to analyze the data for clues about what might be going on. Neither man wanted to halt a $40 million experiment in which both had invested years of their lives only to discover they had overlooked some obvious factor.

The numbers already told one story. The results for two drugs—Tambocor and Enkaid—were notably different than for the third, Ethmozine. The trend toward harm was confined to Tambocor and

Enkaid. The significance of even this obvious difference was difficult to determine because Ethmozine was a second-choice drug, and taken by far fewer patients. It was used if Tambocor and Enkaid failed to suppress premature beats, and in patients with heart failure, where it was feared the other two drugs might further depress already-inadequate cardiac output. Therefore Ethmozine was being given to a different patient population—if anything, a slightly sicker population at greater risk of dying. While the Ethmozine numbers were small, they pointed toward benefit.

Hallstrom thought the bottom-line death totals had another peculiar feature. The placebo group had fewer deaths than expected among typical survivors of a recent heart attack. In other studies, including the pilot for CAST, the first-year mortality was approximately 10 percent. Only 4 percent of the placebo group had died over about nine months on placebo. This made Hallstrom suspicious. The random assignment of patients to a control and treatment group is intended to create two patient populations that are similar. Through some fluke could a disproportionate number of healthier patients have ended up in the placebo group?

Friedman and Hallstrom discussed two ways to answer that question. The CAST central computer files contained an immense collection of medical data about the participants. By combing through the data they might uncover any significant differences between the two patient groups. Hallstrom had another idea he thought might save the trial. Under the guise of needing to check out medication that had mysteriously "degraded," they could recall all the bottles and secretly switch the Tambocor and Enkaid patients to a placebo. The patients would be taken off a potentially harmful medication. Also, with both groups on placebo, it would be possible to observe whether a difference in death rates continued, or the results became similar. Friedman was uncertain about the second plan.

Hallstrom returned to Seattle to analyze the data at length, looking for some other factor that might explain the difference. Until this analysis was complete, the two men decided not to share the troubling results with anyone in the chain of command of CAST or at the National Heart, Lung, and Blood Institute. However, unless Hallstrom turned up some complicating factor, the results for Tambocor and Enkaid seemed definitive. When given to heart attack survivors, more than twice as many died on the active drug, compared with a placebo. The most dramatic differences occurred in the very event the drug was intended to prevent—sudden death or cardiac arrest. Compared with a placebo, those on the active drug were three times more likely to have their heart abruptly stop beating. Dozens of additional deaths had occurred while an effective dose was being established, before the trial death count officially commenced. It had taken fourteen years after Tambocor was given to the first patients in testing to make this discovery. Hallstrom and Friedman were still not certain the finding was valid.

Hallstrom analyzed the Tambocor and Enkaid data exhaustively. He had 60 different measures with which he could compare those on placebo (755 patients) with those on an active drug (772 patients).* Such was the power of randomization that the similarity between groups was nothing less than remarkable. Here are some examples:

	Placebo Group	Treatment Group
	(in percent)	
Smokers	40.1	39.5
No chest pains	80.7	81.4
Bypass surgery	18.9	17.7
Prev. cardiac arrest	3.0	2.4
Male sex	82.5	81.4
Took 4 other drugs	20.8	19.7
Ejection fraction	38.1	38.7
Age (average yrs.)	61.0	60.8
Initial PVCs per hour	132.6	131.7

Perhaps the most sensitive single indicator was a measure of damage to the heart, the ejection fraction. With each contraction, a normal heart ejects at least 55 percent of the blood in the main pumping chamber, the left ventricle. If enough heart muscle cells are destroyed in a heart attack, the ejection fraction falls. It is also a major predictor of survival. When Hallstrom compared the two groups, they contained roughly equal numbers of the high-risk patients—those with an ejection fraction below 30 percent. When analyzed as separate groups, the adverse effects of the drug were compelling among both those with more and less severely damaged hearts. An unexpectedly healthy placebo group did not explain the difference in the test results.

*For more detail on results see the chapter notes.

As Hallstrom examined the records of those who died and those who survived, no telltale patterns emerged to suggest some other unique factor to explain the deaths. He looked at dose. He looked for signs of interaction with other medications. He wondered whether it was safer to wait until several months after the heart attack to start the drug. He could define a subgroup of patients at high risk—for example, those beginning to experience heart failure from dangerously low cardiac output. He could focus on seemingly low-risk patients—those without chest pains, with low cholesterol, and without high blood pressure. The death rates varied among these groups, depending on their underlying health status. But in each analysis the death rate was higher among those taking the active drug compared with placebo.

In mid-February Hallstrom and Friedman discussed by telephone the compelling results of Hallstrom's analysis. Both men now knew there was no escaping the conclusion that the CAST was providing hundreds of patients with medication that might kill them. They also realized they could keep the facts to themselves no longer. Friedman notified his boss, William Harlan, director of the Division of Epidemiology and Clinical Applications. Harlan quickly passed on word to Claude Lenfant, director of the National Heart, Lung, and Blood Institute. Lenfant didn't tell them what to do, but he emphasized that the situation required decisive action. What he didn't want was an endless debate. Friedman and Hallstrom also telephoned J. David Bristow, chairman of the CAST Data Safety and Monitoring Board. They informed him of the results, and Hallstrom dispatched a packet of charts and tables displaying the results of his data analysis. Bristow decided the material should be shared with the entire board without waiting for the regular April meeting. A conference call was set for March 2.

Hallstrom prepared a package for each member of the Data Safety and Monitoring Board. The first element was 50 pages of charts and tables. In accord with the board's policy to remain "blinded," the treatment and placebo groups were not identified. The results were labeled Group X and Group Y. When arrayed graphically to plot deaths over time, one trend was immediately visible. Bigger, Woosley and the other doctors who had helped develop Tambocor and Enkaid assumed that any adverse effects of the drug would appear within the first two weeks of starting the drug. As the lines plotting survival stretched across Hallstrom's chart, the opposite conclusion was immediately apparent. The longer the trial continued, the greater contrast in deaths between the two groups.

In a separate, sealed envelope, marked "DO NOT OPEN," Hallstrom had enclosed the codes identifying X as placebo and Y as treatment. The sealed packet also included the results by specific drug. In a cover letter, Hallstrom warned the board members not to leave the materials lying around. But he remained noncommittal about the results.

"It appears that there is a reasonable likelihood that we may cross one of the boundaries discussed at the last meeting by the time of our next meeting," Hallstrom told them. The reason for providing the material early, he explained, was the "high likelihood" that the board would recommend changes in CAST at its April meeting. But without opening the sealed envelope, the recipient could not know whether CAST had produced a larger than anticipated benefit or a major hazard to life.

Fifteen persons joined in the conference call. Seven members of the Data Safety and Monitoring Board were joined by Friedman and by three associates at the National Heart, Lung, and Blood Institute who helped him coordinate CAST. Hallstrom participated, along with his three most senior colleagues at the Seattle Coordinating Center. Despite the sealed envelopes, there was little suspense about the results. By the time that Bristow, the chairman, started the meeting, everyone knew the data indicated harm.

As the discussion proceeded, few doubted the results were valid. However, the harmful effects appeared to be restricted to Tambocor and Enkaid. If one included in the overall totals the seemingly more favorable results for Ethomizine, the trial was still inconclusive in formal statistical terms. (Officially, they were not testing individual drugs but the effect of suppressing premature beats.) Therefore, one choice was to halt the trial, announcing only that the treatment was unlikely to prove beneficial. One participant said this would actually be a loss for drug therapy. They would have failed to prove the expected benefit. Another participant—perhaps more sensitive to the power of drug company marketing—thought the opposite would occur. Unless the drugs were proven harmful, many physicians would still prescribe them. This had happened when the negative but inconclusive results for Mexitil in the IMPACT trial seemed to have generated more questions about the trial than about the safety of the drug. Thus, the board had to grapple with conflicting moral obligations. If the members focused on their responsibility to the study participants, they ought to stop as soon as possible. The only serious future prospect was of observing increased harm. However, to meet the needs of a greater society—and protect the safety of the hundreds of thousands of patients now taking these drugs—a definitive result was essential.

A second thread also ran through the conversation. The safety board had worked together since the beginning of the pilot study in 1983. Why did Tambocor and Enkaid look so safe in the pilot study, and so lethal in CAST? Nobody had an answer.

The safety board also had to address a sensitive question of medical politics. They had excluded one key figure from the meeting—J. Thomas Bigger, Jr., chairman of the Steering Committee and a prominent proponent of the suppression hypothesis. He would normally attend their April meeting in a few weeks. Bigger was also a principal investigator for the Columbia University site in New York City; knowing the results would breach the double-blind design and place him in a difficult ethical position as a physician responsible for dozens of patients. The board decided to tell him nothing of the results. They agreed to start the April meeting one day early—on a Sunday afternoon in Seattle—without informing Bigger. By the time he arrived as scheduled on Monday, they expected to have reached a firm recommendation on the fate of the Cardiac Arrhythmia Suppression Trial.

To prepare for the April meeting, Hallstrom did some further double-checking. The board wanted the Seattle Coordinating Center to verify the assignment to treatment and placebo for the entire CAST population. Hallstrom also ordered a procedure called a vital status sweep. Sometimes the CAST staff at a hospital site would not learn of a patient death until they attempted to schedule the next four-month follow-up visit and discovered that the participant had died. Current status was determined through a telephone check of all the patients. Because conclusions of great importance were going to be drawn from relatively small numbers, even a small difference mattered.

The Data Safety and Monitoring Board met in Al Hallstrom's office on Sunday, April 17. The Coordinating Center occupied half the third floor of an office building on 45th Street Northwest, a main thoroughfare that leads past the gates of the nearby University of Washington campus. It was a utilitarian office. Four worktables were pulled together to form a large conference table, surrounded by plain wooden chairs. In Seattle, a city of splendid views of the water, a row of windows overlooked only passing traffic on 45th Street. J. David Bristow, the chairman, presided. Lawrence Friedman was joined by William Harlan, his boss at the National Heart, Lung, and Blood Institute.

In a summary similar to the closing arguments of a courtroom trial, Al Hallstrom reviewed the rules that the board had adopted to monitor CAST and outlined the latest results. When the treatment group was compared with the placebo group, the evidence convincingly showed the drugs were harmful. Members of the treatment group were twice as likely to experience cardiac arrest or sudden death as those in the placebo group. The chances were much less than 1 in 100 that these results could have occurred by chance. Additional patient deaths occurred while establishing that the drugs suppressed premature beats, and these deaths were not counted in the results. The board had established an advisory boundary for harm at 0.025, or 2.5 chances in 100 that the results occurred by chance. Current results showed the probability of a statistical fluke was from 1 to 2 in 1,000. Hallstrom had conducted statistical studies to see if other differences between patients could explain the excess deaths in the treatment group. They did not.

Amidst this uniformly compelling mass of evidence of harm were only a few countervailing trends. The harmful effects seemed to be confined to Tambocor and Enkaid. In fact, the Ethmozine results looked somewhat promising but only a small fraction of the expected number of total deaths had occurred. Also, by stochastic curtailment—the technique to determine the chances of success—they were technically not out of the ball game. The trial was still ongoing. If the results suddenly changed to the predicted benefit, the trial still had nearly a 50 percent chance of succeeding. Finally, a large share of the patient deaths had occurred among those with not a single heart attack but two or more. If patients with two or more heart attacks were removed from consideration, the drugs did not look so dangerous. However, when a clinical trial produces a surprising finding, it is usually possible to find the strongest effects in one or two subgroups. The statisticians present knew that these were likely a chance effect and not a valid finding.

While few questioned that the evidence unmistakably showed harm, opinion was not immediately unanimous that the trial should be halted. Some asked whether the evidence was definitive enough to convince the medical community. As Friedman described the concern, "Will we have sacrificed everyone in the trial to no benefit if people aren't convinced?" Another board member put it more bluntly. "The drug companies might try to argue against the finality of the results." The opposing view was simple: the board's responsibility to protect CAST patients outweighed the need to convince the medical community at large.

The board completed its discussion Sunday night, postponing a decision until the next morning. Bristow outlined three options: They could continue the trial seeking a more definitive result. Bristow said he detected no support for this position. They could stop the trial altogether. But Bristow noted they would leave unanswered the question whether Ethmozine was beneficial. In light of the promising but inconclusive results with Ethmozine, they also would not have settled the arrhythmia suppression hypothesis. Finally, Bristow said, they could continue the trial with Ethmozine, but extend the protocol to include deaths occurring during the first two weeks testing for effective suppression. The chairman, it was clear, wanted to continue the trial with Ethmozine. But the board appeared satisfied with the evidence that Tambocor and Enkaid were harmful in these patients.

The Data Safety and Monitoring Board met again the following morning at 7 A.M. They were ready to decide. While some members still worried that the results were not definitive enough to change existing medical practice, no member wanted to retain Tambocor and Enkaid. Everyone wanted to continue with Ethmozine. Only one new element emerged. The original purpose in having three drugs was to prove the truth that suppressing premature beats prevented cardiac arrest and sudden death. The CAST investigators did not want to test any particular company's product. Now they were faced with the possibility of spending millions of dollars of the taxpayers' money to do just that, to demonstrate the benefit of DuPont's drug, Ethmozine. To avoid this situation, the safety board proposed adding another drug to CAST.

For the Monday session, the board had summoned three men: Thomas Bigger, the CAST Steering Committee chairman, Raymond Woosley vice chairman, and a third committee member, George Wyse, a cardiologist from Alberta, Canada. As the three doctors filed into the session in Al Hallstrom's office, none knew anything about the results. Thomas Bigger and Raymond Woosley had spent years helping to develop and promote antiarrhythmic drugs. Woosley had helped persuade Bristol-Myers that Enkaid was a viable drug. He encouraged 3M to bring Tambocor to market. Woosley and Bigger had reassured 3M that the surprising cardiac arrests that had halted clinical testing were a problem of excessive dose. When the troubling results of Mexitil came before the FDA advisory committee, Bigger represented

the manufacturer and Woosley sat on the committee; both dismissed
the adverse results. As marquee professors, the two men had starred
at 3M's symposium in Bermuda, and Bristol-Myers' symposium in
Scottsdale. They had been so confident of the value of these antiarrhythmic drugs that they proposed a clinical trial designed only to
establish benefits, providing no data on their potential danger. On
this Monday morning in April these men were going to learn that
the gold standard of medical evidence—results from a randomized
clinical trial—showed they had been terribly wrong.

When he heard, Thomas Bigger turned ashen white. To some observers, Raymond Woosley looked almost relieved to know the answer. But as Woosley remembered it, he was simply shocked. The
third senior investigator summoned for the meeting, Wyse, was
mainly worried about his patients. Although it happens every day in
modern medicine, the moment a doctor realizes he has harmed a
patient is still terrible. However, the superstars of medicine do not
become paralyzed and wring their hands even when faced with a
disaster. They were soon back at work with the committee, briskly
planning what was going to happen next.

There was plenty of work to be done. CAST needed a new protocol.
They had to figure out how to communicate the results to the other
312 doctors, nurses and other researchers who had worked on the
trial. Hundreds of CAST patients had to be taken off Tambocor and
Enkaid immediately.

The meeting was over by 9:45 A.M. As the group filed out of Al
Hallstrom's office in Seattle, it was not immediately clear how many
of them understood the magnitude of events that were going to
happen next. The world at large was going to learn that hundreds
of thousands of people were taking drugs that might cause them to
drop dead at any moment. Someone, presumably, was going to ask
how such drugs ever got approved and prescribed for so many
people.

Chapter 21

"YOU ARE IMMORAL"

ON THE FRIDAY after the decision to stop CAST for Tambocor and Enkaid, Steering Committee vice chairman Raymond Woosley was on the podium at a medical meeting in Philadelphia. He was describing CAST to a group of cardiologists, and outlining how it was testing the benefits of suppressing premature beats. Since no announcement had yet been made, he could not reveal that the treatment had proved harmful. However, he did focus on the major innovation in CAST—the two-week tryout to verify that an active drug effectively suppressed the premature beats. In the question and answer period after Woosley's talk, one doctor rose to speak. He was plainly angry.

"You are immoral!" he cried. "You are immoral!" His concern was that once the investigators had established that the drug was effective, it was improper to deny this benefit to the one half of the patients randomized to the placebo. The angry doctor was not unique. More than half of America's doctors were treating premature beats, believing they were helping their patients. On that Friday in April, Woosley knew that thousands of doctors were about to learn that they had been killing their patients without meaning to. Already, the complicated machinery to deliver this unhappy message had been set in motion.

Although evidence of the lethal effects of Tambocor and Enkaid had been slowly accumulating for six months, once the evidence was definitive the National Heart, Lung, and Blood Institute did not delay even one day before taking the CAST patients off these two drugs. On Tuesday, the Coordinating Center had sent all sites by electronic mail a message marked "CONFIDENTIAL."

"All patients on CAST-ENC and CAST-FLEC blinded therapy should have their drug therapy discontinued. A list is enclosed of these patients at your center, and we recommend that you contact them (and their private physicians) by telephone." However, the actual results of the trial remained closely held. The message said only, "it is unlikely benefit could be demonstrated over the projected duration of the trial and likely that these drugs are harmful." The message promised details later, and said the Ethmozine arm of the trial would continue. Word of this action, however, did not leak out beyond CAST.

From the minute he arrived back in Washington on Tuesday, the man in the hot seat was Lawrence Friedman, the CAST project officer. He had already informed his boss, William Harlan, and the director of the National Heart, Lung, and Blood Institute, Claude Lenfant.

Lenfant, the institute director, set up a crisis management team. The coordinator was Peter Frommer, the deputy director. Frommer had been a senior institute official for more than two decades and was already deputy director when Lenfant was named to head the institute. A third member of the team was Michael White, associate director for Education, Prevention and Control, the institute's senior public information officer.

It was Wednesday, April 19, when Frommer became involved, and the first thing he wanted was a careful look at all the data. It was his penchant to review situations from a detached perspective, looking for factors that might have been overlooked. Friedman gave him the fat package of graphs and tables that had been prepared for the Data Safety and Monitoring Board, and hurried away to make the first round of notifications of outside agencies.

Friedman called Robert Temple, director of the Office of Drug Evaluation I, at the FDA. Friedman gave him only the barest outline of the facts. They agreed to meet Thursday to go over the data. By fax, he sent letters to the two drug companies, 3M and Bristol-Myers.

After saying the trial had been halted, Friedman's letter to 3M said, "This action was taken because of the extremely low likelihood that Tambocor could be shown to be beneficial and the strong possibility that it is harmful in this patient population."

However, the companies initially got no further details. "We realize your interest in this and your need to learn more," Friedman wrote. "We would be pleased to share our results with you. A manuscript, which is being prepared for publication, will contain the data upon which this decision was based."

At this early moment, Friedman may have underestimated how quickly the events he had set in motion were going to unfold. Research doctors prefer to release important discoveries through medical journal reports. Press conferences are suspect, and have an aura of grandstanding before a less sophisticated audience. In fact, many journals reject articles about discoveries that have been previously publicized. It was the nation's doctors that needed to be convinced, and Friedman knew the way to do that was through providing compelling detail in a medical journal article. He telephoned Arnold Relman, the editor-in-chief of the *New England Journal of Medicine*, to see how fast the journal might publish the CAST results. Even the most accelerated schedule would not allow publication for several months. However, Friedman arranged to expedite the manuscript, and Relman granted him an exemption to the rule that the journal would not consider previously publicized material. Because CAST had sites in Sweden and Canada, Friedman also had to notify those nations' agencies that regulated drug safety. The word on CAST was now rapidly flowing out.

By the time that Friedman had finished his round of telephone calls, Deputy Director Peter Frommer had finished his independent review of the CAST data. He was the first outsider to see the information. If one uncertainty had haunted the Data Safety and Monitoring Board, it was whether the medical community would find the data convincing. The packet of charts and graphs was intended for internal use and not designed for easy reading, even by experienced outsiders. After he examined the material, page by page, Frommer was a believer. "It was very persuasive data," he said.

The next stop was the FDA. Friedman and Frommer went over to the FDA headquarters in Rockville to brief Robert Temple and Raymond Lipicky, director of Cardio-Renal Drugs. These two drug experts could not be expected to accept, without pointed questions, evidence that reflected so directly on the wisdom of their previous decisions. After Friedman presented the data, the two men were readily convinced of the validity of the CAST findings.

At that point the FDA officials had three options available. They could press the manufacturers to withdraw the drug. They could change the labeling to restrict the drugs to a smaller patient population. Or they could do very little, except perhaps include a summary of the trial results on the drug labeling. When a World Health Organization clinical trial of the cholesterol-lowering drug Atromid showed a 29 percent excess mortality in the treatment group, the finding attracted virtually no attention in the United States, and the FDA response had been to describe the results on the label. If one wanted to get legalistic, the CAST patients mostly were not among those for whom the drug was indicated. Most of them had premature beats and no symptoms. The addition of the word "symptomatic" to the Tambocor label provided at least a technical claim that the drug was never intended for the patients in CAST. On the other hand, Temple and Lipicky had stood by, worrying, while 3M and Bristol-Myers had marketed the drug to that population, drug label notwithstanding.

Temple and Lipicky took the middle course. Not only would more restrictive labeling be required, the companies would have to send hundreds of thousands of doctors a special letter warning of the newly discovered dangers. As they absorbed the results of CAST, Temple and Lipicky had to face an additional problem. None of the Class I antiarrhythmic drugs had demonstrated therapeutic benefits to patients in well-controlled trials. Temple and Lipicky had accepted a surrogate endpoint for patient benefit, the suppression of premature beats, or PVCs (premature ventricular complexes). For the first time, CAST had produced a definitive test of a surrogate endpoint. Not only did effective suppression of premature beats fail to prevent sudden deaths; with these two drugs it apparently caused them. Even if one wanted to hope that other Class I drugs were less toxic than Tambocor and Enkaid, it was hard to imagine that suppressing premature beats with them would prove beneficial. CAST had destroyed the basis for approval of the entire class of drugs. That was a most serious problem. The other nasty question was how and why the FDA had approved a drug that caused people to drop dead.

While no serious questions had emerged about the validity of the CAST findings, pressures immediately began to build not to publicize the results. These increasing pressures came to bear directly on Claude Lenfant, longtime director of the National Heart, Lung, and Blood Institute, and veteran of Washington biomedical politics. Born and educated in France, Lenfant's medical research career had begun at the University of Washington in Seattle. He had joined the institute in 1972 to establish and head the division devoted to research on lung disorders. A decade later—just as the pilot for CAST began—he was selected to direct the overall institute.

Both 3M and Bristol-Myers were urging the institute to make no public statement about CAST without consulting first with them. Soon they had won a convert to their cause, Frank Young, the commissioner of the FDA since 1984. When Lenfant met with Young to discuss the CAST results, Young urged him to postpone any press conference. This would provide time to disseminate the findings through a "dear doctor" letter that the companies would send to physicians. It would protect the FDA and the drug companies' credibility within the physician community, and be a much lower-key announcement. Some at the FDA feared that a press conference revealing the capacity of Tambocor and Enkaid to cause cardiac arrest might alarm the public. "The FDA thought it [a press conference] was a mistake," recalled Jeff Nesbit, the FDA associate commissioner for public affairs. "It would scare people." Some people who needed these drugs might stop taking them.

Lenfant was not persuaded. "It would have been extraordinary not to release these findings," he said later. There were thousands of patients taking Tambocor and Enkaid who were being harmed; that warranted an immediate public announcement. This argument convinced Frank Young, who was also invited to join the press conference. An event featuring two such senior health officials was virtually certain to be front-page news. By Friday—just four days after the decision to halt CAST—a press conference was set for the following Tuesday.

The drug companies, meanwhile, were becoming anxious and angry. They were complaining to the most accessible high-level FDA official, Robert Temple. On Friday, he heard from Thomas Hayes of Bristol-Myers, who complained, "Bristol was being asked to make important changes in their labeling for Enkaid and/or send a dear doctor letter without any information."

Temple told them, "Once the [heart institute] showed the figures for mortality for the treated versus untreated groups that Bristol would be as convinced as we were that fairly immediate action was needed." He added, however, that it was not up to him to give out the data.

The next morning, Saturday, Temple heard again from Bristol-Myers, which had now learned about the press conference. This time the caller was Allen Fox, representing Bristol-Myers. He expressed the company's "distress" at learning that the heart institute was going to schedule a press conference. Fox told Temple, "It was only fair we get to see more of the data." He added, "The people at Bristol were all quite surprised by the outcome and thought that all their other data went the other way." But Temple, the man who knew the data, told Fox he was wrong. He reminded Fox of the Enkaid postapproval promotional study in which the company paid hundreds of doctors to put patients on their new drug. Thirty-nine patients had died in just six weeks. He conceded, however, that without a control group there was "no way to determine if this was excessive." Now the first study with an adequate control group had revealed such results were indeed excessive.

3M and Bristol-Myers were also talking to Peter Frommer, the deputy director of the National Heart, Lung, and Blood Institute. He promised the companies a full briefing on the CAST results on Monday afternoon. The press conference, however, would still be held as scheduled on Tuesday morning. Bristol-Myers was strongly opposed to the press conference and wanted to stop it.

It was a moment that tested the power of a modern pharmaceutical giant. Bristol-Myers had the money, organization, and know-how to pull dozens of levers of power. In just a week's time, its drug detailers could present their case, face-to-face, to a substantial fraction of the nation's practicing physicians. In just hours, its public information department could pump faxes into newsrooms from coast to coast. It employed Washington lawyers with the right political connections. It had biostatisticians to comb through the CAST findings. Its medical consultants included the most important and prestigious experts in the country. Over the weekend, the Bristol-Myers team began to assemble in Washington to manage the Enkaid crisis. One key target remained the event mostly outside their control—the National Heart, Lung, and Blood Institute's planned press conference. At the same time, 3M began a similar course of action. The two company teams even assembled at the same hotel, a Marriott located near the National Institutes of Health in Bethesda, just outside Washington, D.C.

The showdown began at 2 P.M. Monday in a conference room a few doors down from Claude Lenfant's office at the NIH campus. The drug company contingent that had gathered in a fifth-floor conference room included lawyers, a biostatistician, and senior members of their medical staffs. The two companies had joined together to use the same medical consultant, Joel Morganroth of Philadelphia. Robert Temple represented the FDA. The heart institute's senior staff were present, as were CAST project officer Lawrence Friedman and Steering Committee Chairman Thomas Bigger.

The company officials were hostile and angry. They demanded that the institute cancel its plans for a press conference, calling the idea "irresponsible." The companies wanted to handle the crisis in their traditional manner; they usually negotiated a disclosure statement with the FDA and circulated it to doctors in a letter. It was quiet, efficient and preserved the drug companies' position as physicians' principal source of information about drug products and safety. A press conference featuring the director of the National Heart, Lung, and Blood Institute and the commissioner of the Food and Drug Administration was going to be national news. No matter how politely the two men might put it, the public would hear that two widely prescribed drugs caused people to drop dead.

As if to make the companies' point on another level, a company lawyer walked down the hallway to the anteroom of Lenfant's office and asked to use the phone to call the White House. A few moments later Lenfant was called out of his office to take an important call from "downtown." In the political insider jargon at NIH, directives from the next higher level, the director of the NIH, are politely described as coming from "Building 1," after the graceful, columned building containing the director's office. The National Institutes of Health are part of the United States Public Health Service, which is headed by the nation's most senior health official, the assistant secretary for health in the Department of Health and Human Services. Calls from this office come from "downtown" because the assistant secretary's office is located in downtown Washington looking out on the historic mall that stretches from the Capitol past the south lawn of the White House. Telephone calls from "downtown" are not taken lightly by officials even of Lenfant's high rank and long seniority. The caller from downtown was not one of the 1,141 aides, analysts and other support personnel on the assistant secretary's staff. It was the assistant secretary himself, James Mason, a physician and Bush administration political appointee. Mason wanted Lenfant to cancel the plans for a press conference. He was getting calls from the White House about it.

While Lenfant talked on the phone, Michael White, the institute's senior public affairs officer, was trying to persuade the drug company delegation it was about to create a public relations fiasco at that very meeting.

"We have a situation where a clinical trial has been stopped not because there was a benefit, but because harm was seen," White said. "It has been shared with all the investigators and hundreds of patients. Chances of it leaking out are quite good.

"You are asking for trouble," White said. "The story might be: 'Pressure from drug companies caused delay. Several people killed in the interim.' " When a senior public affairs official with dozens of news media contacts makes such a statement, it is impossible to know whether he is predicting an event that might somehow happen or describing the story he personally intends to leak. Whatever White's intention, the drug company lawyers present were beginning to nod in agreement.

Lenfant, meanwhile, was explaining the CAST findings to assistant secretary Mason. He described the results and the public health importance. He explained that no delay was warranted while hundreds of thousands of people took a drug that might cause cardiac arrest. The correct scientific and ethical thing to do, Lenfant said, was to release this information to the public immediately. Mason told Lenfant, "Do what you think is right."

In the rarefied air of insider Washington, these words, too, carry hidden meanings. When the nonpartisan director of one of the largest biomedical research organizations in the world begins to discuss "scientific" and "ethical" responsibilities, he is putting his prestige and his job on the line. At this moment, Mason was unlikely to overrule Lenfant. On the other hand, such occasions are rarely forgotten.

Meanwhile, the drug company delegation was hearing the full details of the CAST findings for Tambocor and Enkaid. Despite the companies' having tested the drugs in thousands of patients, they had not conducted one controlled trial of this kind. Among 730 patients taking the two drugs, 33 suffered cardiac arrest in less than one year. Among similar patients on placebo, just 9 cardiac arrests occurred. This meant almost four times as many cardiac arrests occurred on the active drug. The chances this finding was a statistical fluke were remote, less than 1 in 1,000. The results also did not depend on how the deaths were classified. Death rates from all causes were almost three times higher among those getting Tambocor and Enkaid rather than a placebo.* Not only were these definitive results from a well-controlled trial, the study had been conducted by the same researchers the drug companies often employed. Morganroth, who represented both drug companies at the meeting, was also a CAST principal investigator. Bigger, who was CAST chairman, had been a consultant to both 3M and Bristol-Myers. For the companies to assail these results required them to disbelieve the data from the most definitive kind of drug experiment; to doubt the assessment of their own consultants from the medical schools; and to question the conclusions of two major health organizations of the United States

---

*For more on the statistics see the chapter notes.

government, the FDA and the National Heart, Lung, and Blood Institute. As the briefing proceeded, the tone of the meeting grew steadily less confrontational.

Lenfant later described what happened next. "I called in the people from the drug company and their lawyer and I said, 'You know that I have discussed this with the department. This is what we are going to have to do. My business is not to harm you or hurt you, but to make sure everybody understands what is going on, and I invite you to participate in the press conference.'"

The convincing data, Lenfant's determination to proceed, and the invitation to participate resolved the dispute. The press conference was going to be held the next morning as scheduled. But as the meeting broke up, Bristol-Myers wanted to control what was said. "Can we help you write the press release?" White was asked. He was surprised. "Are you kidding me?" he replied. "I'll just tell the press, here is the release, as rewritten by industry."

As notices for the press conference went out, the drug companies and the FDA still had not agreed on labeling changes and a "dear doctor" letter. As the company teams huddled at their Bethesda hotel, Joel Morganroth helped them draft a joint letter. "It was like shuttle diplomacy. They were both in the same hotel but, being drug companies, wouldn't talk to each other." Morganroth also planned to attend the press conference in his capacity as a CAST principal investigator. "I was a special government employee [of the FDA] by that time so I guess theoretically I represented them too."

Michael White also stopped by the hotel to share a copy of the press statement with the Bristol-Myers team. "Let us give you our reaction," White was told. He replied, "That isn't necessary," and departed immediately.

Despite an evening of deliberations, the "dear doctor" letter was still not ready by the Tuesday morning of the scheduled press conference. By 8 A.M. drug company teams were huddled around a table with Robert Temple and other FDA officials, hammering out a final text. The result was just six paragraphs long, finished shortly before the 11 A.M. press conference. The key finding came at the end of the first paragraph. "Tambocor should be reserved for patients with life-threatening ventricular arrhythmias, such as ventricular tachycardia. It should not be used in less severe ventricular arrhythmias, even if the patients are symptomatic." To those doctors who read as far as the middle of the letter, it described the CAST results in technical terms. "An analysis of the data has resulted in the removal of Tambocor from CAST due to the unexpected observation of a 2.2-fold higher rate of total morality and nonfatal cardiac arrest in the patient group on Tambocor compared to the placebo group." It was self-evident why the drug companies hoped to announce these findings in a low-key, technical manner. The press conference for the national news media would be much more straightforward and direct.

Perhaps due to the short notice, only 15 reporters turned out for the press conference. But among them were Warren Leary of *The New York Times*, Robert Hager of NBC's Washington bureau, and Paul Recer, Washington science correspondent for the Associated Press wire service. These three outlets alone were sufficient to guarantee the story of the CAST findings would be immediately disseminated around the world. Claude Lenfant hosted the press conference, but he shared the podium with FDA Commissioner Frank Young, Robert Temple, and CAST chairman Thomas Bigger. The job of describing the CAST results was assigned to Bigger, who confessed that "I was truly stunned and shocked."

Instead of a "press release," which would have required the participation of higher authorities downtown, the institute distributed a "background statement." It was direct, but not inflammatory. The first paragraph revealed that the institute had removed "two antiarrhythmic drugs" because "the data showed no benefit from the drugs in the type of patients studied, while suggesting a possible harmful effect in this clinical population." The press materials, plainly designed to let the facts do the talking, featured a chart comparing 56 deaths or cardiac arrests occurring among patients on the active drug, and 22 on placebo. A second chart showed an even larger disparity in the very event the drugs were intended to prevent, an electrical breakdown of the heart resulting in sudden death or cardiac arrest. Among those on Tambocor or Enkaid, 33 sudden deaths or nonfatal cardiac arrests had occurred, compared to 9 among those on placebo.

FDA Commissioner Frank Young described his agency's actions, and how they would affect the roughly 200,000 patients taking Tambocor or Enkaid. He noted that a letter to doctors would urge they discontinue the medication in those with moderate or mild rhythm disturbances. He urged patients not to discontinue the drug without checking with their doctor—a warning that was included in most but not all news accounts.

Robert Temple had a brief opportunity to explain why he had

approved the drugs in the first place. He conceded that he had relied on small studies showing that the drugs suppressed premature beats, and said CAST proved the value of large randomized trials.

The two drug companies were allowed to have representatives at the press conference, to distribute press releases, and talk to reporters afterward. They did not question the CAST findings. Bristol-Myers, which had fought the press conference so bitterly, was the most forthright. It announced that it was suspending all marketing activities for Enkaid, and would give consumers a refund on any unused medication. The more noncommittal 3M said it was still studying the matter but would notify doctors of the CAST results.

The press conference was front-page news in New York and Washington, D.C., in Houston and San Francisco, Milwaukee, Miami and San Diego. It was an item on NBC's evening news report. It was featured in 35 newspapers, on Cable News Network and in *U.S. News & World Report*. By any measure, it was a major national news story. The reports, by and large, were briskly factual and hewed closely to the presentations at the press conference. Several reports focused on the clinical trial results, mostly leaving it to the reader to make any inferences about the risks to other patients. The most widely used version was Paul Recer's report for the Associated Press. It began:

"Federal officials ordered new restrictions on two heart drugs that have been used for years to treat mild heartbeat irregularities, saying they were 'shocked and stunned' after a clinical study showed patients dying unexpectedly."

The most daring and direct version came from Michael Specter of *The Washington Post*, who missed the press conference but then covered the story through telephone interviews. He wrote:

"Federal officials warned doctors to halt most uses of two drugs widely prescribed to treat mild heartbeat irregularities, saying they were 'shocked' to find that studies showed the drugs appeared to be killing patients."

Overall the news coverage was cautious and correct. Partly because of Claude Lenfant's and Michael White's astute sense of how to handle the news, national media interest in the story died out abruptly. Key officials from the heart institute, the FDA, industry and the medical schools had been assembled in one room and had said their piece. No dissent was evident. It was an awesome united front of medical authority. Few troubling loose ends were left dangling, and apparently there were no unanswered questions provocative enough to encourage reporters to start digging deeper.

However, the answer to just one question might have transformed the press conference into the beginning of a major national scandal. Not one story contained an estimate of how many lives might have been lost through the inappropriate use of these drugs. Those present remember the issue being broached tentatively by some of the reporters; no answer was provided. It might have been that the participants had been under too much pressure to think through the larger question of how many deaths might have been caused by Tambocor and Enkaid. It might be that men like Robert Temple and Thomas Bigger were not able just then to face the magnitude of the misjudgment they had made in approving or promoting these drugs without evidence of benefit from well-controlled clinical trials. Whatever the reason, nothing was said. It was more likely the result of unconscious denial by physicians who could not believe they had harmed their patients rather than any conscious conspiracy to withhold facts.

The materials required for a reasonable estimate of patient deaths were available at the press conference. Frank Young and the two companies revealed that approximately 200,000 persons were taking Tambocor and Enkaid, "a majority" for mild or moderate rhythm disturbances. To be conservative, assume "a majority" means only half the patients. So it was reasonable to apply the findings of CAST directly to those 100,000 patients. Among the 730 CAST patients on the two active drugs, 34 excess deaths had occurred in 10 months. Adjusting these results to a standard annual rate, that meant of every 1,000 persons taking Tambocor or Enkaid, 56 would die in a year. In a population of 100,000 that is a death total of 5,600 persons in one year's time. This figure is likely to be conservative. It assumes that half the 200,000 people who took Enkaid and Tambocor did so without any risk of death, which is highly unlikely.

A man-made disaster claiming 5,600 lives in a single year is a tragedy of the first order. For example, in that same year, 1989, deaths from inappropriate use of these two drugs exceeded all deaths from airplane crashes (1,123); all deaths in fires (4,716); all deaths involving boating and water transportation (989). Even these comparisons underrate the magnitude of the medical misjudgment in giving antiarrhythmic drugs to so many thousands of people without having first determined whether there would be a benefit. The losses in fires or air transportation are not single episodes; they are the annual totals for a whole national system. This was two drugs, 5,600 lives, one year.

The press conference also included no mention of another uncomfortable fact well-known to the participants with expertise in antiarrhythmic drugs. By April 1989, Tambocor and Enkaid had captured only a 20 percent market share. For the preceding seven years one doctrine about adverse effects had guided the drug companies, the FDA, and the medical school experts who were consultants and did the clinical testing. Since the proarrhythmic effects were first widely recognized in 1982 the experts concluded the toxicity of the different drugs in the family was similar. This conclusion was reflected in the labeling of Tambocor and other drugs, which said "Tambocor, like other antiarrhythmic agents, can cause new or worsened arrhythmias." In a 1987 analysis of proarrhythmia published in the *American Journal of Cardiology*, Joel Morganroth rated the risk of serious proarrhythmia as "low" for four drugs in the family, including Tambocor and Enkaid. He rated the risk as "moderate" or "high" for the three best-sellers: quinidine, procainamide and Norpace. At this moment it was therefore prudent to assume similar drugs had similar toxicity. The CAST study had not discovered that Tambocor and Enkaid were uniquely toxic. The drugs were simply the only drugs in the family to have been adequately tested for therapeutic benefit in a controlled trial. If one could assume comparable toxicity in the 80 percent of the patients taking other drugs in the same family, then the one-year death total would reach 28,000. Even this estimate assumes that one-half the patients taking these drugs—about 400,000 people—did so at no risk. This means that more than 50,000 persons died from taking antiarrhythmic drugs in the two-year period during which patients were being enrolled in CAST. In modern United States history the toll is comparable with events such as the wars in Vietnam or Korea, which each claimed the lives of approximately 50,000 soldiers over a longer period of time.*

What should have been immediately clear was that the United States had experienced the largest medical drug disaster in modern history. The FDA acquired its legal authority to regulate drug safety following a 1932 drug tragedy in which a manufacturer sold a sulfa drug dissolved in the chemical equivalent of automobile antifreeze.

---

*The mortality figures for antiarrhythmic drugs are not precise and only establish an order of magnitude of the damage. A more technical analysis contrasting results of various methods and assumptions appears as an appendix.

Roughly one hundred children were killed. The thalidomide tragedy involved about 30 cases in the United States and several hundred worldwide. In winning a ban on the diabetes drug phenformin, drug safety critic Sidney Wolfe argued the drug caused 1,000 deaths a year from lactic acidosis. The tragedy involving Tambocor and the other antiarrhythmic drugs was without precedent in modern medicine.

It may seem surprising that experienced medical reporters and the nation's major health authorities gathered in the same room to discuss deaths from Tambocor and Enkaid without anyone insisting on a death total. So great is the collective faith in the good done by American medicine that the true scale of the disaster was, at that moment, beyond their imagining. They could conceive of a medical experiment in which 20 or 30 patient deaths resulted from unforeseen factors. But the media, the public and even many medical professionals simply could not believe that the same system that brought tremendous benefits to millions of people was capable of harm on this scale.

A similar episode not only illustrates that the American medical system is capable of harm on this scale, but also shows that convincing evidence is ignored even when the facts are readily available.

In 1991 a team from Harvard University completed a landmark study of malpractice in New York state hospitals. The study team included experts drawn from Harvard's schools of medicine, law, and public health. The study employed some of the same techniques that give a clinical trial such great power to yield definitive findings: clearly defined standards, a systematic approach, and random selection of hospitals and cases. They were measuring the number of patients harmed rather than helped by medical treatment. The results were published in the *New England Journal of Medicine*. The key findings were described in the same dry, medical manner that Claude Lenfant used to present the CAST findings. "Adverse events occurred in 3.7 percent of the hospitalizations (95 percent confidence interval, 3.2 to 4.3)...." As a study of malpractice in New York, the report was also headline news for a single day.

Just as with CAST, neither the study's team of experts, the *New England Journal*'s editors nor the news media focused on the obvious implications of the Harvard malpractice study. The team reviewed an emotionally manageable number of actual deaths from adverse events—a total of 168. The study, however, was intentionally designed to reflect accurately conditions in New York state as a whole, just as a carefully conducted opinion poll reflects, within known bounds, the attitudes of a much larger population. These results indicate that 13,445 deaths occurred in New York state in one year due to medical mistakes in hospitals. It is reasonable to assume that New York's doctors and hospitals are neither uniquely safe nor unusually hazardous. It is likely they are typical of hospitals across the country. That means that medical mistakes in United States hospitals kill 168,000 persons each year. Once again this figure is an order of magnitude—an approximation for a range of 150,000 to 200,000 deaths each year. That makes medical mistakes of doctors and hospitals the nation's third largest cause of death, surpassed only by heart disease and cancer, and exceeding stroke.

A medical mistake or adverse outcome, however, does not necessarily imply malpractice or negligence, a failure to exercise due care. The Harvard study noted that an adverse event might be a mistake that could not have been foreseen. For example, a patient might die from an adverse drug reaction that was unusual and could not have been anticipated from the drug labeling or other available information about its toxic effects. This is still a medical mistake because the patient was killed by the decision to give this particular drug. "Negligence" means a medical mistake that would not have been committed by a trained person exercising due care. A death caused by giving the wrong dose or failing to adjust for a well-documented interaction with other drugs might well involve negligence. The Harvard study concluded that 51 percent of the deaths from adverse events occurred through medical negligence, and therefore could have been prevented. Thus, preventable deaths from medical negligence in hospitals total 86,000 a year, easily outnumbering annual deaths from auto accidents (48,000) and murder (26,000). Among hospital deaths from medical mistakes, adverse reactions to prescription drugs were the most common cause. Despite these seemingly shocking results from a landmark study, just one reporter—Michael L. Millenson of *The Chicago Tribune*—explored the national implications of the Harvard medical mistakes study. "A Chilling 166,000 Deaths," wrote Millenson, apparently using a slightly different method to calculate a national estimate. Elsewhere, the reaction was a remarkable silence.

Thus, while the deaths from antiarrhythmic drugs such as Tambocor were unprecedented for a single family of agents, this was only an illustration of a medical system capable of providing not only great benefits but also harm on a monstrous scale. Because those who

tested, developed, approved and promoted Tambocor and Enkaid
meant well, they could not imagine such an outcome. Even when
the facts were in front of them, most simply couldn't see them.
Medical school experts Morganroth, Bigger and Woosley knew that
patients on antiarrhythmic drugs dropped dead with an unusual form
of cardiac arrest. Robert Temple had sensed the dangers and wanted
to restrict the drugs; he knew that only a placebo-controlled trial
could define their dangers. He approved them, persuaded by the
medical school experts. Both drug companies held worried summit
meetings with top medical consultants about the unexplained cardiac
arrests observed during the clinical testing of Tambocor and Enkaid.
Yet somehow these same companies professed to be surprised and
shocked when the CAST results proved the drugs caused cardiac
arrests. And they were angry because Claude Lenfant at the National
Heart, Lung, and Blood Institute insisted that the hundreds of thousands of patients taking these drugs had a right to know this danger
immediately.

While the news media had overlooked the most sensational dimension of the story, they faithfully reported the essential facts. This
was more than sufficient to trigger a powerful and painful reaction
from the American medical system. What happened next would speak
volumes about how that system works when faced with definitive
evidence of a medical misjudgment of monumental size.

Chapter 22

OUTCRY

IN ANNOUNCING THE CAST results immediately, Claude Lenfant believed he was fulfilling his duty as director of the National Heart, Lung, and Blood Institute. He had allowed no delay in telling the public that two widely used drugs might cause cardiac arrest. CAST was also a scientific discovery of the first order. At least half of America's physicians had assumed that they were preventing sudden death by suppressing premature beats and other mild rhythm disturbances. CAST provided clear evidence that this widespread medical treatment was harmful. On either scientific or public health grounds, it would seem hard to fault his action. However, the intensity of the outcry from the medical community surprised even the veteran Lenfant.

Without intending to, Claude Lenfant, M.D., had violated one of the most sacred unwritten rules of medicine: *Thou Shalt Not Tell*. Doctors do not reveal how frequently they harm their patients, even kill them. The shadowy outlines of the *Thou Shalt Not Tell* pledge can be seen in the adamant refusal of most physicians to testify in malpractice cases, no matter how great the negligence involved. *Thou Shalt Not Tell* explains why, as noted earlier, 168,000 persons could die every year in hospital care accidents with so little said. In the aggressive culture of can-do modern medicine, *First Do No Harm* has been quietly replaced by *Thou Shalt Not Tell*. And it was this rule that Lenfant had broken.

A small but essential warning issued at the press conference had the inadvertent effect of guaranteeing that thousands of doctors were going to get angry. Among the 200,000 patients taking Tambocor and Enkaid were a small minority who indeed had life-threatening rhythm disorders, mainly a sustained rapid heartbeat, or ventricular tachycardia. In some of these patients, the problem would recur if they halted the medication. And among these few patients, a recurrence could be life-threatening. Both Lenfant and FDA Commissioner Frank Young had anticipated this danger. At the press conference, they emphasized that patients should not halt their medication without first consulting their doctors. Most of the news stories featured this pronouncement prominently. At first glance it sounded like one of those harmless legalistic admonitions, like the notice on remedies for acid indigestion to consult a physician if symptoms persist. But in the context of a national press conference about two drugs that made people drop dead, the warning had a sensational effect. It motivated tens of thousands of Enkaid and Tambocor patients to telephone their doctors immediately. No matter how politely and tentatively a patient might put it, the message had to be, "Why have you been giving me a drug that might kill me?" As local newspaper reports around the country indicated, this created anger and chaos. Although the story died after one day in the national press, many local newspapers and medical publications covered the patient and physician reaction.

"Physicians have been angry about the news coverage of the Cardiac Arrhythmia Suppression Trial (CAST)," reported *Medical World News*. In Detroit, cardiologist Felix Rogers told the *Free Press*, "We have received a phone call from probably every patient who is taking either of these two medications." In Iowa, one cardiology group practice in Des Moines reported 100 phone calls the first day. It was no more tranquil in Florida. "It's a mess. There are so many people on these drugs it's unbelievable," cardiologist Scott Pollack told the *Orlando Sentinel*. In West Palm Beach, cardiologist Robert Chait told the local daily, "This is the most irresponsible thing to have done. To let the media know about it before the physicians. . . . It's like shouting 'fire' in a crowded theater." To Chait's kind of complaint, the Food and Drug Administration had a simple enough response. Spokesman Bill Grigg told one newspaper, "If you have something that is killing people, you can't get the information out quickly enough." In short, there really was a fire in the theater.

A sampling of how physicians handled the patient calls can also be seen through the local and medical press coverage. One response was the classic physician assurance:

"These two drugs are very, very good drugs—not perfect—but basically good," said Jacksonville cardiologist Scott Baker. "If you select patients for the drug carefully, you're not going to have problems." In California, Ronald Miller told the *San Diego Tribune* he did not intend to take any patient off the Tambocor or Enkaid, but would schedule appointments anyway "to put them at ease."

Some doctors switched to other drugs in the same family. Ramulul Eligeti told the *Ocala Star-Banner* he was going to use Mexitil and Tonocard. In Des Moines, Chad Williams told the *Des Moines Register*, "Personally, if there's an alternative drug, I'm switching them to it."

Other physicians seemed oblivious to the message of CAST, at least in published comments. One important lesson from CAST was the danger of physicians using drugs for purposes that were unproven, and therefore not yet approved by the FDA. One doctor wrote FDA Commissioner Frank Young, "I have received approximately 20 distress calls from patients and an equal number from equally distressed referring physicians and colleagues." In the next paragraph he told Young that he was mainly using the drugs for an unapproved use for which no safety data was yet available—for rhythm disorders of the atria, the two small upper chambers of the heart. "The FDA advice runs counter to our experience," he concluded. Based on the same kind of uncontrolled patient experience, Tambocor had seemed equally safe to Joel Morganroth and numerous other experts who had touted it for suppressing premature ventricular beats. In Florida, the *Orlando Sentinel* quoted a cardiologist saying, "The drugs have been very effective in treating atrial arrhythmias with few side effects." He told the paper he "may decide to keep those patients on the medication." The fact that Tambocor had been proven lethally dangerous in one mild rhythm disturbance did not deter this doctor from continuing the drug in another mild rhythm disturbance in a setting where safety had not been established.

Still another doctor told the *San Diego Tribune* that "No indication was found of danger for the many arrhythmia patients who have never had heart attacks." Yet CAST had not found heart attack survivors uniquely vulnerable; they were simply the only patients who happened to be included in the study.

Others attacked the new restrictions on the two drugs. An angry Idaho cardiologist wrote Young saying, "The knee-jerk response of withdrawing the indication for [Tambocor] and [Enkaid] in the treatment of patients with ventricular premature beats of other than a life-threatening nature makes no scientific sense at all and does nothing but promote hysteria among patients who have been safely taking the drug all along."

The American medical system is no more a monolith than any other system. Despite this massive outpouring of physician denial, some doctors saw the truth with icy clarity. Princeton cardiologist John F. Hagaman wrote to the FDA:

"As a cardiologist what I find so offensive about these two drugs is that they were recommended by the drug company for the treatment of potentially life-threatening arrhythmias, namely PVC's, and the drugs turn out to be more dangerous than the placebo.

"What greatly offended me about the advertising of the two companies involved was the use of the term 'potentially lethal rhythms.' In fact what we were dealing with was a potentially lethal drug."

In Youngstown, Ohio, cardiologist Paul Wright also saw the bigger picture. The *Youngstown Vindicator* quoted him saying there were "substantial risks associated with all of the drugs used to control irregular heartbeats, not just the two mentioned in the study."

Wright evinced no anger about the enormous number of calls he received. "What we are faced with appears to be a competent study which says the drugs may be detrimental to some patients in some cases beyond what we thought. This information is new to us and will necessitate educating the public about them."

Another physician who heard from other doctors was Roger Winkle, the Stanford cardiologist who had written of the dangers as early as 1981 and warned all the experts at the Bermuda symposium on Tambocor back in 1983. This bleak view didn't earn him many invitations to drug company symposia, but when he had the opportunity, he had spoken out about the dangers of the drugs. "I had a lot of physicians call me up and thank me for giving these talks because they ended up not putting half as many people on the drug," Winkle said.

A more systematic assessment of physician reaction came from two Columbia University colleagues of CAST chairman Thomas Bigger. James A. Reiffel and James R. Cook questioned 374 heart rhythm specialists and reported the results in the *American Journal of Cardiology*. Given the "dear doctor" letter and other FDA warnings restricting the drug to life-threatening arrhythmias, the response of these specialists was instructive. Eighty-one percent of the respondents said they were not limiting the drugs to these life-threatening situations as the FDA had urged. Despite the highly publicized CAST results, the responding cardiologists "were not dissuaded from continuing them in a majority of patients already on drug therapy." In short, 81 percent of these doctors did not take their patients off these drugs, despite the newly discovered dangers. This would have required calling the patients and revealing that a mistake had been made, thus violating the unwritten rule, *Thou Shall Not Tell*. However, 79 percent said they were using the drug less frequently in new patients. The authors concluded, "Substantial percentages of respondents used Enkaid and Tambocor for unapproved uses before CAST and continue to do so now. . . ." A broader measure of physician response is the prescription volume of the two drugs. The CAST results were announced just at the end of the first quarter of 1989. In the second quarter, the prescription volume fell 25 percent. Thus, in three out of four cases, the immediate response of doctors was mainly to reassure patients, not to take them off the drug. *Thou Shalt Not Tell* was a rule of great power.

The attitudes of individual physicians were also reflected through their various medical organizations. CAST was manifestly a scientific experiment of great importance and would save uncounted thousands of lives by warning about an important danger in existing medical practice. One might suppose that Claude Lenfant of the National Heart, Lung, and Blood Institute, and Frank Young of the FDA might have been congratulated for rapidly disseminating a definitive finding. Instead, both men were widely condemned. The Alameda–Contra Costa Medical Association pronounced itself "astonished and frustrated at having received no advance notice." President Roger W. Hoag urged the FDA "to consider altering the manner in which information of this nature is released so that physicians will have an opportunity to review it and take appropriate action in the treatment of patients." The letter contained no hint that the association saw any need for educational work among its members about prescribing drugs for unapproved uses in hopes of unproven benefits. On similar grounds, Lenfant and Young were criticized by the American Medical Association and the American College of Cardiology. A few months after the episode, Frank Young was removed as FDA commissioner by James Mason, the assistant secretary of Health and Human Services who had called Lenfant to halt the press conference. Little explanation was provided for Young's abrupt reassignment to a lesser job; other factors likely contributed. Lenfant, who had civil service protection, continued as director of the heart institute.

So great was the outcry that it reminds one of Henrik Ibsen's classic play, *An Enemy of the People*. The local doctor is a greatly beloved figure in the community until he warns that the waters of the community's resort spa are dangerously contaminated. So this was how American medicine reacted to the news of one of the biggest medical misjudgments in modern history—with an assault on the messengers. The response of the pharmaceutical industry proved equally revealing.

Within a matter of days Boehringer Ingelheim had realized that it might seize market share for Mexitil at the expense of Tambocor and Enkaid. As noted earlier, a troubling but inconclusive trial of Mexitil had provided an important early warning about the dangers of trying to suppress mild rhythm disturbances. Six years before CAST, the IMPACT trial had recorded excess deaths but was halted short of conclusive evidence of harm. Already senior officials at both the FDA and the heart institute realized the findings of CAST almost certainly applied to some degree to similar drugs—such as Mexitil. But in the first days after CAST, the FDA stuck narrowly to the most firmly established facts—the dangers of taking Tambocor and Enkaid in anything except life-threatening situations. This created a marketing opportunity. Mexitil had been excluded from CAST in part because of concerns that the IMPACT results suggested it might be harmful. Now Boehringer Ingelheim was going to try to profit from the fact that it wasn't selected for CAST. The company launched a marketing campaign to get doctors to switch their patients to Mexitil—most of whom were the same patients who should never have been put on an antiarrhythmic drug from the start.

Boehringer Ingelheim sent thousands of doctors a "priority letter" that began, "The FDA has released a Talk Paper entitled 'Enkaid and Tambocor Use in Non-Life-Threatening Arrhythmias Halted,' a copy of which is enclosed." The "Talk Paper" was the FDA press release which had been issued at the CAST press conference.

"Should you have questions regarding the transfer of patients from Enkaid or Tambocor, the following dosage schedule is for your consideration," the letter said. It closed by suggesting doctors call their local drug detailer. Needless to say the promotion did not include the warning that Curt Furberg of the heart institute had given an FDA advisory committee: On three occasions investigators had sought to prove benefits in preventing sudden death with Mexitil and three times excess deaths had been seen among patients on the drug. Since these findings fell short of conclusive proof, Boehringer Ingelheim had an opportunity to plunge through the loophole in the evidence and labeling.

The Mexitil marketing campaign also came to the attention of Robert Temple, director of the FDA Office of Drug Evaluation I. "We knew about it. We rolled our eyes. We wondered what to do about it. We would have difficulty doing anything about it until we changed the labeling. It would not have been easy to stop them from promoting." While Temple rolled his eyes, Boehringer Ingelheim was enormously successful in wooing doctors. In the twelve months after CAST it increased the sales of Mexitil by 45 percent.

Parke-Davis was not far behind with a new promotional campaign for the old-timer procainamide. Nine months after CAST, Parke-Davis began a series of monthly promotional letters. "There is no *conclusive* evidence to indict all I-C antiarrhythmics as a class" (emphasis in the original), the letter said. "Labeling changes have been proposed for Tambocor and Enkaid."

The key marketing problem for procainamide was that only quinidine rivaled this drug in the severity and frequency of adverse effects. As noted, concern about the widespread side effects of this drug was an important factor behind the search for safer antiarrhythmic drugs. Procainamide could cause an often-fatal depression of the bone marrow. It produced symptoms of a serious immune system disorder in 15 percent of the patients, and laboratory test evidence of the disorder in about 60 percent. Since the FDA monitored the accuracy of advertising claims, trying to advertise this drug as having a favorable safety profile was almost certain to trigger a complaint from the FDA medical officer for the drug, Sughok Chun. One can almost imagine the Parke-Davis advertising team struggling to find some language to describe an antiarrhythmic drug with an adverse effects profile so bad that some experts doubted whether it would be approved under modern drug law. Citing a trade name of procainamide, Procan-SR, the Parke-Davis brochure said "Procan-SR ... A familiar side effect profile." It was an accurate slogan—side effects were so frequent they ought to be quite familiar to prescribing physicians.

In another tortured rendition of the facts, Parke-Davis described the slow and insidious onset of the most severe side effects in this safety slogan: "A low likelihood of causing side effects that present as emergencies." A company would also like to claim its drug is effective. But in fact, Procan was one of the least effective antiarrhythmic drugs. This forced Parke-Davis to settle for the toothless slogan: "As familiar as it is reliable." It urged doctors who detected early laboratory test evidence of an immune system disorder to wait until actual symptoms appeared.

G. D. Searle sought to increase the market share for Norpace through public relations spin control. On the day that the full CAST results were published in the *New England Journal of Medicine* it wired a bulletin to newsrooms across the country, alerting editors and reporters that the results were about to be published. This would help generate press reports about the dangers of Tambocor and Enkaid. Later, came Searle's punch line. "There are, in fact, nearly 10 other drugs which can effectively and safely control mild to moderate arrhythmias in the proper clinical setting," the press alert said. It urged reporters to call Searle's marquee professor, Lyle Siddoway, a Vanderbilt colleague of Raymond Woosley's. Searle identified Siddoway as a CAST investigator; the medical journal report did not include his name among the participants.

Such was the response of the pharmaceutical industry to the logical conclusion that perhaps half a million people should not be taking any of these drugs until both safety and a genuine benefit were demonstrated in a controlled trial such as CAST. A torrent of gifts and other incentives assured the drug companies a comfortable partnership with the nation's doctors—who were, in any event, busy directing their ire at the FDA and the National Heart, Lung, and Blood Institute rather than the companies who had convinced them to prescribe these potentially lethal drugs.

The companies' relationship was not nearly so cozy with the other major force involved in the CAST results: the news media. Immediately following the press conference, the national media dropped the story. After a day or two of follow-up stories about outraged doctors, coverage had also died out in the local press.

In the meantime, both the doctors and the drug industry were evolving a strategy for dealing with troublesome questions about antiarrhythmic drugs. The news media are carefully and attentively monitored by the FDA, the heart institute and the drug companies. All have public affairs departments that systematically collect every word published about a given subject. Many have friends and contacts in the media. Reporters tend to regard public affairs representatives with habitual suspicion ("flacks" in reporters' jargon) but tend to talk openly with anyone who might have a story. It's not clear exactly how it happened, but a strategy emerged to handle media questions about the safety of these drugs. The strategy was to say it was too dangerous to write about these drugs; it might cause patients to die because they stopped their medication. On its face, it seemed a strange approach, since the point of the announcement was to discourage use of the drugs. Even the first stories after the CAST press conference contained the first hints of this idea. For example, the *Orlando Sentinel* quoted a local cardiologist, saying: "The worst thing patients can do is stop taking the medication without consulting their physician." He said, "Some people with a serious arrhythmia could die without the drugs or a substitute."

There was panic at the FDA when a television reporter said a Florida cardiologist had told him three patients had died because they had stopped their Tambocor. As the history of the drug has demonstrated, such individual claims are nearly impossible to evaluate. But if a medical doctor made such a claim to the press, it was going to be difficult to refute.

Another such case with Enkaid occurred in southern California and was presumably reported to Bristol-Myers. On the day of the CAST press conference, a physician named Gregory Thomas received a call from a 70-year-old patient who had heard a news broadcast. Since the patient was similar to those in CAST—a heart attack survivor without symptoms—Thomas discontinued the drug a month later. Five days afterward the patient died of a cardiac arrest from which he could not be resuscitated. Deaths shortly after drug withdrawal had been reported during the testing of Tambocor and Enkaid. And it was conceivable that this was still another danger of these drugs. What CAST had proved beyond question was that Enkaid did not prevent cardiac arrests; it caused cardiac arrests. However, since placebo patients also experienced cardiac arrests, it was possible that Thomas's patient died from causes that Enkaid would not have prevented anyway. Nevertheless, the event sounded ominous.

The FDA also heard from a Washington lawyer representing 3M, Edward Basile. He wanted to know if 3M should report as an adverse reaction a patient who had died after Tambocor had been withdrawn. According to an FDA memo, Basile said, "3M had received 2,000 calls from angry doctors who said their patients have stopped taking this drug because of news announcements and some of their patients had died because of recurrence of their arrhythmias."

Such an argument had little effect on Robert Temple at the FDA, who had no doubts about restricting the drug. "That was a controversy at the advisory committee meeting," Temple said later. "Doctors were saying, 'He's doing well and he's on it, what am I supposed to do?' The answer: Get him off as quickly as possible. 'But some of them will die.' The answer: Yes, but fewer."

The astute observer might even have seen the jaws of a trap slowly opening, ready to snap shut on the reporter who began a serious inquiry into how many people had been killed through taking anti-arrhythmic drugs. The doctors were not going to blame themselves for prescribing a drug without first insisting on proof of benefit. Nor were they going to blame the drug companies for encouraging them to use drugs in a manner that caused the deaths of thousands of patients. Instead, the real problem was that frightening news media reports were keeping patients from taking the drugs they needed.

The first reporter to start tracking down the broader implications was a 30-year veteran medical writer named Alix Kerr. She had been writing about medicine since working for *Life* in the 1950s, when it was one of the largest and most important magazines in the country. In July of 1989, she worked for *Physician's Weekly,* a large-type, full-color "poster" displayed in special glass cases in more than 2,000 hospitals. A drug company advertisement is stripped across the bottom. The publication resembles a *USA Today* for doctors, with short, snappy stories and bright color graphics. While *Physician's Weekly* had a tiny, controlled circulation, Kerr had more experience than most medical writers on far larger newspapers. Soon after being assigned a story on CAST, she was on the telephone to CAST chairman Thomas Bigger.

An early estimate of the lives lost from inappropriate uses of Tambocor and Enkaid had begun to circulate just a few weeks before Kerr called. It had come from Al Hallstrom of the CAST Coordinating Center in Seattle. In an e-mail message to the 27 CAST sites, Hallstrom had estimated that CAST results had saved 4,000 lives. Without CAST, Hallstrom said, "There would have been an excess of about 4,000 deaths per year in a patient population similar to that of CAST." The purpose of the message was to rally the flagging morale of the troops, who had been appalled to learn they had been harming the patients they cared for. The spin on his message was, "Look at the lives we have saved."

In an interview with Kerr, Bigger confirmed he was a proponent of the arrhythmia suppression hypothesis and added, "I haven't a clue" what went wrong. He also revealed that 4,000 patients might have died, but offered little additional detail. Not surprisingly Kerr could find no published figure. But she did find that Bigger and Joel Morganroth had published the results of a marketing survey of physician prescribing practices. It showed that before CAST was halted, about half the physicians surveyed were treating patients like those enrolled in CAST.

Kerr was thorough. She tracked down the history of the arrhythmia suppression hypothesis and its roots in Bernard Lown's doctrine. She found the published articles challenging the validity of the theory. And she interviewed Robert Temple, who told her revised labeling would restrict the drugs. But he added that they were still useful in some patients with severe rhythm disturbances. She turned in her story and went on jury duty. The story fell into the hands of Managing Editor Mark Bloom, who immediately wanted more on the death toll. He interviewed Morganroth, who provided an even more detailed estimate.

The world of heart rhythm research had come full circle. It was Morganroth's assurances that Tambocor was extremely safe in patients with mild rhythm disturbances that had persuaded Temple to abandon his proposed restrictions. It was a tragic miscalculation. Now, four years and thousands of deaths later, Morganroth was being asked to estimate the death toll. Amazingly he did, in considerable detail, but using assumptions that construed the findings of CAST in a narrow if precise manner. He estimated 1,500 to 2,000 deaths a year, continuing for two years, a total of 3,000 to 4,000.*

Kerr's story, headlined "Sudden Death Debacle" was only eighteen paragraphs long, but was remarkably complete. It began, "Before a trial given to block sudden death actually triggered it, thousands may have died prematurely." It quoted Bigger and included details of Morganroth's estimate of deaths.

That might have been the end of the matter except Kerr's story quickly came to the attention of Paul Recer, the Associated Press reporter who had covered the CAST press conference three months earlier. It was immediately evident to Recer that a death toll of 3,000 or 4,000 was major news. And while a sensational story on a poster-sized newspaper displayed in 2,000 hospital corridors might be overlooked, the Associated Press was instantly available to practically every daily newspaper, and every major radio and television outlet in the country.

Recer immediately set out to write his own version of the story. The national implications were going to be obvious to every doctor he called. He interviewed Bigger and Morganroth. "They were both very brusque, but they gave me an interview," Recer said, "which I taped so I know damn well what they said."

While Kerr had quoted eight key figures in the field, Recer's story focused on Morganroth and the survey he had conducted with Bigger of physician prescribing practices. This time Morganroth reduced the death total to a range of 2,250 to 3,000 deaths over two years. The

---

*The estimate is lower than that in the previous chapter because Morganroth's calculations conservatively assumed the following: The two drugs had no risks except for patients exactly like those enrolled in CAST; and no similar drug had similar risks.

total, which Bigger had initially placed at 4,000 annually, was now down to 2,250 over two years. It was still a large enough number to command national attention.

The story created a frenzy of activity minutes after it moved on the AP wire. The Associated Press is an all-electronic wire service for subscribers, who are free to edit and shape the story as they see fit. Different versions move at different times, and errors can be introduced or corrected by editors downstream.

So despite dozens of printed clippings, it is not absolutely clear what Recer wrote. But he concedes the story contained some "confusing" language. The results of the CAST trial—with 1,445 patients—somehow got mixed up with the results of Morganroth's survey of physicians. It was necessary to combine data from both sources to support the mortality estimate. The version published in the *Philadelphia Inquirer* contained a serious error. The lead said:

"As many as 3,000 patients may have died prematurely in a nationwide trial of two drugs that were intended to prevent irregular heartbeats, but which actually caused heart attacks, according to a survey of cardiac specialists." The implication that 3,000 people died while participating in the trial was, of course, completely incorrect.

Other papers never published the mistake. *The New York Times,* the *Seattle Times,* the *Illinois State Journal* either caught the mistake or got a correction from AP. A small editing change fixed up the lead: "Up to 3,000 patients may have died prematurely *before* a nationwide trial discovered..." (emphasis added).

In response, Recer recalled, "suddenly there was this blizzard of faxes from coast to coast." They contained a statement from Morganroth warning of "gross errors in Paul Recer's Associated Press story." By the next morning Bristol-Myers was wiring newspapers across the nation an even stronger Morganroth denunciation. "I am outraged with the gross errors in Paul Recer's Associated Press story. The implication that thousands have died in a nationwide trial is erroneous and irresponsible."

Recer was also flooded with calls from doctors. "Almost instantly," he said, "I got angry calls from cardiologists accusing me of killing patients [because they would stop their needed medication]."

The assault made Recer angry too. "They were absolutely blind to the fact that patients have been going to the doctor for four or five years, maybe the second or third most intimate relationship. A three- or four-hundred-word story was not going to wipe out that relationship."

But the assault by Morganroth, Bristol-Myers and the angry doctors left Recer shaken and concerned. He called the Food and Drug Administration and asked to speak to an expert on antiarrhythmic drugs. He wanted an outside, unbiased opinion. Recer was soon talking to Robert Temple, apparently not aware he was interviewing the official whose misjudgment had allowed the new generation of antiarrhythmic drugs into the marketplace. As might be expected, Temple emphasized the positive aspects of the drugs, not the dangers uncovered in CAST. Temple told Recer that Tambocor and Enkaid were still important for treating life-threatening arrhythmias.

Recer wrote another story, this time praising Tambocor and Enkaid for helping some patients. "Expert Says Heart Drugs OK for Some" was the headline in the *Philadelphia Inquirer*. The version in that paper also quoted Morganroth, who was now refusing to give any specific figures. The story quoted him saying:

"There probably were some deaths, but it's hard to say how many. One cannot attribute any individual patient's death to the drugs."

Thus the only national effort to probe the death toll from inappropriate use of antiarrhythmic drugs ended in a widely circulated news account praising the drugs. Confusing language in Recer's story was used as a pretext to disown a mortality estimate.

Morganroth continued to assail the Recer story in an interview with *Medical World News*. The story carried a headline, "An investigator in antiarrhythmic drug study blamed one report for some deaths." The text said:

"More recently, one of CAST's principal investigators went further, blaming a ripple of deaths among frightened patients on an Associated Press story he said overstated the dangers of Enkaid and Tambocor.

"After the story appeared across the country, some patients with life-threatening arrhythmias 'stopped the drugs themselves because of what they read,' said Dr. Morganroth."

Both Robert Temple and Joel Morganroth have since acknowledged that the real death toll was much higher than reported in Recer's flawed 1989 story. Their answers came in a different context and might have relied on some information unavailable when the two men talked to Recer.

Robert Temple raised the subject himself in a June 1992 speech to the Drug Information Association. He said:

"Had a claim for treatment ... to prevent sudden death ... been approved and promoted the consequence undoubtedly would have been the premature death of tens of thousands of patients. While the claim was never sought by a sponsor, many physicians did in fact use antiarrhythmic drugs in this way."

Temple was asked to clarify the quote in an interview with the author:

Q: It would be difficult to escape the conclusion that in fact tens of thousands of people did die prematurely in this case.
A: That could be.

In a later interview, Morganroth confirmed that the death toll for Class I antiarrhythmic drugs was at least as great, if not greater, than what Temple described. When asked whether it was possible that tens of thousands of patients died from these drugs, Morganroth replied, "You are underestimating by a lot. . . . We can guess at some arbitrary number. Because that's what you're talking about." He then went on to say, "Pick any number you want—50,000; 500,000. It all depends . . . Any number you pick, it's OK with me. The issue is, which is much more important, is that despite all these articles . . . and despite the legal community running after this . . . two things have happened. One is that the public's ignored it, because there has been very little litigation. Number two, the physicians have ignored it, because sales of quinidine stayed where it was or went up."

Recer's embattled Associated Press account was the closest the national news media ever came to assessing the full impact of the nation's worst prescription drug disaster. However, one major player in the game had yet to move. One would suppose that after such an enormous loss of life, the FDA itself would commence an inquiry into what had gone wrong. Six months after the CAST results were announced, such a proceeding did take place. It too would reveal much about how the system works.

Chapter 23

THE FDA INQUIRES

WHEN A COMMERCIAL airliner crashes, the federal government begins a practiced, nearly instantaneous response. Within minutes, a team of professional investigators without ties to the airlines or the FAA is dispatched to the scene. At the end of a massive fact-gathering process, the findings are publicly presented to an independent panel, the National Transportation Safety Board. It issues written findings and recommendations. The military response to a disaster is less rigidly structured, and perhaps less effective. A high-level commander often appoints a board of inquiry made up of senior officers not involved in the incident. The loss of a U.S. Navy ship can involve a formal military court trying specific charges against the captain of the ship. Faced with a disaster, business corporations turn to outside experts—management consultants, lawyers or accountants. The FDA response worked quite differently.

Despite being a physician and commissioner for five years, Frank Young had little medical background in the specialized field of antiarrhythmic drugs until he had to discuss Tambocor and Enkaid at a national press conference. Not long after the dust had settled, Young asked Robert Temple, the FDA official who had approved the two drugs, for a report. Within a matter of days Young had the response.

The explanation of how Tambocor was approved was three pages long and consisted mostly of passages lifted from the Summary Basis of Approval, the document that summarizes clinical testing for release to the public. By way of justification for what had been done, it described what might be called the quinidine defense. It said:

"It was therefore obvious that [Tambocor] was an antiarrhythmic drug and that in comparison to quinidine, as a 'tried and true' standard, [Tambocor] was more able to suppress ventricular ectopy [irregular beats] and was, in general, far better tolerated." This was accurate except that the director of Cardio-Renal Drugs, Raymond Lipicky, believed quinidine couldn't be approved under the 1962 law and existing guidelines. A six-page summary described Enkaid and ended with an identically worded paragraph with only the drug name changed. This report, along with the lengthy public-release summary for each drug, was sent to Young for his weekend reading on May 2, 1989. The document originated in Lipicky's office; Temple added a one-paragraph note.

Young was removed as FDA commissioner before any further action was taken, and control of the agency passed to an acting commissioner, Mark Novich. The chain of command included one more key figure. Temple reported to Carl Peck, the director of the Center for Drug Evaluation and Research. Peck had taken charge of the center two years earlier after a career in military medicine. He had been pressing hard to get drugs approved more quickly, and to do so had reduced Temple's control over drug approvals. He had taken away from Temple the authority to approve roughly half of all drugs, and assigned it to a newly created office headed by Temple's former deputy, James Bilstad. Peck was also under intense pressure to approve cancer and AIDS drugs more quickly and had been forced to take personal charge of AIDS drugs, working as a division director. The antiarrhythmic drug disaster had dropped out of the public eye, and Peck ordered no outside review.

By default, the responsibility for addressing what had gone wrong in the approval and promotion of Tambocor fell on the FDA official who had approved the drug, Robert Temple. Although he was, in fact, the federal official most clearly responsible, he also emerged as the senior federal official who most clearly saw the need for action. But higher-level inaction left him an unusually free hand to handle the matter in his own style.

Six months after the CAST results made headline news, Temple took the problem to the advisory committee for the Cardio-Renal Drug Division. The very committee that had ignored the early warnings in 1983 and 1984 was now going to consider what its failures had achieved. Temple, however, was not simply going to drop this hot potato in the lap of a committee made up mostly of doctors with close ties to the drug industry. He had an agenda for action. He and Lipicky wanted backing from the medical school experts for broad new restrictions on antiarrhythmic drugs. Temple also had a chance to pick the jury. He and Lipicky invited an additional five antiarrhythmic drug experts to join the committee, four as nonvoting "guests" and one as a voting member. Although some faces had changed over the years, it was really another gathering of the medical elite of antiarrhythmic drug research. The advisory body that had helped make one of the worst medical misjudgments in history was now going to be pressed to do something about it.

When the Cardio-Renal Drug Advisory Committee sat down on the stage at the modernistic Jack Masur Auditorium on the NIH campus, they became special government employees for that day. That made them subject to conflict-of-interest laws that prohibit federal officials from having a financial interest in matters on which they might act or vote. As the ten members of the committee assembled on October 5, 1989, seven had a conflict of interest within the meaning of federal law. The members did not conceal their drug company work; it was described on financial disclosure forms available to FDA officials but not released to the public. The FDA allowed all seven to participate despite their conflicts of interest, granting them waivers in writing. In some cases, the conflicts of interest were substantial. For example, Edward L.C. Pritchett of Duke University was receiving $20,000 a year for consulting with Searle, which sold Norpace. He received $20,000 from 3M (Tambocor). He received $10,000 from American Home Products (Cordarone) and $10,000 from Bristol-Myers (Enkaid). He was also negotiating a consulting fee with a company that sold quinidine. The FDA was knowingly allowing a doctor on the payroll of four drug companies selling antiarrhythmic drugs to consider whether these drugs should be restricted.

Not only did the committee members have financial ties to the drug industry, many were active advocates of antiarrhythmic drugs. Pritchett was a specialist in using these drugs for rhythm disorders of the atria, the two small upper heart chambers that work as primer pumps. Member Jeremy Ruskin of Harvard was a leading proponent of using programmed electrical pulses to identify effective antiarrhythmic drugs. Invited guest Philip Podrid was a longtime colleague of Bernard Lown—an originator of the arrhythmia suppression hypothesis. Podrid had tested Ethmozine in Russia. Douglas Zipes of the University of Indiana was deeply involved in developing the new generation of antiarrhythmic drugs. The chairman, Craig Pratt of Baylor University, had worked with DuPont on the development of Ethmozine; as a CAST investigator, he had also helped get Ethmozine included in the trial. Most of these men headed medical research units specializing in antiarrhythmic drug treatment and development.

The drug companies knew this and were already playing on their fears. The companies were hinting that too many restrictions would mean a cutback on antiarrhythmic drug development. This was hardly an idle concern for these men. Peter Kowey was a Philadelphia-based research physician and a committee consultant with voting rights. He also was doing drug studies for DuPont, which sells Ethmozine, Parke-Davis (procainamide), Bristol-Myers (Enkaid), and American Home Products (Cordarone). He told the drug-industry-supported publication *Cardio,* "The pharmaceutical industry has reacted to the CAST report by curtailing development of new antiarrhythmic drugs." Not only did these men have conflicts of interest that met some technical legal definition, they were judging a matter in which they had a major professional stake.

Robert Temple and Raymond Lipicky had considerable power, too. They had scripted the drama that was going to unfold in front of a large audience in Jack Masur Auditorium at the National Institutes of Health.

During the first segment of a day-long program, antiarrhythmic drugs were not on trial. The first question was whether the CAST results were valid. To defend its findings, the National Heart, Lung, and Blood Institute had dispatched a heavyweight team to brief the committee on CAST. It included Lawrence Friedman, the project officer, and Al Hallstrom, the CAST coordinator and biostatistician. Curt Furberg, who had briefed the committee in 1983, was available to put CAST in context with other clinical trials. Rounding out the team was an Indian-born, Oxford-educated expert on clinical trial statistics, Salem Yusif. Any partisan who chose to attack the findings had to take on a knowledgeable and high-powered group.

The heart institute team provided a crisp summary of the basic findings of CAST. Only one new finding emerged. Hallstrom had discovered that antiarrhythmic drugs effectively suppressed premature beats only in the healthier patients. In those with more severely damaged hearts, the drug often didn't work. This meant that doctors would be deceived by their own observations as they used antiarrhythmic drugs. It would appear that patients they treated with drugs did better because only the healthier patients could tolerate the drugs. The very best health prognosis was for the CAST patients getting the placebo. In the original two-week tryout they had been proved healthy enough to tolerate the drugs. But by taking the placebo they were not exposed to the risks of the drugs. This explained why the placebo group in CAST seemed to have an unusually low death rate.

Curt Furberg reviewed the overall results from clinical trials of antiarrhythmic drugs over the past decade. His conclusion was that the evidence showed that, overall, treatment was harmful and increased patient deaths.

The CAST briefers had to deal with only one serious challenge to the validity of the results. It came from Donald Berry, a University of Minnesota statistician who was a consultant for 3M. He observed that most of the excess deaths had occurred among patients who had experienced two or more heart attacks. The implication was that outside this small group of patients, Tambocor would therefore be quite safe. The heart institute interpretation was that the two drugs were dangerous to the entire population in which they were tested, not one small subgroup.

Yusif used an analogy to explain why Berry's idea was wrong. If one picked apart any body of data carefully enough, it was always possible to find some group that seemed to have enjoyed special benefit or was put at greater risk. He described a clinical trial that had proved that giving aspirin after a heart attack reduced deaths by 25 percent. But major differences emerged when patients were divided into separate groups by astrological sign. Even though aspirin reduced mortality overall, when Gemini was compared with Libra, treatment appeared to have an adverse effect.

"Being an Indian, I thought this was really true," Yusif joked.

Berry sought to defend his position with increasingly technical arguments. Yusif responded, "Basically an incorrect analysis is an incorrect analysis."

One of the most important questions that Temple was taking before the committee was whether, after CAST, the arrhythmia suppression hypothesis was dead. The whole family of drugs was approved on the surrogate endpoint of suppressing premature beats. Not only was it the prime measure of antiarrhythmic activity, the assumption was that suppressing premature beats was beneficial. Did CAST mean that the entire foundation for approval of these drugs had crumbled? If so, Temple needed some other basis for approving antiarrhythmic drugs.

An answer was proposed by the next witness, one of the committee's own members, Jeremy Ruskin of Harvard. Ruskin was a leading promoter of the technique that used programmed pulses of electricity to trigger a heart rhythm disturbance. Then various antiarrhythmic drugs were tested to find an agent that blocked the arrhythmia. Although Ruskin was a committee member, and one of the judges, he now was arguing that this technique proved that antiarrhythmic drugs were effective. His basic argument was the essence of simplicity. After being given antiarrhythmic drugs, it was no longer possible to induce artificially a heart rhythm disturbance in some patients. While an antiarrhythmic drug worked in only a minority of patients, each case where it worked proved the drug was effective.

The critical question, however, was whether outside a special laboratory, did giving the antiarrhythmic drugs benefit the health of the patients, preventing them from dying from dangerous rhythm disorders? On this issue Ruskin had no evidence from well-controlled clinical trials. He said, "In conclusion, the antiarrhythmic drug efficacy . . . with regard to the use of electrophysiological testing [with programmed pulses] can be surmised or postulated, at best, from several indirect pieces of evidence. It certainly remains unproven." Thus it appeared that Robert Temple was going to substitute Ruskin's unproven theory for the now highly questionable arrhythmia surpression hypothesis.

The advisory committee, however, proved unready to abandon Lown's arrhythmia suppression hypothesis even after dozens of attempts to prove it had failed, and great harm had resulted. While one member—Milton Packer of Mt. Sinai Medical Center in New York— voiced a litany of objections to the theory, others sprang to its defense. Ruskin dismissed the CAST trial as a "preliminary result on two drugs." Peter Kowey of the Medical College of Pennsylvania took up the argument made before—the failure of all the previous studies doesn't disprove the theory. The right study might prove benefits.

It was late in the afternoon before the committee turned to the specific written questions that Temple and Lipicky had posed. Pratt, the chairman, said, "The question is how to conduct this and get the most out of all the extremely brilliant people whom we have invited here." The guests could not vote, but could comment on each issue before the committee.

He began with the only easy question. "Do you think CAST found a clear difference in mortality between Enkaid and Tambocor and their respective placebos."

The finding was so obvious only one member answered. Ruskin said, "Yes."

On the next agenda question, Temple could also hope for speedy

approval. He wanted the committee to endorse the use of antiarrhythmic drugs in immediately life-threatening rhythm disorders.
Temple had already limited Enkaid and Tambocor to this use, and it
was the least controversial. However, no placebo-controlled clinical
trials had ever been attempted in this patient population. And federal
law required evidence from well-controlled trials that benefits outweighed the risks.

"The data are not available in a rigorous, controlled prospective
study," said Douglas Zipes. "They just do not exist."

Temple and the status of the whole family of antiarrhythmic drugs
now stood precariously on the edge of the cliff. In well-controlled
trials, the drugs were proved harmful in mild and moderate rhythm
disturbances. As Zipes had noted, there was no evidence of benefit
in more serious disorders. The legal basis for selling and prescribing
these drugs had been destroyed in a public session.

The only evidence that Robert Temple could cite was the experiments with programmed pulses of electricity that Ruskin had described. And even Ruskin had conceded no health benefits had been
established in clinical trials.

Nevertheless, the committee voted in favor of Temple's proposition that the drugs provided a clinical benefit for patients with life-
threatening disorders. Only the committee's biostatistician, Frank
Harrell, voted against it. "I will say I do not know," he said. Given
that no evidence of benefit existed, Harrell was the only committee
member to vote the facts.

Next Temple wanted the committee to ratify the restrictions he
had already placed on Tambocor and Enkaid. The "dear doctor" letter
sent after the CAST press conference had limited the drugs to life-
threatening situations.

The first to object was Albert Waldo, a CAST investigator and
Cleveland medical school professor. "If you are a strict construc-
tionalist, you say we only know about CAST," he said. "We are dealing
with some imponderables." He opposed the restrictions on
Tambocor.

Peter Kowey supported Waldo. "Physicians have to be given some
latitude," he said.

Philip Podrid of Boston College said, "I think it is fair to say we
do not know either the risk or the benefit in that group of patients.
Perhaps physicians should individualize and consider the risk-benefit
ratio."

Temple observed they had overlooked their legal responsibility to
insist on evidence that a drug's benefits outweigh its dangers.

"What you want to do is really not legal," Temple said. "We just cannot put in a wishy-washy statement that we are not sure the benefits outweigh the risks."

Lipicky said, "I am not being facetious now; I am being serious. What happens if you violate the law?"

The audience laughed anyway.

Temple, perhaps the only one to appreciate how many patients had died through inappropriate use of antiarrhythmic drugs, got angry.

"One of the impressions I keep getting is that the enormous magnitude of what we are seeing here is not appreciated," Temple said. "This is, in fact, bigger than anything we have ever encountered in a mortality trial except AZT. The idea that has no implications for other people with ischemic heart disease . . . the idea that has no implications seems sort of farfetched to me. I do not understand it. Yes. We did think it had implications for other populations."

Milton Packer, who had assailed the arrhythmia hypothesis earlier, was also amazed. "I cannot believe what I am hearing in part. There is no proven benefit to the treatment of ventricular arrhythmias in 99 percent of the patients who receive them. There is a proven deleterious effect in a substantial amount of patients who received these drugs. There is no reason to believe that risk does not apply to other patient populations.

"If you think that a drug is killing one patient population, then it is very likely that it is not going to do any good in another patient population that is not all that different."

This did not persuade Douglas Zipes. "Do not tie my hands at the present time," he said. "I do not know that any patient I give Tambocor or Enkaid to I am going to end up killing."

Zipes argued in favor of letting doctors decide, and Temple's proposed restrictions failed on a 5–5 tie vote.

Temple's agenda items marched relentlessly forward in a logical progression. First he wanted restrictions on Tambocor and Enkaid. The next question was whether CAST findings should apply to the closest chemical relatives of the two drugs. The whole family was known as Class I drugs. Tambocor, Enkaid, Rythmol, and indecainide were in a subgroup, in Class I-C. The question was whether the findings should apply to all four Class I-C drugs.

Again, the proposition faced heavy opposition. David Lowenthal of Hahnemann University in Philadelphia, objected. "We only have data for the drugs used in CAST, and to generalize across the board to all I-Cs just would not be proper at this time," he said.

Temple was now truly outraged.

"I want to be very clear. I mean, we do not know they kill people for sure yet," he said. "So we should recommend use?"

Lowenthal said, "Although Rythmol and indecainide fit into I-C, we do not have data to impugn their use."

Lipicky said, "So go ahead and kill people until we find out that you are?"

Ruskin rallied to the defense of the embattled Temple and Lipicky. "We are kidding ourselves if we pretend there are no similarities among these drugs. The fact is there are striking similarities," he said. "Until we prove that, in fact, there is not some overlap with regard to this potential for toxicity, I do not think it is reasonable to pretend that the results of CAST do not exist."

Temple won that restriction by a 7–3 margin. But his next proposition was more difficult. Should the entire family of drugs be restricted, including quinidine, Norpace, procainamide, and Mexitil? Should the committee assume, as Furberg's analysis suggested, that all these drugs cause patient deaths, and put this information on the drug label?

In disagreeing, the committee members embraced a variety of arguments. Waldo, the Cleveland medical professor, argued it didn't much matter what they put in a drug label.

"I was just thinking to myself how many times I have read a package insert [label] to tell me whether a drug is indicated and I could not remember a single time," Waldo said. "I do not know whether it is totally germane or not." It seemed an unusually frank admission that doctors usually get their information from journal reports, drug detailers, company advertising, and drug company symposia.

Lipicky tried to focus the discussion. "The question is whether people who do not have life-threatening arrhythmias should be treated with an antiarrhythmic agent. What evidence is there to say, yes, they should?"

No one had any such evidence to cite. Still, the broader restriction failed. Only Harrell, the committee biostatistician, voted for it. The committee did recommend including the CAST results in the drug label without actually restricting the use of the drugs.

It was nearing the end of a long day, but Temple still had another important agenda item. He had new drugs to review as well as dealing with the many already in wide use. Temple sought the committee's support for more rigorous standards of safety and efficacy testing for future drugs. The discussion did not get far before a pharmaceutical company man delivered the standard threat. His name was Craig

Saxton, and he represented Pfizer, which was developing a new antiarrhythmic drug.

"I suspect I speak not just for Pfizer but for most of the people
left in this room [drug company representatives]," Saxton said.

"There is a danger in the Cardio-Renal Division of moving away
from where the rest of the agency is moving," he said, "in response
to some challenges from . . . the area of AIDS and oncology."

Saxton was describing a whole series of pressures—some from the
National Cancer Institute, from AIDS activists and industry—to relax
the safety and effectiveness standards to make drugs available more
quickly. They were pressing for increased use of surrogate endpoints
instead of actual proof of patient benefit.

Saxton noted that 50 people die every hour from heart disease,
many from cardiac arrest.

"We are concerned that you are going to demand mortality as a
measure for approval of an antiarrhythmic," he said.

"If that is the case . . . the chance of investment is going to drop
remarkably, and you are the sort of people who are the most interested in seeing new tools for the treatment of these patients for this
public health hazard."

Saxton, in other words, was concerned that for a drug intended
to save lives, the FDA might require proof that it did so. Surrogate
endpoints were much easier and cheaper. If forced to prove an actual
benefit to patients, Saxton was threatening that the industry might
focus on areas where the safety and efficacy standards were being
relaxed, putting the doctors who did antiarrhythmic drug development out of business.

The normally well-controlled Temple blew up.

"I cannot believe what I heard!" Temple said. "I mean, what is the
idea? That with luck you can get fifty [deaths] per hour up to two
hundred? The CAST study suggests that one surrogate people were
using—suppression of PVCs—not only was not adequate to show
improvement, it hid an extreme degree of harm."

But in the very next statement, a calmer Temple revealed he was
not nearly as tough as he sounded.

"If you were listening," Temple said, "the committee agreed on
the use of certain surrogates." He explained that they would abandon
PVCs as a surrogate, but accept another unproven surrogate, preventing rhythm disturbances artificially induced with programmed
pulses of electricity.

Once Temple explained his relatively mild position, the drug company man was satisfied.

Saxton said, "The question we are more concerned about is whether any surrogate is going to be acceptable, or is it only going to be mortality."

The advisory committee refused to vote on new standards for approving future antiarrhythmic drugs. But in a summary of their deliberations published in the *American Journal of Cardiology*, the committee hastened to reassure the drug industry.

"The committee is sensitive to avoiding excessively strict guidelines that might discourage new drug development," the summary said. "The members of the committee realize that it is not realistic to require mortality trials for each antiarrhythmic drug and specific patient population."

While the committee was ruling out expensive and lengthy mortality trials, it was uncertain what standards should be established. "Many decisions must be made with imperfect data," it said. "There was inadequate time for our committee to address changes and clarifications."

That statement reflected exactly what the leading experts on antiarrhythmic drugs had learned from the CAST study. No matter how many people died, their main concern was over the drug development programs that sustained their positions. However, as the advisory committee concluded its inquiry, another major investigation into the FDA's actions in approving Tambocor and Enkaid was already well under way.

Chapter 24

TEMPLE ON TRIAL

DURING THE SAME period that a young doctor named Robert Temple was getting his first Washington experience, another youth from New York City also paid a seminal visit to the nation's capital. He was a Brooklyn high school kid named Mitchell Zeller, and he arrived in May 1971 to witness a large protest demonstration against the war in Vietnam. He was instantly enthralled. To Zeller, it was the essence of a vital democratic system, citizens demanding a redress of grievances, a change in a major policy. At that moment, his course in life was set. At Dartmouth College he majored in government and got a student internship to work at the White House. While in law school at American University in Washington, he worked part-time representing Vietnam veterans trying to upgrade their discharges. After graduation, he won an Equal Justice Foundation fellowship to pursue public interest legal causes. He spent several years working on food safety issues before getting a job as counsel to the House Subcommittee on Human Resources and Intergovernmental Relations. For years, the chairman, New York Democrat Ted Weiss, had used the subcommittee's vague legislative jurisdiction to focus on congressional oversight of the Food and Drug Administration.

Mitch Zeller had spent six months on the subcommittee staff when he got a call from the FDA on April 25, 1989, warning him an important announcement was about to occur. As soon as he heard the results of CAST, Zeller knew he had his first major drug investigation. Within days, the FDA had a letter requesting all files, documents, letters and other materials relating to the approval of Tambocor and Enkaid. Over the course of the summer, Zeller negotiated with 3M, which agreed to turn over without a subpoena more than 30,000 pages of corporate documents. From this growing mountain of paper, Zeller labored for months to piece together the story of the approval and marketing of Tambocor and Enkaid. Because it was his first case involving drug approval rather than food issues, and because cardiac rhythm disturbances involve unusually complex medical issues, it was a daunting task.

Over many months of analyzing thousands of pages of documents, Zeller pieced together many important episodes in the Tambocor story. He learned about Temple's early safety concerns and intention to restrict Tambocor. He discovered Denver Presley's behind-the-scenes advice to 3M to press its case. He found out about Temple's change of heart and the revised, more lenient labeling. Other documents recorded the FDA's concerns about Tambocor and Enkaid advertising as the two companies pursued the larger market of patients with mild and moderate rhythm disturbances.

Once Zeller had the essential facts in hand, he had to shape this mountain of material into a form suitable for a congressional hearing. An investigative hearing is a stylized drama, played out according to a set of rules. Zeller needed medical experts to testify about what mistakes had been made, perhaps to suggest changes in drug law. This was, in a courtroom analogy, the prosecution. That was followed by the defense; typically a team of senior FDA officials appeared to explain their actions. The subcommittee members took turns asking questions; they might play prosecutor and attack, or assume a defense lawyer role and try to help a witness.

When Zeller tried to build a prosecution team of expert witnesses, he ran into trouble. He had little difficulty finding cardiologists who had earlier expressed concerns about how antiarrhythmic drugs had been used. "None of them had changed their views," Zeller recalled. "If anything some of them were even more outraged and concerned when we were talking informally on the phone." It was entirely another matter, though, when he began to discuss the possibility that they might testify in public. At least half a dozen turned Zeller down. He too had run into the rule *Thou Shalt Not Tell*. In some cases, Zeller discovered doctors had another reason for refusing.

"The doctors run research facilities that take money from the drug companies. If they went public with their criticisms of these drugs, they were concerned that they would lose future funding from the drug companies." Two doctors even told Zeller exactly that; most simply gave no reason for declining.

He called Joel Morganroth in Philadelphia after seeing the Associated Press news story about 3,000 deaths from the two drugs. "He said the wire service story was wrong. He basically disavowed his effort [analysis]. He went out of his way to say it was unscientific." That was as close as Zeller got to establishing a death toll from the inappropriate use of antiarrhythmic drugs. Ultimately, Zeller did find two witnesses to make his case. Bertram Pitt of the University of Michigan was prepared to testify that the advisory committee had wanted to restrict Tambocor to life-threatening rhythm disturbances. (This was problematical since that wasn't, in fact, what the committee had done back in 1984. It had explicitly opened up a loophole when it recommended the drug for symptomatic arrhythmias.) Thomas Graboys, a Harvard colleague of Bernard Lown's, was prepared to testify that it was a mistake to approve Tambocor and Enkaid for other than life-threatening conditions. (That was also problematical, since Graboys himself used these drugs in some mild disturbances.) A third witness, a critic of the arrhythmia suppression hypothesis, withdrew at the last minute. That was the strongest case Mitch Zeller could build. The hearing was set for April 10, 1991, almost two years after the CAST press conference. It could be expected that Robert Temple would mount a vigorous defense.

By the morning of the hearing, it was already clear that the news media turnout was going to be minimal. If an investigative hearing resembled a legal case, the media was the vital link that forwarded the essential facts to the larger court of public opinion. As Zeller put it, "If you have a hearing that is not well attended, it's like if you're not in the forest when the tree falls and there is a noise." He blamed the low turnout to his own failure to find a victim of Tambocor. (There were, of course, thousands, but they were dead.)

Graboys was the lead witness. As expected, he voiced his opinion that the two drugs should have been limited to life-threatening ar-rhythmias. He also provided a fresh insight into why physicians might have prescribed the drugs so widely. It was not the effect that these rhythm disturbances had on patients—which was usually minor—but the impact on physicians as they read the test data.

"These rhythm problems are complicated. They create a lot of anxiety on the part of the physician," Graboys told the subcommittee.

"Given the high tide of anxiety among physicians in the country and the fact that these drugs had a low incidence of side effects—at least noncardiac side effects—it's no wonder the [drugs were] used, I think, quite frequently." He also charged that the advertise-ments played to these concerns. "The advertisements portrayed kind of everyday folks on the street who had extra beats and emphasized the fact that these drugs would suppress these extra beats. Buried way down in the bottom of the ads was the disclaimer." Beyond that,

Graboys gave few clues how this misjudgment occurred, and said nothing of its cost in human lives.

Bertram Pitt went second, and as in 1984, he equivocated. He recalled his prophetic warning about the dangers of failing to require a clinical trial to prove these drugs had the assumed benefit. He told the committee what he had said: "What happens if it turns out, when the studies are done, that far more of those people died who got the drug?" Pitt conceded that he and other committee members had not insisted on such a study because "It was felt it might be unfair, in fact, to some of the pharmaceutical companies that started trials many years before." He emphasized the need for clinical trials and at the same time he defended the committee for approving the drugs without them.

What was conspicuously absent was any specific information about the loss of life, the magnitude of the error that had occurred. Subcommittee member Democrat Rosa DeLauro of Connecticut seemed to sense the disaster, almost as if by radar.

She said, "There were 800,000 prescriptions and we don't know the results of those 800,000 prescriptions. If you are looking at any percentages, there is probably a high percentage of people who died because there wasn't an outcry or there wasn't a willingness to push the issue . . .[of] the mortality tests."

In response, Pitt seemed to duck the question. He said, "I think these are important things that have to be looked at very thoroughly as the process evolves."

Before DeLauro could press the issue, her five minutes for questioning had expired. But the next questioner also wondered about the deaths. Wyoming Republican Craig Thomas wanted to know if offering these drugs without mortality testing might have also saved lives. Graboys said, "I would have no idea because we don't have follow-up on these kinds of patients."

Neither Graboys nor Pitt would criticize the FDA.

"Where do you think the FDA fell short, if indeed they did?" Thomas asked.

Graboys said, "I'm not an expert in what occurred with the FDA in the mid-1980s in terms of the approval of this drug."

Thomas asked Pitt the same question.

"I don't want to comment on where the FDA fell short or didn't," Pitt said.

By the time it was Rosa DeLauro's turn to ask questions again, she was manifestly displeased by the answers. "We had a reluctance or really a nonanswer on discussing the competency of the physicians who studied the issue, and reluctance in terms of commenting on whether the FDA process is adequate or not adequate.

"There were enough grave doubts about this issue at the first part of the process, in taking a look at whether this potentially could kill a patient.

"Yet there was no minority report, there was no outcry to say to the rest of the process, we need to do it, it's worth the time, it's worth the money to do mortality tests."

She understood that the key failure was the medical school experts who had tested the drugs, advised the FDA and helped the companies sell them.

"This is the responsibility of the people who sit around the table who are the experts in these diseases," she said. "Those of us who sit up here are not." For this diaster, she noted, "There has to be some kind of moral responsibility or outrage."

Pitt's defense was that they had done nothing in secret. "We spoke out at the time of the committee hearings about the potential of killing patients, about the potential of these drugs to cause harm. It wasn't put under the table."

With a weak and equivocal body of testimony about what went wrong, Robert Temple had few difficulties mounting a defense of his actions. Accompanying him was Raymond Lipicky, director of Cardio-Renal Drugs. As usual, Temple came prepared. He remembered the facts and was ready to discuss them at length. He had written a 42-page statement. Even after he had crossed out most of it, it remained so lengthy he promised "to talk fast" to squeeze it into his ten minutes allotted time.

He said he did nothing wrong, had made no mistakes, and had already taken any necessary action. This is not surprising since Temple *was* the system. He approved drugs, set the standards, helped pick the advisory committee members, worked on the legislation and helped write regulations that interpreted the laws. Of course, Temple by no means worked in a vacuum. The drug companies, and the medical school doctors who helped them, had formidable powers and could mobilize doctors, influence the media, or act through the political system. Those who observe individuals with great powers rarely appreciate the pressures that limit them. He believed he had done the best he could. He had no apologies to offer or mistakes to acknowledge.

He said, "We believed the data . . . supported the approval of Tambocor and Enkaid for use in symptomatic patients with arrhythmias that were not life-threatening. The CAST interim results presented FDA with new information and we acted swiftly, and with cooperation from the drugs' sponsors, to remove that indication from the labeling of both products. Labeling for all antiarrhythmic drugs has been, or will be, affected."

He was somewhat less assured about how the FDA had dealt with the drug advertising.

"The promotion of the two drugs has presented FDA with a difficult regulatory situation," he said. "There were numerous interactions with the sponsors and many requested labeling changes. The points of disagreement with the firms on their promotion were subtle enough to make development of a strong legal case difficult, but we believe other remedies can be effective in such cases. We are clearly prepared to prosecute cases that merit this step."

It did not take Ted Weiss long to focus on Temple's critical decision to abandon the restrictions he had initially proposed for Tambocor. Noting that the safety of Tambocor had not been established in controlled trials, Weiss said, "There were serious flaws in the evidence submitted by [3M] to prove that Tambocor was safe for use by persons with mild or moderate arrhythmias. Isn't that correct?"

"Yes," said Temple.

A few minutes later, Weiss zeroed in on the pivotal moment in the approval. Addressing Lipicky, he said, "If you and Dr. Temple had stuck to your guns and not approved Tambocor for mild or less than life-threatening arrhythmias fewer people would have died unnecessarily."

Even though Lipicky once had told 3M, "This drug kills people," he would not acknowledge how many thousands of deaths were linked to that decision.

"You don't know how many people died as a consequence of Tambocor," Lipicky said. "You have absolutely no knowledge of that and I don't think that is an established fact. So I don't understand the question."

Temple had a different answer. He said, "The people [that] it is reasonable to assume were harmed by Tambocor are those in the population [of heart attack survivors] who were treated. That use was never recommended by us." His defense, in short, was that the deaths occurred among patients whom doctors chose to treat for unapproved uses.

All this showed another Temple capacity—under pressure he was capable of fast footwork, of cutting the fine legal point. While Temple did not "recommend" the use of Tambocor in heart attack survivors, he had abandoned restrictions that would have helped prevent Tambocor from being so widely used in such patients.

Although little note was taken at the hearing, Temple also had announced an important decision about the labeling of antiarrhythmic drugs. He was restricting the entire family of similar drugs, the advisory committee's reservations notwithstanding. He said, "We are in the process of relabeling essentially all antiarrhythmic drugs to recommend their use only in immediately life-threatening illnesses; to say that use in lesser arrhythmias is generally not recommended; to say that the implications of CAST should probably be applied to all these other drugs."

The following July, Temple did relabel Boehringer Ingelheim's Mexitil, but not before its advertising campaign to win over Tambocor and Enkaid patients had increased prescription sales by 37 percent over pre-CAST levels. He also restricted Searle's Norpace and procainamide. In 1994, Lipicky said that quinidine should be relabeled in the immediate future.

These quiet steps appeared to have little effect on the overall sales of antiarrhythmic drugs. A slow, steady decline that began even before CAST results continued into the early 1990s. The only dramatic changes were in Tambocor and Enkaid—whose dangers were highlighted at Lenfant's press conference. Over two years their sales fell by two thirds from the peak just before CAST.

This was by no means the only time that the FDA had discovered new dangers in approved drugs that required a major change in labeling. A year earlier the U.S. General Accounting Office had examined labeling changes in 198 drugs approved over a decade's time. It found 51 percent of approved drugs had serious risks not discovered during clinical testing prior to approval.

America loves to heap scorn on members of Congress and to view doctors with admiration. But at the hearing, it was the legislators without medical degrees who saw most clearly what had happened. Pitt and Graboys, senior men of the medical system, couldn't find any grounds for criticism of their colleagues. Democratic representative Donald Payne of New Jersey had another view.

"If you have deaths from medication, as opposed to prolonging life," Payne said, "then I think regardless of whether there were all Einsteins on board, the results are certainly different from the intent of medication. To me, the evidence was there was some poor judgment in permitting this drug to be prescribed."

At another moment, Temple was explaining why he hadn't required a controlled mortality study to ensure that the drugs benefited patients.

He said it was too expensive. "We would like to be able to apportion the resources of the industry to answer questions that we would like, but we are not completely able to do that."

Weiss interrupted, with a simple and direct point. "The FDA has the obligation to make sure the toxicity of the drug is not such that it ends up killing people."

To Weiss the lessons of Tambocor were plain. In summing up the hearing, he said, "The FDA made a serious mistake when it approved Tambocor and Enkaid for mild arrhythmias because the agency did not know if the drugs were safe for that use. No one expects the FDA to detect every harmful effect from an approved drug. With Tambocor and Enkaid, the FDA knew prior to approval that these drugs could kill people whose lives were not jeopardized by their conditions. In this case, the FDA failed to uphold its statutory duty to protect the public from unsafe drugs."

An investigative hearing is a battlefield in the primal confrontation between the independent executive and legislative branches of government. Each side jealously guards its powers and prerogatives. Temple had emerged from the poorly attended hearing unscathed, his position still secure. Without media, without a public outcry, the committee's thoughtful criticisms were mostly without force or effect. That outcry likely would have been loud and sustained had the subcommittee investigation established the tens of thousands of lives lost through the FDA's misjudgment. When the hearing ended, Temple knew he had won a battle in the ongoing struggle. What might have been a dangerous attack had fizzled. As the hearing room emptied out, Temple walked up to Mitch Zeller.

"You still don't get it," Temple said. And then he smiled, and left the room.

Other medical experts hastened to reassure the Weiss subcommittee that the system they ran had worked well. While they did not testify, two doctors who worked on Tambocor sent testimonial letters for the record. One came from Edward Pritchett of Duke University. He was an advisory committee member who voted against restrictions on antiarrhythmic drugs at the same time he was a consultant for the companies that sold them. He wrote to the committee—

openly acknowledging that 3M had asked him to write—and said, "The approval of Tamcobor for the treatment of ventricular arrhythmias in 1985 was a very appropriate action."

The Weiss subcommittee got a letter from another medical school doctor who had helped develop Tambocor, Jeffrey Anderson of the LDS Hospital in Salt Lake City. Anderson, while still working with Bertram Pitt at the University of Michigan, had written the first endorsement of Tambocor. ("An important addition to the antiarrhythmic drug armamentarium.") Working with Morganroth, Anderson had helped write the safety study that led Temple to misjudge the risks of Tambocor in patients with mild rhythm disturbances. Anderson praised the existing system.

"As a physician involved in clinical trials," Anderson wrote, "I would like to indicate the system has functioned well in the development process of new drugs including the antiarrhythmic drugs Enkaid and Tambocor."

Raymond Woosley was another medical expert who came away from the tragedy without a criticism of the system.

"I think the system worked beautifully," Woosley said in an interview. "Unfortunately some people had to die, but they were dying anyway, they were dying from other causes, and there are still people dying from things that are not tested.

"There are things going on in the practice of medicine every day that affect just as many people that are not being studied."

As Woosley thought about his answer—almost the physician's reflex response that laymen ought to leave these matters to the experts—he was uncomfortable. He couldn't bring himself to agree there was a problem, but conceded that there was "an unfulfilled need" for unbiased medical information, free of drug company influence.

One of Mitch Zeller's fears about the hearing was in fact realized. The tree did fall in the forest with no one around to hear. There was no television coverage, no AP story, practically no news coverage at all. The only parties who seemed to have learned the lessons of the episode were the members of Congress. Those who liked the system as it was prevailed increasingly, although not without controversy.

Conflicts of interest on advisory committees drew strong complaints from Sidney Wolfe and the Health Research Group. They reached the ears of a new, reform-minded FDA commissioner, David A. Kessler. He asked the Washington-based Institute of Medicine, a division of the National Academy of Sciences, to study the problem and prepare proposals for reform. A panel made up mostly of medical school professors issued a report recommending that the procedures for granting conflict-of-interest waivers be "codified." When it considered the larger question of whether doctors could make objective judgments about drugs they helped develop, the committee threw up its hands, saying "intellectual bias" was a problem far outside its abilities.

The issue of surrogate endpoints—using theoretical but quantifiable benefits rather than proven benefits—also came under review by both Kessler and Robert Temple. Without surrogate endpoints for effectiveness, Tambocor and Enkaid could never have been approved without a clinical trial that would have revealed the drugs' lethal properties. However, the two officials were not responding to concerns over the arrhythmic drug disaster; they were reacting to the incessant industry and medical pressure to make new drugs available more quickly.

With Temple as principal author, the FDA proposed a new, more lenient regulation providing "accelerated approval" of drugs for life-threatening diseases. It defined life-threatening with great liberality, including chest pains, depression and arthritis. It urged increased use of surrogate endpoints. The proposed regulation said:

"Approval of a drug on the basis of a well-documented surrogate endpoint can allow a drug to be marketed earlier, sometimes much earlier, than it could be if a demonstrated clinical benefit were required."

This major move attracted little or no media attention or outside criticism. It did, however, draw outraged comments from two FDA division directors, officials who knew the real costs of approving inadequately tested drugs.

Paul Leber, director of Neuropharmacological Drugs, strongly disagreed and filed a public dissent. He charged the regulation was nothing more than a "proposal to rely on the speculations of experts about the capacity of un-validated surrogate indicators to predict the efficacy of experimental new drugs." As an example of what could go wrong with relying on expert opinion, he cited CAST.

Raymond Lipicky, director of Cardio-Renal Drugs, said in an interview, "It is the antithesis of all the lessons that have been learned in this whole business. We have no accelerated approvals here in this division."

If anyone ought to understand the dangers, it was Lipicky. Nevertheless, his division was soon in trouble with another surrogate endpoint. It had also accepted a surrogate endpoint for drugs used in heart failure patients, those with hearts too severely damaged to pump an adequate supply of blood. The experts reasoned that in a patient whose heart couldn't pump quite enough blood, a drug that increased cardiac output ought to be beneficial. Like suppressing premature beats, it had a kind of surface plausibility. On the other hand, it was not so obvious. The heart is a muscle. Suppose one was treating an individual with legs so near to failing he could hardly walk. Would not a drug that spurred him to take a few steps more quickly be as likely to prove harmful as it would to prove beneficial? After Manoplax was approved to increase cardiac output, a randomized clinical trial was finally held to answer this question. It proved that while the recommended dose of Manoplax did increase cardiac output, patients were 50 percent more likely to die than those getting the inert placebo. Three months after a low-key "dear doctor" letter attracted little press notice, the drug was voluntarily withdrawn by the manufacturer, Boots Pharmaceuticals.

So it was business as usual in the approval of drugs at the FDA. However, the remarkable CAST still had one more lesson to teach the medical system. The whole reason for expensive testing of prescription drugs is that the results can provide both ugly and pleasant surprises.

Chapter 25

CAST II

BATTERED BUT UNBOWED, the Cardiac Arrhythmia Suppression Trial had continued with a new protocol. When the Data Safety and Monitoring Board had stopped the trial for Tambocor and Enkaid, it had also suggested continuing with the third drug, Ethmozine. For those who continued to believe in the arrhythmia suppression hypothesis, Ethmozine still provided a ray of hope. The safety board did not release the interim results for Ethmozine, but the recommendation to continue was a strong hint that the trend must be neutral or perhaps even in favor of the drug.

So CAST continued, but not without controversy and serious problems. The safety board wanted to add another drug. It wanted a true test of the suppression hypothesis rather than what was in effect an expensive drug development program for DuPont conducted at public expense. That recommendation triggered a major debate. The question of selecting an additional drug was assigned to a subcommittee headed by Raymond Woosley. Other members included Joel Morganroth and Jeffrey Anderson. Many of the same issues that had been debated five years earlier arose once again. David Salerno of the University of Minnesota wanted to include quinidine, the old standard that doctors trusted most. Woosley was against it. He thought the drug was probably harmful. Also it was not very effective in suppressing premature beats. The investigators considered Cordarone—the French-owned drug that had been approved without any clinical trials. Richard Katz of George Washington University argued that its undetermined efficacy and known toxicity made it ethically unacceptable.

Joel Morganroth pushed for Ethmozine. He was, of course, familiar with Ethmozine, and in 1989 had received more than $38,000 from DuPont in connection with the drug. Morganroth told the subcommittee that since the safety board had not removed Ethmozine from the trial, it must be trending toward the positive. Since the results were tallied for all drugs together, adding any other drug that might cause increased deaths might cancel some portion of the benefit of Ethmozine. "It is imperative," he said, "that any drug chosen does not have significant potential for causing increased mortality." While some investigators complained about doing drug company research, Morganroth's position prevailed. The CAST trial continued with Ethmozine as the only drug.

The investigators agreed to make another important modification to the CAST protocol. The mortality count in CAST had not begun until the patient had survived two weeks on the drug with premature beats effectively suppressed. This tryout period to establish an effective dose was called titration. Since the physicians who developed these drugs believed that most drug-related deaths occurred during this early period, omitting the first two weeks of danger made it easier to prove the suppression theory. The safety board had been uncomfortable about the 45 deaths reported during the two-week titration period during CAST I. The board could not tell whether this figure was excessive without a control group of untreated patients. It was exactly the same problem that had faced Temple when he had received reports of unusual numbers of Enkaid patient deaths shortly after approval. This time, however, a group of investigators, led by Donald S. Beanlands of the University of Ottawa, proposed the logical solution. They argued it was unethical to continue the trial without a placebo group for the initial dose titration period. A placebo group would also provide an independent measure of the risks of simply starting patients on Ethmozine. It was not surprising the CAST investigators agreed to this proposition; on the contrary, it was amazing that this test had not been undertaken before, given the large number of early drug-related deaths uncovered during testing of antiarrhythmic drugs.

For project officer Lawrence Friedman, the biggest headache was lagging patient recruitment. The trial already had more than 300 patients randomized to Ethmozine or a placebo. The nurse coordinators were able to persuade many original CAST participants to reenter the trial on another drug, but it was still an uphill battle. Many of the nurses responsible for patient recruitment had been demoralized by the CAST findings. It was the nurses who had the face-to-face contact with the patients who had been harmed. Physicians who had first refused to let patients participate because they didn't want patients on placebo now declined out of fear of the active drug. By May 1990, recruitment was 40 percent below the goal. With

27 sites, perhaps 100 hospitals, and more than 300 researchers, CAST was recruiting only 6 to 12 patients a month.

With a one-drug trial, and some of the investigators smelling a winner, Friedman was also worried about conflicts of interest. He was concerned when he learned that DuPont was sponsoring a symposium on Ethmozine at an Arizona resort. It would feature presentations by many CAST investigators. As the investigators met in Banff, Alberta, the meeting minutes said:

"Dr. Friedman raised the issue of conflicts of interest posed by a meeting on Ethmozine sponsored by DuPont to be held in Flagstaff, Arizona. He urged the investigators to be sensitive to the appearance of conflict of interest, reminding them of the scrutiny that Congress and the press have been applying to this issue." Woosley suggested that CAST physicians pay their own way and donate their honoraria to charity. There was no record whether this happened.

Some investigators were so sure of victory that they were rushing to leap aboard the Ethmozine bandwagon. But the Alberta meeting minutes indicate there were also a few words of caution.

John McNulty of Oregon Health Sciences University said, "Many investigators' responses imply that we have answered the suppression hypothesis." He added that he did not think so. Friedman also counseled caution. He warned the investigators that there were not that many total deaths in the Ethmozine arm when Enkaid and Tambocor were discontinued. He added, "We have shown suppression alone is not sufficient."

When DuPont held its Ethmozine symposium in Arizona, few such words of caution could be heard. Even though CAST had not yet produced any definitive results, several prominent investigators were all but ready to anoint a winner. The proceedings were headed by Thomas Bigger, the CAST chairman, and Joel Morganroth. The conference was later published as a supplement to the *American Journal of Cardiology*.

In providing an overview, Bigger and Morganroth summed up the case. "Ethmozine's unique electrophysiologic profile, reasonable efficacy, excellent tolerance profile and convenient dose schedule make it an attractive new antiarrhythmic drug. However, in the aftermath of CAST our primary concern for any agent is its long-term safety. Fortunately, Ethmozine to date in CAST has not raised any safety concerns. Its continuation in CAST will uniquely provide us with enough long-term mortality data to establish its safety to an unprecedented degree."

Jeffrey Anderson, the Salt Lake City cardiologist who had told the

Weiss committee how well the system had worked, was enthusiastic. "A promising new antiarrhythmic agent when profiled against other drugs," he proclaimed. He acknowledged that a favorable mortality effect was "still being tested." But noted, "The adverse mortality effects, recently shown for Tambocor/Enkaid, have not been suggested for Ethmozine. This favorable profile makes Ethmozine an agent of unique interest."

Craig Pratt of Baylor University, the FDA advisory committee chairman who opposed Temple's restrictions on antiarrhythmic drugs, focused on the risks of Ethmozine. He found it unusually safe, saying it had "a low proarrhythmic potential in the populations tested, including patients presenting with lethal ventricular arrhythmias."

Although Pratt had no placebo-controlled trial data, he was particularly optimistic about the safety of Ethmozine during the first two-week period when a dose was established. For patients like those now being enrolled in CAST, Pratt concluded the risk of drug-related death was 1 in 5,000. He too emphasized the CAST angle. Ethmozine, he said, "has been judged safe relative to proarrhythmia in CAST." He showed little evidence of sharing the concerns of the CAST investigators who had insisted on a placebo controlled trial for the two-week titration period.

A few months after the Arizona symposium, in June 1990, Robert Temple approved Ethmozine, but limited it to life-threatening rhythm disturbances. However, if the CAST II trial proved that it prevented cardiac arrest, as the early results seemed to hint, a new label indication and enormous profits would soon follow.

Approval was the lead story in the *Newspaper of Cardiology*. "Ethmozine Now Available—Effective *And* Safe." It quoted Morganroth, Bigger and Pratt with enthusiastic comments similar to those at the symposium. The article seemed to claim that CAST had endorsed the safety of Ethmozine.

"The [Data Safety and Monitoring Board] found no increase in mortality among the post-MI [heart attack] patients compared with those given a placebo," the article said.

It now looked as if the breakthrough that had eluded 3M and Bristol-Myers was within reach of DuPont. It had a drug many experts had declared safe. If CAST made it the only agent proved to prevent sudden death, DuPont might hope for a market with a million patients. However, one critical problem had come to the attention of Sara Armstrong Mahler, the doctor who was responsible for Ethmozine at DuPont. By late 1990, it appeared that CAST might never prove the benefits of Ethmozine for lack of a sufficient number of patients.

Recruitment in CAST had continued to lag, and a result might not be available until 1994, if then. To speed this process DuPont decided to offer something it had in large quantities: money.

It was an object lesson in pharmaceutical economics. Robert Temple had not required the controlled mortality studies he knew were needed because he was under the impression that no drug company could afford them. (He briefly did urge 3M to conduct such a study in 1985, but did not pursue the matter.) In one sense Temple was right. Since the FDA was not requiring such studies, and doctors widely prescribed the drugs without evidence they worked, no company was willing to shoulder a large, unnecessary expense. Thus, Temple had a self-fulfilling prophecy. However, when CAST findings made it clear that no drug was going to win a large new market without proof that it saved lives as promised, DuPont was immediately ready with its checkbook. (As this is written, Bristol-Myers is also sponsoring a mortality trial of sotalol.) Whether from the dictates of medical opinion in the drug marketplace or the requirements of the FDA, companies would sponsor expensive clinical trials when they had to.

Sara Mahler was soon ready with an offer for Peter Frommer, deputy director of the National Heart, Lung, and Blood Institute. She offered the institute $6 million. In return, she wanted an unwritten understanding that the money would be used to speed up CAST. She had another proposal. DuPont wanted to include seven additional medical school research centers to participate as CAST sites. All had previously done clinical testing of Ethmozine. To qualify the sites as federal contractors would take months and involve elaborate procedures—perhaps even competitive bidding. As a shortcut, the DuPont centers were quietly added as "subcontractors" to existing sites.

Recruitment improved, but it was still a problem when the CAST Data Safety and Monitoring Board met in April 1991, near Lawrence Friedman's office in Bethesda. Al Hallstrom, head of the Seattle Coordinating Center, had a report. The trial had 1,050 patients enrolled but would fall short of the goal of 2,000 patients at current recruitment rates.

Next came a refrain that must have sounded familiar to this veteran safety board with nine years service. Al Hallstrom revealed that a problem had emerged once again. When CAST had halted in 1989, the trend for Ethmozine was favorable, but inconclusive by any measure. Four deaths had occurred on the active drug, compared with 11 on placebo. Further, an unusually large number of deaths, at least

17, had occurred during titration to establish an effective dose of Ethmozine. Thus CAST rules—omitting the first two-week tryout—had excluded more than half the deaths that had occurred on Ethmozine. Once again the board was receiving the results blinded to the true identity of Group X and Group Y. In the two-week tryout period, a difference had emerged between the two groups, and it was increasing with each passing week. The difference was so dramatic that the board immediately voted to unblind itself. Hallstrom then revealed that the excess deaths were occurring on Ethmozine. The numbers did not cross the advisory boundary indicating conclusively that harm had occurred, but they were close. In the main study, the results were also discouraging. The trend in favor of Ethmozine had disappeared with increasing numbers of patients. The chances of proving the expected benefit had declined to 30 percent. The board took no action beyond scheduling a meeting in three months, rather than the customary six months. Hallstrom was going to comb through the master file looking for some hidden factor to explain the deaths. But those present knew that only a miracle would save CAST II. Back in Seattle, Hallstrom continued to get a brief summary of the results each week. The number of deaths among patients on the active drug continued to grow. He analyzed the data carefully looking for hidden factors. "We found nothing to explain it," Hallstrom said.

The safety board met again in Bethesda on July 31, 1991. In addition to the usual members were Peter Frommer, the deputy director of the heart institute, and Thomas Bigger, the CAST chairman who had been so enthusiastic at the Ethmozine symposium. The new figures left little ground for doubt. In the two-week titration period 17 patients had died on Ethmozine, compared with just 3 on placebo. Using the special statistical rules that apply to data that is being repeatedly examined, the results were slightly short of the advisory boundary for harm. But with routine statistical tests, or merely by common sense, it was evident that it was quite hazardous even to start patients on Ethmozine. Titration alone killed 2 percent of the patients exposed to the drug. The finding was of special importance because the risks of starting patients on these drugs had not been explored in a randomized clinical trial. Back in 1987 Temple had worried when 3 percent of the Enkaid patients had died in the first six weeks of Bristol-Myers' program to introduce cardiologists to the drug. The titration result was also significant because Ethmozine was supposed to be the most benign member of the family of Class I drugs; the others might be worse. It did not take the safety board long to agree that no more patients should be started on Ethmozine. It now seemed awfully important for doctors to know immediately the risks they were taking even starting their patients on drugs in this family.

The results were less definitive in the longer and larger main study. In the long-term study, 102 of the treated group died, compared with 86 of the placebo group. In statistical terms, this is still an inconclusive result, but once again excess deaths had occurred among treated patients on an antiarrhythmic drug. Hallstrom had another technique for presenting these results, expressing them as the chance that they could still prove a benefit. The odds were 93–7 against their succeeding. After a modest debate, the board agreed to halt CAST II immediately and take all patients off the medication.

CAST II was nevertheless an important scientific achievement. For the first time, it had provided definitive proof of the dangers of merely starting patients on antiarrhythmic drugs. For the many doctors who insisted lessons of CAST applied only to Tambocor and Enkaid, here was additional proof of the dangers of still another drug in the family. Not one drug in the family had been proven to benefit patients, and harm had been documented in the drug widely considered to be the most benign. Excess deaths had now been reported on Mexitil, Tambocor, Enkaid and Ethmozine. How much evidence was enough to persuade doctors to abandon a theory that had been accepted without proof in the first place? It was, therefore, reasonable to assume these findings would have an immediate and important effect on the use of the whole family of antiarrhythmic drugs. While sales had continued to decline slowly, more than half a million patients still took them every day in 1991.

As the safety board discussed how to disseminate the CAST findings, a consensus quickly emerged. Consensus is the most common mode of medical decision-making. Doctors' training, background and perspective are so similar that they develop almost a chemical sense of their colleagues' sentiments. As the board began to consider how to disseminate the results of CAST II, it was quickly clear that those present wanted to say as little as possible about what they had found. To have proved that still another approved drug was dangerous was a medical embarrassment. According to the minutes, Lawrence Friedman said, "These results are not nearly as urgent as CAST I. One, there is no proof of harm, and two, if practicing physicians were following the package insert they were not using the drug for CAST type patients anyway." Friedman's argument seemed feeble. The titration period showed clear proof of harm; previous experience had shown how frequently physicians did not follow label restrictions. Thomas Bigger found another reason for making no public announcement. He said the FDA would not have to rewrite the label, since Ethmozine was already restricted to life-threatening situations. That too seemed questionable. If Ethmozine immediately killed 2 percent of the patients who started the drug, this was fairly relevant to the physicians trying to weigh whether the benefits of this drug outweighed the risk. Peter Frommer noted they would have to tell the investigators something. He suggested that it should not be "hysterical" and "simple enough that a local journalist would not have to rewrite it." Bigger suggested announcing something at the American Heart Association meeting in November. Friedman thought they might be able to wait for journal publication. With a committee needed to write the report, this might take a year. *Thou Shalt Not Tell* was so deeply embedded in medical culture that the board members never seriously considered a major public announcement. With consensus in hand, the board voted to dissolve itself. The vote was unanimous. The Cardiac Arrhythmia Suppression Trial was over.

It happened to fall to Peter Frommer, deputy director of the National Heart, Lung, and Blood Institute, to notify higher authority. He sent a memo to Bernadine Healy, the director of the National Institutes of Health, summarizing the results. He added, "We do not plan a public announcement at this time, but results will be reported at the American Heart Association meeting in November, and publication will be expeditious."

Records and recollections are not clear, but it was apparently DuPont's Sara Armstrong Mahler who derailed the plans to say nothing. She wanted to send a "dear doctor" letter advising physicians of the findings immediately. One hundred thousand letters would surely generate questions about why the heart institute had said nothing. In response, a press release was prepared that said next to nothing. The institute made the document available in the darkest period of the news cycle: late Friday afternoon when almost all reporters had already filed their weekend stories.

The DuPont letter to doctors put the best face on the situation. It revealed that CAST II had been terminated "due to unfavorable trends having evolved and the remote likelihood of showing net benefit in reducing sudden cardiac death with continued therapy." It did not even mention the finding that had caused the trial to be terminated on safety grounds: the 17 versus 3 deaths during the two-week titration test. There was no explanation why DuPont failed to inform doctors of a newly discovered danger of this magnitude. The FDA should have insisted on this disclosure.

The press release was similarly low-key. It too omitted any mention of the significant new hazard discovered during the trial—the many deaths experienced during dose titration. It was all handled so skillfully that just two newspapers carried a brief wire story, a small southern Indiana paper, *Brown County Chronicle*, and the Detroit *Free Press*.

It was in this manner that the saga of antiarrhythmic drugs sputtered to a quiet and inconclusive close. Among the entire family of drugs, only one was withdrawn. Shortly after the CAST II findings were released, Bristol-Myers voluntarily withdrew Enkaid. DuPont sold Ethmozine to another company, Berlex. The others are still sold, although the drug labels now carry additional restrictions and warnings. The drugs are widely used today for different kinds of irregular heartbeat—those of the atria, the small chambers at the top of the heart that serve as primer pumps. These kinds of rhythm disturbance are rarely as severe as those affecting the ventricles, the main pumping chambers. Doctors are still free to exercise their medical judgment and may prescribe antiarrhythmics for patients with premature beats. Except for drug company marketing programs, no system in organized medicine today exists either to determine how physicians are using the drugs or to discourage uses that are manifestly dangerous.

Meanwhile, many of the key players in the story of antiarrhythmic drugs are still active.

- Albert I. Murphy, the heart attack survivor who joined CAST, was in the group that took the inactive placebo. He is alive and leads an active life.
- Representative Ted Weiss died of a heart attack six months after the Tambocor hearing. No other member of Congress has taken up his interest in oversight of the FDA.
- Mitchell Zeller, who did Weiss's Tambocor investigation, went to work for the FDA.

- Roger Winkle, who warned early of the dangers of these drugs, quit a tenured position at Stanford to focus exclusively on patient care.
- Thomas Bigger is chairing another clinical trial. This one will test whether implantable defibrillators prevent sudden death in heart surgery patients.
- Raymond Woosley, now at Georgetown University, called for creating a government institute to provide drug information and research free of the influence of the pharmaceutical industry.
- Joel Morganroth heads a company developing computer software to help the FDA review drug testing data. He still works part-time for the FDA reviewing drugs and consults for the drug industry.
- Lawrence Friedman was promoted to head the National Heart, Lung, and Blood Institute's Division of Epidemiology and Clinical Applications.
- Robert Temple and Raymond Lipicky hold the same jobs at the Food and Drug Adminstration, where pressures continue to approve drugs more quickly and with less clinical testing.

ACKNOWLEDGMENTS

SOON AFTER THE 1989 publication of my first book, *Heart Failure*, I received a visit from a 77-year-old pediatric cardiologist named John Nestor. He had sought me out because of my expressed concerns about the safety and excessive use of cholesterol-lowering drugs. He handed me a copy of the Cardiac Arrhythmia Suppression Trial results and suggested that it showed an even greater lapse in drug regulation. How right he was! Over the intervening years I came to know Nestor as a truly indefatigable crusader for drug safety, whose concerns and activities span four decades. He generously shared his large library of documents and his thoughts on many issues, and reviewed the section of this book on drug approval.

However, the conclusions, analysis, and any shortcomings are entirely my own responsibility. Nestor, and the many other individuals who assisted me have a wide variety of backgrounds, perspectives and opinions; they do not necessarily share mine.

Special thanks also go to Sidney Wolfe, another lifelong crusader for an improved medical system. Almost a decade ago, Wolfe gave a seminar that first stimulated my interest in writing about medical topics. For this book, he generously shared his thoughts, experience, and the files of the Public Citizen Health Research Group.

Mitchell R. Zeller also played an important role in this book. While counsel to a House subcommittee, he was the first investigator of the events recounted in this book. Not only did he assemble an important hearing and exhibits, he generously shared his experiences and guided me through the public files of the Subcommittee on Human Resources and Intergovernmental Relations.

It is also important to acknowledge the cooperation of the principal figures in this book, and the two major government agencies, the Food and Drug Administration and the National Heart, Lung, and Blood Institute. Of the main characters in this book, only J. Thomas Bigger, Jr., could not find time for an interview despite repeated requests over many months time. Robert Temple, Lawrence Friedman, Raymond Lipicky, and Joel Morganroth all spent many hours with me despite the pressures of senior positions and heavy competing demands on their time. The FDA also produced thousands of pages of documents requested under the Freedom of Information Act. While my requests were legal and valid, it nevertheless was a substantial burden, especially on the Cardio-Renal Drug Division. In particular, I appreciate the efforts of Gerald Deighton, director of the FDA's Freedom of Information Act staff. All of this cooperation was particularly noteworthy considering that I have been a public critic of the National Heart, Lung, and Blood Institute, and would find much had gone wrong at the FDA in the approval of antiarrhythmic drugs.

I am also indebted to the individuals who reviewed and commented on the manuscript. Dean T. Mason, M.D., editor of the *American Heart Journal*, examined the text from a cardiologist's perspective. Robert Beardall, M.D., and Kevin B. Weiss, M.D., M.P.H., reviewed it from a public health and internal medicine viewpoint. As noted, John Nestor, M.D., reviewed the section on drug approval. Edward N. Krapels, Ph.D., reviewed the book from the perspective of a lay reader with personal experience with the lifesaving properties of prescription drugs. Milton Carrow provided many helpful suggestions.

I also appreciate the technical assistance and comment for some of the specialized sections. For Chapter 2, Martin Johnson, Ph.D., of the George Washington University Department of Chemistry, provided technical assistance, and Alice Mauskopf, a former medicinal chemist now a medical student at Duke University, reviewed it. For the section on the FDA, I benefited greatly from the background and insights provided by FDA veterans Wayne Pines, Marion Finkel, M.D., John Villforth, Mark Novitch, M.D., and Jeff Nesbit. Alan Garber, M.D., Ph.D., of Stanford University, and Lawrence Friedman, M.D., provided helpful comments on the mortality estimates. The account of CAST benefited greatly from the assistance of James A. Curtin, M.D., chairman of the Department of Medicine at Washington Hospital Center. He helped obtain the many permissions necessary to show a clinical trial at the patient and medical center level. Margrit Scholz and Ruth McBride of the CAST Coordinating Center in Seattle spent much time helping me understand the center's operations.

George Washington University continued to provide a stimulating environment for my research and writing. I appreciate the interest and support from Rodrick French, Ph.D., vice president for academic affairs, and Peter Budetti, M.D., J.D., director of the Center for Health Policy Research. At the center, Denise Parris and Lee Ann Bernick provided invaluable administrative support; at the Himmelfarb Health Sciences Library, George Paul continued to provide invaluable assistance in locating the many medical studies.

Kevin Mills provided extensive research assistance on the pharmaceutical industry, especially on marketing practices, and helped compile the lengthy bibliography.

I could never have done this book without the support of Bob Bender, my editor at Simon & Schuster, and the assistance of my agent, Esther Newberg.

The book might have gotten started, but it certainly would never have been finished, without the moral support and many editorial suggestions from my wife, Barbara.

Excess Mortality Estimates

POPULATION ESTIMATES OF death have political, moral and policy implications that often are difficult to separate from the technical considerations. In most extreme cases, officials simply decline to estimate deaths because they do not want to know the number. The classic example was the Bush administration's refusal to estimate the number of Iraqi combat deaths in the Persian Gulf War and its dismissal of a Census Bureau population specialist who attempted to do so. Antiarrhythmic drug mortality was a less extreme example. However, it is important to begin by separating a political or psychological preference for ignorance from the question of whether it is scientifically feasible to make reasonable calculations from the imperfect data available. In the case of antiarrhythmic drugs, adequate information is available to make estimates of an accuracy that is comparable with other population estimates used for public health and other policy purposes.

The main task of such estimates is to establish an order of magnitude of the overall problem; adequate data are seldom available to guarantee the literal truth. Great approximations and shaky assumptions underlie many widely used health figures. For example, estimates of the number of people infected with HIV are not determined by random sampling of representative populations; they are inferred from the results of tests in selected specialized populations, such as inductees into the Armed Forces or blood donors. Further, each source of data can be accurate or inaccurate in particular aspects. Death certificates, for example, provide a highly accurate absolute count of deaths and, except in the very oldest individuals, accurate data on age at death. On the other hand, medical cause of death information is extremely suspect, and independent audits have disclosed error rates of up to 50 percent. Other important public health information depends on rather gross assumptions. For example, the Centers for Disease Control and Prevention maintain a national surveillance system to track influenza. The underlying data, however, are not based on confirmed diagnoses of influenza, which would require isolating the virus in each sampled individual. They are inferred from physician counts of respiratory cases and community totals of deaths from pneumonia and related respiratory disease. What appears to

be a widespread agreement on many public health estimates does not necessarily come from underlying quality of the data. Normally everyone uses
the same numbers because of a political agreement to accept, with all its
flaws, a particular method. Estimating deaths from antiarrhythmic drugs with
different methods produces different answers, not because it is an unusually
rough approximation, but because of a lack of an existing scientific consensus, since most experts involved did not choose to consider the issue.

A mortality estimate requires three elements. The first is the size of the
population at risk. The second is the magnitude of the risk. This is typically
expressed in two ways, as a relative risk (e.g., it increases the chance of
death by 3 times) or an absolute risk (e.g., 5 percent of those exposed
died). The third element is the time period. Mortality estimates are usually
calculated on an annual basis. This whole can be divided into an unlimited
number of separate components, and the population, risk, and period of
exposure calculated separately. Then the individual pieces can be summed
to create an overall total. The more separate calculations, the more "refined"
the estimate, but usually either the data are not detailed enough to allow
further subgroup analysis, or the results do not vary significantly enough
among subgroups to alter the overall total in a meaningful way. In short,
fairly simple and straightforward estimates frequently are as good as very
sophisticated calculations and contain fewer buried assumptions.

The fundamentals can be observed with the simplest possible approach.
During 1989–90, an average of 733,000 persons were exposed to the six
largest-selling Class I antiarrhythmic drugs at any particular point. The CAST
I results showed an absolute annual risk of death of 5.88 percent of the
participants (the difference in total mortality between the treatment group
and the placebo group, divided by the size of the treatment group, adjusted
for a one-year period). This yields an initial one-year mortality estimate of
43,106 persons. All other additions, subtractions and refinements can be
considered in reference to this central calculation.

The first consideration is statistical variation. The results of a randomized
clinical trial should represent accurately the experience of a larger similar
population, but the figure is only a possible point within a range or zone.
Statistical theory holds that if the CAST trial were repeated many times we
would expect to observe the excess mortality as much as 33 percent lower
and 50 percent higher—but most of the outcomes should be quite similar
to CAST. This is important in two ways. It communicates the idea we can
be 99 percent certain that the "true" excess mortality lies somewhere within
this zone, but much less certain it is exactly the figure reported. Second, it
is possible that a statistical aberration pushed the CAST result toward one
extreme or another. We would suspect this if other definitive studies produced notably higher or lower estimates. Since there are no other studies
with statistically significant results, it leaves us more or less dependent on

the CAST for the risk estimate. However, the initial crude calculation of 43,106 annual deaths should be considered a point estimate in a zone of possible results that range from approximately 28,000 to 65,000 deaths.

The next step is a careful examination of the exposed population for sources of overestimate or underestimate. The estimate of 733,000 persons is the essence of simplicity. Pharmacy sample data show that over the two-year period, a total of 1.6 billion tablets were dispensed in the United States. Applying the manufacturer's recommended daily dose (two per day for Tambocor and Enkaid, three for Mexitil, three to four for quinidine, etc.) over two years yields an average patient exposure of 733,000. This is an underestimate of at least 20 percent because it assumes perfect patient compliance. Even with the intensive and professional follow-up of a well-run clinical trial, only 80 percent of the CAST medication was taken. In the daily clinical practice, compliance was almost surely even lower in a patient population without symptoms. There are two reasons for not adjusting the exposed population estimate upward. First, on theoretical grounds it might be that if the danger comes from the medication, the risk applies only if the medication is taken. Second, sources of error will occur in both directions. Estimating errors tend to cancel each other out unless the investigator is biased and adjusts for factors only on one side of the equation. In sum, this appears to be a conservative estimate of the exposed population and certainly not a source of a possibly inflated estimate.

A greater danger of a flawed result might come because the CAST patients do not represent the entire population taking the five antiarrhythmic drugs. On one side, CAST excluded a small number of the most seriously ill; on the other hand, it excluded many patients because they were too healthy. Either they had not previously experienced a heart attack, or they did not have enough premature beats to qualify. In clinical testing, gross death rates suggested that the hazard of these drugs was proportional to the underlying condition of the left ventricle—the greater the damage, the greater the risk. For this reason, the relative risk might be a better measure of risk than the absolute risk. The CAST relative risk of 2.5, for example, asserts that in an individual with a 1 percent chance of dying in a year's time, the risk would rise to 2.5 percent. But in someone with a 20 percent chance of dying—for example, a patient in severe heart failure—the annual risk would rise to 50 percent. When Alfred Hallstrom analyzed the more and less healthy patients in CAST he found a reasonably consistent relative risk, but a varying absolute risk of death. Therefore, the alternative approach, using the CAST data, is to assume it increases the underlying risk of death by 2.5 times. This, however, raises the question of determining the health status of the patient population taking the six antiarrhythmic drugs. Previous estimates were based only on a crude pill count.

The best information on patient characteristics comes from the National Ambulatory Medical Care Survey (U.S. HHS, NCHS 1990), a random sample of the 700,000 annual office visits in the years 1989 and 1990. The author's analysis of these data tapes reveals the basic information about the office visits of patients reported to be on one of the six antiarrhythmic drugs. The data show 2.5 million annual office visits by individuals taking these drugs. (These are office visits being measured, not individuals, and this analysis assumes each patient visited the doctor about three times a year.) The main patient characteristics are shown in Table 1. Inspection reveals two notable features, one possible source of a higher death estimate, and one lower. At an average age of 70, this is a much older patient population than in CAST, where the average age was 61. On the other hand, even under the assumption of typical health status for their age group, the office visit population had a 3.8 percent annual risk of death, as shown in Table 2. This risk multiplied by 2.5 yields an excess death total of 69,340—much higher than by the previous technique. However, the consensus view was that CAST risks applied most clearly to patients with already damaged hearts. On this basis, we could exclude 39 percent of the population because these NAMCS records disclosed no evidence of structural heart disease. A recalculation yields an estimate of 42,298 deaths per year. This is remarkably close to the results of the first technique. However, this figure also represents a likely underestimate. First, it assumes that antiarrhythmic drugs have no risk whatever in the population without structural heart disease. While it is possible that the risk might be substantially lower, it seems unlikely that the drugs had no risk at all. Second, the NAMCS data is not a complete patient medical record and may omit many diagnoses of heart disease. Third, it assumes that the patient population with structural heart disease has the same life

TABLE 1. CHARACTERISTICS OF PATIENTS
6 CLASS I ANTIARRHYTHMIC DRUGS
National Ambulatory Medical Care Survey
1989–90 Combined

		Drug		Diagnosis	
Male	0.65	Quinidine	0.56	CHD	0.56
Female	0.35	Procainamide	0.18	Hypertension	0.21
		Norpace	0.10	CHF	0.10
Avg. Age	70.6	Mexitil	0.09	Valve disorder	0.03
		Tambocor	0.05	Conduction	0.02
Age Quartiles		Enkaid	0.03	Cardiomyopathy	0.01
1 >77				Any Structural*	0.61
2 71-77					
3 64-70					
4 <64					

* *Excludes hypertension*

Table 2. Baseline Mortality in General Population
U.S. LIFE TABLE FOR 1990

Estimating Patients 1989/90		Source
Office Visits	2,500	NAMCS Data
Prescriptions	2,192	IMS Data 6 leading class I
Units	199,954	IMS Est. of tablets/capsules
Patients	732,866 @ 3 tablets per person per day	
	(or 3 visits per year per patient)	

Exposed Population in 1990

Male	62.0%	454,377
Female	38.0%	278,489

Baseline Mortality in General Population
U.S. LIFE TABLE FOR 1990

	Age Quartile	Quartile Age for Point Estimate	Male Age Death Rate	Female Age Death Rate	Male Deaths	Female Deaths
1	78-90	82	0.0877	0.0482	9,959	3,352
2	72-79	75	0.0534	0.0259	6,064	1,802
3	64-72	68	0.0303	0.0157	3,437	1,095
4	22-64	60	0.0130	0.0079	1,476	551
Total Mortality		27,736			20,935	6,801
Baseline Risk		0.037846				

expectancy and mortality rate as the general population. Clearly they do not. The major reference on this subject, *Medical Risks* (Lew 1990) provides only the most meager assistance, showing the excess risk in the heart disease population ranges from as little as 10 percent to as high as 1,000 percent. However, the general trend was that the later in life that heart disease is diagnosed, the less the excess risk compared with people of comparable age. This occurs for two reasons. Coronary heart disease tends to be more malignant the earlier in life that clinical indications appear. Also, underlying death rates rise exponentially with advancing age, meaning that while these individuals had structural heart disease, an increasing proportion of the age cohort had other serious disorders. If in a final adjustment, we assume that structural heart disease increases the underlying risk of death by 50 percent compared with the general population, then the excess death total rises to 63,446. In technical terms, this estimate is most refined, in taking the most factors into account.

The third major factor that influences the results is the question of whether the toxicity found for Tambocor and Enkaid applies to other drugs in the Class I family. In the post-CAST world, intuition and clinical experience led many cardiologists interviewed for this book to assert that the two drugs were unusually toxic, especially compared with major sellers quinidine and Mexitil. If that were true, then the figures above could be significant overestimates. However, before the CAST results were known, these same experts asserted exactly the opposite. In journal reports quoted in the text, they proclaimed Tambocor and Enkaid unusually safe and well tolerated. In earlier comparisons of proarrhythmic effects, these drugs did not disclose significant differences in toxicity, nor did the FDA labeling (Morganroth 1988, Podrid 1987). This reveals only that anecdotal clinical judgments are not useful for this purpose. If one had to assume anything it would be the opposite: a group of experts that consistently underestimated the dangers of these drugs continues to do so now. The more important question is what the evidence shows. No clinical trial evidence exists to assert that any of the drugs in the family are either more or less toxic than Tambocor and Enkaid. Therefore the reasonable assumption is to conclude they are similar, absent convincing evidence to the contrary. The Ethmozine data from CAST II are as close as we can get to a second toxicity estimate for another drug in the family. It was also regarded as the most benign of the agents. While the differences are not statistically significant, the absolute mortality results are similar. In the Ethmozine arm, 2 percent excess mortality occurred during titration, and during the long-term trial, 4 percent. In CAST the absolute mortality was 4.9 percent during trial, or a 5.88 percent annual rate. (Titration mortality could not be estimated without a control group, the gross numbers suggest it was lower than for Ethmozine.) The other drug comparison comes from a meta-analysis of the clinical testing trials that compared quinidine with four other drugs. Morganroth and Goin (Morganroth 1991) concluded that quinidine had a 60 percent higher risk of death than the combined results for Tambocor, Enkaid, Mexitil, and Tonocard. The FDA position is that quinidine is more harmful than other Class I drugs (Lipicky interview). Inconclusive information on Mexitil is also available from the IMPACT trial discussed in the text. The absolute excess mortality was lower than in CAST, 2.8 percent. Overall, none of these data refute the general proposition that similar drugs have similar toxicity. We could assume that Mexitil is slightly safer and quinidine is more toxic. The group average remains similar to what was seen in CAST. Alternatively we could assume that these separately inconclusive results are statistical variation well within the range of possible outcomes established in the CAST study. In any event there appears no scientific basis to support an assertion that the other drugs are less toxic.

One important published study appears to support a lower toxicity estimate. A published meta-analysis (Teo 1993) finds the use of Class I drugs "associated with increased mortality." However, when it consolidates the results from 138 clinical trials, it reports a relative risk in the heart attack population of 1.14, much lower than the 2.5 found in CAST. The difference between the two estimates is not a difference in data, it lies in conceptual approach. The Teo study does not yield an annual mortality estimate. It calculates the results of "treatment" which varied from one hour to one year. It also includes the results of unapproved drugs (aprindine), rarely used drugs (imipramine), and IV drugs (lidocaine) and obsolete drugs (phenytoin). It is a useful study in establishing that antiarrhythmic drug treatment with Class I drugs is harmful in a wide variety of clinical settings, and for a large number of drugs. The methodology used, however, does not yield an annual mortality estimate. The results of this analysis should provide a more accurate measure of annual mortality than the Teo approach.

The final source of underestimate in this analysis is that it omits some of the Class I drugs—lidocaine, imipramine, phenytoin and Tonocard, in particular. The effects of the omission, however, are not large. Imipramine is seldom prescribed for this purpose; lidocaine is not used in the outpatient setting, and Tonocard had a small fraction of the market of the other drugs. The effects of the Class III drugs—Cordarone and sotalol—can only be guessed at; they behave so differently that no reasonable inference can be made from the CAST results. They also were not included.

Therefore, these data show that mortality in 1989–90 was from 40,000 to 70,000 lives per year from the six largest-selling Class I drugs. The estimate in the chapter text was lower (28,000) because it tried to use the exact information readily available to the press conference participants. The only significant difference was that cardiologists assumed that CAST risk applied only to patients with ventricular arrhythmias, not to those with atrial rhythm disturbances, even in the presence of structural heart disease. Reducing the population at risk by one half reduces the estimated annual mortality by a similar amount.

These estimates are an annual estimate for 1989–90. This is a fairly representative period, since sales where higher in the years before 1989 and lower after 1990 (see Chart 1). In computing a final death toll from the inappropriate use of antiarrhythmic drugs, how many years should be included? There is no obvious answer. But throughout the decades, these drugs have been prescribed, it is clear that hundreds of thousands died prematurely, an estimate in which two experts, Woosley and Morganroth concurred in interviews. Robert Temple did not go beyond his published approximation of tens of thousands of deaths. Lawrence Friedman agreed that the number of annual deaths was large, but he could not say for certain whether it was a few thousand a year or tens of thousands a year.

It is unfortunate that the annual mortality estimates cover such a wide range—from 24,000 deaths to 70,000 (see Table 3). However, a mortality estimate only has to be sufficiently accurate for the public health purpose to which it is applied. For this account, what matters is the public realization that the events reported in this book constitute the greatest medical drug disaster in history, causing deaths of the scale of major military conflicts such as Korea and Vietnam. It also shows that CAST saved tens of thousands of lives by sounding the alert, although the benefits of this important study were diminished by the failure to wage an educational campaign to halt inappropriate use of antiarrhythmic drugs, which continues to this day.

TABLE 3. POPULATION BASED ESTIMATES

Method 1 Apply CAST absolute annual mortality

Patients - 1 qtr 1989	818,703
CAST - like fraction	409,352
Annual mortality @ 0.0588	24,070

Method 2 Class I drugs increase risk of death 2.5 times in exposed population

Population 89/90	732,866
Expected deaths	27,736
Excess deaths	69,340

Method 3 Class I drugs increase risk 2.5 times only in patients w/ structural heart disease

Population 89/90	732,866
Structural heart disease	447,049
Excess deaths	42,298

Method 4 Class I drugs increase risk 2.5 times only in patients w/ structural heart disease
1.5 times higher baseline risk

Population 89/90	732,866
Structural heart disease	447,049
Excess Deaths	63,446

Method 5 Apply absolute risk of CAST to structural heart disease population

Population 89/90	732,866
Structural heart disease	447,049
Annual mortality @ 0.0588	26,286

GLOSSARY OF MEDICAL TERMS

angina Chest pains that are a symptom of coronary heart disease and can indicate that the heart is not getting sufficient blood supply.

arrhythmia Any disturbance of the heart rhythm or the electrical signals that regulate it.

asymptomatic A medical condition without symptoms that are detectable by the patient.

asystole Complete electrical death of the heart.

atria The two small chambers that contract to prime the main pumping chambers, the left and right ventricles.

atrial fibrillation The electrical disorganization of the two smaller chambers that serve as primer pumps for the ventricles. The two atria are electrically isolated from the ventricles. This condition is far less serious than ventricular fibrillation. It can produce mild symptoms, fatigue, and can reduce cardiac output by 20 percent. Atrial fibrillation is terminated with antiarrhythmic drugs or a direct-current shock.

bradycardia A slower-than-normal heartbeat. Tachycardia describes a rapid beat.

cardiac arrest A complete halt in the heart's pumping activity.

coronary Having to do with the heart.

coronary heart disease The medical term for a series of conditions linked to obstructions in the arteries that provide the heart's own blood supply. A heart attack is the sudden and complete obstruction of one or more coronary arteries. Angina is chest pains from an obstruction large enough to produce an insufficient blood supply under some conditions.

couplet Two premature ventricular contractions in a row.

EKG *(or sometimes ECG)* Common medical abbreviation for electrocardiogram.

electrocardiogram A graph of the electrical activity of the heart. The classic EKG involves 12 leads, but other monitors may use fewer leads.

electrophysiological testing The same as *programmed electrical stimulation.*

exercise stress test An electrocardiogram taken while the patient is subjected to increasing levels of exercise on a treadmill. Most common use is to seek evidence that obstructions exist in the coronary arteries. If serious blockages are present they may prevent the heart from getting the increased blood supply demanded with exercise. This stress produces alterations in the electrocardiogram.

fibrillation   The electrical disorganization of the heart causing the individual cells to contract at random, therefore producing no pumping effect. The two main pumping chambers, the ventricles, are isolated electrically from the two smaller primer pumps, the left and right atria. Fibrillation can occur in either the atria or the ventricles with dramatically different effect. See *ventricular fibrillation* and *atrial fibrillation*.

heart attack   Lay term for acute myocardial infarction. In this condition a coronary artery is suddenly obstructed, which cuts off the blood supply to an area of heart tissue. Unless this obstruction is relieved, the cells die. Heart cells cannot be replaced.

Holter monitor   A portable device that records an EKG for a 12- or 24-hour period on magnetic tape.

nonsustained ventricular tachycardia   Usually defined as three or more PVCs in a row without a normal beat. See *sustained ventricular tachycardia*.

pacemaker of the heart   A small node of tissue that emits the periodic electrical signal that begins a heart contraction.

premature ventricular complex   Premature contraction of the left and right ventricles prior to when the periodic signal arrives. Also called ectopic beat, ectopy, premature beat and premature ventricular contraction. Abbreviated as PVC.

programmed electrical stimulation   A major diagnostic procedure in which an electrode is inserted in a vein in the groin, and then threaded into the right ventricle. A special computer is programmed to emit both regular pulses to contract and irregular pulses, simulating premature ventricular contractions. The purpose of the procedure is to see whether these premature beats trigger sustained ventricular tachycardia. In some treatment routines, antiarrhythmic drugs are then administered to see if they prevent induction of the tachycardia.

sudden cardiac death   Death caused by cardiac arrest. In some definitions it is classified as any cardiac death occurring within one hour of the onset of symptoms.

supraventricular   A condition involving the atria of the heart rather than the ventricles.

sustained ventricular tachycardia   A self-perpetuating rapid heartbeat that occurs when the electrical signal to contract circulates continuously around the ventricles. In only the most serious cases is "sustained" ventricular tachycardia incessant. Usually it comes and goes, and a diagnosis of sustained ventricular tachycardia is given for a period as brief as several minutes.

tachycardia Rapid beat of the heart.

ventricles The main pumping chambers of the heart. The right ventricle pumps blood to the lungs, the left ventricle to the rest of the body.

ventricular fibrillation The electrical disorganization of the ventricles with the individual cells contracting randomly. The output of the heart falls to zero in cardiac arrest. Ventricular fibrillation is lethal without a direct-current shock, which frequently restores a normal rhythm.

ANTIARRHYTHMIC DRUG GUIDE

Drugs prescribed for irregular heart rhythms are divided into four classes, I through IV. Many have other unrelated medical uses or indications. If you are interested or concerned about a drug you are now taking, the most detailed information comes on the drug label, or package insert, which can be obtained from your pharmacist. It also appears in publications such as *Drug Facts and Comparisons* and *Physicians' Desk Reference (PDR)*. A medical dictionary is often helpful in understanding the technical language. As noted earlier, the generic or chemical names are in lower case; brand names are capitalized.

CLASS I

Cardioquin (quinidine)
disopyramide
encainide
Enkaid (encainide)
Ethmozine (moricizine)
flecainide
mexiletine
Mexitil (mexiletine)
moricizine
Norpace (disopyramide)
procainamide
Procan (procainamide)
Pronestyl (procainamide)
propafenone
Quinaglute Dura-Tabs (quinidine)
Quinalan (quinidine)
quinidine
quinidine gluconate
quinidine sulfate
Quinora (quinidine)
Quinidex Extentabs (quinidine)
Rythmol (propafenone)
Tambocor (flecainide)
tocainide
Tonocard (tocainide)

This family of drugs is the focus of the book. They work by slowing, at the cellular level, the conduction of the electrical signal to contract. They are chemically related to (or in some cases are) local anesthetics. Mainly as a result of the events described in this book, the FDA urges restricting the use of these drugs to "documented life-threatening" heart rhythm disturbances. There are a few exceptions. Tambocor was also given an indication for use against disorders of the atria—the two small primer pumps— in patients who have no other heart trouble. The evidence was most definitive that Tambocor and Enkaid caused cardiac arrest in patients who already had damaged hearts. There was evidence that similar effects might have occurred with Ethmozine and Mexitil, but it was not as conclusive. There was less extensive testing of propafenone, quinidine, procainamide and disopyramide. But the FDA's warning for this group of less extensively tested drugs says it is "prudent" to assume that these drugs have similar capacity to trigger cardiac arrest, although they might be either more toxic or less toxic than Tambocor and Enkaid.

Class II

acebutolol	metoprolol
atenolol	propranolol
Blocadren (timolol)	Sectral (acebutolol)
Brevibloc (esmolol)	Tenormin (atenolol)
esmolol	timolol
Inderal (propranolol)	Toprol (metoprolol)
Lopressor (metoprolol)	

These Class II drugs are called beta-blockers because they block the beta receptors in heart and other muscle cells. These receptors receive signals from hormones that stimulate the cardiovascular system to increase blood circulation. The hormones are secreted in response to stress, anxiety, fear and excitement. In the case of the heart, the Class II drugs block signals calling for a greater pumping effort.

Generally, beta-blockers are quite different from the Class I drugs, and are used for a wide variety of medical purposes: for high blood pressure, for chest pains and for some heart rhythm disturbances. Some are used to combat migraine headaches; one beta-blocker has a contraceptive effect in women. They often are prescribed for heart attack survivors because a clinical trial showed beta-blockers reduced the risk of death in this patient group.

Despite a good safety record, the limitation to many beta-blockers is their side effects, which include fatigue, lassitude, impotence and depression.

Class III

amiodarone	Cordarone (amiodarone)
Betapace (sotalol)	sotalol

This family of drugs also alters how the muscle cells conduct the impulse to contract, but with a different mechanism from Class I drugs such as Tambocor. Class III drugs lengthen the brief period when the cells cannot respond to an electrical signal to contract. The two drugs in Class III are quite different from each other. The limited testing of Cordarone prior to approval was discussed in Chapter 15. Sotalol is unusual because it also has beta-blocking effects. However, the FDA has approved it only for life-threatening rhythm disturbances. Use of amiodarone is even more restricted, limited to life-threatening situations when other drugs have not worked.

CLASS IV

bepridil	Isoptin (verapamil)
Calan (verapamil)	Vascor (bepridil)
Cardizem (diltiazem)	verapamil
Dilacor (diltiazem)	Verelan (verapamil)
diltiazem	

This group of drugs are called calcium channel blockers because they affect a cell's ability to move calcium ions through the membrane. The electrical pulses of the heartbeat involve movement of calcium and sodium ions. While most commonly prescribed for high blood pressure, calcium channel blockers are also used for rhythm disorders of the atria, and in disorders of the specialized heart muscle tissues that help time the contraction. Vascor or bepridil is unusual because it shares some of the characteristics—and the dangers—of the Class I drugs such as Tambocor and Enkaid.

Notes and Sources

Several general conventions were observed throughout the book. As noted at the beginning, drugs have two names, a brand name and a chemical name, but only the brand name was used for each drug in this book. Drug names were substituted within quotations without the brackets or other notation.

Another minor source of potential confusion comes because medical journal articles typically have several authors, and the citations appear in the bibliography indexed by the first author. Frequently the senior research physicians who were characters in the book were the last-named author. Therefore the notes will show, for example, an article attributed in the text to Raymond Woosley as "Roden 1980" because Dan M. Roden was the first-named author, and that's how it should be looked up in the medical journal indexes. In a book unfolding over more than two decades, the names of organizations, titles of individuals and their academic affiliations often changed. As much as possible, the text uses one name, title or affiliation. The most important changes were: Until 1989, 3M Pharmaceuticals was called Riker Laboratories; it is called 3M Pharmaceuticals throughout. In 1989, Bristol-Myers merged with Squibb. Except for the first reference it is referred to only as Bristol-Myers. The FDA was reorganized repeatedly; in 1988 the Office of Drug Evaluation, headed by Robert Temple, was divided into two units, Office of Drug Evaluation I and Office of Drug Evaluation II. Temple remained head of Office of Drug Evaluation I. All drug evaluation and approval activities were under the Bureau of Drugs until 1980, then from 1980 until 1987 the National Center for Drugs and Biologics; thereafter it was called the Center for Drug Evaluation and Research. Raymond Woosley is referred to as affiliated with Vanderbilt University. After 1988, he was chairman of the Department of Pharmacology at Georgetown University. Joel Morganroth's academic affilation changed repeatedly, and sometimes he had two affiliations at the same time, with a medical school and hospital. His principal affiliations were: 1975–78, University of Pennslyvania; 1978–82, Lankenau Medical Research Center; 1982–87, Hahnemann University Hospital; 1987–92, the Graduate Hospital of Philadelphia.

For published sources, the formal citation appears alphabetically in the bibliography. In these notes, the source document is cited in shortened style. For example, Moore 1989 indicates a bibliographic entry:

Moore, Thomas J. *Heart Failure*. New York: Random House, 1989.

The large number of government documents—and the cumbersome citations—create problems for those trying to locate these references. However, Kate Turabian (Turabian 1987) argues convincingly that without these full citations, the documents cannot be readily located through most library retrieval systems. Most federal government health agencies are part of the U.S. Department of Health and Human Services, which is abbreviated U.S HHS. FDA documents, for example, appear in the bibliography as: U.S. Department of Health and Human Services, Food and Drug Administration, but are cited below as U.S. HHS,FDA 1980. Similarly, National Heart, Lung and Blood Institute documents as U.S. HHS,NHLBI 1989.

Chapter 1.   A GENIE GETS OUT

Details of the 3M press conference were assembled from the 3M press release, from contemporaneous news reports, records of the National Press Club, and interviews with Gary Gentzkow and Joel Morganroth. The 1985 ranking of 3M is from Fortune 1986; and the most admired list is from Fortune 1985a, the press reports appeared as *New York Times* 1985, and Chemical Marketing Reporter 1985. The 3M spending estimate is from Carlson 1989. The number of office visits involving irregular heartbeats comes from the National Ambulatory Medical Care Survey (U.S. HHS, National Center for Health Statistics 1992). The volume of prescriptions for antiarrhythmic drugs is from Hine 1989. Readers should note that the number of prescriptions is much higher than the number of patients, since each prescription for these drugs is filled repeatedly over a year's time. The testing and animal studies for Tambocor were described in U.S. HHS,FDA 1989.

The ability of many cancer chemotherapy drugs to cause cancer was from an interview with the pharmacologist Joe Graedon. For a survey of the toxic properties of these drugs, sample the entries under "antineoplastics" in *Physicians' Desk Reference* 1994. Belladonna is described in Clark 1992 and curare in Moore 1989. The pyschoactive drugs blamed for suicides are Halcion and Prozac. The experimental drug that harmed the liver was reported in Schwartz 1993, the cholesterol-lowering drug that apparently caused heart attacks was dextrothyroxine and was reported in Coronary Drug Project 1972.

The case of the 16-year-old boy was from an adverse reaction report summarized by FDA medical officer Sughok Chun. The genie quote appeared in Lasagna 1964. Supporting evidence for the death toll from these drugs appears in Chapter 21 and the section on mortality estimates. The comparisons, along with Kenya's 1985 GNP, are from U.S. Dept. of Commerce 1992.

Chapter 2. DISCOVERY

Roger Winkle was interviewed. For a history of 3M see 3M 1977, Drucker 1985, various 3M annual reports, *Business Week* 1989, *Economist* 1991, *Forbes* 1976, Muskowitz 1980. The history of drug research and development came from Baumer 1965, Krantz 1974, LaWall 1927, Leake, 1975. Current research and development practices and policies are explored in Spilker 1989, Smith 1992, and Reekie 1979. The number of drugs screened in 1970 was from Schwartzman 1976, p. 60. For a gripping modern narrative of a drug development project see *The Billion-Dollar Molecule,* Werth 1994.

There are few recent books about the industry. Important works include Sliverman 1974 and Harris 1964. For the investigative perspective see Mintz 1967.

The synthesis of R-818 and other related compounds is elaborately described in Banitt 1975 and Banitt 1977. Hudak 1984 outlines the history of the development program. The mouse screening technique appears as Lawson 1968, and Banitt reported using this exact technique.

Chapter 3. A RACE BEGINS

Arthur Leon was interviewed about the first Phase I experiment. Donald Hunninghake provided additional details by correspondence. The experiment itself is described in Conard 1988, and in U.S. HHS,FDA 1989. Pitambar Somani was interviewed, and described the first effectiveness trial in Somani 1980.

Chapter 4. THE MAKING OF A MARKET

For medical detail about electrical disorders of the heart, the most thorough standard treatment can be found in four chapters in Braunwald 1992. Lown's background comes from Deriewicz 1990 and Lown's curriculum vitae (CV). His talk is reprinted in Lown 1979. The earliest formulation appears as Lown 1971. Also, for the risks of premature beats see Coronary Drug Project 1973, Ruberman 1977, Bigger 1978, and Bikkina 1992. Winkle's opposite view is in Winkle 1979. Woosley was interviewed and 3M's deliberations described in Hudak 1984, and the volume of prescriptions for 1979 was estimated from Hine 1989.

Chapter 5. THE RISE OF MORGANROTH

The Philadelphia symposium proceedings were published as Morganroth 1984. Details on Joel Morganroth came from an interview and his CV. His medical school essay appears under the name of his coauthor as Ruby 1970.

His early testing of Ethmozine is described in Morganroth 1979, and the problem of measuring suppression was published as Morganroth 1978.

The 3M decision to accelerate development is reported in Hudak 1984. The three identical oral dose-ranging studies of Tambocor appeared as Anderson 1981, Duff 1981 and Hodges 1982. The three abstracts were Anderson 1981a, Hodges 1981 and Duff 1980. Dean Mason was interviewed.

Chapter 6.   TAMBOCOR IN TROUBLE

Roger Winkle described his early concerns about the safety of Enkaid in an interview, and in the *American Heart Journal* (Winkle 1981). The upbeat Enkaid reports appear as Roden 1980, with Woosley as senior author, and Meissner 1986, with Morganroth as the senior author. Gary Gentzkow described his background and the atmosphere at 3M in an interview; additional details appear in Summary Basis of Approval U.S. HHS, FDA 1989. Lawrence Griffith was interviewed and additional facts appear in an abstract Griffith 1984. The additional studies the FDA required are described in Morganroth 1986.

Chapter 7.   SUMMIT MEETING

The account of the 1982 Tambocor summit meeting was drawn from many sources. Morganroth, Woosley, Griffith and Gentzkow were interviewed. It is described at length in the Tambocor Summary Basis of Approval (U.S. HHS,FDA 1989), and at an FDA advisory committee hearing (U.S. HHS, FDA 1984). Morganroth summarizes it at a symposium (Morganroth 1984). The Enkaid crisis is described in that drug's Summary Basis of Approval (U.S. HHS,FDA 1988). Lester Soyka describes the safety of Enkaid in Soyka 1986).

Chapter 8.   A QUESTION OF BENEFIT

Morganroth's third symposium was published as Morganroth 1983. The sotalol trial and other details were from an interview with Morganroth. The only published report appears as an abstract (Spielman 1985). Raymond Woosley provides an overview of sotalol in Hohnloser 1994. The trial of Mexitil was reported as IMPACT Research Group 1984. Another important dissent to the arrhythmia suppression hypothesis was Josephson 1986.

Chapter 9.   SHOWTIME

Thomas Bigger's career background comes from his curriculum vitae CV, with a few details from Rothfeder 1989. The sleepy intern study is Friedman 1971, and the editorial Kranes 1971. Morganroth's lectures are from his CV. The conference is described at length in a series of papers and comments

published together in the *American Journal of Cardiology,* as supplement
B in the February 27, 1984, issue. The papers quoted are listed individually
in the bibliography as Hudak 1984, Woosley 1984, Anderson 1984, Morganroth 1984, Hodges 1984, and Reid 1984. See Bero 1992 for an analysis
of the questionable practice of publishing drug company symposia in otherwise peer-reviewed medical journals.

Chapter 10. QUESTIONS FOR TEMPLE

The hearing on Zomax was reported as U.S. Congress, House 1983. The
FDA statistics were from Cooper 1991, page 149. The risks of chloramphenicol were from a pharmacology text (Clark 1992), and an internal
medicine text (Wyngaarden 1992). Temple's background was from an interview and his CV. Sidney Wolfe was interviewed. The case of the conscientious objectors is described at great length in the valuable report U.S.
Dept. HEW,FDA 1977. For more about how doctors use drugs for unlabeled
indications see U.S. General Accounting Office 1991, and U.S. Congress,
House 1991. For the case of Lopid, the cholesterol-lowering drug, compare
the drug label (*Physicians' Desk Reference* 1994) and Parke-Davis 1992.
August Watanabe's comments and Temple's rejoinder were reported in
Morganroth 1981, beginning at page 299.

Chapter 11. THE TAMBOCOR REVIEW

Sughok Chun was interviewed. The side effects of quinidine and procainamide are, as noted, from the antiarrhythmic drugs chapter of Gilman
1985. Charles A. Resnick was interviewed. Additional animal study details
appear in his review and are incorporated in the Tambocor Summary Basis
of Approval (U.S. HHS, 1989). Conard's statement at the Tambocor symposium is from Conard 1984. The case of aprindine and the dogs was
outlined in documents included in U.S. Congress, House 1982, page 150,
and elsewhere.

The drug adverse effects come from the following sources. *Physicians'
Desk Reference* 1992 is abbreviated *PDR.* Halothane (*PDR*); Declomycin,
(*PDR* and John Nestor interview); Mer/29 (Fine 1972 and Nestor inteview);
Zomax U.S. Congress, House 1983; Lopid, (*PDR*); Oraflex (U.S. Congress,
House 1982), Capoten and Coumadin (*PDR*). The case of Atromid-S and
cancer is described in Oliver 1978, the effects of the cholestrol-lowering
thyroid hormone, dextrothyroxine, was reported in Coronary Drug Project
1972. The cancer-causing properties of DES are in *PDR.*

Chapter 12. THE EXPERTS SPEAK

Raymond Lipicky was interviewed. The transcripts of two sessions of the
Cardio-Renal Drugs Advisory Committee are listed as U.S. HHS,FDA 1983

and U.S. HHS,FDA 1984. Curt D. Furberg also expanded and published his presentation in Furberg 1983. The Anderson and Pitt article was Anderson 1981.

Chapter 13. TEMPLE DECIDES

Robert Temple and Raymond Lipicky's memoranda describing their thoughts and concerns are published as exhibits to U.S.Congress, House 1991. The Philadelphia symposium is reported in Morganroth 1985.

Chapter 14. PANIC AT 3M

Some of 3M's concerns and actions are described in exhibits to U.S. Congress, House 1991, as were some of Florence Wong's conversations with Denver Presley. As noted, Temple, Lipicky, Chun, Morganroth and Gentzkow were interviewed.

Chapter 15. PERSUASION

The pivotal meeting between Robert Temple and the 3M team was described in Florence Wong's minutes, and included as an exhibit to U.S. Congress, House 1991. Bramh Singh was interviewed. The advisory committee meeting on Cordarone is listed as U.S. HHS,FDA 1984. The medical review of Cordarone was provided to the author in lieu of the Summary Basis of Approval, and is listed as U.S. HHS,FDA June 28, 1983.

Chapter 16. SELLING TO DOCTORS

The survey of pharmaceutical marketing practices in this chapter was assembled from dozens of sources. Among the most important was Sen. Edward Kennedy's landmark hearing (U.S. Congress, Senate 1990). The world of drug detailing is portrayed in several articles by Edward Roseman, listed under his name in the bibliography. See also Myers 1992, Bleidt 1992, Cetera 1992, Deardorff 1992, Eastman 1978, Labson 1979, O'Brien 1983, Beardsley 1992, Carlucci 1982, Caudil 1992. The story of an angry detailer can be seen in U.S. Congress, House 1978, beginning page 223. The free drug samples are described in a report forming an appendix to the Kennedy hearing, op. cit., as are the statistics on symposia. The list of gifts and reminder items was compiled mainly from colleagues of the author in active clinical medicine; a few came from articles in *Medical Marketing and Media*. An excellent overview of marketing can be found in Part Two of Donald Drake and Marian Uhlman's 1992 newspaper series on the pharmaceutical industry. In 1992 they list higher totals for spending for marketing ($10 billion versus my 1988 estimate of $8 billion) and for the drug detailing sales force (45,000 verus my 20,000). The number of detailers remains something of a mystery. The 20,000 figure is cited repeatedly (Deardorff 1992, Altamore 1979, and Pekkanen 1976) but the basis of the estimate or Drake's is not clear. My estimate of marketing spending was derived from figures in an excellent report on pharmaceutical industry R & D written by the U.S. Congress Office of Technology Assessment (U.S. Congress,OTA, 1993), and confirmed with Judith Wagner, a principal author of the report. It is substantially higher than the $5 billion figure cited in the Kennedy hearing, op.cit. The higher estimate, however, is based on much more de-tailed figures. The details of Joel Morganroth's financial and other activities were gathered from an interview, his CV and financial disclosure statements submitted to the FDA and obtained by the author. Thomas Graboys was interviewed. His article about overuse of antiarrythmic drugs is listed as Graboys 1986. Woosley's appraisal of Tambocor appears as Roden 1986.

The Wilkes study of misleading drug advertising is listed as Wilkes 1992. Examples reporting the industry response include Dickinson 1992 and Cas-tagnoli 1992. The Australian study is Wade 1989, and Jerry Avorn's analysis of influences on physician judgment is listed as Avorn 1982. The advertising violations and controversies of 3M are from FDA documents provided cour-tesy of the Health Research Group, which obtained them under the Freedom of Information Act. The FDA was unable to locate its drug advertising files on 3M.

Chapter 17. ENKAID IN TROUBLE

The Bristol-Myers advertising campaign and the FDA reaction to it was explored in U.S. Congress, House 1991. The Enkaid Phase IV trial, consult-ants' report and related material, and the adverse reaction reporting on Tambocor are from the author's files. For a typical mortality rate in a heart failure population, see Cohn 1986; for a postmyocardial-infarction popula-tion, see Coronary Drug Project 1973.

Chapter 18. THE FREAK OF CHANCE

Albert I. Murphy, Diane Law and Janna Harrison were interviewed. Mur-phy described his out-of-body experience in an unpublished manuscript chapter he was kind enough to share. As noted in the text, most of the history of the clinical trial came from Matthews (in press). For ethics see Freund 1969 and U.S. Congress, House 1973. Richard Riegleman's book appears as Riegleman 1991. For a complete description of CAST procedures see the manual of operations, listed as U.S HHS, NHLBI 1987, and the pro-tocol, U.S. HHS, NHLBI 1988. The psychosocial indicators are described in Gorkin 1993.

Chapter 19. A SIGNIFICANT DIFFERENCE

Lawrence Friedman and Alfred Hallstrom were interviewed, and shared many papers. Additionally, the author reviewed the minutes of the Data Safety and Monitoring Board and Steering Committee. Hallstrom addressed the data monitoring during CAST in Pawitan 1990, and Friedman discussed it in Friedman 1994. Morganroth's article about the new drugs is listed as Horowitz 1987. Note that when Hallstrom analyzed the interim results, he studied only those patients in whom a drug had been found to effectively suppress premature beats in a two-week preliminary period. Because some patients died during this two-week period and in others no drug would work, it was smaller than the total number recruited by that date.

Chapter 20. NO LONGER BLIND

Lawrence Friedman, Alfred Hallstrom and Raymond Woosley were interviewed. Additional detail came from the minutes of the Data Safety and Monitoring Board. Hallstrom's analysis, which was sent to the board members, was reviewed. Friedman and Hallstrom's published accounts, op. cit., also provided detail. For Thomas Bigger's perspective on these events see Bigger 1990.

Chapter 21. "YOU ARE IMMORAL"

For this chapter Raymond Woosley, Lawrence Friedman, Peter Frommer, Claude Lenfant, Michael White, Joel Morganroth, Robert Temple, and Jeff Nesbit were interviewed. Press accounts include Leary 1989, Associated Press 1989, and Specter 1989. The author also reviewed the press conference "background statement," listed as U.S. HHS, NHLBI 1989, and other press conference materials. The CAST results were published as Cardiac Arrhythmia Suppression Trial (CAST) Investigators 1989 and Echt 1991. See also Greene 1989. For detail on the mortality calculations see Appendix I. The Morganroth estimate of proarrhythmic effects is listed as Morganroth 1988. The Harvard malpractice study of New York hospitals is Brennan 1991. The comparative figures are from *Statistical Abstracts of the United States* (U.S. Dept. Commerce 1992). The antiarrhythmic drug section comparisons are for 1989 and the auto and homicide figures for 1990. Note that the mortality results cited at the press conference appear to be worse than those reported to the Data Safety and Monitoring Board just a few days earlier. The safety board initially considered the combined results for all three drugs in the trial. In these overall results, treatment appeared less harmful because at that time Ethmozine results were positive, with fewer deaths occurring among those taking the active drug.

Chapter 22. OUTCRY

The newspaper reports about doctors' reactions are attributed directly in the text. Page numbers were not available. The local reports in the Detroit *Free Press, New Haven Register, Ocala Star-Banner, Des Moines Register, Florida Times-Union,* and *Orlando Sentinel* appeared on April 27, 1989. The stories in the *Palm Beach Post* appeared on April 28, 1989. The drug company promotions to capture Tambocor and Enkaid's market share are from the author's files. The *Physician's Weekly* story is listed as Kerr 1989. Recer's Associated Press story ran in many newspapers on July 26, 1989. *The New York Times* version is listed as Associated Press 1989 and did not contain the confusing language. Joel Morganroth's rebuttal moved on the P.R. Newswire on July 26, 1989. The second story praising the drugs also appeared in many papers. *The New York Times* version is listed as Associated Press 1989. Robert Temple and Joel Morganroth were interviewed about the mortality estimates.

Chapter 23. THE FDA INQUIRES

The chapter was created from the transcript of the October 5, 1989, meeting of the Cardiovascular and Renal Drugs Advisory Committee. The conflicts-of-interest details were taken from FDA public files granting waivers to the seven participants. The memorandum to Frank Young is from the author's files.

Chapter 24. TEMPLE ON TRIAL

The House hearing on Tambocor and Enkaid is listed as U.S. Congress, House, 1991. Mitchell Zeller and Raymond Woosley were interviewed. Edward Pritchett and Jeffrey Anderson's comments were in letters included among the exhibits in the hearing book. The Institute of Medicine study of conflicts of interest on the advisory commitees is Rettig 1992. The landmark General Accounting Office study of serious labeling changes is listed as U.S. General Accounting Office 1990. The case of Manoplex is described in an April 26, 1993, FDA press release on the letterhead of the U.S. Department of Health and Human Services. The withdrawal of the drug was announced in Associated Press 1993.

Chapter 25. CAST II

The findings of CAST II appeared as Cardiac Arrhythmia Suppression Trial II Investigators 1992. Additional details came from the minutes of the Data Safety and Monitoring Board and from interviews with Lawrence Friedman, Alfred Hallstrom, Raymond Woosley and Peter Frommer. For an example of how it appears elsewhere see Greene 1992.

BIBLIOGRAPHY

Abitbol, Hugo, et al. "Use of Flecainide Acetate in the Treatment of Premature Ventricular Contractions." *Am. Heart J.* 105 (February 1983): 227–230.

Altamore, Philip, et al. "The Pharmaceutical Sales Representative—Opinions and Observations." *Med. Mark. & Med.* 14 (August 1979): 28–46.

Anderson, Jeffrey. "Experience with Electrophysiologically Guided Therapy of Ventricular Tachycardia with Flecainide: Summary of Long-Term Follow-Up." *Am. J. Cardiol.* 53 (February 27 1984): 79B–86B.

Anderson, Jeffery L., et al. "Oral Flecainide Acetate for Elimination of Ventricular Arrhythmias in Man." *Am. J. Cardiol.* 47 (February 1981): 482. (Abstr.)

Anderson, Jeffrey L., et al. "Oral Flecainide Acetate for the Treatment of Ventricular Arrhythmias." *N. Engl. J. Med.* 305 (August 27 1981): 473–477.

Anderson, Jeffrey L., et al. "A Proposal for the Clinical Use of Flecainide." *Am. J. Cardiol.* 53 (February 27 1984): 112B–119B.

Anderson, Jeffrey L., et al. "Relation of Baseline Characteristics to Suppression of Ventricular Arrhythmias During Placebo and Active Antiarrhythmic Therapy in Patients After Myocardial Infarction." *Circulation* 79 (March 1989): 610–619.

Antonaccio, Michael J., et al. "Dosing Recommendations for Encainide." *Am. J. Cardiol.* 58 (August 29 1986): 114C–116C.

Associated Press. "2 Heartbeat Drugs Restricted After Deaths." *Chicago Tribune.* April 28 1989.

Associated Press. "Researcher Estimates Heart Drugs Killed 2,250 in Last 2 Years." *New York Times.* July 26 1989, page A13.

Associated Press. "2 Heart Drugs Called Useful Though Dropped from Study." *New York Times,* July 28 1989, page A9.

Associated Press. "Heart Drug Is Withdrawn." *New York Times.* July 20 1993, page C-3.

Avorn, Jerry, et al. "Scientific versus Commercial Sources of Influence on the Prescribing Behavior of Physicians." *American Journal of Medicine* 73 (July 1982): 4–8.

Baker, Charles E., Jr. "Desk-Top Media Provide Cost-Effective Targeted Promotion." *Med. Mark. & Med.* 27 (April 1992): 68–74.

Banitt, E. H., et al. "Antiarrhythmics. N-(Aminoalkylene)trifluoroethoxy-benzamides and N-(Aminoalkylene)trifluoroethoxynaphthamides." *J. Med. Chem.* 18 (1975): 1130–1134.

Banitt, E. H., et al. "Antiarrhythmics. 2. Synthesis and Antiarrhythmic Activity of N-(Piperidylalkyl)trifluoroethoxybenzamides." *J. Med. Chem.* 20 (1977): 821–826.

Bartone, Nicholas. "The Role of Marketing Research During Drug Development." *Journal of Drug Issues* 22 (1992): 295–303.

Bauer, Raymond A., et al. "Doctor's Choice: The Physician and His Sources of Information About Drugs." *J. Mark. Res.* 3 (February 1966): 40–47.

Baumer, Ernst. *In Search of the Magic Bullet.* London: Thames and Hudson, 1965.

Beardsley, Rusty. "Building a Winning Sales Team." *Pharm. Exec.* (February 1992): 42–50.

Beary, John F., III. "Pharmaceutical Ads in Journals" (letter). *Annals of Internal Medicine.* 117 (Oct. 1 1992): 616.

Becker, Marshall H., et al. "Differential Education Concerning Therapeutics and Resultant Physician Prescribing Patterns." *J. Med. Educ.* 47 (February 1972): 118–127.

Beeson, P. B., and W. McDermott, editors. *Textbook of Medicine.* 14th edition, Philadelphia: W.B. Saunders Co., 1975.

Bero, Lisa A., et al. "The Publication of Sponsored Symposiums in Medical Journals." *N. Engl. J. Med.* 327 (October 15 1992): 1135–40.

Bhandari, Anil, et al. "Frequency and Significance of Induced Sustained Ventricular Tachycardia or Fibrillation Two Weeks After Acute Myocardial Infarction." *Am. J. Cardiol.* 56 (November 1 1985): 737–742.

Bigger, J. Thomas. "Antiarrhythmic Treatment: An Overview." *Am. J. Cardiol.* 53 (February 27 1984): 8B-16B.

Bigger, J. Thomas. "Long-Term Continuous Electrocardiographic Recordings and Electrophysiologic Testing to Select Patients with Ventricular Arrhythmias for Drug Trials and to Determine Antiarrhythmic Drug Efficacy." *Am. J. Cardiol.* 58 (August 29 1986): 58C–65C.

Bigger, J. Thomas. "Methodology for Clinical Trials with Antiarrhythmic Drugs to Prevent Cardiac Death: U.S. Experience." *Cardiology* 74 Suppl.2 (1987): 40–56.

Bigger, J. Thomas. "The Events Surrounding the Removal of Encainide and Flecainide From the Cardiac Arrhythmia Suppression Trial(CAST) and Why CAST Is Continuing With Moricizine." *J. Am. Coll. Cardiol.* 15 (January 1990): 243–245.

Bigger, J. Thomas, et al. "Risk Stratification after Acute Myocardial Infarction." *Am. J. Cardiol.* 42 (1978): 202–210.

Bigger, J. Thomas, et al. "The Relationships Among Ventricular Arrhythmias, Left Ventricular Dysfunction, and Mortality in the 2 Years After Myocardial Infarction." *Circulation* 69 (1984): 250–258.

Bigger, J. Thomas, Jr., and Brian F. Hoffman. "Antiarrhythmic Drugs," in *The*

Pharmacological Basis of Therapeutics, 7th ed., ed. by Alfred Goodman Gilman, Louis S. Goodman, Theodore W. Rall, and Ferid Murad, 748–783. New York: Macmillan Publishing Company, 1985.

Bikkina, Mahesh, et al. "Prognostic Implications of Asymptomatic Ventricular Arrhythmias: The Framingham Heart Study." *Ann. Int. Med.* 117 (December 15 1992): 990–996.

Bleidt, Barry. "Marketing Activities: The Keystone of Capitalism—Increasing the Availability of Prescription Drugs Through Pharmaceutical Promotion." *J. Drug Issues* 22 (Spring 1992): 277–293.

Braunwald, Eugene. *Heart Disease: A Textbook of Cardiovascular Medicine*, 4th ed. Philadelphia: W. B. Saunders Company, 1992.

Brennan, Troyen A., et al. "Incidence of Adverse Events and Negligence in Hospitalized Patients." *N. Engl. J. Med.* 324 (February 7 1991): 370–383.

Bristol-Myers Squibb Company. Annual Reports, 1983–1993.

Brody, Howard. "The Lie That Heals: The Ethics of Giving Placebos." *Annals of Internal Medicine* 97 (July 1982): 112–118.

Burns, J. J. "Modern Drug Research," in *The Economics of Drug Innovation: The Proceedings of the First Seminar of Economics of Pharmaceutical Innovation*, ed. Joseph D. Cooper, 55–62. Washington D.C.: Center for the Study of Private Enterprise, School of Business Administration, The American University, 1970.

Capone, Robert J., et al. "Events in the Cardiac Arrhythmia Suppression Trial: Baseline Predictors of Mortality in Placebo-Treated Patients." *J. Am. Coll. Cardiol.* 18 (November 15 1991): 1434–38.

Cardiac Arrhythmia Pilot Study(CAPS) Investigators. "The Cardiac Arrhythmia Pilot Study." *Am. J. Cardiol.* 57 (January 1 1986): 91–95.

Cardiac Arrhythmia Pilot Study(CAPS) Investigators. "Effects of Encainide, Flecainide, Imipramine and Moricizine on Ventricular Arrhythmias During the Year after Acute Myocardial Infarction: The CAPS." *Am. J. Cardiol.* 61 (March 1 1988): 501–509.

Cardiac Arrhythmia Suppression Trial (CAST) Investigators. "Preliminary Report: Effect of Encainide and Flecainide on Mortality in a Randomized Trial of Arrhythmia Suppression after Myocardial Infarction." *N. Engl. J. Med.* 321 (August 10 1989): 406–412.

Cardiac Arrhythmia Suppression Trial II Investigators. "Effect of the Antiarrhythmic Agent Moricizine on Survival After Myocardial Infarction." *N. Engl. J. Med.* 327 (July 23 1992): 227–33.

Carlson, Scott: "3M After Tambocor." *St. Paul Pioneer Press.* March 18 1989, 1D.

Carlucci, John F. "From Detail Man to Pharmaceutical Consultant." *Med. Mark. & Med.* 17 (October 1982): 40–48.

Carpenter, Kenneth J. *The History of Scurvy & Vitamin C*. New York: Cambridge University Press, 1986.

Castagnoli, William G. "Critics Dissect, Authors Defend Wilkes Paper on Advertising." *Medical Marketing & Media.* 27 (December 1992): 14.

Caudill, T. Shawn, et al. "The Influence of Pharmaceutical Industry Advertising on Physician Prescribing." *J. Drug Issues* 22 (Spring 1992): 331–338.

Cetera, Pasquale. "Pharmaceutical Marketing: This Means War." *Pharm. Exec.* (July 1992): 50–58.

Chemical Marketing Reporter. "3M Heart Drug Approved." November 11 1985, p. 1.

Clark, Wesley G., D. Craig Brater, and Alice R. Johnson. *Goth's Medical Pharmacology*, 13th ed. Baltimore: Mosby Year Book, 1992.

Clyne, Christopher A., et al. "Drug Therapy: Moricizine." *N. Engl. J. Med.* 327 (July 23 1992): 255–260.

Cohn, Jay, et al. "Effect of Vasodilator Therapy on Mortality in Chronic CHF: Results of a Veterans Administration Cooperative Study." *N. Engl. J. Med.* 314 (June 12 1986): 1547–52.

Conard, G. J., et al. "Plasma Concentrations of Flecainide Acetate, a New Antiarrhythmic Agent, in Humans." *Clin. Ther.* 6 (1984): 643–652.

Conard, Gordon J., et al. "Metabolism of Flecainide." *Am. J. Cardiol.* 53 (February 27 1988): 41B–51B.

Cooper, Richard M. *Food and Drug Law*. Washington, D.C.: Food and Drug Law Institute, 1991.

Coronary Drug Project Research Group. "The Coronary Drug Project: Findings Leading to Further Modifications of Its Protocol with Respect to Dextrothyroxine." *JAMA* 220 (May 15 1972): 996–1008.

Coronary Drug Project Research Group. "Prognostic Importance of Premature Beats Following Myocardial Infarction." *JAMA* 223 (March 5 1973): 1116–1124.

Council on Ethical and Judicial Affairs, American Medical Association. "Gifts to Physicians From Industry." *JAMA* 265 (January 23/40, 1991): 501.

Coyle, James D., et al. "An Interim Perspective on the Removal of Encainide and Flecainide From the Cardiac Arrhythmia Suppression Trial." *DICP, Ann. Pharmacother.* 23 (June 1989): 478–79.

Croog, Sidney H., et al. "The Effects of Antihypertensive Therapy on the Quality of Life." *N. Engl. J. Med.* 91 (June 26 1986): 314:26.

Deardorff, Frank W. "What's the Key to a Sales Rep's Performance?" *Med. Mark. & Med.* 27 (November 1992): 82–87.

Denes, Pablo, et al. "Prevalence, Characteristics and Significance of Ventricular Premature Complexes and Ventricular Tachycardia Detected by 24-Hour Continuous Electrocardiographic Recording in the Cardiac Arrhythmia Suppression Trial." *Am. J. Cardiol.* 68 (October 1 1991): 887–896.

Deriewicz, Bill. "Bernard Lown Speaks from the Heart." *Harvard Public Health Review*. Winter 1990.

Dickinson, James G. "New Source of Bias: Published Symposia?" *Med. Mark. & Med.* 27 (December 1992): 100–104.

DiMasi, Joseph A., Natalie R. Bryant, and Louis Lasagna. "New Drug Development in the United States from 1963–1990," *Clinical Pharmacology & Therapeutics* 50 (November 1991): 471–486.

DiMasi, Joseph A., Ronald W. Hansen, Henry G. Grabowski, and Louis Lasagna. "Cost of Innovation in the Pharmaceutical Industry," *Journal of Health Economics* 10 (1991): 107–142.

Douglass, James B. "What Type of Database Is Right for Your Sales Force Evaluation Needs." *Med. Mark. & Med.* 27 (July 1992): 52–58.

Drake, Donald C., and Marian Uhlman. "Making Medicine, Making Money." *Philadelphia Inquirer.* December 13–17 1992, p. 1.

Drucker, Peter F. *Innovation and Entrepreneurship: Practice and Principles.* New York: Harper & Row, 1985.

Duff, Henry J., et al. "Abolition of Resistant Ventricular Arrhythmias by Twice Daily Dosing of Flecainide. *Circulation* 62 (Oct 1980): 687. (Abstr.)

Duff, Henry J., et al. "Suppression of Resistant Ventricular Arrhythmias by Twice Daily Dosing with Flecainide." *Am. J. Cardiol.* 48 (December 1981): 1133–1140.

Duran, Dumar, et al. "Suppression of Complex Ventricular Arrhythmias by Oral Flecainide." *Clin. Pharmacol. Ther.* 32 (November 1982): 554–561.

Eastman, Margaret. "The Day the Detail Man Talked." *Am. Pharm.* N.S.18 (October 1978): 8.

Echt, Debra S., et al. "Mortality and Morbidity in Patients Receiving Encainide, Flecainide, or Placebo." *N. Engl. J. Med.* 324 (March 21 1991): 781–88.

Egan, John W., Harlow N. Higinbotham, and J. Fred Weston. *Economics of the Pharmaceutical Industry.* New York: Praeger Publishers, 1982.

Epstein, Andrew E., et al. "Events in the Cardiac Arrhythmia Suppression Trial(CAST): Mortality in the Entire Population Enrolled." *J. Am. Coll. Cardiol.* 18 (July 1991): 14–9.

Epstein, Andrew E., et al. "Mortality Following Ventricular Arrhythmia Suppression by Encainide, Flecainide, and Moricizine After Myocardial Infarction." *JAMA* 270 (November 24 1993): 2451–55.

Estes, N. A. Mark, et al. "Electrophysiologic Properties of Flecainide Acetate." *Am. J. Cardiol.* 53 (February 27 1984): 26B–29B.

Feather, Kenneth R. "The FDA Does Not Regulate CME But . . ." *Med. Mark. & Med.* 26 (September 20 1991): 28–32.

Fessenden, Ralph J., and Joan S. Fessenden. *Organic Chemistry*, 4th ed. Pacific Grove, California: Brooks/Cole Publishing Company, 1990.

Fine, Ralph Adam. *The Great Drug Deception.* New York: Stein and Day: 1972.

"500 Largest U.S. Industrial Corporations." *Fortune.* April 28 1986, p. 182.

Fowler, Noble O. *Cardiac Diagnosis and Treatment.* Philadelphia: Harper & Row, 1980.

Freund, Paul A., editor. *Experimentation with Human Subjects.* New York: George Braziller, 1969.

Friedman, Lawrence M., et al. *Data Monitoring in the Cardiac Arrhythmia Suppression Trial*. Bethesda, MD: National Heart, Lung, and Blood Institute, 1994.

Friedman, R.C., T.J. Bigger, and D.S. Kornfeld. "The Intern and Sleep Loss." *N. Engl. J. Med.* 285 (July 22 1971): 201.

Furberg, Curt D. "Effect of Antiarrhythmic Drugs on Mortality After Myocardial Infarction." *Am. J. Cardiol.* 52 (September 22 1983): 32C–36C.

Gabe, Larry. "You Can Reach the Hard-To-See M.D.!" *Med. Mark. & Med.* 19 (October 1984): 63–69

Gentzkow, Gary D., et al. "Extracardiac Adverse Effects of Flecainide." *Am. J. Cardiol.* 53 (February 27 1984): 101B–105B.

Gilman, Alfred Goodman, et al. *Goodman and Gilman's The Pharmacological Basis of Therapeutics*. New York: Macmillan Publishing Company, 1985.

Goldfinger, Stephen E. "A Matter of Influence." *N. Engl. J. Med.* 316 (May 28 1987): 408–9. (Letter).

Gomoll, Allen W., et al. "Electrophysiology, Hemodynamic and Arrhythmia Efficacy: Model Studies on Encainide." *Am. J. Cardiol.* 58 (August 29 1986): 10C–17C.

Gorkin, Larry, et al. "Psychosocial Predictors of Mortality in the Cardiac Arrhythmia Suppression Trial-1 (CAST-I)." *Am. J. Cardiol.* 71 (February 1 1993): 263–267.

Grabowski, Henry, and John Vernon. "A New Look at the Returns and Risks to Pharmaceutical R&D," *Management Science* 36 (July 1990): 804–821.

Graboys, Thomas B. "The Stampede to Stimulation—Numerators and Denominators Revisited Relative to Electrophysiologic Study of Ventricular Arrhythmias." *Am. Heart J.* 103 (June 1982): 1089–90.

Graboys, Thomas B. "Ventricular Arrhythmias: To Treat or Not to Treat?" *Hospital Practice*. November 30 1986, pages 7–8.

Greenberg, Henry M., and Edward M. Dwyer, Jr., editors. *Sudden Coronary Death*. New York: The New York Academy of Sciences, 1982.

Greene, H. Leon, et al. "Classification of Deaths After Myocardial Infarction as Arrhythmic or Nonarrhythmic (The Cardiac Arrhythmia Pilot Study)." *Am. J. Cardiol.* 63 (January 1 1989): 1–6.

Greene, H. Leon, et al. "The Cardiac Arrhythmia Suppression Trial: First CAST . . . Then CAST-II." *J. Am. Coll. Cardiol.* 19 (April 1992): 894–898.

Griffith, Lawrence, et al. "Persistent Ventricular Tachycardia/Fibrillation—a Possible Adverse Interaction Between Flecainide and Class I Antiarrhythmic Drugs." *J. Am. Coll. Cardiol.* (1984) (Abstr.)

Hallstrom, Alfred P., et al. "Prognostic Significance of Ventricular Premature Depolarizations Measured 1 Year After Myocardial Infarction in Patients

With Early Postinfarction Asymptomatic Ventricular Arrhythmia." *J. Am. Coll. Cardiol.* 20 (August 1992): 259–64.

Hamer, Angas, et al. "Prediction of Sudden Death by Electrophysiologic Studies in High Risk Patients Surviving Acute Myocardial Infarction." *Am. J. Cardiol.* 50 (August 1982): 223–229.

Harris, Richard. *The Real Voice.* New York: The Macmillan Company, 1964.

Harrison, Donald C., et al. "A Symposium: Encainide. Introduction." *Am. J. Cardiol.* 58 (August 29 1986): 1C–3C.

Harrison, Donald C., et al. "Relation of Blood Level and Metabolites to the Antiarrhythmic Effectiveness of Encainide." *Am. J. Cardiol.* 58 (August 29 1986): 66C–73C.

Hawks, John W., et al. "Boosting Script Yield: Healthy Rx for the Nineties." *Pharm. Exec.* (April 1993): 44–51.

Hellestrand, Kevin J., et al. "Electrophysiologic Effects of Flecainide Acetate on Sinus Node Function, Anomalous Atrioventricular Connection, and Pacemaker Thresholds." *Am. J. Cardiol.* 53 (February 27 1984): 30B–38B.

Hemminki, Elina. "Factors Influencing Drug Prescribing—Inquiry Into Research Strategy." *Drug Intell. Clin. Pharm.* 10 (June 1976): 321–329.

Hemminki, Elina. "Content Analysis of Drug-Detailing by Pharmaceutical Representatives." *Med. Educ.* 11 (1977): 210–215.

Herman, Colman M., et al. "Communicating Drug Information to Physicians." *J. Med. Educ.* 51 (March 1976): 189–196.

Hine, Louis K., et al. "Meta-Analysis of Empirical Long-Term Antiarrhythmic Therapy After Myocardial Infarction." *JAMA* 262 (December 1 1989): 3037–3040.

Hine, Louis K., et al. "Outpatient Antiarrhythmic Drug Use From 1970 Through 1986." *Arch. Int. Med.* 149 (July 1989): 1524–1527.

Hodess, Arthur B., et al. "Electrophysical Effects of a New Antiarrhythmic Agent, Flecainide, on the Intact Canine Heart." *J. Cardiovasc. Pharmacol.* 1 (July/August 1979): 427–439.

Hodges, Morrison, et al. "Flecainide Acetate, a New Antiarrhythmic Agent: Dose-Ranging and Efficacy Study." *Am. J. Cardiol.* 47 (February 1981): 482. (Abstr.)

Hodges, Morrison, et al. "Suppression of Ventricular Ectopic Depolarizations by Flecainide Acetate, a New Antiarrhythmic Agent." *Circulation* 65 (May 1982): 879–885.

Hodges, Morrison, et al. "Flecainide Versus Quinidine: Results of a Multicenter Trial." *Am. J. Cardiol.* 53 (February 27 1984): 66B–71B.

Hohnloser, Stefan H., and Raymond L. Woosley. "Drug Therapy: Sotalol." *N. Engl. J. Med.* 331 (July 7 1994): 31–38.

Horowitz, Leonard N. "Encainide in Lethal Ventricular Arrhythmias Evaluated by Electrophysiologic Testing and Decrease in Symptoms." *Am. J. Cardiol.* 58 (August 29 1986): 83C–86C.

Horowitz, Leonard N., et al. "Can We Prevent Sudden Cardiac Death?" *Am. J. Cardiol.* 50 (September 1982): 535–538.

Horowitz, Leonard N., et al. "Proarrhythmia, Arrhythmogenesis or Aggravation of Arrhythmia—A Status Report, 1987." *Am. J. Cardiol.* 59 (April 30 1987): 54E–56E.

Horowitz, Leonard N., et al. "Second Generation Antiarrhythmic Agents: Have We Reached Antiarrhythmic Nirvana?" *J. Am. Coll. Cardiol.* 9 (February 1987): 459–63.

Hudak, John M., et al. "Discovery and Development of Flecainide." *Am. J. Cardiol.* 53 (February 27 1984): 17B–20B.

Hurst, J. Willis, editor-in-chief. *The Heart.* New York: McGraw-Hill, 1986.

Huston, Phillips. "Those Promotional Dinners: Food for Thought?" *Med. Mark. & Med.* 24 (October 20 1989): 78–90.

Huston, Phillips. "Doctors Want More Industry-Sponsored Meetings." *Med. Mark. & Med.* 28 (March 1993): 48–53.

Huszar, Robert J. *Basic Disrhythmias: Interpretation and Managment.* St. Louis: C.V. Mosby Company, 1988.

Hutton, Cynthia. "America's Most Admired Corporations." *Fortune* January 6 1986, p. 1.

IMPACT Research Group. "International Mexiletine and Placebo Antiarrhythmic Coronary Trial: I. Report on Arrhythmia and Other Findings." *J. Am. Coll. Cardiol.* 4 (December 1984): 1148–63.

Joglekar, Prafulla, and Morton L. Paterson. "A Closer Look at the Returns and Risks of Pharmaceutical R&D." *J. Health Economics* 5 (1986) 153–177.

Jones, K., et al. "Indications for Flecainide." *The Lancet* (June 17 1989): 1383. (Letter).

Josephson, Mark E. "Treatment of Ventricular Arrhythmias After Myocardial Infarction." *Circulation.* 74 (October 1986): 653.

Josephson, Martin A., et al. "Effects of Flecainide on Ventricular Function: Clinical and Experimental Correlations." *Am. J. Cardiol.* 53 (February 27 1984): 95B–100B.

Kerr, Alix. "The Sudden Death Debacle." *Physician's Weekly.* July 31 1989.

Kesteloot, H., et al. "Clinical Experience of Encainide (MJ 9067): A New Anti-Arrhythmic Drug." *Eur. J. Clin. Pharmacol.* 6 (1979): 323–26.

Kjekshus, John, et al. "A Double-Blind, Crossover Comparison of Flecainide Acetate and Disopyramide Phosphate in the Treatment of Ventricular Premature Complexes." *Am. J. Cardiol.* 53 (February 27 1984): 72B–78B.

Kleinman, George. "The Physician's Drug Adoption Process. Re: Product Risk." *Med. Mark. & Med.* 14 (November 1979): 46–50.

Konopacki, Allen. "Turn Medical Trade Shows into Moneymakers." *Med. Mark. & Med.* 19 (April 1984): 36–42.

Konopacki, Allen. "Getting More Meat From Meetings." *Med. Mark. & Med.* 23 (September 1 1988): 52–60.

Korschgen, Ann J., et al. "What 'Makes' a Rep?" *Med. Mark. & Med.* 19 (October 1984): 42–45.

Kranes, Alfred. "Sleepy Interns." *N. Engl. J. Med.* 285 (July 22 1971): 231.

Krantz, John C. *Historical Medical Classics Involving New Drugs*. Baltimore: The Williams & Wilkins Company, 1974.

Kvam, Donald C., et al. "Antiarrhythmic and Electrophysiologic Actions of Flecainide in Animal Models." *Am. J. Cardiol.* 53 (February 27 1984): 22B–25B.

Labson, David. "Conversations with a Detailperson—Part II." *Med. Mark. & Med.* 14 (February 1979): 16.

LaPlaca, Peter J. "Meshing Sales Compensation With Strategic Goals." *Med. Mark. & Med.* 17 (June 1982): 32–36.

Lasagna, Louis. "The Diseases Drugs Cause." *Perspectives in Biology and Medicine*. (Summer 1964): 457–470.

——— . "Constraints on Innovation in Drug Development and Use," in *The Economics of Drug Innovation: The Proceedings of the First Seminar on Economics of Pharmaceutical Innovation*, ed. Joseph D. Cooper, 229–240. Washington, D.C.: Center for the Study of Private Enterprise, School of Business Administration, The American University, 1970.

——— . Review of *Academic Scientists and the Pharmaceutical Industry: Cooperative Research in Twentieth Century America*, by John P. Swann. In *JAMA* 260 (December 9 1988): 3349.

——— . "Can Outside Reviews Speed NDA Approvals?" *Med. Mark & Med.* 26 (January 1991): 40–42.

Lasagna, Louis, and William M. Wardell. "The Rate of New Drug Discovery," in *Drug Development and Marketing*, ed. Robert B. Helms, 155–163. Washington, D.C.: American Enterprise Institute for Public Policy Research, 1975.

LaWall, Charles H. *The Curious Lore of Drugs and Medicines: Four Thousand Years of Pharmacy*. Garden City, New York: Garden City Publishing Co., 1927.

Lawson, James W. "Antiarrhythmic Activity of Some Isoquinoline Derivatives Determined by a Rapid Screening Procedure in the Mouse." *J. Pharmacol. Exp. Ther.* 160 (1968): 22–31.

Leake, Chauncey D. "Protopharmacology: Prehistoric Empirical Drug Lore." Chap. in *An Historical Account of Pharmacology to the 20th Century*. Springfield, Illinois: Charles C. Thomas Publisher, 1975.

Leary, Warren E. "Warning Issued on 2 Heart Drugs After Deaths of Patients in Test." *New York Times*. April 26 1989, page 1A.

Lew, Edward A. and Jerzy Gajewski. *Medical Risks: Trends in Mortality by Age and Time Elapsed*. New York: Praeger Publishers, 1990.

Lewis, George P., et al. "Interaction of Flecainide with Digoxin and Propranolol." *Am. J. Cardiol.* 53 (February 27 1984): 52B–57B.

Lewis, Howard R. "How to Get Your Message Across to Doctors." *Med. Mark. & Med.* 14 (December 1979): 26–28.

Liemer, Geri, et al. "Use Satellite Communications to Beam Your Message to Physicians." *Med. Mark. & Med.* 27 (October 1992): 22–30.

Lown, Bernard. "Sudden Cardiac Death: the Major Challenge Confronting Contemporary Cardiology." *Am. J. Cardiol.* 43: (February 1979), 313–328.

Lown, Bernard, and M. Wolfe. "Approaches to Sudden Death from Coronary Heart Disease." *Circulation* 44 (January 1971): 130–142.

Mahoney, Tom. "The Risks of Research: Hurdles for New Drugs." Chap. in *The Merchants of Life: An Account of the American Pharmaceutical Industry.* New York: Harper and Brothers Publishers, 1959.

Marchlinski, Francis E., et al. "Identifying Patients at Risk of Sudden Death After Myocardial Infarction: Value of the Response to Programmed Stimulation, Degree of Ventricular Ectopic Activity and Severity of Left Ventricular Dysfunction." *Am. J. Cardiol.* 52 (December 1 1983): 1190–1196.

Markel, Michael L., et al. "Encainide for Treatment of Supraventricular Tachycardias Associated with the Wolff-Parkinson-White Syndrome." *Am. J. Cardiol.* 58 (August 29 1986): 41C–48C.

Mars, Jerome P. "Measuring the Marketing Power of Meetings." *Med. Mark. & Med.* 25 (September 1 1990): 20–27.

Mason, Jay W. "Basic and Clinical Cardiac Electrophysiology of Encainide." *Am. J. Cardiol.* 58 (August 29 1986): 18C–24C.

Mason, Jay W., et al. "Antiarrhythmic Efficacy of Encainide in Patients with Refractory Recurrent Ventricular Tachycardia." *Circulation* 63 (March 1981): 670–675.

Matthews, J. Rosser. *Quantification and the Quest for Medical Certainty: The Emergence of the Clinical Trial.* Princeton: Princeton University Press, (in press).

Mattison, Nancy, A. Gene Trimble, and Louis Lasagna. "New Drug Development in the United States, 1963–1984." *Clin. Pharmacol. Ther.* 43 (March 1988): 290–301.

May, Charles D. "Selling Drugs by 'Educating' Physicians." *J. Med. Educ.* 36 (January 1961): 1–23.

McIvor, Patrick. "Are You Getting Your Money's Worth on the Exhibit Floor?" *Med. Mark. & Med.* 20 (March 1985): 11–18.

Meissner, Marc D., et al. "Oral Antiarrhythmic Agents for Ventricular Arrhythmias." *Clin. Ther.* 8 (1986): 595–604.

Menzel, Herbert, et al. "Social Relations and Innovation in the Medical Profession: The Epidemiology of a New Drug." *Pub. Opin. Quarterly* 19 (Winter 1955–56): 339–352.

Miall, W.E., and Gillian Greenberg. *Mild Hypertension: Is There Pressure to Treat?* Cambridge: Cambridge University Press, 1985.

Milton, W.L., et al. "A New Measurement of Salesforce Effectiveness—The ACE Approach." *Med. Mark. & Med.* 14 (July 1979): 20–26.

Mintz, Morton. *By Prescription Only*. Boston: Houghton Mifflin, 1967.

Moore, Thomas J. *Heart Failure*. New York: Random House, 1989.

Morganroth, Joel. "Premature Ventricular Complexes." *JAMA* 252 (August 3 1984): 673–676.

———. "The Ventricular Premature Complex." *Geriatrics* 39 (October 1984): 109–112.

———. "Ambulatory Holter Electrocardiography: Choice of Technologies and Clinical Uses." *Ann. Int. Med.* 102 (January 1985): 73–81.

———. "Comparative Evaluation of Antiarrhythmic Agents." *Drugs* 29 Suppl. 4 (1985): 14–20.

———. "Encainide for Ventricular Arrhythmias: Placebo-Controlled and Standard Comparison Trials." *Am. J. Cardiol.* 58 (August 29 1986): 74C–82C.

———. "Comparative Efficacy and Safety of Oral Mexiletine and Quinidine in Benign or Potentially Lethal Ventricular Arrhythmias." *Am. J. Cardiol.* 60 (December 1 1987): 1276–81.

———. "Differential Utility of Antiarrhythmic Agents." *Cardiology* 74 Suppl. 2 (1987): 57–66.

———. "New Antiarrhythmic Agents: Mexiletine, Tocainide, Encainide, Flecainide, and Amiodarone." *Rational Drug Ther.* 21 (April 1987): 1–5.

———. "Placement of Moricizine in the Selection of Antiarrhythmic Drug Therapy." *Am. J. Cardiol.* 65 (February 20 1990): 65D–67D.

———. "Proarrhythmic Effects of Antiarrhythmic Drugs: Evolving Concepts." *Am. Heart J.* 123 (April 1992): 1137–39.

Morganroth, Joel, et al. "Pseudohomozygous Type II Hyperlipoproteinemia." *J. Pediatrics* 85 (November 1974): 639–643.

Morganroth, Joel, et al. "Limitations of Routine Long-Term Electrocardiographic Monitoring to Assess Ventricular Ectopic Frequency." *Circulation* 58 (September 1978): 408–414.

Morganroth, Joel, et al. "Ethmozin: A New Antiarrhythmic Agent Development in the U.S.S.R. Efficacy and Tolerance." *Am. Heart J.* 98 (November 1979): 621–628.

Morganroth, Joel, et al. "Flecainide: Its Proarrhythmic Effect and Expected Changes on the Surface Electrocardiogram." *Am. J. Cardiol.* 53 (February 27 1984): 89B–94B.

Morganroth, Joel, et al. "Comparative Efficacy and Safety of Oral Tocainide and Quinidine for Benign and Potentially Lethal Ventricular Arrhythmias." *Am. J. Cardiol.* 56 (October 1 1985): 581–587.

Morganroth, Joel, et al. "A Review of the Uses and Limitations of Tocainide—A Class 1B Antiarrhythmic Agent." *Am. Heart J.* 110 (October 1985): 856–863.

Morganroth, Joel, et al. "Comparative Study of Encainide and Quinidine in the Treatment of Ventricular Arrhythmias." *J. Am. Coll. Cardiol.* 7 (January 1986): 9–16.

Morganroth, Joel, et al. "Efficacy and Tolerance of Ethmozine (Moricizine HCL) in Placebo-Controlled Trials." *Am. J. Cardiol.* 60 (October 16 1987): 48F–51F.

Morganroth, Joel, et al. "Antiarrhythmic Drug Therapy 1988: For Whom, How and Where?" *Am. J. Cardiol.* 62 (September 1 1988): 461–465.

Morganroth, Joel, et al. "Pharmacologic Management of Ventricular Arrhythmias After the Cardiac Arrhythmia Suppression Trial." *Am. J. Cardiol.* 65 (June 15 1990): 1497–1503.

Morganroth, Joel, et al. "Treatment of Ventricular Arrhythmias by United States Cardiologists: a Survey Before the Cardiac Arrhythmia Suppression Trial Results Were Available." *Am. J. Cardiol.* 65 (January 1 1990): 40–48.

Morganroth, Joel, et al. "Quinidine-Related Mortality in the Short-to-Medium-Term Treatment of Ventricular Arrhythmias: A Meta-Analysis." *Circulation* 84 (November 1991): 1977–1983.

Morganroth, Joel, and Leonard N. Horowitz. "Are There Unnecessary Delays in the Development of New Cardiac Drugs in the United States?" *Am. J. Cardiol.* 58 (December 1 1986): 1265–1267.

Morganroth, Joel, and E. Neil Moore, editors. *Cardiac Arrhythmias: New Therapeutic Drugs and Devices.* Boston: Martinus Nijhoff Publishers, 1985.

Morganroth, J., and E. Neil Moore, editors. *Sudden Cardiac Death and Congestive Heart Failure: Diagnosis and Treatment.* Boston: Martinus Nijhoff Publishers, 1983.

Morganroth, Joel, E. Neil Moore, Leonard S. Dreifus, and Eric L. Michelson, editors. *The Evaluation of New Antiarrhythmic Drugs.* Boston: Martinus Nijhoff Publishers, 1981.

Mossinghoff, Gerald J. "Pharmaceutical Manufacturers and Self-Regulation of Drug Advertising and Promotion." *J. Drug Issues* 22 (Spring 1992): 235–243.

Muskowitz, Milton et al., editors. *Everybody's Business: An Almanac.* New York: Harper & Row, 1980.

Myers, Maven J. "Marketing and Pharmaceutical Development." *J. Drug Issues* 22 (1992): 221–234.

Naccarelli, Gerald V., et al. "Assessment of Antiarrhythmic Drug Efficacy in the Treatment of Supraventricular Arrhythmias." *Am. J. Cardiol.* 58 (August 29 1986): 31C–36C.

Naimark, George M. "Making the Sales Rep Your Differential Advantage." *Med. Mark. & Med.* 19 (September 1984): 106–109.

Napoliello, Michael J. "The Physician's Role in Pharmaceutical Sales Education." *Med. Mark. & Med.* 14 (March 1979): 21–25.

Nelson, Cheryl R. "Drug Utilization in Office Practice: National Ambulatory Medical Care Survey." *Advance Data* n.s. 232 (March 25 1993): 1–12.

Nelson, John C. "A Snorkel, a 5-Iron, and a Pen." *JAMA* 264 (August 8 1990): 742.

Nestico, Pasquale F., et al. "Bepridil Hydrochloride for Treatment of Benign or Potentially Lethal Ventricular Arrhythmias." *Am. J. Cardiol.* 58 (November 1 1986): 1001–1004.

Nestico, Pasquale F., et al. "New Antiarrhythmic Drugs." *Drugs* 35 (1988): 286–319.

Nestor, J.O. "Results of the Failure to Perform Adequate Preclinical Studies before Administering New Drugs to Humans." *S. Afr. Med. J.* 49 (22 February 1975): 287–290.

O'Brien, Bill. "Toward an Adult Doctor-Sales Rep Relationship." *Med. Mark. & Med.* 18 (September 1983): 48–50.

O'Reilly, Brian. "Drugmakers" *Fortune* 124 (July 29 1991): 48–63.

Oetting, George D. "Are Your CME Programs Gathering Dust?" *Med. Mark. & Med.* 17 (June 1982): 38–41.

Oliver, M. F., et al. "A co-operative trial in the primary prevention of ischaemic heart disease using clofibrate." *British Heart Journal* 40 (1978): 1069–1118.

Packer, Milton. "The Placebo Effect in Heart Failure." *Am. H. J.* 120 (December 1980): 1579–1582.

Packer, Milton, et al. "Effect of Oral Milrone on Mortality in Severe Chronic Heart Failure." *N. Engl. J. Med.* 325 (November 21 1991): 1468–75.

Palmer, Roger F. "Drug Misuse and Physician Education." *Clin. Pharmacol. & Ther.* 10 (January-February 1969): 1–4.

Parke-Davis division of Warner-Lambert Company. "Important Prescribing Information" on Lopid. *JAMA* 268 (August 5 1992): 667–668.

Parnham, M. J., and J. Buinvels, editors. *Discoveries in Pharmacology.* Vol. 2, *Hemodynamics, Hormones & Inflammation.* New York: Elsevier, 1984.

Pawitan, Yudi, et al. "Statistical Interim Monitoring of the Cardiac Arrhythmia Suppression Trial." *Stat. Med.* 9 (1990): 1081–1090.

Pekkanen, John. "The Impact of Promotion on Physicians' Prescribing Patterns." *J. Drug Issues* 6 (Winter 1976): 13–20.

Pharmaceutical Manufacturers Association. *Statistical Fact Book.* September 1991.

Physicians' Desk Reference, 46th ed. Medical Economics Data, 1989, 1992, 1994.

Podrid, Philip J., et. al. "Aggravation of Arrhythmia by Antiarrhythmic Drugs—Incidence and Predictors." *Am. J. Cardiol.* 59 (April 30 1987): 38E–44E.

Pool, Peter E. "Treatment of Supraventricular Arrhythmias with Encainide." *Am. J. Cardiol.* 58 (August 29 1986): 55C–57C.

Pratt, Craig M., et al. "Clinical and Regulatory Implications of the Cardiac Arrhythmia Suppression Trial." *Am. J. Cardiol.* 65 (January 1 1990): 103–105.

Prichett, Edward L.C., et al. "Mortality in Patients Treated with Flecainide and Encainide for Supraventricular Arrhythmias." *Am. J. Cardiol.* 67 (May 1 1991): 976–980.

Quart, Barry D., et al. "Drug Interaction Studies and Encainide Use in Renal and Hepatic Impairment." *Am. J. Cardiol.* 58 (August 29 1986): 104C–113C.

Reekie, W. Duncan, and Michael H. Weber. "Whence They Came and What They Do." Chap. in *Profits, Politics and Drugs.* New York: Holmes & Meier Publishers, 1979.

Reid, Philip R., et al. "Evaluation of Flecainide Acetate in the Management of Patients at High Risk of Sudden Cardiac Death." *Am. J. Cardiol.* 53 (February 27 1984): 108B–111B.

Reidenberg, Marcus. "The State of Drug Development in the United States in 1990: A View from the Academic Community," *Clin. Pharmacol. Ther.* 48 (July 1990): 1–9.

Reiffel, James A., et al. "Physician Attitudes Toward the Use of Type 1C Antiarrhythmics After the Cardiac Arrhythmia Suppression Trial (CAST)." *Am. J. Cardiol.* 66 (November 15 1990): 1262–1264.

Rettig, Richard A., Laurence E. Earley, and Richard A. Merrill, editors. *Food and Drug Administration Advisory Committees.* Washington, D.C.: National Academy Press, 1992.

Richards, David A., et al. "Ventricular Electrical Instability: A Predictor of Death After Myocardial Infarction." *Am. J. Cardiol.* 51 (January 1 1983): 75–80.

Richards, Robert K., et al. "Industry's Role in Continuing Medical Education: Is It Good for Doctors, for Industry, for the Public?" *Med. Mark. & Med.* 14 (October 1979): 47–62.

Riegelman, Richard K. *Minimizing Medical Mistakes: The Art of Medical Decision Making.* Boston: Little Brown and Company, 1991.

Roberts, Kay. "Sampling Solution: Safer and More Effective." *Pharm. Exec.* (May 1992): 87–90.

Roden, Dan M., et al. "Total Suppression of Ventricular Arrhythmias by Encainide." *N. Engl. J. Med.* 302 (April 17 1980): 877–82.

Roden, Dan M., et al. "Disposition Kinetics of Encainide and Metabolites." *Am. J. Cardiol.* 58 (August 29 1986): 4C–9C.

Roden, Dan M., and Raymond L.Woosley. "Medical Intelligence: Drug Therapy: Flecainide." *N. Engl. J. Med.* 315 (July 3 1986): 36–40.

Roseman, Ed. "Where the Changing Promotional Mix Is Headed." *Med. Mark. & Med.* 24 (June 1989): 10–20.

———. "How to Establish Quality Control of the Sales Force." *Med. Mark. & Med.* 27 (October 1992): 44–51.

———. "How Good Are Sales Representatives As Field Testers of Sales Promotion Materials?" *Med. Mark. & Med.* 14 (June 1979): 40–42.

———. "How Healthy Is the Sales Force?" *Med. Mark. & Med.* 17 (September 1982): 82–88.

————. "Determining the Right Promotional Mix." *Med. Mark. & Med.* 18 (June 1983): 23–27.

————. "They're Revamping Sales Forces to Cope With New Demands." *Med. Mark. & Med.* 18 (November 1983): 52–56.

————. "Unlocking the Physician's Psyche." *Med. Mark. & Med.* 18 (April 1983): 28–34.

————. "When Your Product Is Displaced from the Selling Cycle." *Med. Mark. & Med.* 18 (February 1983): 40–43.

————. "Are You Over-Sampling?" *Med. Mark. & Med.* 19 (October 1984): 72–78.

————. "Getting More Value From Leave-Behinds." *Med. Mark. & Med.* 20 (June 1985): 27–32.

————. "How to Gain Your Fair Share of Sales Time." *Med. Mark. & Med.* 20 (February 1985): 24–28.

————. "Make Sure Your Sales Force Delivers the Right Message." *Med. Mark. & Med.* 20 (September 1985): 90–95.

————. "Designing Promotion for the Prospect Under Pressure." *Med. Mark. & Med.* 21 (March 1986): 58–63.

————. "10 Ways to Overcome Physicians' Resistance to Detailing." *Med. Mark. & Med.* 22 (August 1987): 22–24.

Ross, Warren R. "Medical Marketing in the Year 2000: The Impact of the New Media." *Med. Mark. & Med.* 17 (August 1982): 25–36.

Rothfeder, Jeffrey. *Heart Rhythms: Breakthrough Treatments for Cardiac Arrhythmia—The Silent Killer of 400,000 Americans Each Year*. New York: Little Brown & Co., 1989.

Ruberman, W., et al. "Ventricular Premature Beats After Myocardial Infarction." *N. Engl. J. Med.* 297 (October 6 1977): 750–757.

Ruby, Allen, and Joel Morganroth. "The Need for a Medical Ideology." *JAMA* 212 (June 22 1970): 2096–97.

Ruskin, Jeremy N. "The Cardiac Arrhythmia Suppression Trial (CAST)." *N. Engl. J. Med.* 321 (August 10 1989): 386–388.

Salerno, David M. "Quinidine: Worse than Adverse?" *Circulation* 84 (November 1991): 2196–98.

Salerno, David M. "Quinidine: Is It a Good Drug or a Bad Drug?" *Postgrad. Med.* 92 (September 15 1992): 131–140.

Salm, Andy. "Why Not Increase Your Sales Activity By Telephone." *Med. Mark. & Med.* 17 (September 1982): 98–107.

Sami, Magdi H. "Acute Intravenous and Long-Term Oral Hemodynamic Effects of Encainide." *Am. J. Cardiol.* 58 (August 29 1986): 25C–30C.

Santarelli, Pietro, et al. "Ventricular Arrhythmia Induced by Programmed Ventricular Stimulation After Acute Myocardial Infarction." *Am. J. Cardiol.* 55 (February 1 1985): 391–394.

Schnee, Jerome E. "The Changing Pharmaceutical R & D Environment," in

The Pharmaceutical Industry: Economics, Performance, and Government Regulation, ed. Cotton M. Lindsay, 91–104. New York: John Wiley & Sons, 1978.

Schumer, Robert. "Speaking Out: Honoraria Thy Physician." *Med. Mark. & Med.* 23 (September 1 1988): 12–13.

Schwartz, Harry. "Pharmaceutical Marketers: A New Breed." *Pharm. Exec.* (May 1992): 28–34.

Schwartz, John. "Company Faulted in Fatal Drug Trials." *Washington Post.* Dec 10 1993, A4.

Schwartzman, David. *Innovation in the Pharmaceutical Industry.* Baltimore: The Johns Hopkins University Press, 1976.

Silverstein, Martin B. "A New Paradigm for Rx Marketing Value." *Pharm. Exec.* (April 1992): 56–64.

Simcox, Steven. "Direct Mail Marketing: a 'Measurable Must.'" *Med. Mark. & Med.* 27 (November 1992): 68–80.

Siwolop, Sana. "Trench Warfare." *Financial World* (May 30 1989): 78–80.

Slatter, Stuart S. P. *Competition and Marketing Strategies in the Pharmaceutical Industry.* New York: Holmes & Meier Publishers, 1977.

Sliverman, Milton, and Philip R. Lee. *Pills, Profits, and Politics.* Berkeley: University of California Press, 1974.

Smith, Charles G. "Screening and Biological Evaluation Systems." Chap. in *The Process of New Drug Discovery and Development.* Ann Arbor: CRC Press, 1992.

Smith, Mickey C. *Pharmaceutical Marketing: Strategies and Cases.* New York: Pharmaceutical Products Press, 1991.

Somani, Pitambar. "Antiarrhythmic Effects of Flecainide." *Clin. Pharmacol. Ther.* 27 (April 1980): 464–470.

Soumerai, Stephen B. "Principles of Educational Outreach (Academic Detailing) to Improve Clinical Decision Making." *JAMA* 263 (January 26 1990): 549–556.

Soyka, Lester F. "Safety of Encainide for the Treatment of Ventricular Arrhythmias." *Am. J. Cardiol.* 58 (August 29 1986): 96C–103C.

Spector, Michael. "U.S. Warnings Against Use of 2 Heart Drugs." *Washington Post.* April 26, 1989, page 1A.

Spielman, Scott R., et al. "Drug Therapy in High Risk Patients Following Acute Myocardial Infarctions: The Results of the Timolol, Encainide, Sotalol Trial." *Circulation* 72: (Oct 1985): III-15. (Abstr.)

Spilker, Bert. "The Nature of Drug Discovery and Development." Chap. in *Multinational Drug Companies: Issues in Drug Discovery and Development.* New York: Raven Press, 1989.

Stillman, Leonard A. "Teach Psychology to Your Sales Force." *Med. Mark. & Med.* 20 (July 1985): 40–45.

Strasburger, Janette F., et al. "Encainide for Refractory Supraventricular Tachycardia in Children." *Am. J. Cardiol.* 58 (August 29 1986): 49C–54C.

Stratton, Joe. "Specialty Advertising: More Than Logos on Coffee Mugs." *Med. Mark. & Med.* 23 (July 1988): 70–75.

Stryer, Lubert. *Molecular Design of Life.* New York: W. H. Freeman and Company, 1989.

Teo, Kook K., et al. "Effective of Prophylactic Antiarrhythmic Drug Therapy in Acute Myocardial Infarction." *JAMA* 270 (October 6 1993): 1589–1595 & NAPS 050504.

3M Company. Annual Reports, 1984–1993.

3M Company. *Our Story So Far: Notes from the First 75 Years of 3M Company.* St. Paul: Minnesota Mining and Manufacturing Company, 1977.

Tobias, Lester L. "Stopping the Sales Turnover Merry-go-round." *Med. Mark. & Med.* 21 (June 1986): 68–74.

Tordjman, Therese, et al. "Safety and Efficacy for Malignant Ventricular Arrhythmias." *Am. J. Cardiol.* 58 (August 29 1986): 87C–95C.

United Press International, "Drug for Heart Rhythm Approved for U.S. Sale." *New York Times.* November 8 1984, p. D 20.

U. S. Dept of Commerce, Bureau of the Census. *Statistical Abstract of the United States 1992.* Washington, D.C.: U.S. Department of Commerce, 1992.

U.S. Congress. House. Committee on Government Operations. *Use of Advisory Committees by the Food and Drug Administration. Hearings Before a Subcommittee of the Committee on Government Operations,* 93d Cong., 2d sess., 1974.

U.S. Congress. House. Committee on Government Operations. *Use of Advisory Committees by the Food and Drug Administration (Part 2). Hearings Before a Subcommittee of the Committee on Government Operations,* 94th Cong., 1st sess., 1975.

U.S. Congress. House. Committee on Government Operations. *Use of Advisory Committees by the Food and Drug Administration.* Eleventh Report by the Committee on Government Operations. Washington, D.C.: Government Printing Office, 1976.

U.S. Congress. House. Committee on Government Operations. *The Regulation of New Drugs by the Food and Drug Administration: The New Drug Review Process,* 97th Cong., 2d sess., August 3, 4, 1982.

U.S. Congress. House. Committee on Government Operations. *FDA's Regulation of Zomax. Hearings Before a Subcommittee of the Committee on Government Operations,* 98th Cong., 1st sess., 1983.

U.S. Congress. House. Committee on Government Operations. *FDA's Regulation of Zomax. Report of a Subcommittee of the Committee on Government Operations,* 98th Cong., 1st sess., December 2 1983.

U.S. Congress. House. Committee on Government Operations. *Oversight of the New Drug Review Process and FDA's Regulation of Merital. Hearing Before a Subcommittee of the House Committee on Government Operations,* 99th Cong., 2d sess., 1986.

U.S. Congress. House. Committee on Government Operations. *FDA's Regulation of the New Drug Versed. Hearings Before a Subcommittee of the House Committee on Government Operations,*100th Cong., 2d sess., 1988.

U.S. Congress. House. Committee on Government Operations. *Promotion of Drugs and Medical Devices for Unapproved Uses. Hearing Before the Human Resources and Intergovernmental Relations Subcommittee of the House Committee on Government Operations,* 102d Cong., 1st sess., 1991.

U.S. Congress. House. Committee on Government Operations. *Problems with FDA's Regulation of the Antiarrhythmic Drugs Tambocor and Enkaid. Hearing Before the Human Resources and Intergovernmental Relations Subcommittee of the House Committee on Government Operations,* 102d Cong., 1st sess., 1991.

U.S. Congress. House. Committee on Government Operations. *Council on Competitiveness and FDA Plans to Alter the Drug Approval Process at FDA. Hearing Before the Human Resources and Intergovernmental Relations Subcommittee of the Committee on Government Operations,* 102d Cong., 2d sess., 1992.

U.S. Congress. House. Committee on Government Operations. *Is the FDA Protecting Consumers from Dangerous Off-Label Uses of Medical Drugs and Devices?* H. Rept. 1992, 102d Cong., 2d sess., 1992.

U.S. Congress. House. Committee on Interstate and Foreign Commerce. *Biomedical Research Ethics and the Protection of Human Research Subjects. Hearings Before the Subcommittee on Public Health and Environment of the Committee on Interstate and Foreign Commerce,* 93d Cong., 1st sess., 1973.

U.S. Congress. House. Select Committee on Narcotics Abuse and Control. *Abuse of Dangerous Licit and Illicit Drugs-Psychotropics, Phencyclide (PCP) and Talwin.* 95th Congress, 2d Session August 1978.

U.S. Congress. Office of Technology Assessment. *Pharmaceutical R&D: Costs, Risks and Rewards,* OTA-H-522. Washington, D.C.: Government Printing Office, February 1993.

U.S. Congress. Senate. Committee on Labor and Human Resources. *Preclinical and Clinical Testing by the Pharmaceutical Industry, 1980— DMSO. Hearing Before the Subcommittee on Health and Scientific Research of the Committee on Labor and Human Resources,* 96th Cong., 2d sess., 1980.

U.S. Congress. Senate. Committee on Labor and Human Resources. *Advertising, Marketing and Promotional Practices of the Pharmaceutical Industry. Hearing before the Committee on Labor and Human Resources,* 101st Cong., 2d sess., 1990.

U.S. Congress. Senate. Committee on Labor and Public Welfare and Committee on the Judiciary. *Regulation of New Drug R.& D. by the Food and Drug Administration, 1974. Joint Hearings Before the Subcom-*

mittee on Health of the Committee on Labor and Public Welfare and the Subcommittee on Administrative Practice and Procedure of the Committee on the Judiciary, 93d Cong., 2d sess., 1974.

U.S. Congress. Senate. Committee on Labor and Public Welfare and Committee on the Judiciary. *Preclinical and Clinical Testing by the Pharmaceutical Industry, 1976. Joint Hearings before the Subcommittee on Health of the Committee on Labor and Public Welfare and the Subcommittee on Administrative Practice and Procedure of the Committee on the Judiciary*, Part II, 94th Cong., 2d sess., 1976.

U.S. Department of Health, Education, and Welfare, Food and Drug Administration. Review Panel on New Drug Regulation. *Investigation of Allegations Relating to the Bureau of Drugs, Food and Drug Administration*. Washington, D.C.: U.S. Department of Health, Education, and Welfare, Food and Drug Administration. April 1977.

U.S. Department of Health and Human Services, Food and Drug Administration. *Requirements of Laws and Regulations Enforced by the U.S. Food and Drug Administration*. HHS Publication No. (FDA) 85–1115.

U.S. Department of Health and Human Services, Food and Drug Administration. *Medical Officer's Review of NDA 17–447 (Norpace)* Washington, D.C.: U.S. Department of Health and Human Services, Food and Drug Administration. December 12 1976.

U.S. Department of Health and Human Services, Food and Drug Administration. *Summary Basis of Approval for Disopyramide Phosphate (Norpace)* Washington, D.C.: U.S. Department of Health and Human Services, Food and Drug Administration. Undated, probably 1977.

U.S. Department of Health and Human Services, Food and Drug Administration. *Division Director's Review of NDA 17–447 (Norpace)* Washington, D.C.: U.S. Department of Health and Human Services, Food and Drug Administration. June 3 1977.

U.S. Department of Health and Human Services, Food and Drug Administration. *Medical Review of NDA 18–972, Cordarone.* Washington, D.C.: U.S. Department of Health and Human Services, Food and Drug Administration. June 28 1983.

U.S. Department of Health and Human Services, Food and Drug Administration. *Statistical Review and Evaluation for Tambocor (Flecainide Acetate) Tablets*. U.S. Department of Health and Human Services, Food and Drug Administration. August 21 1984.

U.S. Department of Health and Human Services, Food and Drug Administration. *Statistical Review and Evaluation for Enkaid (Oral Encainide HCL)*. Washington, D.C.: U.S. Department of Health and Human Services, Food and Drug Administration. February 28 1986.

U.S. Department of Health and Human Services, Food and Drug Administration. *Summary Basis of Approval for Mexiletine Hydrochloride*. Washington, D.C.: U.S. Department of Health and Human Services, Food and Drug Administration. November 10 1988.

U.S. Department of Health and Human Services, Food and Drug Administration. *Summary Basis of Approval for Oral Encainide HCL.* Washington, D.C.: U.S. Department of Health and Human Services, Food and Drug Administration. February 12 1988.

U.S. Department of Health and Human Services, Food and Drug Administration. *National Committee to Review Current Procedures for Approval of New Drugs for Cancer and AIDS.* September 13 1989.

U.S. Department of Health and Human Services, Food and Drug Administration. *Summary Basis of Approval for Flecainide Acetate.* Washington, D.C.: U.S. Department of Health and Human Services, Food and Drug Administration. July 25 1989.

U.S. Department of Health and Human Services, Food and Drug Administration. *Summary Basis of Approval for Ethmozine.* Washington, D.C.: U.S. Department of Health and Human Services, Food and Drug Administration. June 19 1990.

U.S. Department of Health and Human Services, Food and Drug Administration, Cardiovascular and Renal Drugs Advisory Committee. *Minutes of the Forty-First Meeting.* November 3, 4 1983.

U.S. Department of Health and Human Services, Food and Drug Administration, Cardiovascular and Renal Drugs Advisory Committee. *A Discussion of Flecainide.* June 21 1984.

U.S. Department of Health and Human Services, Food and Drug Administration, Cardiovascular and Renal Drugs Advisory Committee. *A Discussion of the Presentation of Boehringer Ingelheim Regarding Mexiletene.* June 20 1984.

U.S. Department of Health and Human Services, Food and Drug Administration, Cardiovascular and Renal Drugs Advisory Committee. *A Discussion of the NDA of Bristol-Myers for Encainide.* July 25 1985.

U.S. Department of Health and Human Services, Food and Drug Administration, Cardiovascular and Renal Drugs Advisory Committee. *A Discussion of Supraventricular Arrhythmias with Encainide.* March 3 1988.

U.S. Department of Health and Human Services, Food and Drug Administration, Cardiovascular and Renal Drugs Advisory Committee. *A Discussion of How the CAST Trial Should Change the Thinking about Antiarrhythmic Drugs.* October 5 1989.

U.S. Department of Health and Human Services, Food and Drug Administration, Cardiovascular and Renal Drugs Advisory Committee. *A Discussion of the NDA of 3M(Riker) for Flecainide,* Volume II. October 6 1989.

U.S. Department of Health and Human Services, Food and Drug Administration, Cardiovascular and Renal Drugs Advisory Committee. *A Discussion of the Implications of the CAST Trial.* January 25 1990.

U.S. Department of Health and Human Services, Food and Drug Administration, Center for Drug Evaluation and Research. *Guideline for the*

Format and Content of the Clinical and Statistical Sections of New Drug Applications. July 1988.

U.S. Department of Health and Human Services, National Center for Health Statistics. "Advance Report of Final Mortality Statistics, 1990." *Monthly Vital Statistics Report* 41 (Jan 7 1993): 20.

U.S. Department of Health and Human Services, National Center for Health Statistics. "Drug Mentions: National Ambulatory Medical Care Survey, 1990."

U.S. Department of Health and Human Services, National Center for Health Statistics. Vital and Health Statistics. National Ambulatory Medical Care Survey: 1989 Summary, April 1992.

U.S. Department of Health and Human Services, National Heart, Blood, and Lung Institute. *Cardiac Arrhythmia Suppression Trial (CAST): Manual of Operations.* September 1 1987.

U.S. Department of Health and Human Services, National Heart, Blood, and Lung Institute. *Cardiac Arrhythmia Suppression Trial (CAST): Protocol.* April 15 1988.

U.S. Department of Health and Human Services, National Heart, Blood, and Lung Institute. *Background statement for release: 11:00 a.m. April 25, 1989, and Remarks by Dr. Claude Lenfant.*

U.S. General Accounting Office. *Federal Control of New Drug Testing Is Not Adequately Protecting Human Test Subjects and the Public.* Washington, D.C., July 15 1976.

U.S. General Accounting Office. *FDA Drug Review: Postapproval Risks 1976–85.* Report to the Chairman, Subcommittee on Human Resources and Intergovernmental Relations, Committee on Government Operations, House of Representatives. Washington, D.C., April 1990.

U.S. General Accounting Office. *Off-Label Drugs: Initial Results of a National Survey.* Briefing Report to the Chairman, Committee on Labor and Human Resources, U.S. Senate. Washington, D.C., February 1991.

U.S. General Accounting Office. *Off-Label Drugs: Reimbursement Policies Constrain Physicians in Their Choice of Cancer Therapies.* Report to the Chairman, Committee on Labor and Human Resources, U.S. Senate. Washington, D.C., September 1991.

Verdouw, Pieter D., et al. "Antiarrhythmic and Hemodynamic Actions of Flecainide Acetate (R-818) in the Ischemic Porcine Heart." *J. Cardiovasc. Pharmacol.* 1 (July/August 1979): 473–486.

Vlay, Stephen C. "How the University Cardiologist Treats Ventricular Premature Beats: A Nationwide Survey of 65 University Medical Centers." *Am. Heart J.* 110 (October 1985): 904–912.

Wade, V. A., et al. "Drug Companies' Evidence to Justify Advertising." *The Lancet* ii (Nov 25 1989): 1261.

Walker, Hugh D. "Research and Development in the Drug Industry." Chap. in *Market Power and Price Levels in the Ethical Drug Industry.* Bloomington: Indiana University Press, 1971.

Ward, David, et al. "Cardiac Arrhythmia Suppression Trial and Flecainide." *The Lancet* (June 3 1989): 1267–68. (Letter).

Wardell, William M. "The History of Drug Discovery, Development and Regulation," in *Issues in Pharmaceutical Economics*, ed. Robert I. Chien, 3–11. Lexington, Massachusetts: D.C. Heath and Company, 1979.

Waspe, Lawrence E., et al. "Prediction of Sudden Death and Spontaneous Ventricular Tachycardia in Survivors of Complicated Myocardial Infarction: Value of the Response to Programmed Stimulation Using a Maximum of Three Ventricular Extrastimuli." *J. Am. Coll. Cardiol.* 5 (June 1985): 1292–1301.

Wellens, Hein J. J., et al. "Electrophysiology in Assessing Supraventricular Arrhythmias: Value of Programmed Stimulation in Predicting and Understanding Efficacy of Encainide." *Am. J. Cardiol.* 58 (August 29 1986): 37C–40C.

Wiklund, I., et al. "Methods for Assessing Quality of Life in the Cardiac Arrhythmia Suppression Trial (CAST)." *Quality of Life Res.* 1 (1992) 187–201.

Wiley, Harvey W. *An Autobiography*. Indianapolis: The Bobbs-Merrill Company, 1930.

Wilkes, Michael S., et al. "Pharmaceutical Advertisement in Leading Medical Journals: Experts' Assessments." *Annals of Internal Medicine*. 116 (June 1 1992): 912.

Wilson, Robert F. "A Fresh Campaign Can Help Wilting Sales." *Med. Mark. & Med.* 17 (November 1982): 76–82.

———. "Find Clones of Your Best Customers." *Med. Mark. & Med.* 18 (March 1983): 30–33.

Winkle, Roger A. "Measuring Antiarrhythmic Drug Efficacy by Suppression of Asymptomatic Ventricular Arrhythmias." *Annals of Internal Medicine*. 91 (1979): 480–481.

Winkle, Roger A., et al. "Treatment of Recurrent Symptomatic Ventricular Tachycardia." *Annals of Internal Medicine*. 85 (1976):1–7.

Winkle, Roger A., et al. "Malignant Ventricular Tachyarrhythmias Associated with the Use of Encainide." *American Heart Journal* 5 (1981): 857–964.

Woosley, Raymond L. "CAST: Implications for Drug Development." *Clin. Pharmacol. Ther.* 47 (May 1990): 553–556.

Woosley, Raymond L., et al. "Flecainide Dose-Response Relations in Stable Ventricular Arrhythmias." *Am. J. Cardiol.* 53 (February 27 1984): 59B–65B.

Woosley, Raymond L., et al. "Pharmacokinetics of Moricizine HCL." *Am. J. Cardiol.* 60 (October 16 1987): 35F–39F.

Woosley, Raymond L., et al. "Medical Intelligence: Drug Therapy: Encainide." *N. Engl. J. Med.* 318 (April 28 1988): 1107–1115.

Wright, David. "Targeted Promotion: Key to a Successful Product Launch." *Med. Mark. & Med.* 17 (May 1982): 44–48.

Wyngaarden, James B., Lloyd H. Smith, Jr., J. Claude Bennett, editors. *Cecil Textbook of Medicine*, 19th ed. Philadelphia: W.B. Saunders Company, 1992.

Wyse, D. George, et al. "Events in the Cardiac Arrhythmia Suppression Trial (CAST): Mortality in Patients Surviving Open Label Titration But Not Randomized to Double-Blind Therapy." *J. Am. Coll. Cardiol.* 18 (July 1991): 20–28.

Young, N.S. "Agranulocytosis." *JAMA* 271 (March 23/30 1994): 935–938.

Ziegler, Edward, and Lewis R. Goldfrank. *Emergency Doctor*. New York: Harper & Row, 1987.

INDEX